The Changing Status of Women in West Bengal, 1970-2000

The Changing Status of Women in West Bengal, 1970-2000

The Challenge Ahead

Edited by

Jasodhara Bagchi

Co-ordinating Editor

Sarmistha Dutta Gupta

Sage Publications
New Delhi ◆ Thousand Oaks ◆ London

First published in 2005 by

Sage Publications India Pvt Ltd
B-42, Panchsheel Enclave
New Delhi 110 017

Sage Publications Inc.
2455 Teller Road
Thousand Oaks, California 91320

Sage Publications Ltd
1 Oliver's Yard, 55 City Road
London EC1Y SP

Published by Tejeshwar Singh for Sage Publications India Pvt Ltd, phototypeset in 10 pt Times New Roman by Star Compugraphics Private Limited and printed at Chaman Enterprises, New Delhi.

Library of Congress Cataloging-in-Publication Data

The changing status of women in West Bengal, 1970–2000: the challenge ahead/edited by Jasodhara Bagchi.
    p. cm.
  Includes bibliographical references and index.
  1. Women—India—West Bengal. I. Bagchi, Jasodhara.

| HQ1744.W47C42 | 305.4'0954'14—dc22 | 2004 | 2004017646 |

ISBN: 0–7619–3242–9 (HB)   81–7829–377–3 (India–HB)

Sage Production Team: Shweta Vachani, Sushanta Gayen and Santosh Rawat

Contents

List of Tables

List of Charts

Foreword

It is a privilege to be asked to write the foreword for this result of a collective enterprise—not only by Women's Studies' scholars, but also by some leading academic institutions in West Bengal that undertook research and who, with some honourable exceptions, have not hitherto demonstrated much sensitivity to the gender dimensions of the transformations experienced by individual states or India as a whole. I must congratulate the entire team and its leaders for this successful mobilization of academic resources.

The authors of *Towards Equality* acknowledged their great debt to the unstinted cooperation extended by individual social scientists from different disciplines, irrespective of their biological identities. In the period immediately following publication of that report, the ICSSR's follow-up measure—the sponsored research programme on Women's Studies—was guided by an interdisciplinary team of eminent social scientists, including B.N. Ganguli, Asok Mitra, Justice krishna Iyer, Iqbal Narain, Leela Dube, Alu Dastur, etc., as well as others who became better known as pioneers in Women's Studies. Unfortunately, the politics within academia has increasingly strengthened the gender divide in the social sciences in recent years. Perhaps this is less so in the humanities, for which again I think this team needs to be thanked. I found the

chapter on culture extremely educative and interesting and hope this area will be developed more in the coming years. It was also an excellent idea to have a separate chapter on tribal women.

I hope that the result of this mobilization effort will stimulate some creative and culturally exciting literature for the young generations—in schools and colleges, in the drama clubs and in the institutions in the interior of the state, and for their counterparts elsewhere. It is also necessary to remember that neo-literates slide back into illiteracy if they do not find something interesting to read. It is a mistake to leave such tasks to official agencies, or educationists, who often remain blissfully unaware of cultural and social transformation in general, and gender issues in particular.

I think I can hear some indignant protests in Jadavpur (!)—'Trust Vinadi to think of more work for us'!!! All I can say in retort is 'Think of the reason. Why?'

Vina Mazumdar
Chairperson
Centre for Women's Development Studies
New Delhi
March 2004

Acknowledgements

A large collective effort like this requires many acknowledgements. The first ones go to Professor Bela Dutta Gupta, the first chairperson of the Women's Commission for setting up the committee for preparing the report on the changing status of women in West Bengal, and the Department of Social Welfare, Women and Child Development, for making the funds available. The major part of the acknowledgement goes to the task force coordinators and the drafting committee members, especially Dr Mukul Mukherjee, who offered us their unstinting support as labour of love. It is difficult to fully acknowledge their contribution.

The chapter on demography was compiled in Sachetana Information Centre by Professor Nirmala Banerjee and Dr Mukul Mukherjee with assistance from Ms Rita Bose. The chapter on health was coordinated and compiled by Maitreya Ghatak after initial consultation with Dr Neena Das. The chapter on education was coordinated and compiled in two parts. The section on school education was done by me and the one on higher and technical education was done by Professor Jaba Guha. For school education, I acknowledge gratefully Maitreya Ghatak's help in compiling the tables. Ms Ranjana Dasgupta assisted both the coordinators. There are two micro studies that are meant to be read in conjunction with this chapter. The one on SC/ST girls' participation in teacher's training in West Bengal was conducted by Mr Kamal Kumar Chatterjee with assistance from Dr Dipali Nag. The one on Muslim girls' education was conducted by Dr Ratnabali Chattopadhyay with some initial input from Ms Saleq but with assistance from Ms Saleha Begum, Ms Swati Biswas, Professor Uttara Chakraborty and Dr Sarmistha Chakroborty. The chapter on culture was co-ordinated by Professor Malini Bhattacharya and Dr Nilanjana Gupta. This chapter needed a large number of assistants and the following students of Jadavpur University were part of this team: Arpita Guha Thakurta, Anshuman Bhowmick, Anindita Banerjee, Anindita Bose, Ellorashree Maitra, Kajori Aikat, Moumita Das, Moupia Mukherjee, Mom Bhattacharya (Viswabharati), Nilanjana Deb, Nandini Dhar, Riju Basu, Reshmi Sengupta, Sambit Saha, Sujata Neogi, Sonali Banerjee, Subrato Dutta. Abhijit Sen and Rumi Mukherjee helped the team with computer assistance. Special acknowledgement to the Folk and Tribal Cultural Centre, Government of West Bengal. The entire team is also acknowledged for the micro study on the women folk artists of Bengal that is presented as an adjunct of the chapter on culture.

For the chapter on economic empowerment, Dr Ishita Mukhopadhyay was assisted by Suratna Ganguly, Sayonti Roy, Anindita Ganguly, Jonaki Sengupta and a team of fieldworkers. For the chapter on political participation Ms Vidya Munshi was assisted by Ms Nibedita Roy, Ms Kamalika Mukherjee and, very briefly, by Ms Swagata Bhowmick. The chapter on law and violence was coordinated by Ms Manjari Gupta, Professor Amit Sen, Chandreyi Alam and Dr Ratnabali Chattopadhyay. Mr Balai Chandra Roy was also consulted. Ms Kalpana Sen rendered assistance to Dr Ratnabali Chattopadhyay. Dr Anuradha Chanda coordinated the chapter on tribal women and was assisted by Ms Ranjana Dasgupta and Ms Moumi Banerjee. Dr Ratna Gupta and Sri Prasenjit Deb Barman of Cultural Research Institute, West Bengal, have also been of great help.

The survey on women's status in Birbhum district was done by a team of scientists from ISI led by Dr Atis Das Gupta. The team included Professor T.J. Rao, Professor Suraj Bandopadhyay, Professor Debapriya Sengupta, Dr Anjali Ghosh and Dr Snigdha Chakraborty. Mr Rabindranath Jana, Dr Anil Kumar Chaudhuri, Mr Dipankar Sen, Ms Sonali Chakraborti, Ms Susmita Bharati, Ms Suparna Som, Mr Kamalaksha Das, Dr Arun Chatterjee, Dr Debashish

Bhattacharya, Dr Molly Chattopadhyay, Mr Ajay Ghosh, Mr Aniruddha Bhattacharya and Mr Shyamal Mukherjee (of the Sociological Research Unit, ISI) participated in various stages of data collection and analysis.

Apart from the core group we look back with gratitude at the early discussions that set us on our feet. Out of this group, we lost Professor Sunil Sen Gupta, one of the early formulators of the rights of the girl child in West Bengal. Ms Saleq and Mr Paramesh Acharya advised us on a few occasions. Mr Nripen Bandyopadhyay continues to give us unstinted support to this day. Ms Anjusree Bhattacharya of the Centre for Studies in Social Sciences helped us with the maps of West Bengal and Ms Jhunu Ghosh provided us with useful information about women bank employees' trade unions in the state.

The librarian of the West Bengal Commission for Women, Ms Deeplekha Sen Gupta and the assistant librarian Ms Subhra Bhadra generously shared their cramped space with the members of the core committee and acquired books and reports and kept us alive by providing tea and biscuits. Ms Ranjana Dasgupta rendered invaluable assistance to many of us. Ms Lopa Guha fed the whole report in the computer and made it possible for all of us to make numerous changes as and when necessary.

This report owes its final form to the meticulous editorial coordination of Ms Sarmistha Dutta Gupta. Maitreya Ghatak has left his signature in too many places to be adequately acknowledged. He passed away in January 2003 while giving final touches to the chapter on health. This text is dedicated to his memory.

Introduction

Coming in the wake of the International Women's Year, *Towards Equality* alerted us to the dynamics of gender in our society, keeping in mind the promised goal of equality between men and women guaranteed in the Constitution. It was an official document to beat all documents, for it succeeded in capturing the vibrant dimension of the Indian polity. One of the major recommendations of the Committee on the Status of Women in India (CSWI) report was that there should be women's commissions to address the issues pertaining to women who appear to have remained neglected and deprived. It was as a fall-out of this recommendation that we find a National Commission set up at the centre and state commissions in many states in India through separate legislations. The National Commission for Women had entrusted Dr Sarala Gopalan to update the report *Towards Equality* (1975), which was published as 'The Unfinished Agenda' in 2002. But so far nothing had been done for the state of West Bengal. Hence, by writing an introduction to a narrative of the changing status of women in West Bengal, compiled under the aegis of the West Bengal Commission for Women, one is repaying a longstanding debt to the mother-document *Towards Equality*.

Professor Bela Dutta Gupta, the former chairperson of the West Bengal Commission for Women, Ms Geeta Sen Gupta, former vice-chairperson, enthusiastic senior members like Vidya Munshi and Manjari Gupta and younger members like Malini Bhattacharya and Ratnabali Chattopadhyay mooted the proposal of compiling a status report for West Bengal. I was entrusted with coordinating the report from the beginning. After lying dormant for some time, the project was re-activated after the present committee took over at the end of 2001. I am happy to be in a position, as chairperson of the State Women's Commission, to be able to bring to an end a collective venture of this magnitude.

The larger committee which had discussed the parameters within which the evolving status of women and children in West Bengal could be best captured had decided on the following: demography, health and nutrition, education, economic empowerment, political participation, law and violence, and culture. At a later stage it was decided to introduce a chapter on tribal women. During the planning period it was further decided to have a number of micro studies (included in the Appendices) to accompany the main chapters covering the parameters mentioned above, to make the qualitative aspect of the data more visible. The Sociological Research Unit of the Indian Statistical Institute was commissioned to do a major survey in the district of Birbhum, focussing on the *Kartri*, (the women head of the household) to gauge the gender dynamics of community, family, assets and workplace.

We have named our document *The Challenge Ahead*. Using some of the basic parameters of our social existence, we have tried to show how women and girls of West Bengal have fared in the last three decades of the twentieth century, so that we can pinpoint the areas of vulnerability as well as those of success. Why did we choose to talk about the 'changing status' rather than the status of women? The last three decades have been especially significant for developments within the women's movement all over India. Starting with the interventions in the Mathura Rape Case which led to the united struggle of women in India, demanding and achieving reform in the rape law, the publication of *Towards Equality*, the launching of the Indian Association of Women's Studies in the early eighties, the founding of the national and state commissions for women in the early nineties, down to the Supreme Court guidelines on sexual harassment at the workplace in 1997. This was also the period in which the Government of India, in 1993, ratified the Convention on the Elimination of All Forms of Discrimination Against Women (CEDAW), accepted by the UN in 1979. Autonomous women's groups, committed to gender justice came into existence in this phase. Towards the end of the eighties two of the major universities of the state, Jadavpur University and Calcutta University, were given women's studies centres by the University Grants Commission. Jadavpur University had already conceived of it as an interdisciplinary School of Women's Studies committed to capturing gender perspectives holistically not compartmentalized by different disciplines.

For most of the 30-year period that this report covers, West Bengal has been under a stable Left Front government and has carried out a regime of land reforms, though the accession to the demand for land reforms came later. The Left Front government had already introduced decentralized planning at the district level and the panchayat level, so that when the 73rd and 74th Amendments were passed, giving 33.3 per cent reservation to rural women, West Bengal was in a position to implement these in a meaningful manner. The report tries to capture conditions of women and girls in West Bengal within the socio-economic and politico-cultural ambience that has marked West Bengal in the last 30 years of the twentieth century and acknowledges that the status of women cannot be conceived as monolithic and static. The direction of gender policy in our state is likely to depend on the analysis of the data emerging from this report.

The uphill task before us is to achieve gender justice that is appropriate to a state like West Bengal. The demographic profile of the state shows certain upward trends, for instance, the life expectancy at birth (LEB) of women have outstripped that of men, thereby making amends for the general sex-ratio. Although just above the national average, the child sex-ratio still shows a disturbing decline in the 0–6 years age group. Son preference, in its many manifestations, appears to stand at the helm of many social evils. It battens on the looming prospect of dowry that stands as one of the prime movers of social injustice and crime against women. The structural adjustment policy that was meant to accompany economic liberalization under the aegis of globalization has hit the opportunities of different classes differently, of which poor women have been hit the hardest. Destitute women in rural and urban areas, assetless widows and female-headed households will need to be specially addressed. We also have to pay attention to the below-poverty-line groups, who deserve special attention.

The signals under LPG, that is, liberalization, privatization and globalization are trying to wean the state away even from the meagre allocation to the social sectors. We expect innovative policies to emerge out of this document that will help the emergence of a truly developmental state in active partnership with the civil society organizations. The nineties saw the intensification of the challenge. While the District Primary Education Programme (DPEP) tried to do some damage control in primary education, health, food security, that can be best ensured through employment, opportunities for women have been challenged by privatization. Primary Health Centres and Integrated Child Development Services (ICDS) programmes—the two main service providers in health for the vast majority of our women—are also feeling the pinch. By distorting the notion of market, unbridled consumerism has been trying to influence the representation of women in the media. While the look of poverty is increasingly getting feminized, forces of masculinity, both frustrated and aggressive, have unleashed tremendous violence against women.

In this perspective, we look forward to larger number of women in decision-making roles, emanating not only from the rich reservoir of women members in the panchayati raj institutions, but from all other walks of life. We look forward to the 33 per cent reservation for women in legislatures, both in the state and at the centre so that women can play a more effective role in spreading the fruit of social justice and entitlements, thereby ensuring the equality guaranteed in the Constitution to all marginal and deprived sections in our society and to their women in particular.

The aim of this report is to capture the process within which women and girls in West Bengal responded to the challenges posed by the CSWI report and the direction the challenges took. Standing at the beginning of the twenty-first century, this study is published with the hope that it will help the people of West Bengal as well as its policy makers to bring into sharper focus the nature of the challenge that lies ahead and the assets that may be picked up from the past struggle for confronting the challenge.

Jasodhara Bagchi
Chairperson,
West Bengal Commission for Women
August 2003

Map 1
West Bengal (Census - 2001)

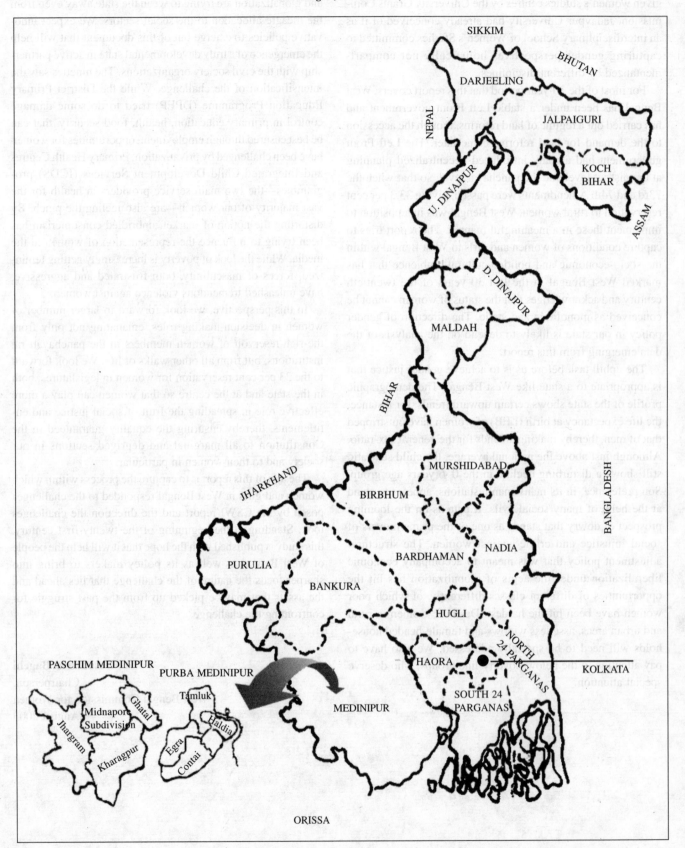

Map 2
West Bengal (Census - 1971)

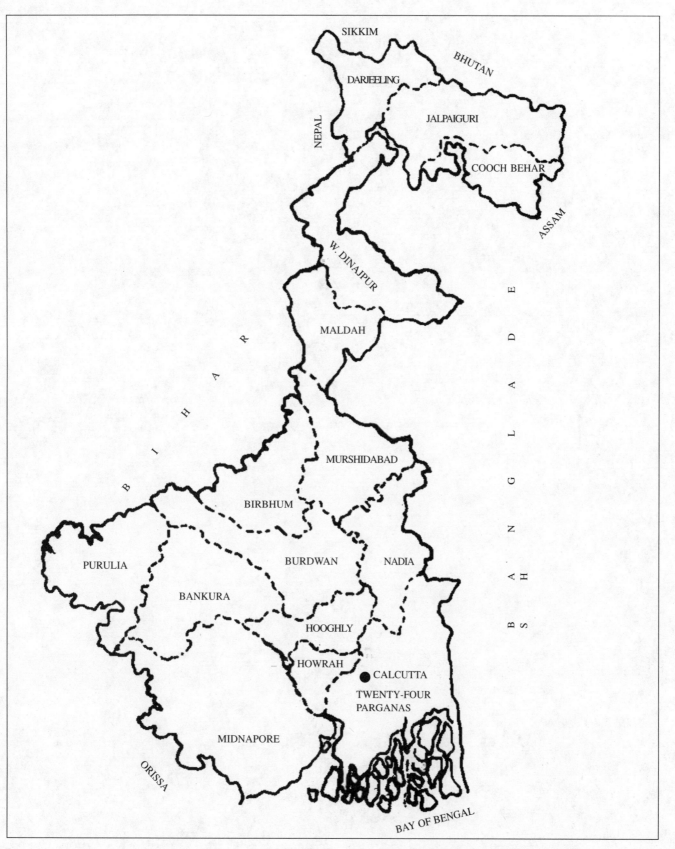

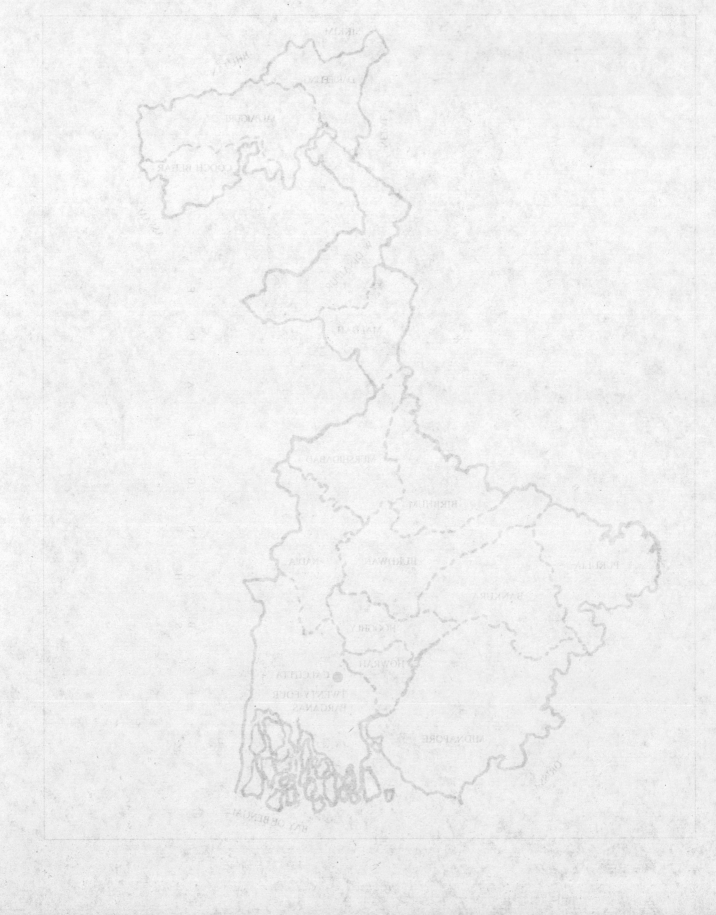

Sectoral Essays

Demography

CHAPTER 1

Nirmala Banerjee and Mukul Mukherjee

Demographic Trends and the Status of Women

An understanding of the demographic background is an important step for exploring the status of women living in a given region. The domain of demography relates to the five basic processes that shape the size and composition of human populations—fertility, mortality, marriage, migration and social mobility. It can be readily seen that these processes have a profound bearing on the quality of life experienced by women and their social position, particularly in a country like India, where women tend to be identified primarily by their reproductive roles. Quite often, a single demographic feature can contain an eloquent summary of women's overall status in society. In the Indian context, for example, this feature is the declining female-male ratio, epitomizing persistent female disadvantage.

It is now increasingly recognized that there is a two-way linkage between women's experiences of empowerment (or disempowerment) and the demographic characteristics/trends that form part of their social existence. On the one hand, many of these demographic attributes affect women's status and autonomy; for instance, early marriage, early motherhood, high levels of fertility and morbidity, low levels of literacy and work participation—all these serve to constrain their progress towards empowerment. On the other hand, women's empowerment itself is known to be capable of influencing demographic outcomes such as fertility patterns, infant mortality rates and child sex-ratio. This chapter, therefore, looks at the situation of women in West Bengal from a broad demographic perspective that includes aspects of population growth; age-wise, sex-wise and community-wise composition of population; expectation of life; fertility and mortality rates; marital status; literacy levels, etc., as well as certain gender-related indicators of women's development that have a demographic context.

Three points may be mentioned about the overview of demographic trends presented in this chapter. First, wherever possible, the situation in West Bengal has been placed in a wider, all-India context; second, gender-based disparities are brought to light since gender is a central stratifying feature in everyday life; third, disaggregation of data has been extended to the district level so that local characteristics can emerge more clearly and to that extent provide a better basis for policy.

Some basic demographic facts relating to West Bengal and India for the period 1971–2001 are given in Table 1.1. Appendix Table A1 provides more details including district-wise data for West Bengal.

Population Growth Rate

The total population of West Bengal (as per its current boundaries) was 17 million in 1901. By 1991, it had risen to 68 million and in 2001 it stood at 80 million. It now comprises about 8 per cent of the all-India population. However, West Bengal's decadal population growth rate showed a welcome decline from 24.7 per cent during 1981–91 to 17.8 per cent during 1991–2001. The corresponding all-India growth rate had declined from 23.9 per cent to 21.3 per cent.

Table A1 shows that Medinipur was the most populous of the West Bengal districts in 1991 and continued to be so in 2001. Closely following it were several of the districts of south West Bengal, including North and South 24 Parganas and Bardhaman. In comparison, the districts of north West Bengal were generally less populous.

District-wise annual population growth rates during the last decade varied significantly from as little as 1.6/1.7 per cent per

Table 1.1
Select Demographic Characteristics of West Bengal and India, 1971–2001

	Year	Population (crore)			Density (Population per km^2)	Urban population (per cent)			Literacy (per cent)		
		Male	Female	Total		Male	Female	Total	Male	Female	Total
West Bengal	1971	2.3	2.1	4.4	504	26.8	22.5	24.8	42.8	22.4	33.2
	1981	2.9	2.6	5.5	614	27.8	24.9	26.5	50.7	30.3	40.9
	1991	3.6	3.3	6.8	767	28.4	26.5	27.5	67.8	46.6	57.7
	2001	4.2	3.9	8.0	904	NA	NA	NA	77.6	60.2	69.2
India	1971	28.4	26.4	54.8	177	20.7	19.1	19.9	39.5	18.7	29.5
	1981	35.0	33.0	68.3	216	24.0	22.6	23.3	56.4	29.8	43.6
	1991	40.7	43.9	84.6	274	26.2	25.2	25.7	64.1	39.3	52.2
	2001	53.1	49.6	102.7	324	29.1	28.6	28.9	75.9	54.2	65.4

Sources: *Economic and Political Weekly,* 21 April 2001 (p. 1,275); Appendix Table A1.
Census of India 1981, Series-23,West Bengal, Paper 1 of 1981.
Census of India 2001, Series-20, Provisional Population Totals, West Bengal, Paper 1 of 2001, Statement 4, p. 51; Table 2, p. 45.
Government of India, *Women & Men in India—2000*.
Central Statistical Organization, Ministry of Statistics and Programme Implementation. New Delhi, 2001, Table 1(a) and Table 53.

annum in Puruliya and Bankura to 3.3 per cent per annum in Nadia and 3.1 per cent in Darjeeling (Appendix Table A1). It seems likely that the faster rates of growth were not entirely due to natural increase; possibly, much of that growth came about through considerable immigration from neighbouring countries. It is worth noting that the districts with relatively faster rates of population growth were all situated along the several international boundaries of West Bengal. By the same logic, it is possible that the extremely low growth rates of the western districts were due to people moving out of those relatively backward areas. Another indicator of the backwardness of the area is also to be found in Appendix Table A1: urban population in those districts accounted for less than 10 per cent of the total in 1991.

Population Density

The 2001 census reveals that West Bengal has now earned the dubious distinction of being the most densely populated state; the density now stands at 904 persons per sq. km, which had shown a rise of 44 per cent over its 1971 level of 504 persons per sq. km. In the decade from 1991 to 2001, West Bengal added another 152 persons per sq. km, while India as a whole added only 57 persons. The all-India average density in 2001 stood at 324 persons per sq. km.

As expected, Kolkata in 1991 still had a density of 23,784 persons per sq. km which was by far the highest among all districts. This figure, however, was substantially lower than its 1971 density which then stood at over 30,000 persons per sq. km. Part of this change can be attributed to the revision of its boundaries since 1971 when many new, less populated areas were amalgamated in it. Partly, Kolkata has also been losing population to its neighbouring districts, especially to 24

Parganas and Haora. In 1991, these districts exhibited higher than average densities as well as rates of urbanization. Although in many West Bengal districts population density had been rising fast, it remained below that of the state as a whole. The districts where population density increased fast between 1971 and 1991 included Hoogli (75 per cent increase), Nadia (73 per cent increase) and Maldah and Murshidabad (about 60 per cent increase).

Urbanization

From 1971 to 1991, the share of urban population in West Bengal increased from about 25 per cent to 27.5 per cent of the total. For India as a whole, urbanization had been growing much faster; it grew from less than 20 per cent in 1971 to 25.7 per cent in 1991.

As mentioned before, Haora and North 24 Parganas had high levels of urbanization and about 50 per cent of the residents were already living in urban areas. Urbanization was also relatively high in the districts of Darjeeling and Bardhaman (30 to 35 per cent). However, till 1991, levels of urbanization in other districts and especially in the districts of Koch Bihar, Maldah in north Bengal and Bankura, Birbhum and Purulia in south Bengal remained as low as 8 per cent to 10 per cent.

It is particularly important to note that, in the decades since 1971, the rate of urbanization among women grew faster than among males. It went up from 22.5 per cent in 1971 to 25 per cent in 1981 and 26.5 per cent in 1991. This was a significant change in the character of West Bengal's urban areas. It is well-known that from the earliest available census records, urbanization in colonial India and particularly in West Bengal was closely associated with industrial development. The labour that came into the cities for work in the industries comprised mainly single male adults. The wages they received from the industrial jobs were too meagre to support families; nor did cities offer sufficient civic facilities for housing them. This had meant that, at one time, the ratio of women to men in Kolkata's population was as low as 612:1000 (1961). Family migration into cities grew at a significantly faster rate after independence. Even though single male migrants still come in large numbers to several cities, including Kolkata and Haora, women also appear to be moving into urban areas.

Nevertheless, there is a significant difference in the character of male and female urbanization. Women moving from rural to urban areas seldom do so for motives of work. In general, they migrate on marriage or when the family as a whole moves city-wards.[1] Recent years have seen a fast rise in the numbers of women who commute to urban areas for work on a daily basis; but they are still counted as rural residents because they continue to live there.

Rising population density and accelerated urbanization usually bring in several problems in their wake and these particularly affect the living conditions of women. These include a growing lack of civic amenities (shelter, sanitation, water supply, etc.), growth of slums and prevalence of criminal activity. According to the second National Family Health Survey (NFHS 1998–99 or NFHS-2), about 40 per cent of households surveyed in West Bengal had electricity (as compared to 60 per cent for all-India and 72 per cent for Kerala) and 45 per cent had sanitary facilities (as compared to 36 per cent for all-India and 85 per cent for Kerala). Only 25 per cent of West Bengal households were reported to have piped water. Obviously, special attention needs to be directed towards improvements in basic civic amenities which will ensure improvement in the quality of life for women, which in turn is a critical constituent of women's status.

Distribution of Population by Community

If we divide the population by its religious affiliations, we find that in 1991, Hindus constituted almost three-fourths of the total population of West Bengal. Muslims accounted for a little less than one-fourth (23.6 per cent). For India as a whole the percentage of Hindus was 79 per cent while that of Muslims was 11 per cent. Christians, Sikhs and Jains together accounted for about 1 per cent of West Bengal's population. The corresponding all-India figure was 4.5 per cent. There was a sizeable Muslim population in some districts of West Bengal, notably in Murshidabad (61 per cent), Maldah (47 per cent) and North and South 24 Parganas (24 to 30 per cent). Cross-border inflows seem to have been a contributory factor behind the religion-based population structure in these districts.

According to the Census of 1991, scheduled caste (SC) population constituted about 24 per cent of the total population of West Bengal as compared to 16.5 per cent for India as a whole. The scheduled tribe (ST) population in West Bengal accounted for less than 6 per cent of the total as compared to the all-India figure of 8 per cent. However, ST population was prominent in Jalpaiguri (21 per cent), Darjeeling (14 per cent) and Purulia (19 per cent); in West Dinajpur and Bankura too, tribal population was about 1/10th of the total.

Distribution of Population by Age Group

The composition of the population of West Bengal and India by age group is given in Table 1.2.

Between 1981–91, the proportion of population in the below 20 years age groups fell marginally in both India and West Bengal. The marginal change went in favour of the

Table 1.2
Percentage Distribution of Population by Age Group, 1981 and 1991

Age group (years)	Sex-ratio		Total population				Male population				Female population			
	1981	1991	1981		1991		1981		1991		1981		1991	
	West Bengal		W.B.	India	W.B.	India	W.B.	India	W.B.	India	WB.	India	W.B.	India
0–14	966	963	38.9	39.5	36.9	37.2	37.8	39.6	35.8	37.7	40.0	39.8	37.5	37.8
15–19	923	901	10.4	9.6	9.3	9.42	10.3	10.2	9.3	10.0	10.5	10.0	9.2	9.5
20–24	908	978	9.4	8.6	9.3	8.9	9.5	8.5	9.1	8.6	9.4	8.6	9.5	9.0
25–29	877	987	8.3	7.6	9.0	8.3	8.5	7.3	8.7	7.9	8.2	7.8	9.4	8.5
30–39	858	873	12.3	12.2	14.0	13.2	12.6	13.1	14.6	12.3	11.9	13.2	13.3	13.2
40–49	811	861	9.3	9.5	9.2	9.4	9.8	9.6	9.7	9.2	8.7	9.7	8.6	9.2
50–59	802	950	5.8	6.3	6.1	6.3	6.2	6.6	6.3	6.2	5.5	6.5	5.8	5.2
60+	992	1,081	5.6	6.8	6.5	6.8	5.3	6.2	6.5	6.3	5.8	6.7	6.7	6.7
Total	911	917	100	100	100	100	100	100	100	100	100	100	100	100

Sources: *Census of India 1981*, Series-23, Part IV-A, Social and Cultural Tables, West Bengal.
Census of India 1991, Series-26, Part IV-A, Social and Cultural Tables, West Bengal.
Institute of Applied Manpower Research, *Man Power Profile: India (Yearbook 2000)*, p. 77.

[1] Mehrotra, G.K., *Birth Place Migration in India. Census of India—Series-1*, Special Monograph No. 1. New Delhi, 1971.

population in the working age groups. For West Bengal there was some increase also in the share of the older age groups, though not for India as a whole. The trends were almost identical for men and women. This trend means that there is possibly a small fall in the dependency rates, i.e., the average number of persons depending on a worker in the country as a whole, but till 1991, this trend was not very clear. Unfortunately, at the time of writing, the figures for age distribution of the district-wise population of West Bengal for 2001 was not available. There is a possibility that, with a fall in West Bengal's birth rate, the share of the population in younger age groups has fallen. At the same time, with rising expectation of life, there would be an increase in the share of the older age groups. Since there is a growing divergence between the situations in West Bengal and India as a whole, the emerging trends are likely to prove interesting.

In 1991 the older age groups of 50–60 years and above accounted for a larger percentage of the female population (12.5) than the male population (11.3). This is a universal trend. According to a UN report, worldwide there are 123 women per 100 men aged 60 years or more, and 189 women per 100 men aged 80 years or more, and between 2000 and 2020, the percentage of older women in the population of South-East Asia is expected to rise from 7 to 13 per cent.[2] We must recognize that older women constitute a specially vulnerable social group as they are more likely to be widowed, are often without regular income, employment and kinship support and are subject to physical infirmity. As such, they too represent a target group for whom it is necessary to devise effective policy interventions.

Woman-headed Households

It is now recognized that woman-headed households tend to be a particularly disadvantaged segment of society and thus need a special focus in development efforts.[3] There are two typical situations giving rise to such households: (*a*) absence of a resident and functional male head (due to widowhood, separation or disability of male members of the family) and (*b*) migration of male members of the household for long periods. Women under the first category are considered *de jure* heads and are more likely to be recognized by investigators and policy makers as compared to the de facto women heads under the second category. According to data available

in NSS 50th Round (1993–94), West Bengal had about 11.6 million and 4.6 million woman-headed households in rural and urban areas, accounting for roughly one-tenth of total households.

Sex-ratio (SR)

As is well-known, India is one of the few countries of the world where there is a deficit in the relative number of women as compared to men. What is more, this ratio between female and male numbers in the population SR had been declining almost steadily in every decade of the twentieth century. Demographers agree that neither the deficit in the overall numbers of women nor the decline in the sex-ratio over the years can be entirely due to natural causes. Further analysis of the facts has shown that the disadvantage in women's capacity to survive arises from a complex play of several socio-cultural forces. These forces operate against women within their own families right from the time of birth or even before that. For parts of India there is a long history of female infanticide and, in recent years, this trend has been further aggravated by the opportunities provided for pre-birth sex verification through techniques of amniocentesis. Although it is now a crime to use amniocentesis tests for verifying the sex of the foetus and disclosing it to the parents, the law does not seem to have stopped widespread illegal use of this test in many parts of the country. Even when girls are allowed to survive till birth, their health needs tend to get neglected as compared to that of the boy in the family. As a result of these practices, the relative number of girls continues to fall throughout childhood, leading to adverse sex-ratios among child populations of age groups 0–1 year, 1–6 years and 0–9 years.[4]

Interestingly, the shortfall in the relative numbers of all women as well as in the numbers of girl children is not spread uniformly over the entire country; there is a definite geographical pattern discernible in the distribution of levels of SRs. Moreover, this pattern has remained fairly steady throughout the twentieth century. Some parts of India, particularly the north western states, have always had a significantly larger deficit in women's relative numbers than elsewhere, while the southern states, particularly Kerala, have generally exhibited more women-friendly trends. This regional pattern of the sex-ratios has excited many researchers to investigate its causes.

---

[2] United Nations, *The World's Women*. New York, 2000.

[3] Lingam, Lakshmi, 'India's Household with Female Heads: Coping with Caste, Class and Gender Hierarchies?' *Economic and Political Weekly*, 19 March 1994.

[4] Agnihotri, Satish, 'Unpacking the Juvenile Sex Ratio in India' in Vina Mazumdar and N. Krishnaji (eds), *Enduring Conundrums: India's Sex Ratio. Essays in Honour of Asok Mitra*. Rainbow Publishers, New Delhi, 2001.

As Table 1.3 will show, West Bengal's sex-ratio has always appeared to be worse than that of India as a whole. Part of its problem arose out of the way Indian urbanization grew during the late nineteenth and first half of the twentieth century. Modern factory industries with large industrial workforce came up in a few locations, mainly in India's larger coastal cities. In these cities, there was an influx of single male migrants coming to work in the factories. These factories were located mainly in Bengal and Bombay provinces of colonial India, and West Bengal and Maharashtra of independent India. As a consequence the decennial census reports for these states continuously recorded a much larger number of men than women in the population. On the other hand, in some other states, particularly Bihar and Uttar Pradesh, from where the majority of men migrated to other states for work, the numbers of men remained relatively low. After independence, this imbalance between states has been gradually corrected. The picture in West Bengal changed rather markedly immediately after partition, when a large number of families from former East Pakistan moved there. Presumably the same process of correcting that imbalance has been going on for the last 40 years or so.

In order to allow for this, Banerjee and Jain[5] had carried out an exercise where each state's population was adjusted for migration by eliminating the inflow of men and women born elsewhere and adding those persons who were born in

that state but were counted elsewhere.[6] The sex-ratios for West Bengal as adjusted for migration are shown in column 3 of Table 1.3. The table shows that West Bengal's figures, when unadjusted for migration, were significantly below the all-India levels for 1971 and 1981. But after allowing for migration (column 3), the sex-ratios for West Bengal for those years stood very close to the all-India level. It is possible that in the decade 1981–91, there had been a significant rise in the numbers of males migrating singly for work into West Bengal from across international borders. We have already talked about this possibility when discussing the district-wise growth rates.

The district level figures included in Table 1.4 in fact corroborate this to an extent. In the districts sharing a border with Bangladesh (Maldah, Murshidabad, Nadia and 24 Parganas), the sex-ratio had fallen significantly in the decade 1981 to 1991.

Table 1.3
Relative Sex-ratios of West Bengal and India

Year	West Bengal	India	West Bengal (adjusted)
1971	891	930	931
1981	911	934	946
1991	917	927	929
2001	934	933	NA

Source: Compiled from Census figures.

Table 1.4
Female–Male Ratio in the Total Population of West Bengal, 1971–2001

District	1971 Total	Urban	Rural	1981 Total	Urban	Rural	1991 Total	Urban	Rural	2001 Total	Urban	Rural
Koch Bihar	916	830	923	935	921	937	934	954	933	949	965	947
Jalpaiguri	886	826	892	909	885	914	927	916	929	941	932	943
Darjeeling	882	792	910	887	831	912	913	868	936	943	917	956
West Dinajpur	921	928	928	937	900	942	929	895	934			
Maldah	948	959	951	949	940	951	940	928	939	948	945	948
Murshidabad	956	930	959	959	966	958	943	960	941	952	970	949
Nadia	947	926	953	947	954	945	936	960	929	947	964	942
Kolkata	636	636		712	712		799	799		828	828	
Purulia	963	886	969	957	898	845	946	892	952	953	918	957
Haora	833	703	941	873	788	950	881	824	941	906	858	958
Hoogli	895	784	939	908	832	942	917	858	945	947	896	974
Medinipur	945	867	952	951	905	956	944	905	949	955	936	958
Bankura	958	924	961	964	946	966	951	933	952	953	954	953
Birbhum	968	894	976	962	922	965	946	924	948	949	950	949
24 Parganas	882	793	935	903	847	941						
24 Parganas (N)							907	879	938	927	913	944
24 Parganas (S)							929	877	938	938	914	943
Bardhaman	886	785	918	897	815	934	899			921	886	942
West Bengal	891	751	941	911	819	947	917	858	940	934	893	950

Sources: *Census of India 1971, 1981, 1991*, Social and Cultural Tables.
Census of India 2001, Provisional Population Totals, West Bengal, Paper 1 of 2001, p. 12.

[5] Banerjee, Nirmala and Devaki, Jain, 'India's Sex Ratios through Time and Space: Development from Women's perspective', in Vina Mazumdar and N. Krishnaji (eds), *Enduring Conundrums: India's Sex Ratio. Essays in Honour of Asok Mitra*. Rainbow Publsihers, New Delhi, 2001.

[6] For comparison over the decades, the sex-ratios calculated are for states as per their current geographical boundaries.

However, sex-ratio had also fallen in another set of districts (Puruliya, Birbhum, Bankura, Medinipur). This sub-regional diversity needs further investigation, because worsening sex-ratios usually imply a worsening socio-economic scenario for women, not just in their chances of survival but also in their access to education, health and employment.

Table 1.5 shows the sex-ratios (unadjusted for migration) for the year 1991 for various social groups. It indicates that in 1991, the sex-ratios for Muslims and scheduled castes (unadjusted for migration) in West Bengal were higher than the comparable all-India figures. On the other hand, for Hindus and for the scheduled tribe population, the ratios were slightly worse.

Table 1.5
Sex-ratio by Community—West Bengal and All-India, 1991

Community	West Bengal	All-India
Scheduled caste	964	922
Scheduled tribe	931	972
Muslim	944	930
Hindu	914	925
Total population	917	927

Source: *Census of India 1991*, West Bengal State District Profiles, 1991.

Child Sex-ratios (CSR)

The child sex-ratios are a better tool to use for assessing women's position, because it is very unlikely that they would be vitiated by single migration of either sex. In a population unaffected by bias against girl children (as reflected in the practice of female infanticide and foeticide), the sex-ratio would favour girls since girls are by nature the stronger of the two sexes. This indeed was true of West Bengal and other states of eastern India till 1981. However, it is a cause for concern that this sex-ratio for children in the age group 0 to 6 years dropped from 1,007 in 1971 to 963 in 2001.

Demographers have already noted with alarm that one of the most dismal aspects of the first results of the 2001 Census was this pervasive downtrend in CSR as shown in Table 1.6. The commissioner has observed in this context 'The imbalance that has set in at this early age group is difficult to be removed and would remain to haunt the population for a long time to come'.[7] According to Bose, migration cannot explain this phenomenon, which must be the consequence of female foeticide on a massive scale, if not female infanticide, and higher female mortality rates. He would like to coin the acronym DEMARU, 'where D stands for daughters and MARU stands for killing',

and on the basis of the statistical cut-off point of 50 points decline (between 1991 and 2001) in the CSR, Punjab, Haryana, Himachal Pradesh and Gujarat would be classified as DEMARU states. For West Bengal, the fall in the CSR (0–6 years) from 1991 to 2001 at –0.4 per cent was relatively negligible. Searching for 'the missing girl child', Mahendra K. Premi has drawn attention to two possible factors.[8] One possibility is that the sex-ratio at birth (SRB) has become more biased against females. This is supported by the data collected by the Office of the Registrar General of India. In various parts of India, SRB stood at 110–12 males per 100 females. This is a significant departure from the standard figure, which should lie around 105/106 boys per 100 girls. Three trends would seem to lie behind the masculinization of SRB: growing adoption of the small family norm, the continuing preference for sons, and increasingly resorting to sex selection at birth through rampant misuse of medical technology.

Table 1.6
Child Sex-ratio—India and States, 1971–2001

	Age group (years)	1971	1981	1991	2001
India	0–4	980	972	955	NA
	0–6	954	962	945	927
West Bengal	0–4	1,019	1,002	972	NA
	0–6	1,007	981	967	963
Orissa	0–4	1,031	1,018	974	NA
	0–6	984	995	967	950
Bihar	0–4	985	1,010	978	NA
	0–6	958	981	953	938
Punjab	0–4	1,117	915	874	NA
	0–6	892	908	875	793

Source: For 1971 and 1981, Banerjee, Nirmala and Devaki Jain, 'India's Sex Ratios through Time and Spece: Development from Women's Perspective' in Vina Mazumdar and N. Krishnaji (eds), *Enduring Conundrums: India's Sex Ratio*. For 1991 and 2001, Bose Ashish, 'Census of India 2001 and After', *Economic and Political Weekly*, 19 May 2001, p. 1,686.

Premi also points to a second possibility. In certain states of India, the female age-specific death rate (ASDR) for the age-groups 0 to 4 years and 5 to 9 years have been found to be higher than the corresponding male rates during 1984–99. In West Bengal, for example, mortality rates for boys and girls aged 0–4 were 26.1 and 26.3 respectively in 1986 and 18.1 and 18.7 respectively in 1994 (calculated at 5-year averages). For the age group 5 to 9 years, mortality rates for boys and girls were 2.6 and 3.2 respectively in 1986 and 1.7 and 2.1 respectively in 1994, pointing to continued neglect/deprivation of the girl child.

[7] Bose, Ashish, 'Census of India and After', *Economic and Political Weekly*, 19 May 2001.
[8] Premi, Mahendra K., 'The Missing Girl Child', *Economic and Political Weekly*, 26 May 2001.

The decline of CSR, therefore, may be partially explained in the light of the above two factors, i.e., the increasing masculinity of SRB (because of foeticide) and the persistent female disadvantage in the ASDR of children aged 0–9 years.

As district level statistics on CSR become accessible through systematic progress in data collection and analysis, it will be possible to work towards a locality-specific exploration and amelioration of factors underlying the girl-specific pattern of child mortality.

Expectation of Life at Birth (LEB)

This is an important indicator of health standards and an important component of human development indices. Recent calculations have shown that both male and female LEB in West Bengal have been rising steadily during 1981–97 (Table 1.7). LEB for women continued to trail below that for men up to 1991. Even in the period 1988 to 1991, the all-India male/female life expectancies at birth were almost equal. But in West Bengal, there was a systematic shortfall in the female LEB as compared to the male one.

Table 1.7
Life Expectation at Birth (years)—West Bengal and India

	1981–85	1986–90	1993–97
West Bengal			
M	56.95	60.00	62.20
F	56.28	59.50	63.60
India			
M	55.40	60.01	60.40
F	55.70	60.00	61.80

Sources: Government of West Bengal, *Family Welfare Statistics at a Glance,* West Bengal, 1995, Table 8.
Government of India, *Women & Men in India—2000.* Central Statistical Organization, Ministry of Statistics and Programme Implementation, New Delhi, 2001.

This situation changed rather dramatically in the early nineties. LEB of both males and females rose fast in West Bengal and the female LEB overtook its male counterpart by a significant margin. For India as a whole, the trends were similar, but the gain of female LEB as compared to the male one was not as large as in West Bengal. It is not clear what explains this significant reversal of the relative positions of West Bengal and India in this short period.

Vital Rates

Table 1.8 provides figures of birth rates (BR) and death rates (DR) for various years for West Bengal and India. It shows that over the years, the birth rates in West Bengal have fallen much faster than in India as a whole. In 1981, the birth rate for India was slightly above the West Bengal figure. But by 1991, the urban birth rate for West Bengal had fallen sharply to 18.5 as compared to India's 24.3. That explains the growing gap between the total birth rate of West Bengal and India. By 1998/99, West Bengal's rural and urban birth rates had fallen much more sharply than their all-India counterparts.

Table 1.8 also shows the death rates for rural and urban West Bengal and India since 1981. West Bengal's combined (rural plus urban) BR and DR, at 27.0 and 8.3 per 1,000 respectively, were decidedly more favourable than the relevant all-India figures of 29.5 and 9.8.

Table 1.8
Vital Rates—West Bengal and India, 1981 and 1999

Year	Birth rate (per 1,000 population)			Death rate (per 1,000 population)		
	Rural	Urban	Combined	Rural	Urban	Combined
1981						
West Bengal	37.0	20.0	33.2	12.2	6.9	11.0
India	NA	NA	33.9	NA	NA	12.5
1991						
West Bengal	30.3	18.5	27.0	8.9	6.7	8.3
India	30.9	24.3	29.5	10.6	7.1	9.8
1997–98						
West Bengal	NA	NA	20.8	7.3	8.7	8.3
India	NA	NA	24.8	NA	NA	9.7
1998–99						
West Bengal	22.9	14.3	20.7	6.8	7.2	7.1
India	27.6	20.8	26.1	9.4	6.3	8.7

Sources: Government of West Bengal, *Family Welfare Statistics at a Glance,* West Bengal, 1995, Table 9.
NFHS-2, 1998–99, India, Tables 4.3 and 6.2.
For 1999, West Bengal: *Economic Review 2000–2001,* Table 2.5, p. 23.

Infant and Child Mortality

Levels of infant and child mortality are acknowledged as basic indicators of the quality of life in a society. West Bengal has consistently had lower levels of infant and child mortality than the national averages. Estimates of five categories of infant and child mortality rates as well as the incidence of still births in West Bengal's population are given in Table 1.9. It can be seen that the all-India death rates for all the age groups are well above the West Bengal figures, the difference in most cases amounting to 30 or more percentage points. In 1998–99 West Bengal's IMR was about 49 per 1,000 live births as compared to about 68 for India as a whole, as reported by the second National Family Health Survey. These figures, however, have to be seen against India's national population policy goals of reducing IMR to 30 by 2010. Moreover, infant and child

Map 1.1
Urban Female Under-Five Mortality Rates in West Bengal (1991)

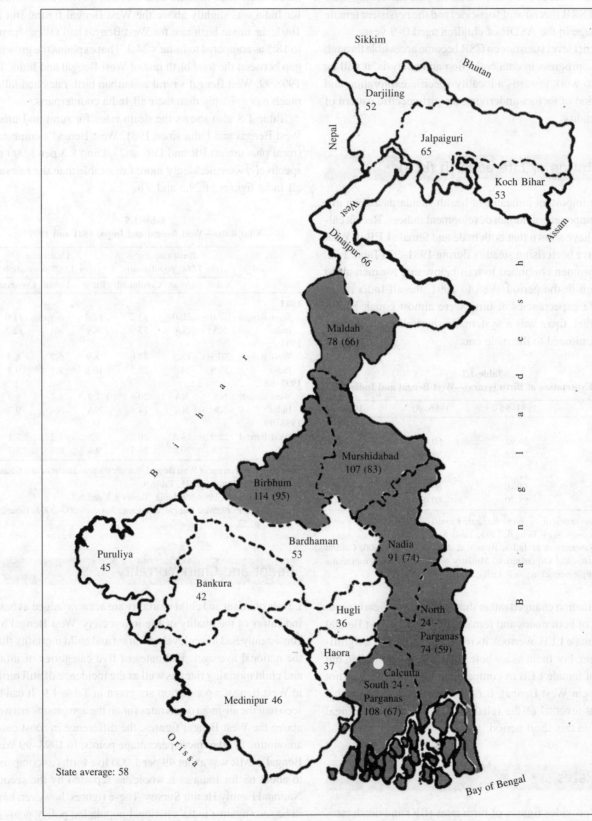

Sikkim

Bhutan

Darjiling
52

Jalpaiguri
65

Koch Bihar
53

Nepal

West
Dinajpur 66

Assam

Maldah
78 (66)

Bihar

Murshidabad
107 (83)

Birbhum
114 (95)

Bardhaman
53

Nadia
91 (74)

Puruliya
45

Bankura
42

Hugli
36

North
24 -
Parganas
74 (59)

Haora
37

Medinipur 46

Calcutta
South 24 -
Parganas
108 (67)

Orissa

Bangladesh

Bay of Bengal

State average: 58

Source: Rajan et al. (1998).

mortality patterns are often characterized by gender differences pointing to female disadvantage.

Table 1.9
Infant and Child Mortality—West Bengal and India, 1991 and 1998–99
Sample Registration System, 1991

		West Bengal	NFHS-2: 1998–99 West Bengal	India
Neonatal mortality rate	R	48.0	NA	46.7
	U	24.7	NA	
	R+U	61.5	31.9	43.4
Infant mortality rate	R+U	71.0	48.7	67.6
Under-5 mortality rate	R+U		67.6	94.9
Child mortality rate (per 1,000 births)	R+U		19.9	29.3
Still birth rate	R	13.6	22.9	26.1
	U	7.2	14.3	27.6
	R+U	12.4	20.7	20.8

Sources: Government of West Bengal, *Family Welfare Statistics at a Glance,* West Bengal, 1995, Table 15.
NFHS-2: *West Bengal Preliminary Report*, August 2000, Table 16.
Notes: 1: probability of dying within the first month of life.
2: probability of dying between birth and exact age of one year.
3: probability of dying between birth and fifth birthdays.
4: probability of dying between the first and fifth birthdays.
All four rates are calculated per 1,000 live births.

Between 1981 and 1991, the under-5 mortality rate in West Bengal fell by 24 per cent. However, this decline is marked by a gender gap, particularly evident in urban areas of the state. This can be clearly seen in Map 1.1 based on Agnihotri's pioneering analysis using mapping techniques.[9] As this map shows, the six districts of Birbhum, Maldah, Murshidabad, Nadia, North and South 24 Parganas formed a contiguous cluster of high mortality rate for under-5 girls ranging from

66 to 108 in urban localities. In contrast, the comparable male rates varied between 59 and 95. The largest gender divide in urban under-5 deaths was found in South 24 Parganas (108 for girls as against 67 for boys).

Marital Status and Age at Marriage

Table 1.10 is based on the 1981 and 1991 census for West Bengal and India; it shows the proportions of never-married, ever-married and divorced/separated persons in five different age groups. In the age group 0 to 14, there were very few males or females who had been married. According to the 1991 Census, only 0.3 per cent among males and 0.6 per cent among females were married in this age group.[10] But in the age group 15 to 19, over 33 per cent of women in West Bengal and 35 per cent in India as a whole were married in 1991. Among males in that age group, marriage was very uncommon for West Bengal males, but not so rare for India as a whole, even in 1991. In the next age group, 20 to 29 years, almost all females had been married both in West Bengal and India, though more than half the males in West Bengal were still unmarried, a substantially higher proportion as compared to India as a whole.

Burdens of Widowhood

As Table 1.10 shows, women's conjugal status seems to change quite significantly when they reach the age group 50 to 69 years: in this particular cohort, in 1991, over 40 per cent of

Table 1.10
Distribution of Male and Female Population by Age Group and Marital Status, India and West Bengal, 1981 and 1991

Age group		Never married Male 1981	1991	Female 1981	1991	Married Male 1981	1991	Female 1981	1991	Widowed Male 1981	1991	Female 1981	1991	Divorced/Separated Male 1981	1991	Female 1981	1991
15–19	West Bengal	96.3	96.3	61.1	66.3	3.6	3.6	37.5	33.0	0.00	0.03	0.03	0.2	0.03	0.03	1.0	0.4
	India	87.5	90.0	55.8	64.3	12.24	9.4	43.4	35.3	0.09	0.07	0.02	0.18	0.08	0.06	0.04	0.02
20–29	West Bengal	54.3	55.0	12.8	13.0	45.1	44.6	83.9	84.9	0.2	0.2	1.5	1.1	0.4	0.2	1.6	1.0
	India	39.7	42.8	9.0	10.8	59.3	56.4	89.1	87.7	0.6	0.5	1.1	0.9	0.4	0.2	0.9	0.6
30–49	West Bengal	6.5	7.7	1.2	2.1	91.6	91.0	86.7	89.4	1.4	0.9	11.1	7.5	0.6	0.3	1.0	1.0
	India	4.0	4.6	0.7	1.2	92.9	93.3	90.5	92.5	2.3	1.8	8.0	5.6	0.5	0.3	0.8	0.7
50–69	West Bengal	2.2	3.0	0.3	0.9	90.2	91.0	46.8	55.5	7.0	5.7	52.3	43.1	0.5	0.3	0.6	0.5
	India	1.7	2.3	0.4	0.7	82.3	88.9	57.9	66.5	10.2	8.4	35.4	32.4	0.4	0.3	0.5	0.5
70+	West Bengal	1.9	9.0	0.4	3.8	78.1	75.7	15.0	20.6	19.4	15.0	84.4	75.4	3.9	0.4	0.2	0.3
	India	1.9	5.4	0.4	2.5	70.4	72.8	21.7	29.9	27.1	21.4	77.6	67.2	0.4	0.3	0.3	0.4

Sources: *Census of India 1981*, Social & Cultural Tables, Table C-1—Age, Sex and Marital Status, Page- 46.
Census of India 1991, Social & Cultural Tables, Table C-1—Age, Sex and Marital Status, Part-IV A-C-Series.

[9] Agnihotri, Satish, 'Infant Mortality Variation in Space and Time: Analysis of West Bengal Data', *Economic and Political Weekly*, 8 September 2001.
[10] Government of West Bengal, *Statistical Abstract: West Bengal, 2001–2002*, Bureau of Applied Economics and Statistics, Table 1.15.

the women in West Bengal were widowed. For India the percentage was much lower. But in both cases, in that age group, there were many more widowed women in the population than men.

The same situation is reflected in Appendix Table A3, with district level data from the 1991 Census and showing percentages of married, widowed and divorced/separated women and men who were aged 60 years and above. In a number of districts, more than 80 per cent of women aged 70–79 years were widowed while the status applied to less than 20 per cent of men in the same age group. The incidence of divorce/separation was negligible among both women and men according to data from the 1981 and 1991 censuses.

We may note here that the observations of the Committee on the Status of Women in India on widowhood, recorded a quarter of a century ago, are still largely and sadly true:

A change in the life style of women after they are widowed is characteristic of Indian society ... with the conception of the man as the breadwinner and the woman as his dependant, the married state for women is considered fortunate and conversely, widowhood is associated with great misfortune ... society's attitude to this unfortunate group has not registered any appreciable change in all these decades.... The large group of widows, whom we met in Banaras, were in a state of destitution.... Majority of them were from Bengal but some were also from South India and Maharashtra.[11] As Martha A. Chen writes,

The sensational circumstances of small numbers of widows receive more attention than the less visible and quiet deprivation of millions. These deprivations do not show up in economic and social statistics, the standard household-level analysis tells very little about widows and their well-being. Female-headed households are not reported by marital status, so widow-headed household cannot be compared with other households.[12]

Aspects of Nuptiality

We now look at some salient points arising from Appendix Table A4. It is to be noted that more than half the women who got married in the period 1981–86, had been married before the age of 18 years. Surprisingly, the percentage for India as a whole was lower. It appears that in rural West Bengal the trend

of women getting married early is more common than in rural India as a whole. In urban India, the West Bengal situation is better than the one for all-India. Table A4 shows that a much higher proportion of urban women aged 20–24 years (37 per cent in 1981 and 1991) remained unmarried as compared to rural women in the same age group (only about 12 per cent in 1981 and 1991) in West Bengal. During 1971–91 all districts reported a steady rise in the proportion of rural women remaining unmarried at least up to the age of 20 years. However, even in 1991 this proportion continued to be less than 12 per cent in a number of districts (for example, Koch Bihar, West Dinajpur, Puruliya, Birbhum, etc.). Between 1981 and 1991, there has been a noticeable fall across districts in the proportion of currently married women who were married before the legal age of 18 years. In West Bengal as a whole, this proportion declined from about 56 to 48 per cent but there were still districts where it varied from 55 to 65 per cent (for example, Koch Bihar, Maldah, Murshidabad, Nadia, the 24 Parganas, Puruliya).

Mean Age at Marriage

During the two decades from 1971 to 1981, the mean age at marriage in West Bengal has remained well above the all-India figure both for men and women. This is evident from Table 1.11 which provides both census data (1971–91) as well as data from the second National Family Health Survey. In West Bengal, during 1971–91, the mean age of marriage for women had gone up from 18 to 19.7 years while that for men had gone up from 24.6 to 25.9 years. The relevant all-India figures for women were 17.2 and 19 years and that for men, 22.6 and 24 years. However, during the last decade, the rise in the mean age of marriage seems to have been marginal both for men and women and in 1998–99 the female mean age for West Bengal and all-India were almost identical at 19.6 and 19.7 years respectively.

Table 1.11
Mean Age at Marriage, West Bengal and India, 1971 to 1998–99

	Sex	1971 census	1981 census	1991 census	NFHS-2: 1998–99		
					Rural	Urban	Total
West Bengal	Male	24.6	26.0	25.9	29.0	25.2	26.2
	Female	18.0	19.3	19.7	22.4	18.67	19.6
India	Male	22.6	23.5	24.0	26.5	24.2	24.9
	Female	17.2	18.4	19.3	21.5	19.0	19.7

Source: IIPS and ORC Macro, NFHS-2, 1998–99, India, Table 2.4.

---

[11] Government of India. *Towards Equality*. Report of the Committee on the Status of Women in India. Department of Social Welfare, New Delhi, 1975.
[12] Chen, Martha A., 'Perpetual Mourning: Widowhood in Rural India', in *The World's Women*, UN, 2000.

Early marriage carries the possibility of early pregnancy and motherhood. These events can severely curtail education and employment opportunities for women and affect their own as well as their children's quality of life. It follows that vigorous education and awareness generation programmes need to be designed for and propagated in areas systematically reporting early marriages for women, i.e., marriage at ages below the legal requirement.

Fertility Rates

Table 1.12 provides information regarding fertility rates for West Bengal and India. The table is based on figures obtained from the Sample Registration System (SRS) for 1991 as well as from the second National Family Health Survey of 1998/99.

According to estimates from NFHS-2, West Bengal's total fertility rate (TFR) in 1998–99 was 2.3 children per woman of childbearing age as compared to the all-India rate of 2.9. The corresponding figures for West Bengal and India in 1991 from the first NFHS (1989–91) and also from the SRS 91 were 2.9 and 3.2, pointing to a steady decline in recent years. TFR refers to the average number of children expected to be born per woman if age specific fertility rate continues to be the same. A high TFR is obviously unfavourable for women because of repeated risks and burdens of child birth and child care.

It is interesting to note that in 1991, according to the SRS, West Bengal's age-specific fertility for all age groups were lower than the all-India figures except for the youngest, i.e., 15 to 19 years age group. Again, according to the NFHS figure for 1996/98, West Bengal's rates for the youngest age group were the same as the all-India one. In all older age groups, the West Bengal figures were lower than the all-India ones. The exception was the small positive difference between the two in the age group 44 to 49 years. This suggests that West Bengal's women in general are more capable of controlling their fertility than their all-India counterparts. But when women are married at a young age and bear children before reaching the age of 20 years, they are as helpless in West Bengal as anywhere else in the country.

SRS figures show that for all age groups, rural fertility levels were considerably higher than urban levels. The difference was most pronounced for age groups 20–24 and 25–29 years, with fertility rates of 2.35 and 1.74 in rural areas as against the urban rates of 1.53 and 1.21.

The age pattern of fertility peaked at age group 20–24 years and declined markedly thereafter. This was a common feature for India as a whole and rural and urban West Bengal. This trend is unchanged.

Table 1.12
Age-specific Fertility Rates,* West Bengal and India

| Age Group | Sample Registration System (1991) | | | | NFHS-2 (1996–98) | |
| | West Bengal | | | India | West Bengal | India |
	Rural	Urban	Combined	Combined	Combined	Combined
Age-specific Fertility Rate*						
15–19	95.6	46.5	83.5	76.1	107	107
20–24	235.5	152.7	212.9	234.0	172	210
25–29	174.1	120.7	157.8	191.3	110	143
30–34	111.1	61.5	96.1	117.0	47	69
35–39	65.6	26.6	54.0	66.8	15	28
40–44	31.5	9.7	24.5	30.6	3	8
45–49	16.2	3.4	12.3	12.1	4	3
Total Fertility Rate**						
	3.6	2.1	3.2	3.6	2.29	2.85

Sources: Government of West Bengal, *Family Welfare Statistics at a Glance*, West Bengal, 1995, Table 10.

Economic Information Technology, Kolkata and International Institute for Population Science, Mumbai (IIPS).

NFHS-2, 1998–99: *West Bengal Preliminary Report*, August 1999, Table 5.

IIPS and ORC Macro, NFHS-2, 1998–99: India, October 2000, Table 4.3.

Notes: * No. of live births in a year to 1,000 women in a specified age group.
** Average no. of children born to a woman experiencing current fertility pattern.

Preliminary findings of NFHS-2 suggest that 39 per cent of the women of West Bengal do not want any more children. An additional 35 per cent cannot have more children because of sterility or infertility of either spouse.

Literacy

Literacy levels for West Bengal have always been much higher than the all-India equivalent figures. For example, according to the 2001 Census, male, female and total population of West Bengal had literacy rates of 78 per cent, 60 per cent and 69 per cent respectively. The comparable figures for India as a whole in 2001 were 76 per cent, 54 per cent, and 65 per cent. The differential between male and female literacy rates in West Bengal has always been lower than the all-India figures. Nevertheless, even for this state it was as high as 21.2 percentage points in 1991. In 2001, it had come down to 18 percentage points. This is by no means an insignificant level and needs special efforts to correct the imbalance.

Appendix Table A2 provides detailed information about total literacy rates as well as female literacy rates of scheduled caste and scheduled tribe populations. The scheduled tribes living in rural areas had the lowest literacy rates in the state. In Maldah and Birbhum districts, for example, less than 5 per cent ST women were found to be literate in 1991. Obviously, special programmes are needed for advancement of literacy of these deprived social groups. The importance of high female literacy cannot be overemphasized, particularly in view of its being linked with lower fertility rates, better child birth practices and child health standards, that have been brought out in many studies. West Bengal's relative advantage in female literacy in comparison with Bihar and all-India has perhaps provided the region with an advantage in this respect, which is reflected (Table 1.13) in the somewhat higher use of family planning devices and higher rates of child immunization that are found here.

Table 1.13
Literacy and Associated Indicators Relating to Ever-Married Women Aged 13–49 Years, 1992–93

Indicators	India	West Bengal	Bihar
Literate among ever-married women (per cent)	36.9	49.5	21.7
Births attended by health professionals (per cent)	35.8	34.8	19.1
Mortality rate for children under 5 years per 1,000 live births	137	128	154
Percentage of fully immunized children			
Male	43.1	43.7	12.1
Female	40.9	43.5	9.0
Percentage of women using family planning methods	40.7	57.7	23.2
Total fertility rate	4.0	3.6	4.8

Sources: Mari Bhat, P.N. and F. Zavier, 'Findings of National Family Health Survey: Regional Analysis', *Economic and Political Weekly*, 16–23 October 1999.
NFHS-2, 1998–99, India, Table 2.10, p. 207.
For Bihar: NFHS, 1998–99, *Bihar Preliminary Report*, Table 14, p. 26.

The advantage that West Bengal's women have through higher literacy rates is also likely to yield them benefits in the labour market in future. Recent data on employment rates has shown that, increasingly, the Indian labour market has come to favour workers with some education. Between 1993/94 and 1999/2000, the employment of women with secondary education went up by 4.1 per cent in rural areas and 30 per cent in urban areas. This took place when the overall employment rates for women were either stagnant or falling.[13]

Indices of Women's Development

Since 1990, the United Nations Development Programme (UNDP) has been publishing Human Development Reports every year. Each of these reports is a rich compendium of statistical data from countries all over the world, throwing light on many chosen aspects of the human condition. Utilizing this huge collection of data, the UNDP has formulated the now celebrated Human Development Index (HDI). It has also developed two new indices or special types of numerical measures for evaluating the relative situation of women. The first is the Gender Development Index (GDI), which, like the HDI, takes into account three important indicators of human welfare: life expectancy, educational attainment and per capita income, as applicable separately for women and men in a given country. A specific numerical score on the basis of these three attributes is then computed, showing the extent of gender-based disparities that affect the situation of women in each country. This score, essentially representing certain basic capabilities that promote a decent life, can ideally reach a maximum value of 1, as in the case of the HDI. The GDI score falls when the achievement levels of both men and women in a given country go down or when the disparity between them increases. The second measure is the Gender Empowerment Measure (GEM), which seeks to throw light on the extent to which women participate in the economic, political and professional spheres of their respective countries. 'While the GDI focusses on expansion of capabilities, the GEM is concerned with the use of these capabilities to take advantage of the opportunities of life.'[14]

In a recent study on GEM values for different states in India, West Bengal is ranked 7 in a list of 16 states.[15] Scholars have also calculated state-level GDI values on the basis of available statistical data. In a study done by K. Seeta Prabhu and others, West Bengal is ranked 9 in a list of 15 states with a GDI score of 0.3643 as against 0.7584 and 0.6999 for Kerala and Maharashtra respectively.[16]

Conclusion

This chapter has provided basic information relating to demographic variables for West Bengal as compared to those for India as a whole. Its focus is specially on the conditions of women in comparison with men. It appears that over the last two or three decades of the twentieth century, West Bengal's population has grown fast but it is increasingly lagging behind the all-India rates. That it did not fall further was perhaps due to illicit immigration across the state's international boundaries.

[13] Banerjee and Jain, 'India's Sex-ratio'.
[14] UNDP, *Human Development Report*, 1995.
[15] Mehta, Asha Kapur, 'Recasting Indices for Developing Countries: A Gender Empowerment Measure', *Economic and Political Weekly*, 26 October 1996.
[16] Seeta Prabhu, K. et al., 'Gender-related Development Index for Indian States', *Economic and Political Weekly*, 26 October 1996.

Women have been moving into urban areas of West Bengal at faster rates than men in recent decades. That has meant that the earlier imbalance in male/female numbers in urban areas has been shrinking.

The sex-ratio of West Bengal, as compared to all-India, has always appeared to be more adverse to women. However, part of this shortfall was due to the single-male immigration of workers into West Bengal in the past. If one corrects for this factor, West Bengal's sex-ratio was standing at a higher level than for India as a whole in 1981. Unfortunately, there was a setback in 1991 which could actually be due to fresh male in-migration from neighbouring countries that has not been reported as such.

Women have made some gains especially in their expect-ation of life at birth (LEB). During the 1990s, LEB improved quite fast and women's gains were larger in this respect than men's. West Bengal's birth rates have fallen rapidly in the 1990s and their gap with the all-India rates has increased. This was particularly true for urban areas. There is a significant gap between urban and rural infant mortality rates that deserves immediate attention of policy makers.

Looking at distribution of the population by age groups and marital status, it appears that for women living longer it may be a mixed blessing since with age comes the possibility of widowhood and the loss of status that goes with it in our country.

While the average age at marriage of women has gone up in the last quarter of the twentieth century, about a third of the women in West Bengal who had been married in the eighties and nineties had been married before the age of 19 years. Early marriages apparently mean that the women have less say in the reproductive decisions. While age specific fertility in West Bengal was lower than the all-India figures for all age groups, it remained at par with India for the youngest age group.

Health and Nutrition

CHAPTER 2

Maitreya Ghatak

Health and Gender

Health of the people is a reflection of the overall social, economic and cultural situation prevailing in a society. Like any other field of social development, women's status in the field of health is characterized by inequality based on gender. In the Indian situation, gender-based inequality is further aggravated when associated with such factors as poverty, illiteracy, rural background, lower caste, widowhood, desertion, disability, single marital status or childlessness.[1]

There has been considerable progress in the states in the last few decades in social and economic development, even though unevenly, in terms of life expectancy, literacy, infant mortality, to mention only a few. Yet, the situation in respect of women's health lags behind gains in other fields and gender-based inequalities continue to persist in most states including West Bengal.

The failure to address the health and nutritional needs of women is often revealed where gender disaggregated data are available. Unfortunately, such data are scanty and largely with a narrow focus. Ever since independence, the health policies of the country in respect of women have been obsessed with demographic considerations, more specifically population control. As early as 1952, promotion of health of women and children was tagged with the national family welfare programme. From the Fifth Plan period (1974–79), maternal health, child health and nutrition services were integrated with family planning services with the primary aim of providing at least a minimum level of public services to pregnant women, lactating mothers and pre-school children. In the early nineties, several key child survival interventions were integrated with safe motherhood and family planning activities. And now, since 1996, the new Reproductive and Child Health (RCH) Programme seeks to integrate maternal health, child health and fertility regulation interventions with reproductive health programme for both men and women and adolescent girls.[2]

Despite frequent changes in packaging, the 'family welfare' component of the programmes has always been accorded a secondary position and the programme thrust has been achievement of demographic targets by increasing contraceptive prevalence (read female sterilization).[3] While assessing the health policy of the country, the Committee on Empowerment of Women recently observed:

> Anaemia, urinary tract infections, malnutrition, repeated child births, adolescent marriage and overwork take a heavy toll on women's lives. But their health and nutritional needs receive little focus. All healthcare programmes for women are tailored for pregnant and nursing mothers for achieving population stabilization....[4]

As a result of this priority, data relating to demography and family planning are more easily available, both at the central and the state government levels, than data relating to other aspects of health and nutrition of women and children. To give a

---

[1] Voluntary Health Association of India. *Report of the Independent Commission on Health in India.* New Delhi, 1997, p. 184.

[2] National Family Health Survey (NFHS-2) (1998–99), India, IIPS, Mumbai, 2000, p. 279.

[3] Jejeebhoy, Shireen J., 'Addressing Women's Reproductive Health Needs: Priorities for the Family Welfare Programme'. Internet-accessed mimeo, Population Council of India, 1995.

[4] Committee on Empowerment of Women (2000–2001), Fourth report submitted to the Lok Sabha on 30 August 2001.

concrete example, before the first National Family Health Survey (NFHS) was conducted in 1992–93, an apparently simple information like immunization coverage used to be published by the governments in such a manner that no one could make out how many children of the relevant age group were fully immunized (all doses of all vaccines), how many were partly immunized, how many were not immunized at all and whether there was any difference between boys and girls in the coverage. The two NFHS (1992–93 and 1998–99) and the Rapid Household Survey under the RCH (1998–99) provide a vast body of information on the health status of women in various states. But even these surveys are primarily concerned with fertility and reproductive aspects of health of women, as if they do not have any other health problem, physical or mental. So any discussion on the status of women in the field of health has to face the problem of inadequate data in respect of matters not related to RCH.

This report aims at analysing the status of women in the state in the field of health and nutrition. The West Bengal situation has been compared with the situation prevailing in 14 other 'most populous' states of India, wherever such data were available. The present situation in the state has also been compared with the situation in the past, where comparable data were available.

Expectation of Life at Birth

There has been considerable improvement in expectation of life at birth (average number of years a child is expected to live under current mortality conditions) in India since independence. It has nearly doubled from 32.1 years in 1951 to 62.4 years in 1995 for the country as a whole. It has nearly tripled from 22.9 years in 1901–11.

Yet, for the country as a whole, it was only in the beginning of the eighties that the expectation of life for women, which has been lagging behind that of men, improved substantially and the gap between men and women was not only gone, but women's expectation of life began to exceed that of men, a normal feature in most countries.

There has been considerable improvement in West Bengal during the period. Expectation of life at birth for women has gone up from 54.70 in 1981 to 64.19 in 1996–2001. But it was only in 1991–96 that West Bengal was able to bridge the gap between men and women in this respect as evident from Table 2.1. Among the 15 major states, West Bengal ranked ninth in terms of expectation of life at birth for women in 1981. The state's relative position remained the same in 1996–2001.

Table 2.1
Projected Values of Expectation of Life at Birth by Sex

| | Base year* Value of e: | | Rank F base year | Projected Values of e* | | | | | | | | Rank female 1996–2001 |
| | | | | 1981–86 | | 1986–91 | | 1991–96 | | 1996–2001 | | |
	Male	Female		Male	Female	Male	Female	Male	Female	Male	Female	
Andhra Pradesh	53.90	57.60	5	56.10	59.98	59.10	62.23	61.40	64.48	63.40	65.93	5
Assam (1)	49.19	48.29	14	52.74	51.98	55.74	55.23	58.74	58.48	61.14	61.18	12
Bihar (2)	53.71	50.71	11	55.21	52.90	58.21	57.00	60.81	60.09	62.81	62.78	11
Gujarat	53.14	55.92	7	55.34	58.30	58.34	61.49	60.94	62.74	62.94	65.59	6
Haryana	59.89	57.21	6	61.41	59.59	63.41	61.97	65.21	64.22	66.21	65.94	4
Karnataka	57.88	59.11	3	60.15	61.06	62.15	63.31	64.15	65.30	65.55	65.56	7
Kerala	64.19	68.95	1	65.23	69.87	66.23	71.12	67.23	72.37	68.23	73.62	1
Madhya Pradesh	51.04	49.25	13	53.24	51.46	56.24	54.71	59.24	57.96	61.50	60.82	14
Maharashtra	57.65	58.56	4	59.85	60.66	61.90	62.91	63.90	65.06	65.45	66.31	3
Orissa	51.93	49.59	12	54.13	51.90	57.13	55.15	60.13	58.40	62.13	61.15	13
Punjab	62.84	62.69	2	64.31	64.34	65.61	65.30	66.61	66.55	67.61	67.80	2
Rajasthan (3)	52.30	52.73	10	54.8	55.44	57.80	58.69	60.50	61.34	62.50	63.59	10
Tamil Nadu	56.05	55.63	8	58.25	57.85	60.85	60.80	62.85	63.05	64.85	65.20	8
Uttar Pradesh (3)	48.86	44.60	15	51.14	46.89	54.14	49.64	57.14	52.84	60.09	56.09	15
West Bengal	55.45	54.65	9	56.95	56.28	59.95	59.53	61.95	61.94	63.95	64.19	9
India	54.10	54.70		55.60	56.40	58.10	59.10	60.60	61.70	62.80	64.20	

Source: *Census of India 1981*, Report of the Expert Committee on Population Projections, Occasional Paper No. 4 of 1988.
Notes: (1) Relates to 1976–78;
(2) Relates to 1981;
(3) Relate to 1978–80.
* For all other states the base year is 1979–80. For India the base year is 1980—SRS estimate R.G. India.

Sex-ratio

The term sex-ratio is being used here to denote the number of females per 1,000 males in the population. All census operations in the country, ever since 1901, have recorded lower proportion of females in the population at the national level. The observations of the Report on the Committee on the Status of Women in India (1974) largely remain valid even today:

> The decline in the sex-ratio ever since 1901 is a disturbing phenomenon in the context of the status of women. Demographers put forward various hypotheses to explain this, like (a) higher under-enumeration of females; (b) the higher mortality rate of the females; (c) the marked preference for sons and the consequent neglect of the female infants; (d) the lower status of women and the general neglect of women at all ages; (e) the adverse impact of frequent and excessive child-bearing on the health of women; (f) the higher incidence of certain diseases on women.... The differential improvement in health conditions must have contributed substantially to the decline in sex-ratio.[5]

Addition of sex-ratio at birth and (sex-selective) migration to this observation would, probably, complete the list today.

Among the major states, Kerala is the only state to record a higher proportion of females (females/1,000 males) *in every census from 1901 to 2001*. Bihar and Orissa maintained this position from 1901 to 1961. In the last 100 years, it is only in the 2001 Census that West Bengal was able to marginally improve its sex-ratio over the all-India average. West Bengal's sex-ratio was 934 in the 2001 Census compared to the national ratio of 933.

In the case of West Bengal (as well as Maharashtra), migration has played an important role in the prevailing sex-ratio pattern for decades as they have attracted migrants from other states for occupational reasons.[6]

However, it is also to be noted that ever since 1941, the sex-ratio of West Bengal has been steadily improving and the trend has been maintained in the 2001 Census. None among the 15 major states, other than West Bengal, has been able to maintain this increasing trend throughout this period, as Table 2.2 would show.

Between 1901 and 1951, West Bengal's rank among the 15 major states had fluctuated between 10 and 14, one of the lowest in the country. Both in 1941 and 1951, West Bengal ranked 14 among the 15 major states. From 1961 onwards, West Bengal's rank steadily improved without any break and in 2001 became sixth.

Another aspect of sex-ratio in West Bengal needs mention. The sex-ratio relating to scheduled caste population compared to total population has been lower at the national level. In 1981, the SC sex-ratio was 932 compared to 935 for the total population. In 1991, the difference was even wider—

Table 2.2
Sex-ratio (Females per 1,000 Males) from 1901 to 2001 in India and 15 Major States

	1901	R	1911	R	1921	R	1931	R	1941	R	1951	R	1961	R	1971	R	1981	R	1991	R	2001	R
Andhra Pradesh	985	5	992	5	993	5	987	4	980	5	986	5	981	5	977	4	975	4	972	3	978	3
Assam	919	12	915	12	896	12	874	12	875	12	868	13	869	13	896	10	910	11	923	7	932	7
Bihar	1,061	1	1,051	2	1,020	3	955	6	1,002	4	1,000	4	1,005	2	957	5	948	6	907	11	921	9
Gujarat	954	9	946	9	944	9	945	8	941	9	952	7	940	7	934	6	942	7	934	6	921	9
Haryana	867	14	835	14	844	13	844	13	869	13	871	12	868	14	867	13	870	15	865	14	861	13
Karnataka	983	6	981	6	969	6	965	5	960	6	966	6	959	6	957	5	963	5	960	5	964	5
Kerala	1,004	4	1,008	4	1,011	4	1,022	3	1,027	2	1,028	1	1,022	1	1,016	1	1,032	1	1,036	1	1,058	1
Madhya Pradesh	972	8	967	7	949	8	947	7	946	8	945	8	932	9	920	8	921	9	912	9	920	10
Maharashtra	978	7	966	8	950	7	947	7	949	7	941	9	936	8	930	7	937	8	934	6	922	8
Orissa	1,037	3	1,056	1	1,086	1	1,067	1	1,053	1	1,022	2	1,001	3	988	2	981	2	971	4	972	4
Punjab	832	15	780	15	799	14	815	14	836	15	844	15	854	15	865	14	879	14	882	12	874	12
Rajasthan	905	13	908	13	896	12	907	9	906	11	921	10	908	10	911	9	919	12	910	10	922	8
Tamil Nadu	1,044	2	1,042	3	1,029	2	1,027	2	1,012	3	1,007	3	992	4	978	3	977	3	974	2	986	2
Uttar Pradesh	938	11	916	11	908	10	903	10	907	10	908	11	907	11	876	12	882	13	876	13	898	11
West Bengal	945	10	925	10	905	11	890	11	852	14	865	14	878	12	891	11	911	10	917	8	934	6
India	972		964		955		950		945		946		941		930		934		927		933	

Source: *Census of India 2001*, Provisional Population Totals, Table 10, p. 154.
Notes: All Data for Bihar, MP & UP are adjusted data after creation of Jharkhand, Chhattisgarh and Uttaranchal respectively. Haryana data are also adjusted retrospectively since 1901.
The 1981 Census was not held in Assam. Hence sex-ratios of Assam have been worked out by interpolated population.
R: Rank.

[5] Government of India. *Towards Equality: Report of The Committee on the Status of Women in India*. Ministry of Education and Social Welfare, New Delhi, 1975, p. 11.

[6] Agnihotri, S.B., 'Missing Females: A Disaggregated Analysis', *Economic and Political Weekly*, 19 August 2002.

922 for the SC population compared to 927 for the total population. But in West Bengal, the sex-ratio of the SC population was better than the total population sex-ratio both in 1981 and 1991. In 1981, the SC sex-ratio was 926 in the state compared to 911 for the total population. In 1991, it was 931 for the SC compared to 917 for the total population. The sex-ratio of the scheduled tribe population is better than the total population sex-ratio both at the national and state level.

Sex-ratio, 0–6 Years

Unlike the overall sex-ratio, the sex-ratio for the 0–6 age group is not likely to be affected by (sex-selective) migration, as there is nothing to suggest that migrating parents bring or leave behind only boys or girls. If both male and female children are correctly reported to the census enumerator, or if the under-reporting is of the same magnitude for male and female children, then sex-ratio for this age group is likely to be primarily the result of sex-ratio at birth and sex differential in survival through infancy and childhood. It has been pointed out by demographers that the overall sex-ratio is the result of past legacy while the sex-ratio of the child population is the outcome of factors operating in the recent past.[7] That is why the steadily declining trend of this ratio in the last four decades (for which data are available) in practically every major state is a matter of much concern.

Table 2.3 shows that the ratio has fallen from 976 in 1961 to 927 in 2001, a fall of 49 points at the national level. The fall has been most considerable between 1991 and 2001, from 945 to 927. A comparison with the earlier table on general sex-ratio would show that for the first time, the child sex-ratio fell below the general sex-ratio of the country.

Ever since 1961, West Bengal has remained the third or second best-performing state in this regard. Assam is the only state which in 1991 and 2001 did better than West Bengal.

But the West Bengal data also show some disturbing trends. In 1961, the child sex-ratio in the state was 1,008. In 1971, it further improved and went up to 1,010 when at the national level the ratio fell from 976 to 964. The only other state in the country where this ratio improved between 1961 and 1971 was Kerala. But, since then, the ratio has steadily declined in West Bengal.

However, it is also to be noted that the sex-ratio decline in West Bengal between 1991 and 2001 by four points (from 967 to 963) is much lower than the decline by 29 points between 1971 and 1981 (from 1010 to 981) or by 14 points between 1981 and 1991 (from 981 to 967). During 1991–2001, West Bengal's decline was also the lowest among all the major states.

Table 2.3
Sex-ratio (Female per 1,000 Males) of Population Aged 0 to 6 years in India and 15 Major States, 1961 to 2001

	1961		1971		1981		1991***		2001***		Change	
	0–6	Rank	0–6	Rank	0–6	Rank	0–6	Rank	0–6	Rank	1961–2001	Rank
Andhra Pradesh	1,002	4	990	4	992	2	975	1	964	1	38	3
Assam*	1,021	2	1,002	3	na	na	975	1	964	1	57	9
Bihar	988	5	964	9	981	4	953	5	938	6	50	7
Gujarat	955	11	946	10	950	11	928	9	878	11	77	11
Haryana**	na	na	899	13	902	14	879	12	820	12	79	12
Karnataka	987	6	979	5	974	6	960	3	949	4	38	3
Kerala	971	10	976	6	970	7	958	4	963	2	8	1
Madhya Pradesh	982	8	976	6	977	5	941	8	929	7	53	8
Maharashtra	978	9	972	8	956	9	945	7	917	8	61	10
Orissa	1,035	1	1,020	1	995	1	967	2	950	3	85	13
Punjab	906	14	899	14	908	13	875	13	793	13	113	14
Rajasthan	950	12	932	11	954	10	916	11	909	10	41	4
Tamil Nadu	985	7	974	7	967	8	948	6	939	5	46	6
Uttar Pradesh	946	13	923	12	935	12	927	10	916	9	30	2
West Bengal	1,008	3	1,010	2	981	3	967	2	963	2	45	5
India	976		964		962		945		927		49	

Sources: All data compiled from *Census of India*.
   1961—Vol I, Part IIC(i), Social and Cultural Tables, Table CIV, Single Year Age Returns, p. 412.
   1971—Series I, Part IIC(ii), Social and Cultural Tables, Table CIV, Single Year Age Returns, p. 135.
   1981—Series I, Social and Cultural Tables, Table CV, Single Year Age Returns, p. 530.
   1991—Series I, Part IV, A-C Series, Social and Cultural Table, Table CII, Age, Sex and Level of Education, p. 168.
   2001—Series I, Provisional Population Totals, Supplement District Totals, Paper 1 of 2001, Table No. 2, p. 118.

Notes: * Assam data not available for 1981 because census was not held there in 1981.
   ** Haryana data are available from 1971. Change also shown from 1971.
   *** Data for Bihar, Madhya Pradesh and Uttar Pradesh for 1991 and 2001 adjusted after recent bifurcation of respective states.

[7] Parasuraman, S. 'Declining Sex Ratio of the Child Population in India'. Internet accessed document. IIPS, Mumbai, 2001.

Nutrition

Widespread poverty resulting in chronic and persistent hunger is the single biggest scourge of the developing world today. The physical expression of this continuously re-enacted tragedy is the condition of under-nutrition, which manifests itself among large sections of the poor, particularly women and children.[8]

The Statement on the National Nutrition Policy (1993) identified several major nutrition problems in the country. Among them is under-nutrition, which results in protein-energy malnutrition (PEM), iron deficiency (anaemia), iodine deficiency, vitamin A deficiency and low birth weight children. Under-nutrition is a condition resulting from inadequate intake of food or some essential nutrients resulting in deterioration of physical growth and health.

Increased food production or its availability may not necessarily result in proportionate rise in actual availability of food, in quantity or quality, for women and children within the household. There are several studies which suggest that there is gender-based discrimination in this respect in various parts of the country.

For the country as a whole, low birth weight, respiratory infections and anaemia are the main causes of mortality among children 0–4 years of age. For the next higher age group of children (5–14), respiratory infection and anaemia become the main causes of mortality.

Under-nutrition is an important contributory factor to mortality among infants and children. For adolescent girls, physical growth and development continues and there is need for adequate nutrition for normal growth. Not only does this need remain unmet for many, there is additional demand for nutrition during pregnancy, which also remains largely unmet and results in malnutrition-related illness for the mother and low birth weight for the baby. As a very large number of marriages for women in the country take place even before a girl is 18, the problem perpetuates both for the mother and the baby. The situation has been described as 'child labour' at its worst, in more senses than one. 'It is "labour" which carries far greater risks than some of the other forms of child labour over which there is public outcry.'[9]

Low Birth Weight Children

It is difficult to give a precise picture simply because a vast majority of the children are not weighed within two days of birth, particularly in rural areas as shown in Appendix Table B1. In 1992–93 (NFHS-1) 73 per cent of the children in West Bengal (India: 79.1 per cent) were not weighed within the stipulated two-day period. In 1998–99 (NFHS-2), 60.6 per cent of the newborns in West Bengal remained unweighed at birth (India: 70.1 per cent).[10] The NFHS-2 findings were more or less corroborated by the Rapid Household Survey under the Reproductive and Child Health Programme, conducted in 1998–99, which showed that only 35.1 per cent of the children were weighed. While the situation was better in West Bengal than the country as a whole, the RCH survey (Appendix Table B2) shows that the situation in respect of weighing is way behind five states, particularly Kerala, Tamil Nadu and Maharashtra. Health workers and Anganwadi workers have been provided with weighing machines for covering deliveries that take place in the home, but apparently they reach only a few in most states including West Bengal. Because of this large 'unweighed' or 'weight unknown' segments, data in these two tables should be seen with caution. Both the tables indicate that the percentage of under-2.5 kg birth weight children is more in West Bengal than in the country as a whole.

Appendix Table B3 provides data from NFHS-1 and NFHS-2 relating to three summary indices of nutritional status of children:

- Weight for age
- Height for age
- Weight for height

Height for age and weight for height data were not collected for West Bengal under NFHS-1 and cannot be compared. Broadly speaking, –2SD under weight for age would mean undernourished and –3SD would mean severely undernourished under that parameter. For height for age, children who are more than two standard deviations below the median of the reference population are considered short for their age or stunted. For weight for height, those below two standard deviations are considered too thin or wasted.[11]

In terms of weight for age, West Bengal fared poorer than the all-India average (below –2SD). Under NFHS-1, its position

---

[8] Government of India, *National Nutrition Policy (Introduction)*, Department of Women and Child Development, Ministry of Human Resource Development, New Delhi, 1993.

[9] Gopalan, C., 'Child Labour in India—Emerging Challenges', in C. Gopalan (ed.), *Towards Better Nutrition: Problems and Policies*. Nutrition Foundation of India, New Delhi, 1993.

[10] See all-India and West Bengal reports of NFHS-1 and NFHS-2.

[11] NFHS-2, India, pp. 265–66.

Table 2.4
Nutritional Status by Sex among Children in West Bengal and India and the Percentage
Classified as Under-nourished in NFHS-1 and 2 (1992–93 and 1998–99)

| | Weight for age | | | | Height for age | | | | Weight for height | | | | Number of | |
| | % below –3SD | | % below –2SD | | % below –3SD | | % below –2SD | | % below –3SD | | % below –2SD | | Children | |
Year	Male	Female	Male	Female	Male	Female	Male	Female	Male	Female	Male	Female	Male	Female
1992–93														
W. Bengal	17.2	19.6	54.7	59.0	NA	NA	NA	NA	NA	NA	NA	NA	839	797
India	20.2	21.0	53.3	53.4	x	x	x	x	x	x	x	x	18,208	17,599
1998–99														
W. Bengal	13.7	19.1	45.5	52.3	14.4	24.5	36.6	47	1.5	1.7	14.8	12.3	586	525
India	16.9	19.1	45.3	48.9	21.8	24.2	44.1	47	2.9	2.7	15.7	15.2	12,822	11,778

Notes: Children are under 4 years in NFHS-1 and under 3 years in NFHS-2.

Each index is expressed in standard deviation units (SD) from the median of the International Reference Population.

Approximately, below –2SD would mean under-nourished and below –3SD would mean severely under-nourished for the given parameter. –3SD is included in –2SD. NFHS Reports for India and West Bengal for respective years.

Height for age, weight for height data were not collected for West Bengal in NFHS-1. So the corresponding all-India figures are not shown.

was 11 which somewhat improved to 9 under NFHS-2. But Appendix Table B3 does not provide any idea about gender differentials, if any. Gender differential details under these indices are provided in the West Bengal state reports of the two NFHSs, which can be compared with the all-India situation. This is done in Table 2.4.

In terms of weight for age, more girls than boys (59 per cent vs 54.7 per cent) were under-nourished (per cent below –2SD) whereas at the all-India level there was no difference. In 1998–99, the gap between boys and girls in terms of under-nourishment increased in West Bengal (52.3 per cent for girls and 45.5 per cent for boys). This gap was higher than the all-India average.

In height for age, the gap in West Bengal was even wider than the all-India situation, 36.6 per cent for boys and 47 per cent for girls (below –2SD). The all-India gap was much less, 44.1 per cent boys and 47 per cent girls were below –2SD.

In weight for height also, girls fared poorer than boys in West Bengal, though the gap was very little (14.8 per cent for boys compared to 12.3 for girls). At the all-India level the gap was much less.

West Bengal ICDS Data

All Anganwadi centres (AWCs) under the Integrated Child Development Scheme (ICDS) in the state submit a monthly report to their block-level projects about the weight of boys and girls covered by them. In the year 2000 (September), there were 359 sanctioned (block level) projects in the state, of which 270 were actually functioning. Under them were 39,813 Anganwadi centres of which 39,234 had sent their monthly reports to their respective project heads. These monthly reports contained weight-related information for a total of 939,476

boys and 921,734 girls, from all the districts of West Bengal including Kolkata. The total number of children for whom data are available is 1,861,210. The AWCs are overwhelmingly located in the rural areas of the state. Table 2.5 has been prepared on the basis of this data for the state as a whole.

Table 2.5
Nutritional Status (Weight for Age) of Children by Sex in West Bengal in September 2000 as Reported by Anganwadi Centres*

Number of children weighed	Male (n =)	Female (n =)	Female/100 Males
By age in years			
Below 1	143,003	138,358	96.75
1 to 3	354,750	349,327	98.47
3 to 5	441,723	434,049	98.26
All ages	939,476	921,734	98.11
% Normal weight			
Below 1	46.21	41.22	89.20
1 to 3	39.04	34.19	87.58
3 to 5	41.27	38.33	92.88
All ages	41.18	37.47	90.99
% Grade I (mild) malnutrition			
Below 1	32.83	35.49	108.10
1 to 3	36.54	36.71	100.47
3 to 5	37.37	36.41	97.43
All ages	36.37	36.39	100.05
% Grade II (moderate) malnutrition			
Below 1	19.16	21.26	110.96
1 to 3	23.05	26.08	113.15
3 to 5	20.17	23.77	117.85
All ages	21.10	24.27	115.02
% Grades III and IV (severe) malnutrition			
Below 1	1.80	2.03	112.78
1 to 3	1.67	2.29	137.13
3 to 5	1.19	1.40	117.65
All ages	1.46	1.83	125.34

(*Table 2.5 contd.*)

(Table 2.5 contd.)

Number of children weighed	Male (n =)	Female (n =)	Female/100 Males
% Grades II–IV malnutrition			
Below 1	20.96	23.30	111.16
1 to 3	24.72	28.38	114.81
3 to 5	21.36	25.17	117.84
All ages	22.57	26.11	115.68

Note: * The table has been prepared from monthly reports (September 2000) submitted by 270 Child Development Project Officers (CDPOs) to the state ICDS office. The data represent reports of 39,234 out of 39,767 functioning rural, tribal and urban AWCs from all the 17 districts as well as Kolkata.

The data in Table 2.5 indicates:

- Among children of all ages, for every 100 boys there are 99 girls.
- In terms of normal weight, girls lag behind boys. For every 100 boys, there are 91 girls in this category.
- In terms of grade I or mild malnutrition, there is no difference between boys and girls of 'all ages'.
- When it comes to moderate or grade II malnutrition, for every 100 boys, 115 girls fall under this category.
- The number of children who have been recorded as severely malnourished (grades III and IV combined) is very small (less than 2 per cent). Under this category there are 125 girls for every 100 boys.

It is not possible to state whether the present situation is any better or worse than what it was earlier without comparing it with the past. It can, however, be said that the ICDS programme in the state has a considerable ground to cover in terms of improving the overall nutritional status of children as well as narrowing down the gap between boys and girls.

Anaemia among Children of 6–35 Months

Anaemia is considered a serious problem for young children as it can result in several other problems including impaired cognitive performance and increased morbidity from infectious diseases.[12]

Under NFHS-2, anaemia level was determined after clinical examination of blood in the field. No past data are available, as NFHS-1 did not check anaemia.

Among the 15 major states, 78.3 per cent children in West Bengal are found to have 'any anaemia' as indicated in Appendix Table B4. The all-India average is lower (74.3 per cent).

The 78.3 per cent who have anaemia may be further subdivided into three other groups: mild anaemia (26.9 per cent), moderate anaemia (46.3 per cent) and severe anaemia (5.2 per cent).

In 'anaemia' and 'mild anaemia', West Bengal is well below the national average. In 'any anaemia', the state is behind nine other major states. But is there any gender differential in the incidence of anaemia among children?

Appendix Table B5 provides data which can make this comparison between the all-India and West Bengal situation. For this age group, there is no gender gap of significance either in West Bengal or at the national level. In fact, in moderate and severe anaemia, girls appear to be marginally better off than boys.

Anaemia among Women

Anaemia among women may have adverse effects on the health of women and may become an underlying cause of maternal and perinatal mortality. It may also result in an increased risk of premature delivery and low birth weight.[13] NFHS-2 actually took blood samples and measured the haemoglobin levels of all ever-married women (excluding those pregnant or gave birth in the last two months). Results for 15 major states are shown in Appendix Table B6.

West Bengal has a much higher prevalence of 'any anaemia' (62.7 per cent) compared to the all-India level (51.8 per cent). Most of those having anaemia in West Bengal (45.3 per cent) fall in the 'mild anaemia' category (India 35 per cent). In moderate and severe anaemia, West Bengal is practically at par with the all-India average.

In West Bengal, prevalence is higher for rural women (64 per cent) compared to urban women (58 per cent). But 61 per cent of all women living in Kolkata have some degree of anaemia. Another point to note is that compared to the state average of 63 per cent, prevalence is as high as 67 per cent among scheduled caste women and 81 per cent among scheduled tribe women.[14]

[12] NFHS-2, India, p. 271.

[13] Seshardi, Subadra, 'Nutritional Anaemia in South Asia', in Stuart Gillepse (ed.), *Malnutrition in South Asia: A Regional Profile*. Kathmandu Regional Office for South Asia, Kathmandu, 1997. Cited in NFHS-2 (India), p. 247.

[14] NFHS-2, West Bengal, p. 156.

Height and Weight-for-Height

The NFHS-2 also measured the height and weight-for-height (body mass index or BMI) of ever-married women for an understanding of their nutritional status. The height of an adult may be the result of several factors including nutrition during childhood and adolescence. A woman of short height may have a difficult delivery because her pelvic size may also be smaller. The risk of having a baby with a low birth weight is also higher for mothers who are short.[15] Height of women vary within a narrow range in the 15 major states.

The mean height for women in West Bengal (150 cm) is one of the lowest among the 15 major states (India, 151.2 cm) and it is better than only two other states—Assam and Bihar, as shown in Appendix Table B7. About one in five (19.2 per cent) women in West Bengal is below 145 cm, compared to only 13.2 per cent women who are below 145 cm at the national level. The only other state in almost the same league with West Bengal is Bihar where 19.5 per cent women are below 145 cm.

In terms of mean body mass index or BMI (weight in kilogram divided by the height in metres squared), West Bengal is behind 12 other states with a mean of 19.7 but there is very little difference with the national average (20.3).[16] Chronic energy deficiency is usually indicated by a BMI of less than 18.5. In West Bengal, 43.7 per cent women are below this point (India, 35.8 per cent). Orissa is the only other state which has more women below this limit (48 per cent). While for West Bengal as a whole 43.7 per cent women are below the BMI of 18.5, the situation is worse for certain socio-economic categories like illiterates (53 per cent), scheduled tribes (64.2 per cent), those working in family farm/business (51.1 per cent) or employed by others (55.8 per cent) and those with a low standard of living (57.1 per cent).[17]

Age at Marriage

Age at which a girl gets married is of considerable interest to demographers because, earlier the marriage, greater the likelihood of more children. But the age at marriage and consequently the age at which they start bearing children have serious implications for the health of women and the children to be born. The slow rise in age at marriage for women in the

country is considered a factor in poor reproductive health. For example, the NFHS-1 showed that for women of 15–49 years, 3.5 per cent pregnancies result in spontaneous abortion in West Bengal. For the 15–19 years age group, spontaneous abortions are as high as 8.2 per cent.[18]

Still births (3.7 per cent) are also higher for this age group compared to 'all ages' (2.3 per cent). This is a common pattern in the country.

A retrospective study of nearly 11,000 pregnancies over a period of five years in a subdivisional hospital of Durgapur in West Bengal clearly indicated that there is higher risk of maternal deaths, low birth weight babies, premature birth and perinatal death in pregnancies at lower ages as shown in Table 2.6.

Table 2.6
Retrospective Study of Pregnancies in a Subdivisional Hospital in West Bengal

Women's age	Maternal death/1,000 births	Average birth weight (kg)	Premature birth	Perinatal death/1,000 births
12–19	3.80	1.90	20	29.6
20–30	2.55	2.50	16	18.4
31+	1.07	2.65	11	4.3

Source: Mishra, S. and C.S. Dawn, 'Retrospective Study of Teenage Pregnancy and Labour during 5-Year Period from January 1978 to December 1982 at Durgapur Subdivisional Hospital', *Indian Medical Journal*, 80 (9): 150–52, 1986.

It took 30 years, from 1961 to 1991, for the singulate mean age at marriage for women to move from 15.9 years to 19.7 years in West Bengal as shown in Appendix Table B8. During the same period, the age of marriage for men moved from 24.3 to 25.9 years. Appendix Table B8 also shows that in 1992–93 (NFHS-1), the age of marriage of women in West Bengal was 19.2. By the time of the NFHS-2 in 1998–99, it rose to 19.6. These are figures for the state as a whole. In rural areas, the age at marriage was even lower.

The RCH study (Appendix Table B8) found that over 51 per cent currently married women in West Bengal were married before they were 18 years old. In terms of the percentage of women getting married before reaching the age of 18, West Bengal's record is quite poor, the state ranking 12 among the 15 major states. The only other states where more women got married before the age of 18 are Bihar, Rajasthan and Madhya Pradesh. If one compares this with Kerala where less than 10 per cent marriages take place before the age of 18, the magnitude of the problem becomes clear.

[15] NFHS-2, India, 1998–99, p. 243.
[16] Ibid.
[17] NFHS-2, West Bengal, p. 154.
[18] National Family Health Survey-1 (NFHS-1) (1992–93), International Institute of Population Sciences, Mumbai, State Report West Bengal, p. 74.

Use of Contraceptives

Launched in a modest way in the early fifties (1952), the country's 'family planning' programme has gone through periodic changes. But all along, the core emphasis has remained demographic, more specifically, reduction in total fertility rate. Till the mid-seventies, some efforts used to be made to put part of the responsibility on men. It is another issue that this used to be done almost entirely through male sterilization and not so much through the promotion of condoms. This reached a peak during the emergency years (1975–77). Since then, there has been a clear policy of de-emphasis on male methods, particularly male sterilization. Almost the entire responsibility of family planning has shifted to women and that, too, through permanent, irreversible or long-lasting methods which leave little choice or autonomy for the user.

The overriding emphasis on demographic considerations has, in effect, overshadowed other aspects of the health needs of women. All sorts of experiments are going on in the country with injectables and implants which are yet to make their appearance on a large scale. In the process, the health, actual needs and the well-being of the users are of little concern. 'Side effects such as menstrual chaos, hypertension, heart disease, cancer, contraceptive induced sterility, etc., were all considered minor in view of the pressing need for population control.'[19] Thus 'targets' and 'incentives' have given away to 'target free approach', mother child health (MCH) has been replaced by reproductive and child health (RCH), but the focus remains the same—permanent methods aimed at women (read female sterilization). Where do women in West Bengal stand in this respect?

It was observed, on the basis of the findings of the NFHS-1:

Figures available clearly suggest that the FP programme has been, through 'quotas', 'targets' and 'incentives' systematically targeting women of the country. It is a disturbing thought that out of every 100 women following any so-called modern method, 75 have been sterilized. This is not an unintended bias that has somehow crept into the programme. This is the result of a systematic policy of the donor bodies, led by the World Bank, IMF, the USAID and a host of other agencies, both bilateral and multilateral, pursued over the last few decades. The governments both at the centre and the states have buckled under the pressure.[20]

Appendix Table B9 provides data on the use of family planning methods in the 15 major states in 1992–93 (NFHS-1) and 1998–99 (NFHS-2). West Bengal is among the top three states in terms of use of 'any' method of family planning, with 57.4 per cent using some method or the other. Kerala tops the list with 63.3 per cent, followed by Punjab (58.7 per cent).

In NFHS-2, the state further improves its position and practically shares the top position with Punjab. Followers of 'any' method' are 66.6 per cent in West Bengal, compared to 66.7 in Punjab, when the national average is only 48.2 per cent. Even Kerala is found to be behind West Bengal with about 64 per cent women following 'any method'.

One distinct feature of West Bengal is the high level of traditional methods. Around one-fifth of the eligible age group (currently married) women in the state use the so-called 'traditional' methods (abstinence, withdrawal, rhythm, etc.). Assam is the highest user of traditional methods with nearly 23 per cent women following them. The unusually high use of traditional methods in West Bengal is revealed by NFHS-1, confirmed by NFHS-2 and corroborated by the Rapid Household Survey under the 1998–99 RCH project.

But when it comes to 'modern' methods (i.e., sterilization, IUD, pills, condoms, etc.), West Bengal presents a different picture. With 37.3 per cent women in the state using modern methods in 1992–93, the state is just above the national average (36.3 per cent) but behind eight states. NFHS-2 shows that 47.3 per cent women in West Bengal (India 42.3 per cent) use modern methods but the state is still behind eight major states.

The use of the terms 'traditional' and 'modern' in this context may be misleading as a 'modern' method implicitly suggests a 'better' method. This may not actually be the case from the standpoint of women's autonomy. In any case, what has been happening in the country and in West Bengal in the name of 'modern' methods is revealed by Table 2.7. The table gives detailed break-ups of the number of women following a specific method out of every 100 women practising modern methods. The table also shows the change between 1992–93 and 1998–99. It shows:

- Female sterilization not only remained the most largely prompted method, but its extent had also substantially gone up between the two surveys in most of the states. It was 75.2 per cent in 1992–93 and almost became 80 per cent in 1998–99 in the country. In West Bengal also, the predominant 'modern' method remained female sterilization.

[19] Mehta, Kalpana, 'War Against People', *Frontier*, 28 (4): 9, 1995.
[20] Ghatak, Maitreya, 'War Against Women', *Frontier*, 28 (3): 74, 1995.

Table 2.7
Percentage Distribution of Women Practising 'Modern Methods' by Type

	Methods targeted at women						Methods targeted at men			
	Female sterilization		IUD		Pill		Male sterilization		Condoms	
	1992–93	1998–99	1992–93	1998–99	1992–93	1998–99	1992–93	1998–99	1992–93	1998–99
Andhra Pradesh	81.9	89.5	1.3	1.0	1.1	0.8	14.2	7.3	1.5	1.2
Assam	61.1	59.0	4.5	7.1	14.1	23.7	11.6	3.8	8.6	6.8
Bihar	80.1	85.7	2.3	2.2	5.1	4.5	6.0	4.5	6.0	3.1
Gujarat	80.0	80.7	6.4	5.8	2.1	2.8	7.5	4.3	3.8	6.6
Haryana	67.0	72.7	7.2	6.8	6.5	3.9	11.3	3.9	5.6	12.8
Karnataka	86.7	91.2	6.8	5.0	0.8	1.1	3.2	1.2	2.5	1.8
Kerala	76.8	86.5	5.0	2.9	0.9	0.7	11.9	4.5	5.3	5.5
Madhya Pradesh	74.4	83.8	3.1	1.9	2.0	2.3	14.4	5.2	6.2	6.8
Maharashtra	76.2	81.0	4.8	3.2	2.7	2.8	11.8	6.2	4.8	6.7
Orissa	81.5	84.1	4.3	2.0	2.6	7.4	9.8	4.2	1.7	2.2
Punjab	61.4	54.5	12.3	11.3	4.3	5.8	4.9	3.0	17.3	25.7
Rajasthan	81.9	80.8	3.9	3.1	1.6	3.9	7.8	3.9	4.9	8.1
Tamil Nadu	83.0	89.9	7.7	5.0	1.3	0.6	4.4	1.6	3.5	3.0
Uttar Pradesh	63.2	67.7	5.9	4.5	5.4	5.5	7.6	3.2	17.3	19.1
West Bengal	70.2	67.7	3.5	3.0	9.4	19.5	11.5	3.8	5.1	6.1
India	75.2	79.9	5.2	3.7	3.3	4.9	9.4	4.4	6.6	7.2

Source: Based on Tables of NFHS-1 and 2.

- Among the modern methods, male sterilization was at 9.4 per cent in the country and somewhat better at 11.5 per cent in West Bengal in 1992–93. But by NFHS-2, the share of male sterilization drastically fell and became negligible both at the national level as well as in West Bengal. In West Bengal, it fell from 11.5 per cent to a mere 3.8 per cent. This was even lower than the national average of 4.4 per cent. This clearly indicates a de-emphasis on male sterilization.

- There was very little increase in male condom use in West Bengal, by about 1 per cent. It rose from 5.1 per cent to 6.1 per cent in 1998–99. This was lower than the national average of 7.2 per cent.

On the whole, the data clearly indicate that the entire responsibility for family planning rests with women, that too through female sterilization. The little efforts which used to be made earlier by placing some responsibility on men have been given up. But there are some other features of the programme in West Bengal which have bearing on the status of women.

- West Bengal is one of the very few states in the country where the share of female sterilization in modern methods has actually recorded a decline, from 70.2 per cent in 1992–93 to 67.7 per cent in 1998–99. The only other states where this has happened are Assam, Punjab

and, very marginally, Rajasthan. Even in Kerala, the share of female sterilization was as high as 86.5 per cent.

- Another positive aspect of the programme in West Bengal revealed by both the surveys is the high share of pills, with hardly any difference between urban and rural areas. In urban areas they account for 19.6 per cent of modern method users and in rural areas 19.3 per cent.[21]

Pills accounted for 9.4 per cent of modern methods in 1992–93 in West Bengal. This shot up to 19.5 per cent in 1998–99. The only other major state in India where this has happened on such a significant scale is Assam. These are also the two states where traditional methods account for a large share of 'any method'. The significance would be apparent when one considers that at the national level, pill-using women (among 'modern method users') were only 4.9 per cent in 1998–99. In Kerala they constituted less than 1 per cent.

Pre-natal, Natal and Post-natal Care

The key elements of the elaborate reproductive and child healthcare system that has been set up in the country over the last few decades, so far as pregnant women and mothers of newborn children are concerned, are the following:

- Provision of antenatal care (ANC), including at least three ANC checkups, iron prophylaxis for pregnant

[21] NFHS-2, West Bengal, Table 5.3.

women and lactating mothers, two doses of tetanus toxoid vaccine, detection and treatment of anaemia and management and referral of high risk pregnancies.

- Encouragement of institutional delivery or home delivery assisted by trained health personnel.
- Provision of post-natal care, including at least three visits.

Where do women in West Bengal stand with respect to these cares? Information based on the two NFHS surveys as well as the Rapid Household Survey under the RCH programme (1998–99) suggest that there is scope for improvement.

Appendix Table B10 shows that 75.3 per cent pregnant women receive at least one ANC check up. This is better than the all-India average (62.3 per cent), but at least 7 of the 15 major states are doing better than West Bengal in this respect. When it comes to all three check ups, 57 per cent women in the state are covered. When it comes to all the recommended ANCs, West Bengal is behind 9 of the 15 major states with only 19.7 per cent women being fully covered.

Appendix Table B11 provides data based on the RCH survey. The RCH survey indicated that over 84 per cent pregnant women in West Bengal received 'any' ANC (India, 65.3 per cent). While this is impressive, only one in three pregnant women in West Bengal (33.4 per cent) received full ANC and the state was behind 6 major states. In certain specific parameters, like receiving ANC in the first trimester, abdominal check ups and IFA tablets, West Bengal's progress was poor and the state was behind 8 to10 states.

Despite the network of sub-centres and PHCs in the state, among those women who received any ANC service, only 18.2 per cent received home visits from health workers in West Bengal (Appendix Table B12). This is below the national average (22.0 per cent) and at least 9 of the 15 major states are doing better than West Bengal in home visits. But there is another side of the picture. Appendix Table B12 also shows that in West Bengal, 49.3 per cent of those women who had any ANC went to government health facilities to avail of the services. The state ranks number one among the major states of the country in this respect. The national average is 31.6 per cent. Another way of interpreting the data is that West Bengal ranks highest among the 15 states in respect of women being conscious (and free) enough to go out of their homes to avail of health services during pregnancy.

Institutional delivery is considered safer compared to home delivery and the government policy is to encourage it. Yet, as Appendix Table B13 would show, women in West Bengal are behind many states in institutional delivery. In 1998–99, NFHS-2 and the RCH survey found that around 60 per cent deliveries take place in homes in West Bengal. About 40 per cent births in the state take place in medical institutions. In terms of those women who deliver at home but are attended by doctor/nurse/ANM, West Bengal is behind 7 major states, with 45.6 per cent home deliveries which may be considered safe.

Women in West Bengal are poorly placed vis-à-vis other states in terms of several other delivery related parameters, as Appendix Table B14 shows. Over 74 per cent pregnant women have pregnancy related complications, against a national average of 63.6 per cent. One in four such women have delivery complications in West Bengal (India, 37 per cent). A very high 59.2 per cent women have post delivery complications, against a national average of 46.7 per cent. West Bengal is behind 12 major states in this. Less than half (46.2 per cent) such women seek treatment in West Bengal, which is almost at par with the national average.

More women in rural areas of West Bengal report that they had 'normal' deliveries compared to women in urban areas, as Appendix Table B15 shows. In fact, West Bengal ranks second in terms of rural women reporting that they had a normal delivery. But there is a sharp drop in West Bengal in terms of normal deliveries in urban areas—only 833 per 1,000 mothers reported they had a normal delivery against a national average of 891.

Appendix Table B15 also shows that 'operation' during delivery is much more prevalent in urban areas than rural areas. Out of 1,000 mothers in rural areas of West Bengal, 13 reported operation during delivery, against a national average of 23. In contrast, in Kerala, 171 mothers in rural areas reported operation during delivery.

In terms of operation during delivery in urban areas, however, West Bengal is much above the national average. Out of every 1,000 mothers, 133 reported operation during delivery, whereas the national average is 76. The only other state with more operations (197) in urban areas is Kerala.

The question remains, whether lesser number of reported operations in rural areas of West Bengal is on medical grounds or because the operations were not performed due to lack of personnel, facilities and equipment. Going by the findings of the Facility Survey conducted in all government facilities in five districts plus Calcutta,[22] there is little doubt that this inadequacy of the health delivery system is a major factor behind lower number of operations during delivery in rural areas.

[22] Reproductive and Child Health Programme Facility Survey in Hoogli, Bankura, Birbhum, Calcutta, Medinipur and Darjeeling. Economic Information. Technology, Calcutta, April 1999.

Morbidities

Gynaecological morbidity has to do with any morbidity of the reproductive system which is not related to pregnancy, abortion or child birth, but which may be related to sexual behaviour. There are many conditions, diseases or dysfunctions which fall under the scope of gynaecological morbidity but which go unreported for a variety of reasons. Because of women's overall position in society, they are less likely to articulate their problem or seek medical help. It is another issue that such help is often beyond the reach of most women in the country.

Because of biological reasons, women are more susceptible to sexually transmitted infections (STIs) than men. Undiagnosed or untreated STIs may cause chronic infections and serious complications later. Women also suffer from reproductive tract infections (RTIs) which can cause pregnancy related complications, congenital infections, infertility and chronic pain.[23] Reproductive tract infections may or may not be sexually transmitted. NFHS-2 collected information on some common symptoms of RTIs. The findings are presented in Appendix Table B16.

In West Bengal, about 36 per cent women reported abnormal vaginal discharge, against a national average of 30 per cent. Only three other states have more women reporting this. West Bengal has a higher proportion of women reporting a symptom of urinary tract infection (18.4 per cent) or any reproductive health problem (45.3 per cent) than the national average. Appendix Table B17 is based on the findings of the Rapid Household Survey under the RCH programme, conducted around the same time as the NFHS-2. It not only shows the gender difference in terms of prevalence of 'at least one symptom of RTI/STI', but it also shows the difference between men and women in terms of seeking treatment for the problem.

At the national level, 12.3 per cent men and 29.7 per cent women reported at least one such symptom. In West Bengal, 30.4 per cent women reported such a symptom, almost at par with the national average.

But the gender difference comes out sharply in terms of those who sought treatment for reported symptoms. Among men, 18.1 per cent spoke of a symptom and out 53.4 per cent out of them sought treatment. But even though 30.4 per cent women spoke of symptoms, only 30.2 per cent out of them sought treatment in West Bengal. In fact, West Bengal is behind 11 other states in terms of women with RTI/STI symptoms seeking treatment. This is also much below the national average of 37.6 per cent women seeking treatment.

Table 2.8 based on the RCH survey shows the difference in awareness about RTI, STI and HIV/AIDS between men and women in 15 major states and India. Surprisingly, the awareness of RTI and STI among men in West Bengal is much higher than the national average. But West Bengal men are below the national average in HIV/AIDS awareness. Women, too, have a higher awareness than the national average of RTI and STI but lag behind 10 states in terms of awareness of HIV/AIDS. The awareness of RTI, STI and HIV/AIDS is higher among men than among women in West Bengal. Part

Table 2.8

Awareness among Men between 20 and 54 Years and Women between 15 and 44 Years about RTI, STI and HIV/AIDS in India and 15 States

| | Awareness among men | | | | | | Awareness among women | | | | | |
| | RTI | | STI | | HIV/AIDS | | RTI | | STI | | HIV/AIDS | |
	%	Rank	%	Rank	%	Rank	%	Rank	%	Rank	%	Rank
Andhra Pradesh	36.5	10	44.0	8	70.2	7	52.3	5	43.8	2	57.9	5
Assam	36.0	11	33.7	11	57.7	9	29.6	13	21.5	12	37.7	9
Bihar	48.6	5	52.8	4	40.7	15	67.0	2	38.9	3	15.1	15
Gujarat	58.5	2	46.9	7	62.7	8	59.9	4	33.6	6	33.6	10
Haryana	48.5	6	49.0	5	75.9	6	62.7	3	25.0	11	38.9	8
Karnataka	11.3	15	19.6	14	76.9	5	14.8	15	12.0	15	60.7	4
Kerala	57.4	3	74.7	1	97.1	1	51.5	6	58.4	1	92.0	1
Madhya Pradesh	23.4	14	24.6	13	44.8	14	17.8	14	12.5	14	24.5	12
Maharashtra	37.6	8	42.0	9	78.2	4	50.2	8	28.6	8	62.3	3
Orissa	45.7	7	34.3	10	56.9	10	37.8	12	17.4	13	40.6	7
Punjab	51.6	4	53.2	3	81.5	3	83.5	1	37.1	4	54.1	6
Rajasthan	37.3	9	26.0	12	51.9	11	48.2	9	26.9	9	22.3	14
Tamil Nadu	25.1	13	48.5	6	85.7	2	43.3	11	31.7	7	89.6	2
Uttar Pradesh	30.3	12	19.3	15	49.1	13	47.9	10	25.3	10	22.8	13
West Bengal	60.3	1	53.5	2	51.3	12	50.7	7	36.4	5	30.9	11
India	37.2		36.4		60.3		45.4		28.8		41.9	

Source: Reproductive and Child Health Programme, Rapid Household Survey (Phases I and II), 1998–99. International Institute of Population Sciences, Mumbai, 2001, Table 7.1, p. 110.

[23] NFHS-2, India, p. 307.

of the explanation probably lies in limited access to information for women.

Appendix Table B18 on communicable diseases is based on data released by the Government of West Bengal and are for the first seven months (January–July) of 2002. The data have been collected from government hospitals and health facilities in all the districts and Kolkata. It is difficult to generalize on the basis of data for such limited period.

Within this limitation, it is interesting to note that women constitute bulk of those who sought treatment for sexually transmitted diseases. Out of nearly 55,000 patients seeking treatment in OPDs and IPDs, about three in four were women. It should be noted that seeking treatment in OPD does not necessarily mean that one has been found to be positive in terms of a particular STD. Yet the data is quite outstanding. Some of the women may be sex workers, who are more vulnerable to STD. It is also possible that more men than women are likely to seek treatment from private sources.

In acute respiratory infections, women are almost at par with men (49.7 per cent), as also in acute diarrhoeal diseases (47.3 per cent) and pneumonia (48.8 per cent). But out of any three who sought treatment for TB, one was a woman.

Abortion

Abortion is an integral part of the issue of reproductive health of women. It is also an extremely emotive and complex issues in many societies, including India, having bearing on their status. Prior to the Medical Termination of Pregnancy (MTP) Act of 1971, induced abortion was a criminal offence under the Indian Penal Code of 1860. While the passage of the 1971 Act was positively a landmark development, it does not provide full right to adult women to terminate pregnancy considered 'unwanted' by her. It allows termination of pregnancy under specific circumstances:

1. Where continuance of pregnancy involves a risk to the life of the pregnant woman or of grave injury to her physical or mental health.
2. Where substantial risk exists of the child being born with a serious physical or mental abnormality.

In separate explanatory notes, the Act clarifies that pregnancy following rape and following failure of contraception may be presumed to constitute grave injury to mental health, justifying abortion.

Apart from the scope of the Act, there is another limiting factor. Under the Act, abortion can be performed only by qualified doctors experience within gynaecology. There is nothing wrong with this clause except that very few doctors have the stipulated training.

A more serious restricting factor is that abortion can be undertaken only at a facility which has been sanctioned by an appropriate authority as meeting the required standards prescribed for securing such permission. Shorn of legal jargon, this, in effect, means that abortions cannot be performed in all facilities providing natal services, public or private. While these doctor/facility related conditions have been kept with a concern for the health of the women seeking abortion, in practically every state of India, including West Bengal, they have severely restricted the access of women seeking abortion. Millions of women in India are forced to seek unsafe abortion from unauthorized individuals and facilities because government recognized facilities and trained doctors are simply not there. Or, if they are there, necessary equipment is lacking. According to an official estimate,[24] between 11 and 14 per cent of all maternal deaths in rural India during 1990–94 were reported to have been caused by abortion related complications. Most of the deaths are preventable. The women had to die simply because they became pregnant when they did not plan to. Official estimates of abortion in West Bengal are based on abortions carried out in officially recognized facilities, which are few. It should also be remembered that unwed pregnant women would never seek abortion in such facilities. So it can be guessed that a very large number of abortions remain outside the official data.

Table 2.9
Medical Termination of Pregnancies in West Bengal, 1972–73 to 1998–99

Year	Number	Year	Number
1972–73	2,200	1986–87	43,699
1973–74	3,375	1987–88	41,112
1974–75	11,623	1988–89	37,930
1975–76	18,655	1989–90	50,564
1976–77	19,436	1990–91	41,054
1977–78	13,778	1991–92	55,673
1978–79	19,180	1992–93	36,803
1979–80	25,472	1993–94	64,273
1980–81	20,293	1994–95	50,687
1981–82	31,225	1995–96	51,926
1982–83	33,904	1996–97	48,635
1983–84	39,802	1997–98	41,229
1984–85	34,458	1998–99	40,800
1985–86	38,567		

Source: Government of West Bengal, *Health on the March in West Bengal*, 2002.

---

[24] 'Causes of Death (Rural) India for the Years 1990–94'. Office of the Registrar General, India, New Delhi, various years.

Table 2.9 shows that starting with 2,200 abortions in the first year after the Act was passed (1972), abortions in West Bengal reached a peak at 64,273 in 1993 and then gradually fell to 40,800 in 1998. The fall cannot be due to lesser number of women seeking abortion from authorized institutions but, in all probability, due to the inability of the governmental institutions to provide the service because of lack of trained personnel and other facilities and equipment.

What is the ground reality in West Bengal in terms of availability of trained personnel and equipment for abortions in government health facilities? According to a study sponsored by the Ministry of Health and Family Welfare, Government of India, in all government hospitals and health centres in the districts of Hoogli, Bankura, Birbhum, Medinipur and Darjeeling,[25] the situation is extremely poor. Out of 428 primary health centres (PHCs) in these districts, only 6 had at least one medical officer trained in MTP and only 13 had MTP suction apparatus.

Above the PHCs, there are 32 community health centres (CHC) in these five districts. The situation is no better there. Only 6 of the 32 CHCs have a gynaecologist/obstetrician. No wonder a very large number of women are forced to seek abortion services from unauthorized people and institutions. According to an estimate made in 1993 (Appendix Table B19) in West Bengal, 493 abortions took place per 1,000 live births when the national average was 452.[26] The same source also estimated that in 1991 West Bengal had a total of 908,000 abortions, of which 544,800 were induced abortions (Appendix Table B20). This is about 10 times the official figures of the state government. Abortion rate per 1,000 couple was 83 for West Bengal (India, 78) while induced abortion rate was 49.8 per 1,000 couple (India, 46.8). It was also estimated that in West Bengal there were 23,000 couples per MTP centre, while there were 8,000 couples per centre in Maharashtra and 12,000 in Kerala.[27]

In a later study,[28] the authors analysed information collected during NFHS-1 to find out what proportion of women covered by the survey (among those who became pregnant) considered their pregnancy 'ill-timed' or 'unwanted'. The exercise was undertaken on the assumption that seekers of induced abortion would largely come from these groups. The study revealed (Appendix Table B21) that among the major states, West Bengal had the second highest proportion (19.9 per cent) of women (India, 13.8 per cent) who considered their pregnancy ill-timed. In terms of 'unwanted', West Bengal

topped the list with 15.3 per cent against a national average of 8.8 per cent.

Finally, the study estimated (Appendix Table B22) that West Bengal had 226,153 induced abortions in 1994 when the state government sources had recorded only 55,673 abortions. In terms of possible induced abortions, West Bengal was behind only one state, Uttar Pradesh. The report firmly concludes that the reported number of induced abortions as per government sources are 'definite underestimates'.

MTP has remained a severely neglected area in the state, endangering the life of a very large number of pregnant women who are forced to go for unsafe abortions. It has received little attention from the government both at the centre and at the state level, who have failed to integrate it with the family welfare and the RCH programme. Nor has it received much attention from researchers, women's groups and activists in the state.

Gender Difference in Immunization Coverage

In the eighties, the Government of India introduced free vaccination programme for protecting children against six killer/crippling diseases like tuberculosis, diphtheria, pertussia, tetanus, poliomyletis and measles. The aim was to fully cover 85 per cent of the children of the country by 1990. Under the existing norms, all children should be fully protected (all prescribed doses of all vaccines) by the time they complete one year. Substantial resources have gone into the programme and an elaborate network cum cold chain system has been developed to cover even the remotest parts of the country. Health and ICDS workers play an important role in implementing the programme.

Despite its importance, the success of the programme was found to be much below the set goal in the first NFHS in 1992–93 as well as in the second NFHS in 1998–99. An assessment of the success of the programme will depend on the number of children of the relevant age group who have received all the necessary doses of all the vaccines, as against those who have been partly immunized or have not received any immunization at all. Another aspect of the assessment would be the difference (if any) between the coverage of boys and girls.

---

[25] Facility Survey, 1999.

[26] Chhabra, Rami and Sheel C. Nuna, *Abortions in India: An Overview*. Veerendra Printers, New Delhi, 1993.

[27] Ibid.

[28] Mishra, U.S., Mala Ramnathan and S. Irudaya Rajan, *Induced Abortion Potential among Indian Women*. Centre for Development Studies, Trivandrum, 1997.

The NFHS-1 found that only 35.4 per cent children in the 12–23 months age group were fully vaccinated, leaving nearly two in three children in the country uncovered or partly covered. The West Bengal situation was marginally poorer than the national average, with 34.2 per cent children fully vaccinated. The state ranked 10 among the 15 major states in this respect in 1992–93.

There was an overall improvement in the situation in the next few years and NFHS-2 found that 42.0 per cent children in the 12–23 months age group were fully covered. The West Bengal situation in 1998–99 was found to be better than the national average, with 43.8 per cent children fully vaccinated. The state's rank among the 15 major states, however, improved only marginally, from the 10th position in 1992–93 to the 9th position in 1998–99.

While poor coverage of children, much below the set target, is a matter of concern, a more pertinent issue for this discussion is the existence of gender difference in full vaccination coverage. At the national level, 34.1 per cent girls were fully vaccinated, compared to 36.7 per cent boys in 1992–93. In states like Andhra Pradesh, Bihar, Gujarat, Haryana, Madhya Pradesh, Orissa, Punjab, Rajasthan, Tamil Nadu, Uttar Pradesh and even Kerala, the coverage of girls was poorer than that of boys. West Bengal, along with only three other states (Assam, Karnataka and Maharashtra), was an exception where the coverage of girls was better than the coverage of boys.

NFHS-2 found that in as many as 11 states the coverage of girls (in full vaccination) was poorer and West Bengal was one of them. However, the difference between the full coverage of boys and girls was negligible in the state as shown in Appendix Table B23. In terms of those children who were not vaccinated at all, the proportion of boys was higher in NFHS-1 in West Bengal (Appendix Table H2). The percentage of boys who remained totally uncovered by any vaccination was 23.6 per cent, compared to 21.3 per cent girls. A disturbing finding of NFHS-2 is that the situation has reversed and there are now more unprotected girls (14.3 per cent) compared to unprotected boys (12.9 per cent).[29]

Soon after NFHS-2, another major national study offering district level data for all the states suggested that 52.5 per cent children (12–23 months) were fully vaccinated in West Bengal. While this suggests better coverage than NFHS-2, West Bengal's relative rank among the 15 major states remained poor, behind nine others in full coverage. The RCH study also confirmed that gender difference in full vaccination coverage in West Bengal was less than 1 per cent; in the coverage of both boys and girls, West Bengal was behind 9 other major states. At the national level, the RCH survey found that 53 per cent girls are fully vaccinated as against 55.3 per cent boys. In terms of full immunization, thus, the overall performance of West Bengal is quite poor but the deficiency is true for both boys and girls to an almost equal extent.

Conclusion

The health status of women and children in West Bengal brings out a rather mixed picture: in certain respects this state has done well but in certain others it lags behind a fairly large number of major states in India. Our detailed state-wise tables help to show the health status of West Bengal's women and children in a comparative perspective.

The ongoing emphasis on demographic considerations and population control has in effect overshadowed other aspects of health needs of women, with the result that data relating to family planning are more easily available than data relating to other important aspects of women's health and nutrition. Finally, because of lack of reliable and readily available data, we have not tried to explore the mental health situation of women and children, though it is well-known that mental illness, particularly clinical depression and stress and anxiety-related mental disorders, are on the rise, both among women and children.

[29] Reproductive and Child Health Programme, Rapid Household Survey (Phases 1 and 2), 1998–99, International Institute of Population Sciences, Mumbai.

Education

CHAPTER 3

Jasodhara Bagchi and Jaba Guha

In this chapter we shall examine the gender dimension of school education and higher and technical education in West Bengal. With the massive international mandate on basic elementary education for all, great attention was paid by experts and activists in the country to examine the Directive Principle of the Indian Constitution's promise to make education compulsory and available to all children up to the age of 14 years. The first section of the chapter deals with the way in which girls and women in West Bengal fared in school education during the last three decades of the twentieth century. In the subsequent section, a gendered analysis of general education above the higher secondary stage and technical education, including vocational courses, is presented.

School Education

Educating the Girl Child

Bengal, since the colonial times, has thought of women and girl child's education as a gateway to liberation, not of the women alone but of entire societies. It was in the context of women's education that we find Lotika Ghosh's poem, *To Our First Champions*, making the point about India seen as a woman in chains. The coming of women's education was fraught with anxieties of nation-building. John Drinkwater Bethune's girls' school began in 1849 with 21 girls, out of which 11 were between the ages of 9 and 14. True to its initial bias of producing adequate *helpmeet* for the respectable *bhadralok* of colonial Bengal[1] or even the suitable mothers of

the incipient *bhadralok,* women's literacy was restricted to the adequate formation of the upper class elite in colonial society. Because of a certain prioritizing of education as a value, literacy among girls in Bengal did spread, though nowhere was it as wide as one would have liked it to be. Here, we will examine how women and children fared in this sector and the social dynamics of the process in West Bengal.

As the title of a recent book on education in India suggests, the terrain occupied by education is a 'contested' one.[2] It is premised on a notion of education that socializes individuals into acquiescing with the nitty-gritty of family and citizenry. Gender division is built into the naturalized order of the family and the state and education becomes a major instrument in keeping this in place. However, the paradox is that it is education that is also the instrument of breaking stereotypes. To quote from a young researcher in the field:

> The tensions in the notion of education I have been describing are found in the very etymology of the word education—the emphasis on 'ducere' or 'leading', on the one hand, and on 'ex', or the movement towards freedom, on the other. This is a dialectic between control and freedom.[3]

It is as a symptom of this ambivalence that 'education' remains under the stranglehold of the major stratifications leading to discrimination and disempowerment in our society, viz., gender, class, caste and religious minority. In a stratified society like ours, education, we must remember, has been a reinforcing agent of privilege. In a state like West Bengal, where partition saw a large-scale exodus of the Muslim middle-class, the spread of mainstream education entrenched the divide between the

---

[1] Borthwick, Meredith, *Changing Role of Women in Bengal, 1849–1905*. Princeton University Press, Princeton, 1984. Murshid, Ghulam, *The Reluctant Debutante: Response of Bengali Women to Modernization, 1849–1905*. Shahitya Samsad, Rajsahi (Bangladesh), 1983.

[2] Bhattacharya, Sabyasachi (ed.), *The Contested Terrain: Perspectives on Education in India.* Orient Longman, New Delhi, 1998.

[3] Bagchi, Barnita, *Pliable Pupils and Sufficient Self-Directors: Narratives of Female Education by Five British Women, 1778–1814*, Tulika, New Delhi.

Hindu majority and the Muslims minority. Compared to the elite aspirations about the efficiency of education as a transforming agent that might lead to windows opening out to the world, the ground-level reality of spreading education among the masses ran into rough weather. Certain major divides continued not only in the total population but also in the underprivileged categories of the scheduled castes and scheduled tribes. It is with the 'disprivileged'[4] that school education has run into its worst challenges in West Bengal and has been utilized by the processes of social stratification that are noticeable especially in rural Bengal. (For a discussion on the state of tribal girls' education in West Bengal, please refer to Section 8.4 of Chapter 8. Two micro studies included in Appendix C of this book deal with the education of Muslim women and the SC/ST women's participation in professional training courses.) The delay in realizing the stated constitutional goal of elementary education for all in 10 years from the commencement of the Constitution signified an absence of political will on the part of the government. J.P. Naik saw this failure as a concession to the demand for class (and caste?) consolidation among the elite. He says: 'In my opinion, the lower priority accorded to elementary education is due mainly to the fact that the intelligentsia which came to power at the end of the British rule is now tending to transform itself from a service group to an exploiting group.'[5] He suspected that the increasing distance between the masses and the intelligentsia was a part of India's hierarchical traditions.

That West Bengal, under the Left Front government which implemented a programme of land reforms, could not break this stranglehold has got reflected in the ways in which it has affected the access of the deprived and toiling section to education. As Amartya Sen has said, 'It is agreed in this report that a powerful new initiative is badly needed right now to reorganize primary schooling in this state.'[6]

Literacy

In order to understand the changing status of girls' school education in West Bengal in the last three decades of the twentieth century, we need to look at several complications that have been noticeable over decades. To quote A.K. Bagchi:

In 1951, West Bengal had a literacy rate of 24 per cent, and was second in terms of literacy among the major Indian states; Kerala being the top state with 40.7 per cent.... Three states were close behind West Bengal; Gujarat with a rate of 23.1 per cent, Maharashtra with 20.9 per cent and Madras (later Tamil Nadu) with 20.8 per cent. By 1961 all the three had overtaken West Bengal; the latter had a literacy rate of 29.8 per cent. Whereas Gujarat, Maharashtra and Tamil Nadu had literacy rates of 30.45 per cent, 29.82 per cent and 31.41 per cent respectively, Kerala had kept its long lead with a rate of 46.85 per cent (Census 1961).[7]

The analysis goes on to comment:

While the relative slowness of progress of literacy in West Bengal was to be observed both for males and females, it was more pronounced in respect of female literacy. The decade 1961–71 was pretty bad in respect of progress of literacy in India and West Bengal. For India as a whole, the literacy rate advanced from 24.03 per cent to 29.45 per cent, and for West Bengal from 29.8 to 33.20 per cent only.[8]

The literacy question remained the largest juggernaut in the management of education for all in India. In the three decades that we are studying, the EFA (education for all) campaign appeared to have borne some fruit in the nineties, at least in

Chart 3.1
All-India Rural–Urban Literacy Rates (in per cent)

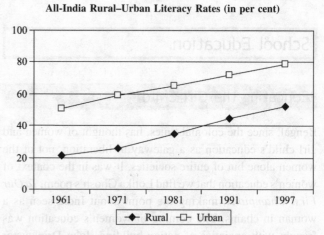

Source: Govinda, R., *India Education Report.* Oxford University Press, New Delhi, 2001.

---

[4] Bhattacharya, Sabyasachi (ed.), *Education and the Disprivileged: Nineteenth and Twentieth Century India.* Orient Longman, New Delhi, 2002.

[5] Sen, Samita, 'A Father's Duty: State Patriarchy and Women's Education', in Sabyasachi Bhattacharya (ed.), *Education and the Disprivileged*, 2002.

[6] Sen, Amartya, 'Introduction', in *The Pratichi Education Report.* Pratichi Trust (India), New Delhi, 2002.

[7] Bagchi, A.K, 'Studies on the Economy of West Bengal since Independence', *Economic and Political Weekly*, 21–28 November 1998, p. 2,973.

[8] Ibid.

Table 3.1

Literacy Rate in India and in 15 Major States by Sex (in per cent)

State	1971 M	Rank	1971 F	Rank	1971 F/100M	Rank	1981 M	Rank	1981 F	Rank	1981 F/100M	Rank	1971–81 change	Rank	1991 M	Rank	1991 F	Rank	1991 F/100M	Rank	1981–91 change	Rank	2001 M	Rank	2001 F	Rank	2001 F/100M	Rank	1991–2001 change	Rank
Andhra Pradesh	38	11	18	6	48	6	45	11	23	10	52	8	4.4	6	55	13	33	11	59	9	7.3	7	71	10	51	9	72	10	12.9	6
Assam	37	12	15	8	40	7	–	–	–	–	–	–	0	–	62	10	43	8	70	3	0	3	72	9	56	8	78	9	8.3	3
Bihar	36	13	10	11	29	11	44	12	16	12	36	13	7.4	11	52	15	23	14	44	12	7.6	12	60	13	34	12	56	12	12.1	12
Gujarat	54	4	29	3	54	3	62	4	37	5	60	3	5.5	3	73	4	49	5	66	6	7.0	6	81	4	59	4	73	6	6.3	5
Haryana	44	9	18	6	40	7	55	7	26	8	46	6	6.2	6	69	5	40	9	58	8	12.0	8	79	5	56	5	71	8	12.6	7
Karnataka	49	6	25	5	51	5	56	6	32	7	57	5	6.3	5	67	7	44	7	66	6	9.1	6	76	8	57	8	75	5	9.4	4
Kerala	77	1	63	1	81	1	85	1	73	1	87	1	5.7	1	94	1	86	1	92	1	5.2	1	94	1	91	1	97	1	4.5	1
Madhya Pradesh	39	10	13	9	34	9	46	10	18	11	40	9	6.0	9	58	11	29	12	49	10	9.8	10	77	7	50	7	65	10	16.2	9
Maharashtra	59	3	31	2	52	4	67	2	39	2	59	5	7.0	4	77	2	52	2	68	5	9.2	5	86	2	68	2	78	2	9.9	3
Orissa	45	8	16	8	36	8	53	8	24	9	45	8	8.4	9	63	9	35	10	55	9	10.1	9	76	8	51	8	67	9	12.2	8
Punjab	46	7	29	3	63	2	53	10	38	4	72	2	9.0	2	66	8	50	4	77	2	4.8	2	76	8	64	4	84	4	7.2	2
Rajasthan	34	14	10	11	30	10	42	10	13	13	32	12	2.1	12	55	13	20	13	37	13	5.5	13	76	8	44	8	58	11	20.8	11
Tamil Nadu	60	2	31	2	52	4	66	2	39	2	60	3	8.1	3	74	3	51	3	70	3	9.8	3	82	3	65	3	78	3	8.6	3
Uttar Pradesh	37	12	12	10	34	9	44	12	16	12	37	11	2.8	10	56	12	25	13	45	11	8.7	11	70	11	43	12	61	11	15.8	10
West Bengal	50	5	27	4	54	3	57	5	34	6	60	3	6.8	3	68	6	47	6	69	4	8.2	4	78	6	60	5	78	6	9.0	3
India	46		22		48		53		28		53				64		39		61		8.0		76		54		71		10.2	

Sources: For 1971 and 1981, Government of India, *Selected Educational Statistics*, Ministry of Human Resource Development, Table no. CP, p. 157.
For 1991 and 1997, Government of India, *Selected Educational Statistics*, Ministry of Human Resource Development, Tables 12 and 12A.
For 2001, *Census of India 2001, Provisional Population Totals, Figures at a Glance.*

Notes:
M = male; F = female.
Up to 1981 figures relate to population age 6+ years. From 1991 figures relate to population age 7+ years.
The decadal change represents the change in the proportion of F/100M.

reducing the gender gap. Not only was it brought down to 20 per cent in the 2001 Census, but also in the late nineties there appeared a converging trend in the rural–urban literacy rate.

The analysis of the tables will show that there has been a substantial increase among literates in the population of West Bengal. The decade from 1990 to 2000 brought the percentage of literacy among males to 77.55 per cent and among females to 60.2 per cent. This brought the decadal growth in population literacy among males to 9.77 per cent and for females to 13.66 per cent. The F/100M (females per 100 males) ratio in the literacy figures show there is a steady rise in the reduction of gender gap in literacy. From 54 females per 100 males in 1971, there has been a steady rise to 78 females per 100 males in 2001. By maintaining a steady national rank, which has remained between four and three, West Bengal has also maintained a standard that has been consistently higher than the all-India figure. From Table 3.1 we see that while the all-India figure has gone up by 23 per cent, West Bengal's has increased by 24 per cent.

Chart 3.2
Literacy Rate of Females/100 Males (in per cent)

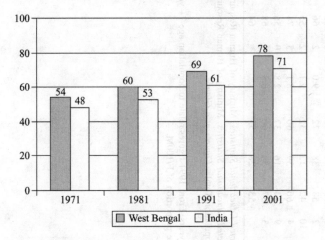

Source: Data provided in Table 3.1.

Table 3.2 clearly shows the cause for concern for the uneven spread of literacy throughout West Bengal. Kolkata seems to get the lion's share in educational facilities, so that it ranks first in all the categories, except among the SC male population. Proximity to Kolkata seems to have helped 24 Parganas (S), except most glaringly among the ST population. The problem clusters appear to be West Dinajpur, Maldah and Murshidabad in the northern part and Bankura, Purulia and Birbhum in the mid south-western part.

Table 3.2
Literacy among Males and Females in Districts of West Bengal, 1991 Census (in per cent)

Districts	Male			Female			Gender gap		
	All	SC	ST	All	SC	ST	All	SC	ST
Darjeeling	67.1	58.1	47.5	47.8	33.3	30.8	71.3	57.2	64.7
Jalpaiguri	56.0	54.8	31.7	33.2	2?.5	12.5	59.3	48.5	39.5
Koch Bihar	57.4	54.3	44.9	33.3	2?.9	19.3	58.1	49.5	43.0
West Dinajpur	49.8	45.7	28.4	27.9	19.1	9.1	56.0	41.7	32.0
Maldah	45.6	46.6	25.1	24.9	20.2	6.4	54.6	43.3	25.6
Murshidabad	46.4	40.5	26.0	29.6	24.4	10.6	63.7	60.2	40.8
Nadia	60.1	55.0	33.5	44.4	34.8	12.6	74.0	63.2	37.7
24 Parganas (N)	74.7	64.7	36.7	58.0	41.2	13.1	77.6	63.7	35.6
24 Parganas (S)	68.5	65.0	36.4	40.6	33.4	12.1	59.3	51.5	33.3
Bardhaman	71.1	47.5	36.7	51.5	24.7	14.8	72.4	52.0	40.4
Bankura	66.8	40.3	50.4	36.6	13.1	13.9	54.8	32.5	27.5
Purulia	62.2	48.9	43.9	23.2	13.5	10.6	37.4	27.5	24.0
Birbhum	59.3	38.5	23.6	37.2	16.1	5.6	62.7	41.9	23.8
Medinipur	81.3	68.7	55.6	56.6	39.8	24.6	69.7	57.9	44.2
Hoogli	75.8	52.8	42.1	65.9	27.8	13.8	87.0	52.7	32.8
Haora	76.1	56.0	51.0	57.8	32.9	32.0	76.0	58.7	62.6
Calcutta	81.9	63.5	64.3	72.1	47.3	42.0	88.0	74.4	65.3
West Bengal	67.8	54.6	40.1	46.6	28.9	15.0	68.7	52.9	37.4

Source: Compiled from Government of India, *Selected Educational Statistics*, Ministry of Human Resource Development, 1997–98, Tables 24 to 26, pp. 95–149.

In a recent analysis of rural West Bengal, G.K. Lieten had referred to the mobilization undertaken for literacy. According to his reading of the 'energetic activism', Lieten claims that,

> By 1997, the overall literacy rate in Bengal had moved up to 74 per cent from 58 per cent in 1991 and thereby had moved in to third place, just behind Maharashtra. The steep increase was very much a reflection of the increasing literacy in rural population, not much above the national average of 30.9 per cent. By 1995 the ratio had gone up to the 52.6 per cent clearly above 39.8 per cent of the national average.[9]

The trend break the author believes is 'on account of involvement of the panchayats and local activists after 1990'.[10] The literacy rate went up to 77 per cent among males and 59.8 per cent among females of West Bengal in the 2001 Census.

The Pre-school Experience

There was a very legitimate objection to the recent constitutional amendment that made education of children of 6–14 years their fundamental right whereas children of 0–6 years were left out of the fold of education. The one major state-led

[9] Lieten, G.K., 'Rural West Bengal after a Quarter Century of Land Reforms'. Unpublished paper.
[10] Ibid.

critical intervention that addresses the problem of 0–6 years is the ICDS, that cuts across different sectors. Started in 1975 in select districts in all states of India, in West Bengal it still remains one of the mainstays of the welfare of 0–6 year-olds, among the rural and urban poor, along with their mothers. As a publication that marks 20 years of ICDS in West Bengal says: 'From a small beginning with two projects in 1975, in West Bengal we have at present 275 sanctioned projects which benefits lakhs of children up to 6 years and their mothers.'[11]

Its original design conceptualized the linkage between pre-school education for children, intergenerational understanding of health issues and the induction of mothers in the arena of human development. Though many NGOs now collaborate with the government and the number has gone up many times over, the original target of one ICDS centre for every thousand people is still far from being reached.

Primary, Upper Primary and Secondary Stages

'Primary' school in West Bengal predominantly means classes I to IV. Of the over 51,000 'primary' schools in West Bengal, there are only 1,700 junior basic schools that teach in classes I to V and can be called 'primary' in the strict sense. This means, as has been rightly pointed out, boys or girls often have to travel quite a distance to get to an upper primary school. The problem is severe for girls. The drop in school attendance among girls after Class IV has a lot to do with the problems of travelling. Consequently, girls drop out a year earlier in West Bengal. In addition, a calculation of girls completing primary education within the state will not be comparable to a similar

Chart 3.3
Enrolment by Stages: Percentage of Girls in West Bengal and India (1986–97)

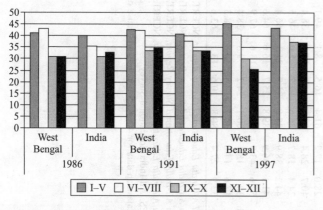

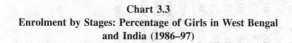

Source: Data from Table 3.3.

calculation in other states because they have not read up to Class V. While in the primary stages (that includes Class V, in conformity with the rest of India) girls' enrolment went up from 41.4 per cent in 1986 to 45.4 per cent in 1997, in the upper primary level girls' enrolment declined from 43 per cent in 1986 to 40.5 per cent in 1997 as shown in Table 3.3. In terms of rank at the upper primary stage, the state seems to have dropped to the ninth place in 1997 from the third in 1986.

This is also borne out by the dismal picture of enrolment in the final year of elementary education. As far as the all-India average goes, West Bengal has lagged way behind. Chart 3.4 shows that in the enrolment to Class VIII there has been a sharp decline in the female to male ratio from 78.3 per cent in 1973, when the state ranked third in the whole of India, to 55.8 per cent in 1993, when it ranked last among the 15 major states.

Table 3.3
Enrolment by Stages, Percentage and Rank of Girls in India and Four Major States

	I–V		VI–VIII		IX–X		Higher secondary stage (10 + 2) new pattern	
	% of girls	Rank	% of girls	Rank	% of girls	Rank	% of girls	Rank
1986								
West Bengal	41.4	9	43.0	3	30.9	9	30.9	8
Kerala	48.6	1	48.9	1	50.4	1	37.3	3
Uttar Pradesh	32.9	13	25.3	13	17.0	15	0	
Maharashtra	45.0	4	38.6	7	33.7	7	31.0	7
All-India	40.1		35.5		30.8		32.7	
1991								
West Bengal	42.7	8	42.4	5	33.4	11	34.6	6
Kerala	48.6	1	48.8	1	50.6	1	43.9	1
Uttar Pradesh	36.5	11	30.5	13	22.3	13	27.9	12
Maharashtra	46.3	3	40.9	7	36.9	7	32.1	11
All-India	41.7		37.7		33.6		33.4	
1997								
West Bengal	45.4	8	40.5	9	30.0	12	25.7	14
Kerala	48.3	1	48.4	1	51.3	1	52.4	1
Uttar Pradesh	36.9	14	31.4	12	24.5	15	32.0	10
Maharashtra	47.4	5	44.4	4	41.1	5	36.4	8
All-India	43.6		40.1		37.4		36.9	

Source: Compiled from Government of India, *Selected Educational Statistics*. Department of Education, Ministry of Human Resource Development.

In less than 20 years the Gross Enrolment Ratio (GER) in West Bengal went up from 67.6 per cent in 1978 to 83.1 per cent in 1993, barely managing to keep its average higher than the all-India one. It has not only remained way below Kerala–which is not surprising—but it has also dipped much lower than Gujarat which ranked first in 1993. However, in the

[11] Government of West Bengal, *Twenty Years of ICDS in West Bengal*, Department of Social Welfare, December 1995.

Table 3.4

For Every 100 Boys and 100 Girls Enrolled in Class I, the Number Enrolled in Classes V and VIII

| | 3rd AES (1973) | | | | | | 4th AES (1978) | | | | | | 5th AES (1986) | | | | | | 6th AES (1993) | | | | | |
| | Class V | | | Class VIII | | | Class V | | | Class VIII | | | Class V | | | Class VIII | | | Class V | | | Class VIII | | |
State	B	G	G/100B	B	G	G/100B	B	G	G/100B	B	G	G/100B	B	G	G/100B	B	G	G/100B	B	G	G/100B	B	G	G/100B
Andhra Pradesh	34.3	31.0	90.4	16.5	10.1	61.2	30.4	25.3	83.2	17.6	10.5	59.7	41.3	34.3	83.1	22.8	15.0	65.8	48.9	43.6	89.2	28.9	20.6	71.3
Assam	27.8	24.9	89.6	20.9	17.0	81.3	31.5	26.7	84.8	17.3	13.2	76.3	39.5	34.1	86.3	22.7	19.6	86.3	36.7	34.4	93.7	25.6	24.6	96.1
Bihar	27.6	22.0	79.7	14.1	6.8	48.2	27.9	19.8	71.0	11.8	4.9	41.5	36.6	30.3	82.8	23.1	13.6	58.9	41.1	34.9	84.9	23.9	15.3	64.0
Gujarat	33.6	26.7	85.4	19.2	14.7	76.6	40.9	34.9	85.3	24.6	19.1	77.6	55.0	46.2	82.2	35.2	23.8	67.6	69.5	61.3	88.2	47.3	36.8	77.8
Haryana	55.1	43.6	79.1	40.7	24.8	60.9	70.5	54.9	77.9	50.4	29.9	59.3	75.8	59.0	77.8	67.1	35.0	52.2	82.2	74.4	90.5	75.1	55.5	73.9
Karnataka	34.3	24.6	71.7	17.9	10.8	60.3	39.8	29.0	72.9	24.6	15.6	63.4	52.9	41.4	78.3	33.3	23.6	70.9	63.5	54.2	85.4	40.8	30.5	74.8
Kerala	85.8	81.6	95.1	43.2	42.8	99.1	92.0	87.6	95.2	81.9	76.3	93.2	101.0	96.5	95.5	81.9	80.6	98.4	114.0	111.0	96.9	111.0	112.1	101.0
Madhya Pradesh	28.0	17.2	61.4	16.5	8.1	49.1	43.8	33.2	75.8	27.3	16.8	61.5	73.0	51.3	70.3	46.7	22.3	47.8	64.7	56.8	87.8	38.0	24.4	64.2
Maharashtra	40.7	28.4	69.8	19.0	11.1	58.4	41.4	31.4	75.8	24.9	14.9	59.8	59.7	48.7	81.6	41.9	26.3	62.8	74.9	66.6	88.9	54.3	42.3	77.9
Orissa	24.4	18.7	76.6	12.7	5.9	46.5	42.0	37.0	88.1	21.5	11.9	55.3	50.2	43.0	85.7	32.7	21.7	66.4	53.4	46.7	87.5	31.8	23.7	74.5
Punjab	44.2	38.9	88.0	31.8	21.1	66.4	46.9	40.9	87.2	35.4	23.9	67.5	66.7	63.3	94.9	53.2	37.4	70.3	82.0	70.3	85.7	57.5	54.0	93.9
Rajasthan	41.1	36.9	89.8	25.7	16.6	64.6	*	*	*	*	*	*	30.5	20.8	68.2	21.5	11.7	54.4	37.0	26.8	72.4	26.6	15.4	57.9
Tamil Nadu	52.6	43.9	83.5	27.4	18.6	67.9	69.3	60.0	86.6	38.9	26.6	68.4	71.6	63.5	88.7	46.3	34.5	74.5	85.7	84.1	98.1	65.7	60.5	92.1
Uttar Pradesh	30.1	18.1	60.1	24.2	9.3	38.4	46.6	35.3	75.8	34.1	18.1	53.1	61.8	52.6	85.1	49.6	31.6	63.7	51.0	43.5	85.3	39.9	29.2	73.2
West Bengal	17.6	14.8	84.1	13.8	10.8	78.3	24.3	21.0	86.4	14.7	12.4	84.4	40.5	35.0	86.4	24.1	19.0	78.8	49.4	42.4	85.8	39.9	22.2	55.6
India	33.9	27.4	80.8	20.6	13.1	63.6	42.0	34.4	81.9	26.3	18.1	68.8	52.5	45.0	85.7	36.0	25.3	70.2	56.7	51.9	91.5	39.9	32.0	80.2

Sources: *3rd All-India Educational Survey Report.* NCERT, New Delhi, 1973, Tables 51, 54, 57, 60, 63, 67, 70, 73, 77, 80.
4th All-India Educational Survey Report. NCERT, New Delhi, 1978, Table 152.
5th All-India Educational Survey Report. NCERT, New Delhi, 1986, Table 177.
6th All-India Educational Survey Report. NCERT, New Delhi, 1993, Table 153.

Notes: AES: All-India Educational Survey.
*Rajasthan data for 4th AES not shown because of apparent inconsistency.

female to male ratio, Gujarat compares unfavourably to West Bengal. The West Bengal total has gone up from 39.7 per cent to 44.8 per cent. The girls/100 boys ratio has gone up from 66.2 per cent to 76 per cent. The fact that Haryana has outstripped West Bengal in girls/100 boys GER is a matter of concern, as shown in Chart 3.5.

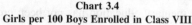

Chart 3.4
Girls per 100 Boys Enrolled in Class VIII

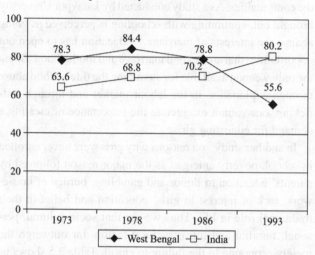

Source: Data from Table 3.4.

Chart 3.5
Girls per 100 Boys Gross Enrolment Ratio in the Upper Primary Stage

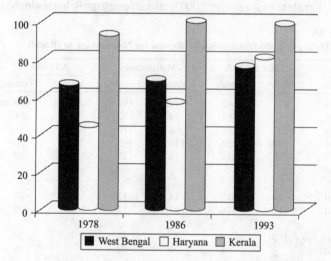

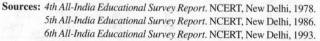

Sources: *4th All-India Educational Survey Report*. NCERT, New Delhi, 1978.
5th All-India Educational Survey Report. NCERT, New Delhi, 1986.
6th All-India Educational Survey Report. NCERT, New Delhi, 1993.

Available calculations show that the number of upper primary schools have not increased at the rate at which secondary, higher secondary and even primary schools have increased in the state. Lack of schools also adds to the limitations of girls who might have had some incentive in completing the elementary education. Withdrawal of opportunities affects children in the age group of 10–14 years, which is the most vulnerable age group as they are easily sucked into child labour, trafficking and early marriage.

Supply Constraints

It was in the seventies that decentralization in the administering of education in West Bengal began. Even in 1968, when the Education Commission of 1964–66 was debated in the Parliament, the state government had played practically no part in determining an education policy.[12] In the light of this, when the Left Front government came to power in its current form in 1977, it went in for administrative decentralization. One of the first steps was to divide the department into school education, higher education, mass education extension, and technical education and training departments. Soon there were four departments of education in place of one, with four sets of ministers, secretaries and the rest of the bureaucratic apparatus. Tapas Majumdar, who used to head the committee on education appointed by the Government of India, comments, 'In spite of the drastic reorganization of the department of education and the added emphasis placed on school (particularly primary) education, the pattern and the structure of the government school system has been allowed to remain static.'[13] The so-called decentralization of education by breaking it into different departments hardly addressed the inner core of the problem.

The quality of education imparted is a cause for serious concern. Interestingly, this is one area that received a great deal of critical attention during the nineties. Of these, the most noted report, apart from the one referred earlier, is by Raghabendra Chattopadhyay and his team from the IIMC.[14] A smaller status report published by the West Bengal Education Network have also thrown some light on the constraints.[15]

The pay revision of school teachers, according to the Majumdar report, has impacted negatively on the quality and spread of education in two ways. First, by creating an obvious

[12] Majumdar, Tapas. 'Elementary Education in West Bengal.' An unpublished report.

[13] Ibid.

[14] Chattopadhyay, R., Sudip Chaudhuri, S.K. Ghosh, A.K. Sinha and V.N. Reddy, 'The Status of Primary Education in West Bengal.' Unpublished report of a project sponsored by the UNICEF and Government of West Bengal, 1998.

[15] Chattopadhyay, Bratin, *Status Report*. West Bengal Education Network, Kolkata, 2000.

income disparity between teachers and children of poor families, whom they are supposed to teach, it has reinforced the class/caste hierarchies that are meant to cripple the democratic potential of the social fabric. A society in which the traditional association of the Shastras and Shariyat with the teaching community already creates social barriers, the presence of school teachers who are way above the community whose children they are supposed to teach has not allowed education to be a step towards equality.

Rampant absenteeism and black-marketeering in education in the form of private tuitions or teachers using their posts as bases for activities like contesting panchayat elections have further vitiated the educational atmosphere and affected the quality of education imparted. In terms of externalities, the poor infrastructure of the schools for the rural and urban poor, the 'slowness' in access to school textbooks and school dresses, and the inability to provide edible, cooked midday meals show a sluggishness and bureaucratic indifference towards educating the poor. From within the educational system these are some of the things which affect the quality of education. But the more palpable casualty is in the spread of education. The revised salary of teachers now accounts for nearly 95 per cent of the state budget and leaves little room for horizontal expansion. As West Bengal is one of the few states that look after the salary of all teachers in school education and higher education, the burden of the pay review as per the recommendations of the Fifth Pay Commission has fallen heavily on the state exchequer.

Demand Constraints

Most of the discussions on constraints have tended to concentrate on the supply as part of school education. However, the problem also needs equally to be understood from the site where the demand for school education is generated. Each of the studies mentioned earlier said that the motivation for girls to complete elementary education has not been created within the communities. As a study conducted by Jadavpur University brought out, continuing with schooling is perceived as going against the interests of marriage.[16] Education has to open out opportunities that are beyond marriage and motherhood. Being the only weapon available for stemming the tide of child abuse through exploitation in the labour market and through trafficking, one cannot exaggerate the importance of creating a demand for educating girls.

In another study[17] on reasons why girls were never enrolled in school, poverty emerged as the major reason followed by parents' addiction to liquor and gambling, burden of housework, lack of interest in girls' education and belief in their traditional role in life. Thus we see that socio-cultural, personal, familial and infrastructural factors far outweigh the merely economic in the failure to enroll. Table 3.5 shows us the reasons most responsible for non-enrolment of rural children. The topmost reason in West Bengal seems to be that parents are not interested in the studies of their children. The female to male ratio per 1,000 is also adverse to girls. Interestingly,

Table 3.5
Proportion (per 1,000) of Never Enrolled Persons (5–24 Years) and Their per 1,000 Distribution by Reason for Non-enrolment (Rural)

Reasons	West Bengal		Kerala		Uttar Pradesh		Maharashtra		All-India	
	Male	Female	Male	Female	Male	Female	Male	Female	Male	Female
Never enrolled	263	350	13	29	272	542	110	194	235	406
No Tradition in the family	11	36	51	76	9	68	14	32	15	54
Child not interested in studies	217	189	49	38	257	155	208	119	205	151
Parents not interested in studies	177	320	Nil	Nil	240	355	171	395	278	356
Education not considered useful	40	24	Nil	Nil	19	16	16	23	27	29
Schooling/higher education facilities not available conveniently	1	1	Nil	Nil	24	16	14	12	20	23
Has to work for wages/salary	26	3	Nil	Nil	12	26	27	17	22	9
Has to participate in other economic activity	14	7	Nil	Nil	108	3	77	47	46	30
Has to look after younger siblings	4	14	Nil	Nil	7	8	0	39	7	16
Has to attend to other domestic activity	1	14	Nil	Nil	0	43	1	36	7	40
Financial constrains	273	171	44	0	235	191	87	95	163	136

Source: National Sample Survey Organization 1995–96, NSS 52nd Round, Department of Statistics, Government of India.
Note: This table is compiled from Table 17R of the NSS report (52nd Round). While Table 17R lists 15 reasons for non-enrolment, this table lists 10 reasons that are more significant. Hence, the relevant figure here may not add up to 1,000.

[16] Bagchi, Jasodhara, Jaba Guha and Piyali Sengupta, *Girl Child and the Family: The Case of West Bengal.* School of Women's Studies, Jadavpur University, Calcutta, 1993.
[17] Bagchi, Jasodhara, Jaba Guha and Piyali Sengupta, *Loved and Unloved: The Girl Child in the Family.* Stree, Calcutta, 1997.

it is more for boys than for girls that education is not considered useful. Availability of schooling/higher education facilities is hardly a factor in West Bengal. Girls count for less than one-eighth of boys in terms of obligation to earn wages. Proportionately boys who have to look after siblings are less than one-third of the girls who have to do so and the boys who have to engage in domestic duties are less than one-fourth of girls who are burdened with domestic chores.

The NSS 52nd Round data (1995–96) shows us (Table 3.6) that as far as average expenditure per male and female student of 5–24 years in urban India is concerned, West Bengal presents the interesting case of more money being spent in the middle level on girls than boys, which again does a turnaround in the secondary/higher secondary stages. Possibly, this is the time for the dowry money to be accumulated! In rural West Bengal (Table 3.7), there seems to be an upward trend in the

Table 3.6
Average Expenditure (in rupees) per Male and Female Student of Age 5–24 Years Pursuing General Education by Board Level of Education in India and 15 Major States (Urban)

| | Board level of education | | | | | | | | | | | | | | |
| | Primary | | | Middle | | | Sec./H. Sec. | | | Above H. Sec | | | All | | |
	Male	Female	Gap*	Male	Female	Gap*	Male	Female	Gap*	Male	Female	Gap*	Male	Female	Gap*
Andhra Pradesh	1,072	884	82.5	1,384	1,256	90.8	2,184	2,415	110.6	3,842	3,481	90.6	1,696	1,591	93.8
Assam	895	878	98.1	1,169	1,256	107.4	1,723	1,553	90.1	2,762	3,595	130.2	1,411	1,341	95.0
Bihar	910	863	94.8	1,264	1,109	87.7	1,741	1,546	88.8	2,641	2,430	92.0	1,444	1,228	85.0
Gujarat	1,007	983	97.6	1,312	1,198	91.3	2,103	1,664	79.1	3,081	1,992	64.7	1,593	1,290	81.0
Haryana	1,841	1,809	98.3	2,447	2,356	96.3	3,175	2,890	91.0	3,438	3,820	111.1	2,352	2,326	98.9
Karnataka	827	727	87.9	1,296	911	70.3	1,506	1,493	99.1	3,293	3,263	99.1	1,392	1,171	84.1
Kerala	1,127	831	73.7	1,446	1,259	87.1	1,534	1,678	109.4	2,741	2,547	92.9	1,490	1,407	94.4
Madhya Pradesh	820	697	85.0	1,137	1,017	89.4	1,624	1,584	97.5	2,164	2,072	95.7	1,181	1,049	88.8
Maharashtra	1,102	1,004	91.1	1,336	1,171	8,7.6	2,128	1,901	89.3	4,441	4,383	98.7	1,725	1,583	91.8
Orissa	868	830	95.6	1,164	1,013	87.0	2,108	1,651	78.3	2,500	2,699	108.0	1,499	1,253	83.6
Punjab	1,903	1,773	93.2	3,124	2,307	73.8	4,408	3,459	78.5	5,000	4,608	92.2	2,970	2,568	86.5
Rajasthan	1,172	1,106	94.4	1,278	1,232	96.4	1,807	1,701	94.1	1,921	2,808	146.2	1,389	1,352	97.3
Tamil Nadu	893	901	100.9	1,290	1,359	105.3	2,037	1,833	90.0	3,780	2,852	75.4	1,487	1,363	91.7
Uttar Pradesh	1,478	1,311	88.7	2,004	1,562	77.9	2,354	2,385	101.3	2,487	2,727	109.7	1,860	1,703	91.6
West Bengal	1,058	1,043	98.6	1,900	2,142	1,12.7	3,874	3,390	87.5	3,977	5,012	126.0	2,115	1,979	93.6
India	1,197	1,092	91.2	1,590	1,456	91.6	2,288	2,136	93.4	3,338	3,260	97.7	1,750	1,609	91.9

Source: National Sample Survey Organization 1995–96, NSS 52nd Round, Department of Statistics, Government of India. Table no. 12U.
Note: * The amount of money (in rupees) spent on female students for every Rs 100 spent on male students.

Table 3.7
Average Expenditure (in rupees) per Male and Female Student of Age 5–24 Years Pursuing General Education by Board Level of Education in India and 15 Major States (Rural)

| | Board level of education | | | | | | | | | | | | | | |
| | Primary | | | Middle | | | Sec./H. Sec. | | | Above H. Sec | | | All | | |
	Male	Female	Gap*	Male	Female	Gap*	Male	Female	Gap*	Male	Female	Gap*	Male	Female	Gap*
Andhra Pradesh	205	270	131.7	473	656	138.7	850	893	105.1	1,734	1,337	77.1	399	417	105.0
Assam	190	211	111.1	412	420	101.9	953	839	88.0	2,403	1,672	69.6	518	489	94.4
Bihar	235	222	94.5	441	442	100.2	972	904	93.0	1,905	3,138	164.7	483	375	77.6
Gujarat	182	160	87.9	372	353	94.9	1,169	949	81.2	2,013	1,626	80.8	466	366	78.5
Haryana	738	621	84.1	1,260	1,076	85.4	2,138	1,889	88.4	2,819	6,450	228.8	1,154	894	77.5
Karnataka	132	132	100.0	360	394	109.4	921	935	101.5	2,346	1,401	59.7	450	362	80.4
Kerala	709	603	85.0	737	662	89.8	1,060	1,211	114.2	2,951	3,671	124.4	897	992	111.0
Madhya Pradesh	196	190	96.9	485	412	84.9	960	811	84.5	1,462	1,854	126.8	389	279	71.7
Maharashtra	266	265	99.6	479	512	106.9	992	949	95.7	1,710	1,754	102.6	556	472	84.9
Orissa	187	213	113.9	625	561	89.8	1,097	969	88.3	1,839	1,668	90.7	571	416	72.9
Punjab	916	856	93.4	1,438	1,167	81.2	2,758	2,693	97.6	4,033	3,432	85.1	1,468	1,297	88.4
Rajasthan	320	308	96.3	649	604	93.1	1,151	1,226	106.5	1,989	1,005	50.5	571	424	74.3
Tamil Nadu	302	225	74.5	586	517	88.2	1,120	1,260	112.5	3,697	3,592	97.2	619	479	77.4
Uttar Pradesh	337	293	86.9	696	668	96.0	1,210	1,075	88.8	2,129	2,048	96.2	587	436	74.3
West Bengal	268	219	81.7	960	1,026	106.9	1,969	1,702	86.4	2,990	2,940	98.3	709	570	80.4
India	305	286	93.8	640	641	100.0	1,192	1,156	97.0	2,283	2,323	102.0	605	516	85.3

Source: National Sample Survey Organization 1995–96, NSS 52nd Round, Department of Statistics, Government of India. Table no. 12R.
Note: * The amount of money (in rupees) spent on female students for every Rs 100 spent on male students.

expenditure on the education of females. This is extremely heartening and calls for a more concerted social intervention.

Since 1994, girls' education has been one of the major components under the District Primary Education Programme (DPEP) which is running in 10 districts of West Bengal at present. These districts have been selected on the basis of female literacy rates that were lower than the national average at the time of commencement of the project. The girls' education unit has focused on activities like awareness generation campaigns by using folk theatre, folk music and innovative programmes, like *Ma-O-Meye Mela*. The unit also tries to sensitize educational administrators, panchayat functionaries, teachers of primary schools, village education committees and, most importantly, parents at block, gram panchayat and subdivisional levels.

Conclusion

The external obstacles that come in the way of girls and women being educated need committed attention. An increase in the teacher–student ratio and gender sensitization of teachers, both males and females, also craves attention. Making community participation mandatory in administering school education and introducing vocational education from the post-elementary level in all schools would go a long way in addressing dropout problems. Besides, the demand for elementary education may be strengthened within the families of schoolgoing children by generating awareness among them about entitlements like free textbooks, school uniforms and midday meals. There is a tendency among the privileged sections to interpret the demand for these things as greed on the part of the poor. However, awareness needs to be raised about children's rights to timely supply of these entitlements. This should affect the supply of the promised free school uniforms and textbooks that the state is committed to provide, in time. On the whole, the gender gap that has persisted in school education through all the changes will have to be addressed as a special social malady.

Higher and Technical Education

In the last section we have seen how girl children fare with respect to school education. In this section we present a gendered analysis of general education above Class XII level, and technical education, including vocational courses. Special attention will be given to technical education of different kinds and at different levels (degrees, diplomas and short certificate courses) because access to technology is one of the critical areas which causes gender-based differences in securing and retaining jobs, in promotion prospects, as well as in potential for self-employment. Together with ownership of land and other assets, and availability of capital and credit, access to technical education and vocational training is one of the crucial determinants influencing potential for women's access to paid work. This assumes greater significance in these days of globalization and speedy technical changes.

This study includes a quantitative and a qualitative aspect. The quantitative aspect looks into matters such as the proportion of women vis-à-vis men in particular areas of study as well as the changes in these proportions over time. The qualitative aspect looks at the areas in which women tend to concentrate as against those in which men concentrate. This is connected with the gender-based role stereotyping that we observe in our society, which in turn yields restrictions on opportunities open to women, lower chances of doing paid work, earning less than men, losing jobs when technical innovations are introduced and so on. For matters to improve in job markets as well as in fields of self-employment, gender-based concentration of women in non-technical areas of study must give way to a more even spread of education, technical or otherwise, across gender.

Education Completed as Proportion of Relevant Population in West Bengal

Table 3.8 shows (cross-section and inter-temporal) what proportion of the relevant population have completed different levels and kinds of education over the period 1971 to 1991. By relevant population we mean people of that age group who may be expected to have completed the levels of education being referred to. To simplify matters and maintain comparability we have taken 20+ to be the relevant population for all education levels in this table. The data has been taken from Census records for the years 1971, 1981 and 1991. It gives us a gendered picture of the different levels of education for the whole of West Bengal. Separate data for rural and urban is available only for the categories, non-technical diploma/certificate (not degree) and technical diploma/certificate (not degree). For all other categories, only urban data is available, possibly because rural figures would not be significant. As expected, the highest figures are for general, i.e., non-technical, graduate and postgraduate degrees. The third highest figures are in the category, technical degree/diploma = graduate or postgraduate in teaching, where the proportion for women is higher than that for men over the entire period. This reflects our gender-based role stereotyping where teaching is considered to be one of the areas suitable for women. In all other categories women lag behind men, the gender-based differences being more substantial in engineering and technology, medicine as well as general graduate and postgraduate degrees. At diploma/certificate levels, the female–male differences are higher for technical as compared to non-technical categories. Chart 3.6 gives an inter-temporal picture of female and male graduate and postgraduate non-technical degree holders (as percentage of relevant population) in West Bengal.

Table 3.8
Level of Education Completed as Proportion of Relevant Population in West Bengal (in per cent)

		1971			1981			1991		
		M	W	P	M	W	P	M	W	P
Non-tech dipl./cert.	(U)	0.024	0.011	0.019	0.029	0.015	0.023	0.063	0.036	0.051
(not degree)	(R)	(0.091)	(0.010)	(0.053)	(0.039)	(0.004)	(0.022)	(0.070)	(0.011)	(0.042)
Tech dipl./cert.	(U)	0.402	0.022	0.252	0.879	0.094	0.548	0.585	0.071	0.344
(not degree)	(R)	(0.091)	(0.012)	(0.053)	(0.277)	(0.027)	(0.156)	(0.202)	(0.026)	(0.117)
Graduate other than										
tech. degree	(U)	6.507	2.961	5.107	8.952	5.116	7.333	13.011	7.522	10.552
P.G. degree other than										
tech. degree	(U)	1.133	0.559	0.906	1.285	0.743	1.056	1.416	0.942	1.204
Tech. degree/dipl. = graduate										
or P.G. engg. and tech.	(U)	0.533	0.016	0.329	0.576	0.012	0.338	0.752	0.078	0.450
Tech. degree/dipl. = Graduate										
or P.G. medicine	(U)	0.352	0.061	0.237	0.282	0.052	0.185	0.366	0.089	0.242
Tech. degree/dipl. = graduate										
or P.G. agri. vet. dairy	(U)	0.005	0.001	0.003	0.016	0.001	0.010	0.027	0.014	0.022
Tech. degree/dipl. = graduate										
or P.G. teaching	(U)	0.142	0.256	0.187	0.364	0.671	0.494	0.464	0.593	0.522
Tech. degree/dipl. = graduate										
or P.G. others	(U)	0.096	0.027	0.069	0.003	0.000	0.002	0.038	0.016	0.028

Source: *Census of India 1971, 1981, 1991*, Social and Cultural Tables.
Notes: (a) Relevant population is the 20+ age group for all categories; (b) U = Urban, R = Rural; (c) M = Men, W = Women, P = Persons.

Chart 3.6
Level of Education Completed as Proportion of Relevant Population in West Bengal (in per cent)

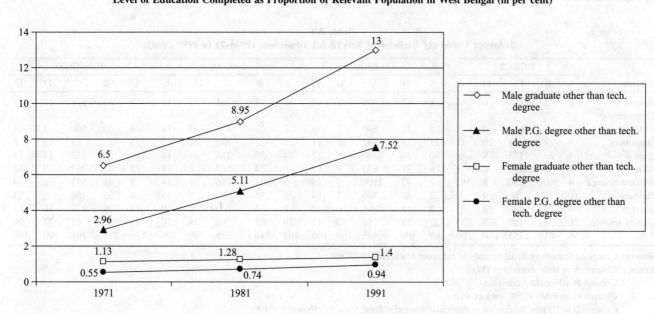

Source: *Census of India 1971, 1981, 1991*, Social and Cultural Tables.

Enrolment—A Case Study of Jadavpur University

We next take up a case study of Jadavpur University in Kolkata where all three streams—arts, science and engineering and technology—are taught at both graduate and postgraduate levels. This will enable us to get a comparative idea of gender differences in arts, science and engineering and technology admissions at degree levels. The data has been collected from the official records of Jadavpur University at four time-periods: 1970–71, 1980–81, 1990–91 and 1999–2000. Thus, an inter-temporal picture will also be obtained. Jadavpur University admission data has been presented in Tables 3.9 to 3.14.

In Table 3.9, admissions in Bachelor of Arts (B.A.) courses have been shown. There are nine subjects—Bengali, comparative literature, economics, English, history, political science, philosophy, Sanskrit and library science. We note that in the B.A. courses, the number of girls for exceed the number of boys enrolled—the overall (female/male ratio) × 100 being 153, 435, 135 and 201 in the years studied. In economics, the F/M ratio is, in general, much lower than for the other subjects, since job prospects are better and there are more options available. One interesting feature is that in library science, the F/M ratio shows a declining trend over time. This may be due to better job prospects. In 1999–2000, the highest F/M enrolment ratios are in political science, comparative literature and philosophy. In English, the F/M ratio has declined continuously over the entire period, once again possibly reflecting better job opportunities for students of this subject.

When we look at the proportion of boys and girls enrolled in different subjects in relation to total enrolment of boys/girls, interesting features emerge. Over the entire period, higher proportions of boys got admitted to library science, economics and English, in this order. For girls, political science has emerged as the subject with the highest enrolment proportion since 1980–81. Philosophy, history, English, Bengali, comparative literature are among the subjects with high enrolment proportions for girls, but the ranks vary over the four years being studied. In general, it seems that girls tend to be clustered in courses which offer a lesser variety of job openings, the main opportunities available are in teaching. Naturally, the competition for enrolment is lesser in the other courses as compared to English or economics.

Table 3.10 presents the M.A. enrolment scenario. There are eight courses being offered. There is no Masters' course in library science. The international relations in M.A. corresponds to the political science course in B.A. In M.A., too, girls' enrolment is much higher than the boys over the entire period. Philosophy emerges as the course with the highest female–male enrolment ratio, followed by comparative literature and international relations. In the seventies and eighties, Bengali had the second highest F/M ratio, but the figures have declined in the later period. Economics is the only subject where boys' enrolment outstrips that of girls'. Once again this may have something to do with job prospects and the fact that many students from the science stream at higher secondary level, who may have failed to get admission in engineering or other courses, shift to economics from B.A.

Table 3.9
Jadavpur University Bachelor of Arts (B.A.) Admissions (1970–71 to 1999–2000)

Subject	1970–71					1980–81					1990–91					1999–2000				
	A	B	C	D	E	A	B	C	D	E	A	B	C	D	E	A	B	C	D	E
Bengali	0	2	NMA	0	3	1	43	4,300	1	14	11	29	264	11	12	17	30	176	13	11
Comparative literature	0	1	NMA	0	2	5	27	540	7	9	7	33	471	7	14	6	30	500	4	11
Economics	14	9	64	26	11	21	34	162	30	11	22	23	105	22	10	25	22	88	18	8
English	4	23	575	8	28	10	36	360	15	12	14	30	214	14	13	19	30	158	14	11
History	0	2	NMA	0	3	6	38	633	9	13	6	34	567	6	14	12	32	267	9	12
Political science	4	10	250	8	12	2	42	2100	3	14	7	34	486	7	14	7	38	543	5	14
Philosophy	10	6	60	19	7	2	42	2,100	3	14	5	31	620	5	13	8	36	450	6	13
Sanskrit	1	4	400	2	5	0	5	NMA	0	2	1	1	100	1	0	13	29	223	10	11
Library science	20	24	120	38	30	22	33	150	32	11	29	25	86	28	10	29	27	93	21	10
Total	53	81	153	100	100	69	300	435	100	100	102	240	235	100	100	136	274	201	100	100

Source: Compiled from the official records of Jadavpur University, Kolkata.
Notes: Column A = Male Admission (M)
   Column B = Female Admission (F)
   Column C = (F/M) × 100, subject-wise
   Column D = {(Male Admission in Particular Subject)/(Total Male Admission)} × 100
   Column E = {(Female Admission in Particular Subject)/(Total Female Admission)} × 100
   NMA = No Male Admission.

Table 3.10
Jadavpur University Master of Arts (M.A.) Admissions (1970–71 to 1999–2000)

Subject	1970–71					1980–81					1990–91					1999–2000				
	A	B	C	D	E	A	B	C	D	E	A	B	C	D	E	A	B	C	D	E
Bengali	3	32	1,066	4	13	7	46	657	8	21	16	39	244	19	12.1	23	45	196	16	12
Comparative literature	4	13	325	5	5	11	29	264	12	13	5	50	1,000	6	16	13	52	400	9	14
Economics	17	16	94	23	7	26	21	81	29	10	28	27	96	34	8	31	31	100	21	9
English	10	43	430	14	18	11	36	327	12	16	9	46	511	11	14	21	49	233	14	14
History	10	31	310	14	13	18	30	167	20	14	12	44	367	15	14	20	39	195	14	11
International relations	13	30	231	18	12	9	15	167	10	7	7	50	714	8	16	14	50	357	10	14
Philosophy	4	43	1,075	5	18	5	15	300	6	7	5	51	1,020	6	16	4	60	1,500	3	17
Sanskrit	13	38	292	18	15	4	27	675	4	12	1	15	1,500	1	5	21	38	181	14	10
Total	74	246	332	100	100	91	219	241	100	100	83	322	388	100	100	147	364	248	100	100

Source: Same as Table 3.9.
Notes: Column A = Male Admission (M)
Column B = Female Admission (F)
Column C = (F/M) × 100, subject-wise
Column D = {(Male Admission in Particular Subject)/(Total Male Admission)} × 100
Column E = {(Female Admission in Particular Subject)/(Total Female Admission)} × 100
NMA = No Male Admission.

level as a viable alternative. Out of the total boys' enrolment, the highest proportion is in economics, followed by Bengali, English and history. For girls, philosophy, comparative literature, international relations and English are the major enrolment areas.

Table 3.11 gives the Bachelor of Science (B.Sc.) enrolment figures, where boys predominate. The overall F/M ratios are declining—46, 28, 27 and 36 from 1971 to 2000. The F/M ratio does not show any clear ranking between subjects and varies over time. The subject proportion among boys enrolled also varies at different time points, but mathematics and physics appear to be most popular in recent times and geological science is the least popular throughout. A similar picture emerges for girls enrolment. For Master of Science (M.Sc.), Table 3.12 shows that, here also, there are substantially more boys than girls. The F/M ratio varies between subjects. Mathematics accounts for the highest proportion of enrolment among both boys and girls.

Table 3.11
Jadavpur University Bachelor of Science (B.Sc.) Admissions (1970–71 to 1999–2000)

Subject	1970–71					1980–81					1990–91					1999–2000				
	A	B	C	D	E	A	B	C	D	E	A	B	C	D	E	A	B	C	D	E
Mathematics	21	14	67	27	39	28	10	36	30	39	49	11	22	34	28	54	21	39	32	35
Physics	22	10	46	28	28	22	9	41	24	35	36	15	42	25	39	51	13	26	30	22
Chemistry	24	9	38	30	25	21	7	33	23	27	35	10	29	24	26	36	17	47	21	28
Geological science	12	3	25	15	8	22	0	0	24	0	24	3	13	17	8	28	9	32	17	2
Total	79	36	46	100	100	93	26	28	100	100	144	39	27	100	100	169	60	36	100	100

Source: Same as Table 3.9.
Notes: Column A = Male Admission (M)
Column B = Female Admission (F)
Column C = (F/M) × 100, subject-wise
Column D = {(Male Admission in Particular Subject)/(Total Male Admission)} × 100
Column E = {(Female Admission in Particular Subject)/(Total Female Admission)} × 100
NMA = No Male Admission.

Table 3.12
Jadavpur University Master of Science (M. Sc.) Admissions (1970–71 to 1999–2000)

Subject	1970–71					1980–81					1990–91					1999–2000				
	A	B	C	D	E	A	B	C	D	E	A	B	C	D	E	A	B	C	D	E
Mathematics	34	19	56	47	50	33	11	33	33	58	35	21	60	36	62	47	16	34	43	32
Physics	15	9	60	21	24	20	4	20	20	21	24	8	33	25	24	29	7	24	26	14
Chemistry	14	9	64	19	24	26	3	12	26	16	19	5	26	19	15	21	16	76	19	32
Geological science	10	1	10	13.7	3	20	1	5	20	5	20	0	0	20	0	13	11	85	12	22
Total	73	38	52	100	100	99	19	19	100	100	98	34	35	100	100	110	50	46	100	100

Source: Same as Table 3.9.
Notes: Column A = Male Admission (M)
 Column B = Female Admission (F)
 Column C = (F/M) × 100, subject-wise
 Column D = {(Male Admission in Particular Subject)/(Total Male Admission)} × 100
 Column E = {(Female Admission in Particular Subject)/(Total Female Admission)} × 100
 NMA = No Male Admission.

In Bachelor of Engineering (B.E.), shown in Table 3.13, there are 15 courses being offered (some of these courses have been introduced only since the nineties). Here, girls' enrolment (as measured by F/M ratio) was only 3 per cent in 1970–71, but has increased gradually to 9, 16 and 11. The F/M ratio is highest in architecture and lowest in mechanical, staying at zero in most years. Among boys enrolled, the highest proportion is in mechanical, followed by electrical, civil and chemical. Among girls, traditionally, architecture occupies the highest positions, but in 1999–2000, admissions in chemical, electrical and civil picked up.

Table 3.14 shows that in Master of Engineering (M.E.), the number of girls was very low in 1970–71, but has been increasing over time. The F/M ratio in M.E. has increased from 2 in 1970–71 to 14 in 1999–2000. The F/M ratios are comparatively high in pharmaceutical and architecture and lowest in mechanical. Among the girls enrolled, relatively high proportions go to pharmaceutical, MCA and electronics and telecommunications, and the lowest go to mechanical. Chart 3.7 gives a diagrammatic representation of Jadavpur University enrolment data for arts, science and engineering given across Tables 3.9 to 3.14.

Table 3.13
Jadavpur University Bachelor of Engineering (B.E.) Admissions (1970–71 to 1999–2000)

Subject	1970–71					1980–81					1990–91					1999–2000				
	A	B	C	D	E	A	B	C	D	E	A	B	C	D	E	A	B	C	D	E
Mechanical	83	0	0	23	0	84	0	0	21	0	96	1	1	18	1	105	0	0	15	0
Electrical	70	1	1	19	10	84	3	4	21	9	78	19	24	14	22	91	14	15	13	18
Civil	45	0	0	12	0	82	5	6	20	15	83	14	17	15	17	91	12	13	13	15
Chemical	50	1	2	14	10	28	7	25	7	21	57	13	23	10	15	54	18	33	8	23
Electronics & tele-communications	30	0	0	8	0	28	2	7	7	6	43	4	9	8	5	56	4	7	8	5
Architecture	–	–	–	–	–	7	10	143	2	29	11	11	100	2	13	19	8	42	3	10
Metallurgical	13	0	0	4	0	12	0	0	3	0	19	3	16	4	4	24	1	4	3	1
Pharmaceutical	44	0	0	12	0	21	4	19	5	12	48	14	29	9	17	58	8	14	8	10
Computer science	–	–	–	–	–	–	–	–	–	–	43	2	5	8	2	56	3	5	8	4
Production	–	–	–	–	–	18	0	0	5	0	31	2	7	6	2	37	2	5	5	3
Printing	–	–	–	–	–	–	–	–	–	–	10	1	10	2	1	19	1	5	3	1
Power plant	–	–	–	–	–	–	–	–	–	–	11	0	0	2	0	36	1	3	5	1
Construction	–	–	–	–	–	–	–	–	–	–	9	1	11	2	1	31	1	3	4	1
Instrumentation	12	0	0	3	0	22	1	5	6	3	11	0	0	2	0	31	5	16	4	6
Food technology & bio-chemistry	17	8	47	5	80	16	2	13	4	6	–	–	–	–	–	–	–	–	–	–
Total	364	10	3	100	100	402	34	9	100	100	550	85	15	100	100	708	78	11	100	100

Source: Same as Table 3.9.
Notes: Column A = Male Admission (M)
 Column B = Female Admission (F)
 Column C = (F/M) × 100, subject-wise
 Column D = {(Male Admission in Particular Subject)/(Total Male Admission)} × 100
 Column E = {(Female Admission in Particular Subject)/(Total Female Admission)} × 100
   – = Subject not offered for study.

Table 3.14
Jadavpur University Master of Engineering (M.E.) Admissions (1970–71 to 1999–2000)

Subject	1970–71					1980–81					1990–91					1999–2000				
	A	B	C	D	E	A	B	C	D	E	A	B	C	D	E	A	B	C	D	E
Mechanical	20	0	0	17	0	18	0	0	13	0	25	0	0	15	0	30	1	3	3	3
Electrical	21	0	0	18	0	23	1	4	16	13	21	1	5	13	3	26	2	8	12	6
Civil	7	0	0	6	0	14	0	0	10	0	19	2	11	12	7	19	2	11	9	6
Chemical	16	0	0	14	0	21	0	0	15	0	9	2	22	6	7	16	3	19	9	9
Electronics & tele-communications	19	1	5	16	50	22	2	9	16	25	23	5	12	13	12	21	5	24	9	15
Architectural	–	–	–	–	–	11	2	18	8	25	4	1	25	3	3	6	2	33	3	6
Metallurgical	–	–	–	–	–	–	–	–	–	–	–	–	–	–	–	–	–	–	–	–
Pharmaceutical	8	0	0	7	0	19	1	5	13	13	19	8	42	12	27	17	10	59	8	30
Computer science	21	1	5	17	50	0	0	0	0	0	7	4	57	4	13	28	0	0	13	0
Production	–	–	–	–	–	–	–	–	–	–	12	0	0	7	0	13	0	0	6	0
Master of computer applications (MCA)	–	–	–	–	–	–	–	–	–	–	27	11	41	17	37	39	6	15	18	18
Food technology & bio-chemistry	5	0	0	4	0	14	2	14	10	25	–	–	–	–	–	–	–	–	–	–
Total	116	2	2	100	100	142	8	6	100	100	162	30	19	100	100	215	31	14	100	100

Source: Same as Table 3.9.

Notes: Column A = Male Admission (M)
Column B = Female Admission (F)
Column C = (F/M) × 100, subject-wise
Column D = {(Male Admission in Particular Subject)/(Total Male Admission)} × 100
Column E = {(Female Admission in Particular Subject) / (Total Female Admission)} × 100
– = Subject not offered for study.

Chart 3. 7
Jadavpur University Admissions in Arts, Science and Engineering (1970–71 to 1999–2000)

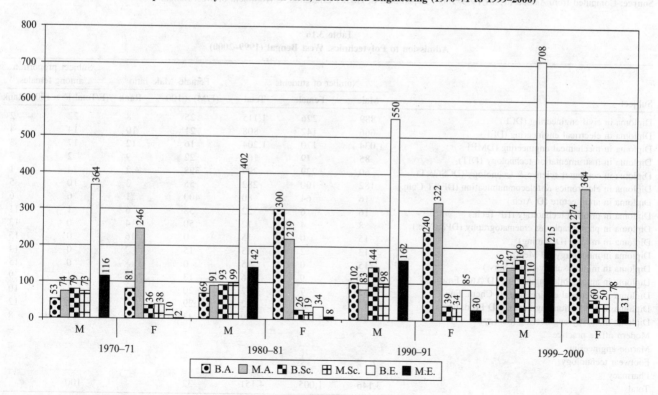

Source: Compiled from the official records of Jadavpur University, Kolkata.

Trends in Examination Results in Higher Studies

So far we have been studying the gendered enrolment scenario. But how do girls fare in different courses when they do enrol and complete the courses? Table 3.15 shows some results in 1999–2000 as obtained from the records of the Department of Higher Education, Government of West Bengal. We observe that in 1999–2000, the proportion of passed to appeared for different streams of higher education reveals that for arts, commerce, science and management, girls have done better than boys. In education the figures are similar, while for engineering and law, boys have done better. These results have been taken from too small a sample to be in any way conclusive. But they

do indicate that, in higher education, girls (women) are in no way intrinsically handicapped by their gender. The handicaps that do exist are societal in nature which can and should be removed.

Technical Education and Vocational Training

In recent times, many programmes have been initiated to encourage and facilitate female enrolment in diploma level technical education and in vocational education and training courses. Women have opportunities to train themselves in polytechnics (diploma courses), community polytechnics, short-term vocational training courses and industrial training institutes.

Table 3.15
Examination Results in Higher Studies, West Bengal (1999–2000)

Areas of study	Boys			Girls			(Girls [A]/ 100 Boys [A])
	Appeared (A)	Passed (P)	(P/A) × 100	Appeared (A)	Passed (P)	(P/A) × 100	
Arts	60,111	36,377	60.51	65,505	49,316	75.28	108.97
Commerce	40,811	25,106	61.51	7,874	6,111	77.60	19.29
Science	25,426	16,136	63.46	12,089	9,511	78.67	47.54
Education	2,783	2,315	83.18	2,270	1,880	82.81	81.56
Engineering	4,006	3,658	91.31	479	414	86.43	11.95
Law	3,389	2,008	59.25	1,049	529	50.42	30.95
Management	324	144	44.44	66	41	62.12	20.37
Total	136,850	85,744	62.65	89,332	67,802	75.89	65.27

Source: Computed from *Annual Report 1999–2000*, Department of Higher Education, Government of West Bengal.

Table 3.16
Admission to Polytechnics, West Bengal (1999–2000)

Subject	Number of students			Female–Male ratio		Subject proportion among females	
	Male	Female	Total	(F/M) × 100	Rank	(F/Total F) × 100	Rank
Diploma in civil engineering (DCE)	889	226	1,115	25	8	22	2
Diploma in electrical engineering (DEE)	666	142	808	21	10	14	4
Diploma in mechanical engineering (DME)	1,034	170	1,204	16	12	17	3
Diploma in instrumentation technology (DIT)	85	19	104	22	9	2	7
Diploma in computer science & technology (DCSC&T)	60	239	299	398	2	24	1
Diploma in electronics & telecommunication (DE&T Com.)	182	100	282	55	3	10	5
Diploma in architecture (D Arch.)	16	64	80	400	1	6	6
Diploma in printing technology (DP Tech.)	16	6	22	38	6	1	11
Diploma in photography & cinematography (DP&Cine.)	8	4	12	50	4	0	13
Diploma in mining (D Mining)	15	0	15	0	16	0	15
Diploma in metallurgy (D Meta)	13	2	15	15		0	14
Diploma in mining survey (Mine Surv.)	15	0	15	0		0	15
Diploma in automobile engineering (D Atuo Eng.)	67	9	76	13	15	1	9
Diploma in chemical engineering (D Chem. Eng.)	35	7	42	20	11	1	10
Diploma in production engineering (D Prod. Eng.)	17	5	22	29	7	1	12
Diploma in survey engineering (Survey)	28	12	40	43	5	1	8
Modern office practice	–	–	–	–	–	–	–
Marine engineering	–	–	–	–	–	–	–
Footwear technology	–	–	–	–	–	–	–
Pharmacy	–	–	–	–	–	–	–
Total	3,146	1,005	4,151	32		100	

Source: Computed from the official records of the West Bengal State Council for Technical Education, Kolkata.
Note: No figures indicate no admission.

Polytechnics

The polytechnics offer diploma level courses of three years, the qualifying level of education necessary for admission being Madhyamik (Class X). The diplomas are recognized at an all-India level. The number of polytechnics in West Bengal has increased from 21 in 1970 to 34 in 2000, and some new ones are being planned. Most of them are co-educational. Two polytechnics have been for men only. A number of women's polytechnics have also been set up. In 1970, there was only one such polytechnic (in Jodhpur Park, Kolkata). Since then, two others have been opened in Chandannagore and Siliguri. There are hostels for girls in Jodhpur Park, Siliguri, Jalpaiguri and Bardhaman. Since 1997, reservation of some seats for women in polytechnics has been introduced, and this has helped increase female enrolment substantially. The examination results of girls are as good as or better than boys.

In Table 3.16 we present the polytechnic scenario in 1999–2000. Twenty types of courses are being offered. Of these some may not be offered in a particular year. The overall female–male ratio in polytechnic admissions is about 32 per cent while the proportion of female to total admission is around 24 per cent. An encouraging finding is that only in mining and mining survey women's admissions are zero. In all other fields, women have taken admission, the numbers being low in metallurgy (2), photo and cinematography (4), production engineering (5), printing technology (6), chemical engineering (7) and automobile engineering (9). Large numbers of women have been admitted in computer science and technology (239), civil engineering (226), mechanical engineering (170), electrical engineering (142), electronics and telecommunications (100) and architecture (64) in this particular year. The highest male admissions are in mechanical engineering (1,034), civil engineering (889), electrical engineering (666), electronics and telecommunications (182), instrumentation technology (85), automobile engineering (67), chemical engineering (35), etc. We find female concentration in computer science and technology, where they outnumber male admissions substantially (the female–male ratio being the second highest, 398), the highest being in architecture (400). When we compare the absolute admission figures in different streams, however, we must allow for the differences in the numbers of polytechnics offering the relevant courses. Thus, while mechanical, electrical and civil engineering are taught in 22, 20 and 18 polytechnics respectively, architecture, printing technology and photo and cinematography are taught in only 3, 1 and 1 polytechnics respectively. Computer science and technology, however, has attracted a good number of female students, although it is taught in only five polytechnics of which two are for women only. If the number of polytechnics offering a wider range of courses increases and the number of women's polytechnics increases, then female admissions may increase over a wider range of technical courses. It is heartening to note that many women are now entering even erstwhile male bastions like mechanical and civil engineering. This shows that given proper opportunity, women can and do enter all technical fields and compete with men. It is mainly a question of providing the necessary facilities and also, very importantly, providing jobs and self-employment opportunities for those women who qualify in these so-called non-conventional technical areas for women. Chart 3.8 gives a pictorial representation of enrolment in polytechnics in 1999–2000.

Industrial Training Institutes (ITIs)

In Tables 3.17 and 3.18, we present the enrolment figures of the certificate level technical courses in West Bengal for 1999–2000. The ITIs offer two kinds of courses—the One-Year Engineering Trades and the Two-Year Engineering Trades. The minimum qualification necessary for admission to these courses is Madhyamik for most courses and Class VIII for a few. On completion of these courses, students get National Trade Certificates issued by the National Council for Vocational Training. In 1970, there were 17 ITIs and 1 industrial training centre in the state. There were no ITIs only for women. In 2000, there where 27 ITIs of which 4 are only for women. There are no reservations for female admissions to ITIs.

Table 3.17 shows the admissions to ITIs of West Bengal for one-year courses in 1999–2000. The types of courses being offered are 18, of which 11 were being offered in 1970. There are no male admissions in dress making, hair and skin care, and secretarial practices. There are no female admissions for courses in carpentery, forger and heat treater (HT), moulder, welder, mechanic diesel, mason and plumber. These male-only or female-only admissions reflect, once again, the gender-specific work stereotyping that we have in our society, where even the women who break the outside-inside barrier to work outside tend to get slotted in particular types of occupations. We observe that in plastic process operations (PPO), sheet metal works (SMW), book binding, manufacturing of footwear (MNF) and leather goods, there is only one female admission, which means that in these areas as well, women's admission is the exception rather than the rule. In general, female admission in ITIs for these one-year courses is very low—only 10 per cent of male admission and 9 per cent of total admission. The largest number of female admissions are in cutting and tailoring, secretarial practices, hair and skin care and dress making, while the highest male admissions are in welder, mechanic diesel, moulder, SMW, carpenter, forger and HT.

Chart 3.8
Polytechnic Admission in 1999–2000

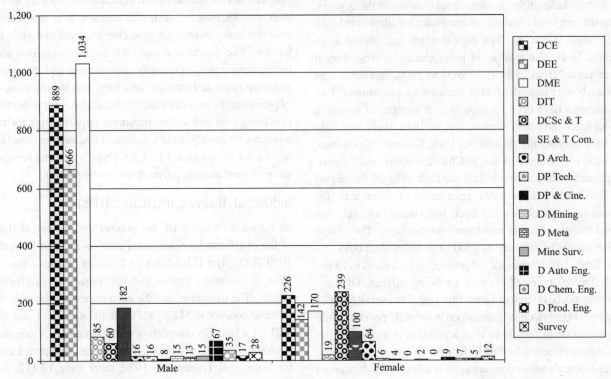

Source: Table 3.16.
Note: Abbreviations given in Table 3.16.

Table 3.17
Admissions in ITIs in West Bengal (1999–2000), One-Year Engineering Trades

Trade	Numbers of trainees			Female–Male ratio		Subject proportion among females	
	Male	Female	Total	(F/M) × 100	Rank	(F/Total F) × 100	Rank
Carpenter*	166	0	166	0	10	0	10
Forger & heat treater (HT)*	83	0	83	0	10	0	10
Moulder*	156	0	156	0	10	0	10
Plastic process operator (PPO)	84	1	85	1	8	1	5
Sheet metal worker (SMW)*	127	1	128	1	9	1	5
Welder*	553	0	553	0	10	0	10
Mechanic diesel*	230	0	230	0	10	0	10
Mason	14	0	14	0	10	0	10
Plumber*	47	0	47	0	10	0	10
Dress making	0	10	10	NMA	1	6	4
Hair & skin care	0	27	27	NMA	1	17	3
Secretarial practice	0	34	34	NMA	1	21	2
Stenography	7	0	7	0	10	0	10
Book binding*	15	1	16	6	6	1	5
Cutting & tailoring*	50	86	136	172	4	53	1
Manufacturing of footware (MNF)*	9	1	10	11	5	1	5
Leather goods maker*	23	1	24	4	7	1	5
Computer operator and programming assistant	–	–	–				
Total	1,564	162	1,728	10			

Source: Computed from the official records of Directorate of ITI Education, Kolkata.
Notes: No figures indicate no admission this year.
   * Courses which were being offered in 1970. The other courses were introduced later at different times.
   NMA = No Male Admission.

There seems to be a clear gender-specific specialization in matters of training, skill formation and, therefore, work, even as late as 1999–2000, as reflected in admissions to one-year ITI courses. Chart 3.9 gives a pictorial representation of enrolment in ITIs for One-Year Trade Courses in 1999–2000.

Table 3.18 shows admissions to ITIs for Two-Year Engineering Trades in 1999–2000. Here the number of courses offered are 19. The fields are not the same as in the one-year course. The subjects for the two-year course are of a more technical nature and are associated with higher earnings. The total number of trainees are much higher for the two-year courses, but the female–male ratio is much lower—only about 4 per cent as compared to around 10 per cent for the one-year courses. The proportion of female to total also is much lower—around 4 per cent as compared to 9 per cent in the other case. This corroborates our hypothesis that given the gender-based role stereotyping and the gender-based specialization in

patriarchal societies like ours, the higher paid, more technical occupations are still very highly male-dominated. There are no female admissions in courses for grinder, turner, mechanic motor vehicle (MMV), agricultural machinery, painter general and pattern maker and very low admissions for refrigeration and air conditioning (R&AC) mechanic, surveyor (only 1 each) and for electricians and machinist (2 each). The highest female admissions are in courses for electronic mechanic (43), radio and TV (24), information technology (17) and draftsman civil (DMC) (16). The highest number of admissions among males are in the fields of fitter (812), electrician (378), turner (345), machinist (323), draftsman mechanical (DMM) (198), MMV (192), wireman (147) and DMC (117). We note that electronic mechanic, radio & TV and DMC, where the women seem to be concentrated, are not the most popular courses among men. Chart 3.10 gives a pictorial representation of admissions in ITIs (two-year courses) in 1999–2000.

Chart 3.9
ITI (One-Year Course) Admissions in 1999–2000

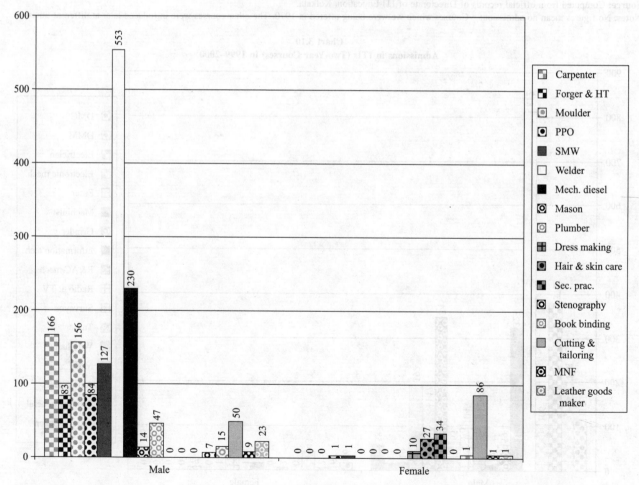

Table 3.18
Admissions to ITIs in West Bengal (1999–2000), Two-Year Engineering Trades

Trade	Numbers of trainees			Female–Male ratio		Subject proportion among females	
	Male	Female	Total	(F/M) × 100	Rank	(F/Total F) × 100	Rank
Draftsman civil (DMC)*	117	16	133	14	4	13	4
Draftsman mechanical (DMM)*	198	6	204	3	6	5	6
Electrician*	378	2	380	1	9	2	7
Electronic mechanic	106	43	149	41	2	36	1
Fitter*	812	0	812	0	11	0	11
Machinist*	323	2	325	1	10	2	7
Grinder*	59	0	59	0	11	0	11
Information technology	12	17	29	142	1	14	3
Refrigeration & air conditioning (R&AC) mechanic*	126	1	127	1	8	1	9
Radio & television mechanic*	104	24	128	23	3	20	2
Surveyor*	65	1	66	2	7	1	9
Turner*	345	0	345	0	11	0	11
Wireman*	147	7	154	5	5	6	5
Mechanic motor vehicle (MMV)*	192	0	192	0	11	0	11
Agricultural machinery	19	0	19	0	11	0	11
Painter general*	17	0	17	0	11	0	11
Pattern maker*	58	0	58	0	11	0	11
Laboratory assistant	–	–	–	–	–	–	–
Instrument mechanic	–	–	–	–	–	–	–
Total	3,078	119	3,197	4			

Source: Computed from official records of Directorate of ITI Education, Kolkata.
Notes: No figures mean no admission; * Courses which we were being offered in 1970. The other courses were introduced later at different times.

Chart 3.10
Admissions in ITIs (Two-Year Courses) in 1999–2000

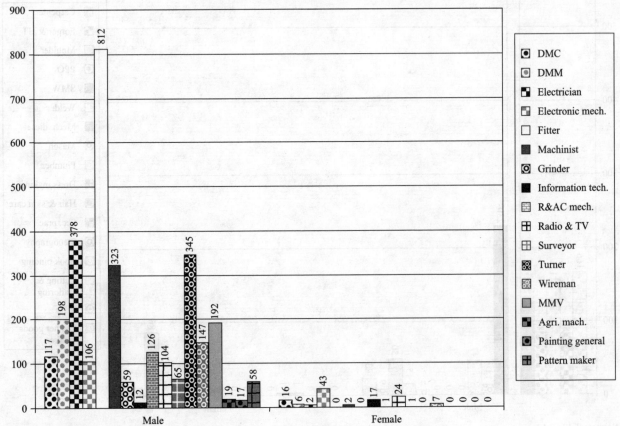

Source: Table 3.18.
Note: Abbreviations given in Table 3.18.

Community Polytechnic Courses

Funded by the Government of India, these courses were started in the seventies in India and in the eighties in West Bengal. These are three to six months' training courses mainly for rural people. Age or sex are no bar and no minimum qualifications are needed. The courses are conducted by polytechnics who have extension centres in various rural and urban locations in their respective districts. Extension centres are opened on request from panchayats, municipalities or NGOs, who also indicate the subject areas in which courses are needed in those centres. Community polytechnic courses in the extension centres are usually run separately for men and women because they demand different types of courses and, especially in rural areas, socio-cultural conditions do not permit men and women to attend courses together. Generally, female teachers are provided for women.

These courses are doing reasonably well. Our panchayat system and decentralized planning process can combine to make these courses useful and effective. Demand for the courses is generated and identified locally. This information is conveyed to the district polytechnics; courses are framed accordingly, with respect to both content and timing; and then the courses are run in the relevant localities from where the demands originated. Panchayats, municipalities and NGOs can interact with the polytechnics in running these courses so as to suit local needs and exploit local potentials. These courses have good possibilities for the really underprivileged women because they require no minimum qualification and are flexible in a lot of other ways. Even women from households below the poverty line can avail of these courses.

Interest in these courses and enrolment has started on an encouraging note, but the problem is of being able to utilize the acquired skills for income generation. Jobs are difficult to come by and more so for women. Self-employment possibilities are severely limited, especially for women, due to lack of capital, credit and marketing channels. If income generation possibilities improve for those who complete these courses, then only will other women be motivated to acquire these skills. If women who have completed these courses are forced to remain idle, then this would have a negative impact on attempts to provide vocational training to women.

Short-term Vocational Training Courses (STVT)

These are six-month courses started around 1995, funded by the Government of West Bengal and run by polytechnics, junior technical schools, industrial training institutes, municipalities, NGOs, and also some select schools and colleges, mostly in rural areas. These vocational training courses run parallel to the general curriculum in these schools and colleges. The minimum required qualification is Class X and the student's age must be below 25 years. The target student group consists of those who pass Class X examination, but are not able to get admission into other courses (technical or general) because of financial and/or academic handicaps. A large number and variety of courses are offered (76 courses in 2000 which increased to 150 in 2003). There are computer-related courses (software and hardware), para-medical courses, agriculture related courses, engineering trades, beautician and related courses, textile and fashion designing and so on. Women's enrolment in these courses is low and measures need to be taken to increase this.

Conclusion

In our analyses, two fields of higher education, namely, medicine and management have not been covered. This gap needs to be acknowledged and filled in later.

In the field of non-technical higher education, Census data (Table 3.8, Chart 3.6) shows that the proportion of graduate population in West Bengal has increased substantially from 1971 to 1991 for both male and female, but the gender gap is wider in 1991 than in 1971. The increase in the proportion of postgraduate population is low, but the gender gap has declined in this case. A possible reason may be that after graduation, boys try to get jobs or go in for job-oriented courses rather than continue with studies in the general stream.

Jadavpur University data shows that in engineering degree courses women were nearly absent in 1971. Enrolment has increased over the years, but the figures are still very low. The F/M ratio, however, shows an upward trend at both B.E. and M.E. levels. Women are also entering a wider variety of engineering fields. But certain prejudices still obstruct women from joining the hardcore engineering fields.

In the area of technical diploma courses, we observe that enrolment quotas helped increase female enrolment in polytechnics over a wide variety of courses. But, training and placement for women has emerged as a sticky problem which is proving very difficult to dislodge. Employees usually do not want to employ women even if their results and interview performances are better. When prospective employees are forced to call women candidates for result-based campus interviews, selections show clear gender-based discrimination against women. Interviews with relevant authorities reveal that would-be employers reject clearly qualified women candidates, offering all kinds of lame excuses to the extent of citing the need to provide separate toilet facilities for them! When women are selected, in many cases they are paid less than their male colleagues. Women are forced to accept this discrimination because of the difficulty they face in getting jobs.

Self-employment possibilities for women are also severely limited due to lack of information regarding available opportunities; lack of capital/credit/materials, etc.; and difficulties in marketing their products.

These difficulties are faced by men as well, especially among the underprivileged sections of society, but the problems are much more severe for women. Unless possibilities for income generation improve, enrolment quotas would be ineffective in the long run. Experience in the polytechnics already corroborates this hypothesis. The boost in women's enrolment in polytechnics, owing to quotas, has been undone by the adverse placement scenario and many women's quota seats remain vacant (later filled up by admitting men students).

In the ITIs, women's enrolment has always been, and still remains, very low. The courses are mainly engineering-industry-oriented, so female employment prospects are very low. The community polytechnic courses can be very useful for women, especially poor women in rural areas. In West Bengal, with an already well-developed and ruling panchayat system, an effective decentralized planning and execution mechanism can make good use of these courses because they are flexible (content-wise and location-wise), have no age or sex bar, require no minimum qualification and can exploit local needs and potential. Employability is once again a crucial factor in ensuring success of these courses. In the short-term vocational training courses, the enrolment of girls has not picked up as yet. Promotional programmes may help in this sphere. There is a need to attract the attention of policy makers to these issues so that gender gaps are reduced at the enrolment level of higher and technical education. This is interlinked with reduction in gender bias, gender-based role stereotyping and wage discrimination at work, which is a matter that craves attention as we shall also see in the next chapter on economic empowerment.

Economic Empowerment

CHAPTER 4

Ishita Mukhopadhyay

Women's Work: Concept and Definition

Much of women's work remains unrecognized and un-valued.... There is no adequate reward or recognition for the burden of work that women carry. Because status in contemporary society is so often equated with income-earning power, women suffer a major undervaluation of their economic status. This is so despite their larger share of the total work burden and notwithstanding the reality that men's paid work in the market place is often the result of 'joint production', much of which might not be possible if women did not stay at home looking after the children and the household.[1]

While discussing women's economic empowerment it is essential to remember that a part of the work that women do is paid and a part unpaid. The proportion of unpaid work done by women is very high compared to that of the paid work. Most of the work that women do is either supplementary or invisible and exhaustive information about this kind of work is practically impossible to obtain. In this report we have mainly tried to assess women's status in West Bengal vis-à-vis paid work performed both outside and at home. (A micro study on 'Women's Work: A Survey in Bankura and Hoogli' is included in Appendix D.) Work outside home as well as home-based work can be documented, but that is not the case with unpaid work. Unpaid work can be analysed through time-use surveys, which estimate the time required to perform each job by women. One time-use study was done for the state by Jain[2] for 1976–77. In that study it was noted that though female work participation rate is low in the state, women have reported

at least three hours of unpaid family labour. Home-based work was also found to be relatively more intensive than farm work for women. Since we have not had any time-use study for women in the state in recent times only paid work by women has been taken into account in this chapter.

An inquiry into women's work has also been essential for assessing women's empowerment. According to the UNDP guidelines, women's economic participation is an important element of the gender empowerment measure (GEM). GEM examines whether women and men are able to actively participate in economic and political life and take part in decision making. It is basically composed of economic, political and professional components. Though here we will not attempt to measure GEM, we will try to infer the contribution of work participation induced economic empowerment to the total empowerment index. Then we will try to look at the extent of marginalization and casualization of female labour from the available official statistics. The extent and varieties of livelihoods based on female economic activity will also be assessed. Both the diversity as well as stereotyping with respect to female economic activity are to be understood for policy recommendations.

In developing countries, where poverty is a burning issue, any question of economic empowerment cannot be dealt with without poverty eradication programmes intertwined with earning opportunities. In fact, there is a consensus among many that employment of women is crucial to poverty eradication. It is around work participation and employment opportunities that the process of social empowerment and bridging of gender inequality can be understood. In West Bengal, work participation went hand-in-hand with social and political participation of women, especially in rural areas. This has been possible

---

[1] *Human Development Report*, 'Valuation of Women's Work'. UN, 1995.

[2] Jain, Devaki, 'Valuing Work: Time as a Measure', *Economic and Political Weekly*, 26 October 1996.

due to a decentralized planning programme implemented through a three-tier panchayat system which has involved women in economic, social and political processes simultaneously at the grassroots level.

The source of data with respect to women's work in West Bengal has been the National Sample Survey (NSS) rounds and the *Census of India*. But they have been also supplemented by the data obtained from the Statistical Abstract[3] and other sources. The NSS rounds which have been considered are the quinquennial surveys of the 55th Round (1999–2000), 50th Round (1993–94) and 43rd Round (1987–88). The census figures are taken for the years 1981, 1991 and 2001.

Coming to the NSS definitions and concepts, the classification of economic activity is according to principal or subsidiary status. The status of activity on which a person has spent a relatively longer time in the preceding 365 days from the date of the survey is considered as principal status, otherwise the status becomes subsidiary. When we look at work participation, we have considered the aggregate of both principal and subsidiary categories. The status of persons classified as being engaged in economic activity is as follows: self-employed in household enterprise, regular salaried/wage employee, and casual labourer. The census division considers only main and marginal workers. The participation has been assessed in terms of work participation rates. Although the concepts used in the different data sources are different and as such non-comparable over time periods, broad trends can be deduced from analysing the data.

Economic Participation as Contribution towards Empowerment

UNDP devised the norms so as to include the question of economic empowerment in the process of gender empowerment as a whole. The reason for inclusion of female work participation in the broader definition of empowerment is obvious as economic earnings are initiators in the process of increasing capabilities and entitlements of women. We have measured equally distributed equivalent percentage (EDEP) of the female population in the state according to the UNDP guidelines. Taking the aversion to inequality parameter as 2 according to the technical specification of the *Human Development Report*, EDEP has been constructed for work participation. This can be stated to be the outcome in economic and political participation.

GEM concentrates on participation—economic, political and professional. EDEP focuses on few select variables. To measure economic empowerment, we need to focus on earned income of the females as well as control over economic resources given by share in professional jobs. This formulation by the UNDP has been moderated by Kapur Mehta[4] and a new measure of GEM as applicable in developing countries has been suggested by her. Going by her measure, GEM has been calculated and EDEP for economic participation has been estimated with respect to the state. Here we are interested in the contribution of economic empowerment in the state towards general gender empowerment. In other words, as gender empowerment is a combination of political and economic empowerment meaning access to economic and political power, the importance of economic power of women in gaining empowerment in general is the focus of this report.

Economic participation has been categorized as administrative and other work, where work appears as a main category. Thereby we ignore the marginal women workers. For participation as administrators, the number of women in the Indian Administrative Service and the Indian Police Service have been taken into consideration. Work participation has been assessed from the Census Main Worker category. Both these contributions have been measured and EDEP for economic participation constructed. The reference time has been the year 2000–2001. The EDEP for economic participation and decision making index for the state emerged as 0.03. The index for participation in the Indian Administrative Service is 0.30 and that for participation in the Indian Police Service is 0.07. The index for main workers is 0.52. However, the contribution of earned income component for GEM is small compared to that of the entire country. The computed EDEP for earned income for West Bengal females is lower than many other states, as well as below the country average, which is 0.04. But the GEM index is higher for the state. This is not only higher than the country average, but also higher than many states in the country. From this we can infer that the contribution of political empowerment has been much higher than economic empowerment in the state. This is also corroborated by the calculations done according to Kapur Mehta guidelines.[5] The calculations show that the state records the highest EDEP for political participation among all Indian states in 2001 with the value as 0.70. This makes economic empowerment a lesser priority for women in West Bengal. Economic empowerment has still a long way to go. Table 4.1 depicts the situation.

[3] Government of West Bengal, *Statistical Abstract of West Bengal*, Bureau of Applied Economics and Statistics, Kolkata, 2001–2002.

[4] Kapur Mehta, Asha, 'Recasting Indices for Developing Countries: A Gender Empowerment Measure', *Economic and Political Weekly*, 26 October 1996.

[5] Ibid.

Table 4.1
Economic Participation and Decision Making
Index in West Bengal

IAS Index	0.30
IPS Index	0.07
Main Workers' Index	0.52
EDEP for income	0.03
EDEP for political participation	0.70
GEM	0.48

Source: Mukhopadhyay, Ishita and Anindita Ghosh, 'Gender Empowerment Measures for the Indian States'. Mimeo, 2003.

Marginalization of Female Labour

Census data is available on the distribution of labour force between main and marginal workers. This provides some clues about the marginalization of female labour force in the state. The data also helps us to compare the situation over the decades with the all-India figures. The proportion of main and marginal workers in the total workforce calculated for both female and male workers in the rural and urban areas provide proof of the extent of marginalization of female labour.

Table 4.2
Marginalization of Female Labour from 1981–2001
(worker-population ratio)

Category	Total 1981	1991	2001	Urban 1981	1991	2001	Rural 1981	1991	2001
Male (main)	48.71	50.50	47.32	48.70	49.12	50.61	48.72	51.04	46.00
Male (marginal)	1.51	0.86	6.91	0.92	0.40	3.47	1.84	1.05	8.30
Female (main)	5.81	8.07	8.86	4.65	5.93	8.82	6.29	8.83	8.87
Female (marginal)	2.26	3.60	9.22	0.94	0.53	2.31	2.70	4.71	11.83

Source: *Census of India.*

Table 4.2 clearly indicates certain trends. First, there has been a general marginalization of the labour force throughout 1981 to 2001. The percentage of marginal labourers in the workforce was 58.29 in 1981, went up to 63.03 in 1991 and reached 72.31 in 2001. Most of the labourers were marginal workers even two decades ago. However, in 2001, the scope of main work has diminished so much that a sizeable majority of the workers are now marginal. Chart 4.1 depicts the extent of marginalization of the workforce in the state.

It is clear from Chart 4.1 that the degree of marginalization from 1991 to 2001 has been faster than from 1981 to 1991. But this phenomenon is common to the country as a whole. Next, the participation of women as main workers has increased

Chart 4.1
Marginalization of Labour

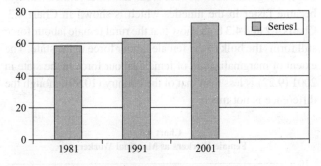

Source: *Census of India 1981, 1991, 2001.*

steadily in these two decades. The proportion was 5.81 in 1981, 8.07 in 1991 and 8.86 in 2001. If we look at the rural–urban break up, the percentage of urban female main workers in the workforce went up from 4.65 in 1981 to 5.93 in 1991 and further to 8.82 in 2001. In the rural areas, it went up from 6.29 in 1981 to 8.83 in 1991 and then to 8.87 in 2001. So, the rate of inclusion in the main worker category has been faster in the rural areas during the eighties and in the urban area in the nineties. Chart 4.2 describes the process of inclusion of female workers in the main worker category in rural and urban areas. The process of mainstreaming of female workforce started in the rural areas much earlier than the urban areas

Chart 4.2
Female Workers as Main Workers

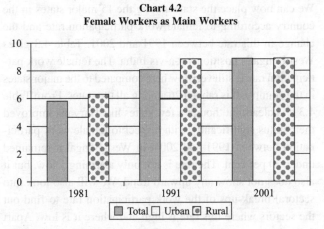

Source: *Census of India 1981, 1991, 2001.*

Marginalization of female labour force is an old trend of the nineties, which is still continuing. Although more women workers have been included as main workers, they have always been engaged as marginal workers throughout. The percentage of female marginal workers was 2.26 in 1981, went up to 3.60 in 1991 and further to 9.22 in 2001. If we again look at the rural–urban break-up, the proportion of urban female marginal workers was 0.94 percentage points in 1981, became 0.53 in 1991 and then went up to 2.31 in 2001. The proportion in the case of rural females was 2.70 in 1981, 4.71 in 1991 and 11.83 in 2001. Marginalization of both urban and rural female workers became faster in the nineties which is shown in Chart 4.3. Charts 4.2 and 4.3 both show that the rural female labour force still forms the bulk of the female labour force in the state. The extent of marginalization of female labour force in the state in 2001 (9.22) is less than that of the country (10.99), though the difference is not much.

Chart 4.3
Female Workers as Marginal Workers

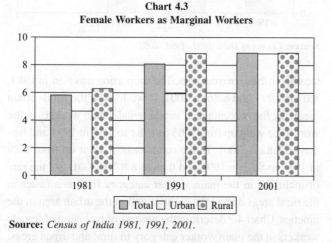

Source: *Census of India 1981, 1991, 2001.*

Female Work Participation Rate

We can now place the state among the 15 major states in the country according to female work participation rate and the change in this rate between 1991 and 2001. Table 4.3 gives West Bengal's position vis-à-vis India. The female work participation rate is still very low here compared to the major states in the country. It is ranked 26 among all the states. From Table 4.3 it is clear that though a few states like Haryana improved their status significantly with respect to female work participation between 1991 and 2001, in West Bengal it remained under 20 per cent. The rate is not only alarmingly low, but it also does not show any upward trend. We will also look into sectoral break-ups of the work participation rate to find out the sectors where this rate is high and where it is low. Apart from the census data, the NSS data has also been used. As the data is not comparable, we start with the NSS 55th Round and gradually trace backwards towards the beginning of the decade. In the 55th Round, we find that female work participation in both the urban and rural areas of the state has declined for the 25 to 49 age group. This once again reasserts the finding that the state shows a low rate of female work participation.

Table 4.3
Female Work Participation Rates from 1991–2001

State	2001	1991
India	25.68	22.25
Himachal Pradesh	43.69	34.82
Andhra Pradesh	34.93	34.32
Rajasthan	33.48	27.40
Madhya Pradesh	33.10	32.68
Maharashtra	32.59	33.11
Karnataka	31.88	29.39
Tamil Nadu	31.32	29.89
Gujarat	28.03	25.96
Haryana	27.31	10.76
Orissa	24.62	20.79
Tripura	21.02	13.76
Assam	20.80	21.61
Bihar	18.84	14.86
Punjab	18.68	4.40
West Bengal	18.08	11.25

Source: *Census of India.*

The gender difference with respect to work participation stands at 36 per cent for West Bengal whereas for the country it is 26 per cent.[6]

We can take a look at Table 4.4 to understand the female work participation in the 43rd Round and the 55th Round of the NSS for the usual category including both the principal and the subsidiary categories. The two rounds are presented to understand the process of change. For the rural population, agriculture is still the main occupation. Though the employment of women relative to men is low in the state compared to the entire country, it is significantly larger in agriculture than in all other occupations. Dependence on manufacturing as an occupation is rising for the rural females in the state. Manufacturing is an important source of livelihood in both the urban and rural areas of the state. But in other parts of the country, we find female livelihood in manufacturing mostly in the urban areas. This means that there exists a significant amount of small-scale and cottage industries in the rural areas which has attracted gainful female employment. Public administration and education is another main area of employment for urban females in the state.

The NSS reports also reveal concentration in pattern of labour use among females. It is observed that rural females do not dominate rural males in agriculture in the state as in India. Both in India and the state, females dominate the manufacturing sector relative to males in the urban area. Trade, hotels, public administration and education emerge as important areas of absorption of female labour in the urban areas.

---

[6] Government of India, *Annual Report*, Department of Women and Child Development, Ministry of Human Resource Development, New Delhi, 2001.

Table 4.4
Per 1,000 Distribution of Usually Working Persons in the Usual Category taken together by Broad Industry Division

State Rounds of the NSS Survey	1 43rd/55th	2 43rd/55th	3 43rd/55th	4 43rd/55th	5 43rd/55th	6 43rd/55th	7 43rd/55th	8 43rd/55th	9 43rd/55th
West Bengal Rural male	722/664	5/4	91/109	1/1	18/27	71/102	31/42	5/4	60/46
West Bengal Rural female	708/541	2/0	196/361	0/0	6/4	26/28	1/0	0/1	61/66
West Bengal Urban female	154/23	20/5	269/286	5/0	13/19	75/132	16/15	15/15	446/505
West Bengal Urban male	47/32	24/9	321/252	10/14	50/72	202/278	108/131	2/47	236/165
Indian Rural male	745/714	7/6	74/73	3/2	37/45	51/68	20/32	1/5	62/56
Indian Rural female	847/854	4/3	69/76	0/0	27/11	21/20	1/1	1/1	30/36
Indian Urban female	294/177	8/4	270/240	2/2	37/48	98/169	9/18	4/25	278/317
Indian Urban male	91/66	13/9	257/224	12/8	58/87	215/294	97/104	5/45	252/165

Sources: Government of India, *Employment Unemployment Survey Report*, NSSO, 43rd Round, 1987–88.
Government of India, *Employment Unemployment Survey Report*, NSSO, 55th Round, 1999–2000.

Notes: 1. Agriculture; 2. Mining and quarrying; 3. Manufacturing; 4. Electricity, gas and water; 5.Construction; 6. Trade and hotels; 7. Transport; 8. Financial business; 9. Public administration and education.

The disaggregated work participation rates with respect to three broad divisions given by the NSS, namely, regular, self-employed and casually employed, have been studied. Charts 4.4 and 4.5 present the relative proportions of the three broad divisions with respect to female employment during the 43rd Round and the 55th Round respectively.

self-employment and casual employment has grown tremendously compared to regular salaried employment for women. This is a country trend for both male and female labour. However, this trend has reinforced itself with respect to working females in the state and has had an impact on their earnings too, which we shall see in the next section.

Chart 4.4
Proportion of Self-employment, Casual and Regular Female Employment in the 43rd Round (1987–88)

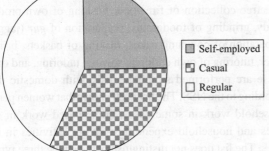

Chart 4.5
Proportion of Self-employment, Casual and Regular Female Employment in the 55th Round (1999–2000)

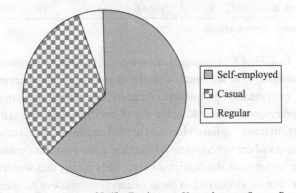

Source: Government of India, *Employment Unemployemnt Survey Reports*, NSSO, 43rd Round, 1987–88.

Source: Government of India, *Employment Unemployment Survey Report*, NSSO, 55th Round, 1999–2000.

It is obvious from the charts that self-employed and casual labour force have grown in size and regular employment has shrunk. In fact, it is mostly self-employed women who are employed as workers. This is true for both the urban and rural areas. One has to recognize the fact that the importance of

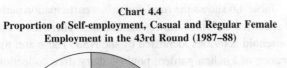

Gender Stereotyping

Gender stereotyping is important from the point of view of women's work in any part of the world, mostly in developing countries. For this we need to look into occupational sex-ratios and identify the occupations where this ratio is high. These occupations are the ones where we find concentration of female labourers over male labourers and which are labelled as 'feminine' occupations. We have a set of activities designated as 'feminine' and another set of economic activities as 'masculine'. This division subjugates women in the field of work. Marginalization of female labour and gender stereotyping go hand in hand. The areas where women are heavily employed are ill-paid occupations. We take a snapshot view of the gender stereotyping process with respect to the 2001 Census data Table 4.5.

Table 4.5
Occupational Sex-ratios in the Districts

State and districts	Cultivators	Agricultural labourers	Household industry workers	Others	Total
West Bengal	0.20	*0.44*	*1.40*	0.21	0.31
Bardhaman	*0.80*	*0.46*	*1.17*	0.19	0.26
Birbhum	0.11	*0.48*	*1.80*	0.25	0.33
Bankura	0.31	*0.94*	*1.41*	0.33	0.56
Medinipur	0.26	*0.55*	*1.79*	0.25	0.40
Haora	0.06	0.10	*0.43*	0.11	0.14
Hoogli	0.14	*0.46*	*1.10*	0.18	0.26
Purulia	0.51	*1.36*	*1.17*	0.20	0.66
24 Parganas (N)	0.06	0.16	*1.09*	0.17	0.19
24 Parganas (S)	0.20	*0.21*	0.70	0.17	0.20
Kolkata	*0.27*	*0.20*	*2.41*	0.17	0.17
Nadia	0.09	0.09	*1.12*	*0.26*	0.23
Murshidabad	0.03	0.07	*2.66*	0.20	0.29
Uttar Dinajpur	0.25	*0.64*	*2.45*	0.27	0.43
Dakshin Dinajpur	0.17	*0.72*	*1.55*	0.35	0.43
Maldah	0.13	0.51	*4.04*	0.33	0.51
Jalpaiguri	0.31	0.77	0.87	0.36	1.19
Darjeeling	*0.49*	*0.62*	0.68	0.36	0.40
Koch Bihar	0.29	*0.68*	*1.24*	0.19	0.38

Source: *Census of India 2001.*

In Table 4.5 the occupational sex-ratios have been computed according to broad census classifications into such categories as cultivators, agricultural labourers, household industrial workers and others. Keeping the district ratio and the state ratio in mind, we have identified in bold and italics those occupations where stereotyping is found and those where sex-ratios are higher than the district average. This means that women are mostly employed in these occupations relative to men. Women mostly emerged as agricultural labourers and household industry workers both at the district and at the state level. Although agricultural labour as an occupation did not emerge as an area of stereotyping for the districts Haora, 24 Parganas (N), Nadia, Murshidabad, Maldah and Jalpaiguri, for all other districts this was true. However, household industry was an area where women were uniformly stereotyped. This also means women prefer to do home-based work simultaneously with other work. If we measure the extent of stereotyping by the district and state occupational sex-ratios, we find that the household industry is a heavily stereotyped occupation.

Participation in Domestic Duties

The preceding sections suggest that most of the work done by women in the state is at home. A part of it is still unrecognized and unpaid. They participate in home-based work and take part in other family occupations, which is mostly unaccounted for. This is a phenomenon which takes place both in the rural and urban areas. The NSS data from the 50th Round in 1993–94 and the 55th Round in 1999–2000 give us the degree of change in domestic economic activities for both rural and urban females. This is shown in Table 4.6. These activities are performed along with household work and females hardly recognize that these can be separate economic activities and that they are also workers in their own right. These home-based activities are all sources of either family income or self-employment in the state. However, there are no official statistics to distinguish between home-based self-employment for women and home-based family occupation. Women mostly prefer these activities as they can be easily combined with household work and they do not have to travel away from their homes. Caring for their families and working for a supplementary income go hand in hand.

Table 4.6 shows the rural and urban participation patterns in specified activities during the nineties. There are 18 such household activities identified by the NSS. These are: maintenance of kitchen garden, poultry, dairy, free collection of fish, free collection of firewood, husking of own-produced paddy, grinding of foodgrains, preparation of *gur* (jaggery), preparation of cowdung cakes, making of baskets, bringing water, tutoring of own children, sewing, tailoring, and others. These are performed simultaneously with domestic duties according to the NSS. The list itself shows that women perform household work in some cases, home-based work in some cases and household expenditure-saving activities in other cases. The list does not distinguish between the three types of jobs done and hence mixes up both paid and unpaid work. In all the categories listed, the proportion of females participating has been declining. This is true for both rural and urban females in all activities except sewing and tailoring for the urban female. This means that women at home are moving away from these activities and switching to non-traditional home-based production.

In the NSS survey of unemployment,[7] we also learn about women's willingness to work under assistance and their preferred activities. Rural women in the state said that they would prioritize home-based work in the following areas: dairy, poultry, tailoring, animal husbandry, spinning and weaving, and manufacture of leather goods and wood and cane products. But they also pointed out some difficulties in carrying out these home-based work and wanted assistance in the form of initial finance on easy terms, working finance facilities, easy availability of raw materials, training and assured market. Urban women mostly preferred tailoring, followed by dairy, spinning and weaving and poultry. The priorities indicate that women prefer home-based self-employment rather than working for the household and being engaged in expenditure-saving activity as unpaid workers. Tailoring is an occupation which women have preferred both in urban and rural areas. But the stiffest obstacle which women face is the unavailability of finance in all these spheres.

Table 4.6
Rural–Urban Female Participation in Household Activities
(Percentage change from 1993–94 to 1999–2000)

Household activity	1993–94		1999–2000	
	Rural	Urban	Rural	Urban
Maintenance of kitchen garden	30.8	9.5	15.3	3.3
Poultry-dairy	69.3	47.5	38.7	3.1
Collection of fish	51.4	8.9	38.7	1.0
Collection of firewood	74.5	44.3	72.8	15.7
Husking paddy	17.6	1.0	13.3	25.3
Grinding of foodgrains	6.5	0.02	4.3	25.3
Preparation of cowdung cakes	73.9	52.3	61.1	8.4
Sewing and tailoring	52.0	55.3	32.6	73.6

Sources: Government of India, *Employment Unemployment Survey Report*, NSSO, 50th Round, 1993–94. Government of India, *Employment Unemployment Survey Report*, NSSO, 55th Round, 1999–2000.

Home-based Production

West Bengal follows the South Asian pattern of women preferring to work at home and both the society and these women generally do not recognize home-based production as part of the general production system of the economy. They look upon this type of production as part of household work. They hardly distinguish between domestic work and home-based production. This is more so for rural females than urban females.

The items of domestic duties involve significant amount of home-based production. This is more so in the latest rounds of the NSS surveys. The items identified in the NSS surveys are listed in the preceding section. The items of home-based production require more data collection and analysis which is not available in existing secondary sources of data. To understand the intensity of home-based production and the vast number of livelihoods it covers, we need to consider primary surveys. However, secondary data sources confirm how over time small-scale and cottage industries are gradually becoming important with home-based production becoming popular with both urban and rural women in general. The items covered under home-based production in NSS surveys are: kitchen garden, poultry, dairy, making of baskets, food processing (*gur*, meat, etc.) and sewing and tailoring. The extent of home-based production depends on the income position of the households to which rural women belong. According to the NSS data sources, if we take three areas of home-based production, namely, kitchen garden, poultry and dairy, and sewing and tailoring, the females participating in these activities mostly come from households with a landownership of 0–7.50 acre. These are households of small and marginal farmers, who mostly possess 0–1 acre of land. Thus, home-based production by females provides supplementary earnings for the households as a whole.

Household industry workers are predominantly female in all the districts. This is exactly what is meant by home-based production. If we rank the districts in order of intensity of home-based production, Maldah ranks first followed by Murshidabad and then Uttar Dinajpur, Kolkata, Birbhum, Medinipur, Dakshin Dinajpur, Bankura, Purulia, Bardhaman, Nadia, Hoogli, 24 Parganas (N), 24 Parganas (S), Darjeeling and Haora. The first six districts show a concentration of home-based production, which implies the existence of a geographical area within the state where we find women actively engaged in home-based work.

Women in the Informal Sector

The preceding sections adequately point out to the gradual informalization of female workers in the state. The importance of non-agricultural off-farm employment for women is on the rise and greater dependence on small-scale and cottage industries is increasing. All of these factors, together with a general increase in countrywide unemployment, have meant swelling up of female labour in the informal sector. The informal workers include wage earners, piece-rate workers, casual labourers, paid and unpaid home-based workers. The NSS and census

[7] Government of India, *Employment Unemployment Survey Reports*, NSSO, 50th Round, 1993–94; Government of India, *Employment Unemployment Survey Reports*, NSSO, 55th Round, 1999–2000.

data as well as the census of small-scale industries point towards certain trends. For the NSS data, the self-employed and the casual workers form the informal sector. If we classify the formal sector as regular employed and informal sector as a combination of self-employed and casual labourers, then the change in the proportion of the informal female workers from the 43rd Round to the 50th Round and the 55th Round comes out clearly as shown in Table 4.7. The census data broadly classify the household industry workers and other workers together as non-agricultural workers. Table 4.8 shows the districtwise decadal increase in female workers from 1991 to 2001. The contribution of non-agricultural sector can also be seen to assess the relative importance of the informal sector for female workers in the districts, as it is the non-agricultural sector that provides for potential informal sector.

Table 4.7 shows that though women were making inroads into the formal sector workforce from 1987–88 to 1993–94, they were again informalized between 1993–94 and 1999–2000.

Table 4.7
Proportion of Informal Sector Female Workers

Category	Formal			Informal		
	43rd (%)	50th (%)	55th (%)	43rd (%)	50th (%)	55th (%)
Rural female	6.1	7.3	5.1	93.9	92.7	94.9
Urban female	42.4	44.1	40.1	57.6	55.9	59.9

Sources: Government of India, *Employment/Unemployment Survey Report*, NSSO, 43rd Round, 1987–88.
Government of India, *Employment/Unemployment Survey Report*, NSSO, 50th Round, 1993–94.
Government of India, *Employment/Unemployment Survey Report*, NSSO, 55th Round, 1999–2000.

Most of the female informal sector workers are engaged in the manufacturing sector in rural areas. In urban areas, it is manufacturing, trade and repair services and education, where they are mostly employed. These are all unincorporated proprietary and partnership enterprises. In rural areas, 25.7 per cent of all rural female workers work in male-owned enterprises, 61 per cent work in female-owned enterprises, and 1.5 per cent work in partnership enterprises within the same household. So majority of them work in female-owned enterprises. In urban areas, 36.9 per cent of urban female workers work in male-owned proprietary enterprises, 36.6 per cent work in female-owned enterprises and 1.3 per cent work in partnership enterprises within the same household. Here, a sizeable portion of female workers work in male-owned enterprises.

Table 4.8 shows the districtwise increase in the number of female non-agricultural sector workers between 1991 and 2001. The non-agricultural sector constitutes the household

industry workers as well as other workers; this is the potential and actual informal sector. The table shows that in Darjeeling, Murshidabad, 24 Parganas (N), Hoogli, Medinipur and Haora, it is this sector that has absorbed female labour during the nineties. It is also this sector which has always grown as far as female labour is concerned and the same is true for male workers too. From the point of view of employment, however, this sector is of more importance to female workers.

Table 4.8
Increase in Number of Female Non-agricultural Sector Workers (1991–2001) (in lakh)

Place	Increase in female non-agricultural sector workers	Net increase in total female workers
West Bengal	23.46	33.40
Darjeeling	1.01	0.38
Jalpaiguri	0.87	1.73
Koch Bihar	0.42	1.69
Uttar Dinajpur	0.61	1.98
Dakshin Dinajpur	0.48	1.17
Maldah	1.86	2.38
Murshidabad	2.11	2.22
Birbhum	0.84	1.27
Bardhaman	1.81	2.61
Nadia	1.81	2.15
24 Parganas (N)	2.65	2.86
24 Parganas (S)	1.57	2.17
Hoogli	1.48	2.21
Bankura	1.07	2.34
Purulia	0.61	0.72
Medinipur	2.61	3.65
Haora	1.15	1.15
Kolkata	1.19	1.20

Source: *Census of India 1991, 2001.*

The third economic census on small-scale industries was done in 1990. This is a record of female employment in small-scale own-account enterprises, that is, mostly self-employed female workers, in different districts. The data in the earlier decade showed that the percentage of female employment was high in the sector producing beverages, tobacco and related products, wood and wood products and cotton textiles. This implies concentration in *bidi* making, weaving and handicrafts and this trend has continued. The census also gave distribution of female workers in non-agricultural own-account enterprises and female employment rates by district. There was high female rural employment rates in the informal sector in the districts of Darjeeling. Dinajpur, Maldah, Murshidabad, Medinipur and Bankura. High urban female employment rates in the informal sector were found in the districts of Maldah, Murshidabad, Medinipur and Bankura. The importance of informal sector with respect to female employment has risen steadily throughout the nineties. The scope and extent of this sector has gone up with product diversification.

Informal occupation also implies participation in multiple jobs. The status of these jobs cannot be analysed without time-use surveys and primary investigation.

Earnings of Female Workers

The difference in earning between males and females is perceptible mostly with respect to casual workers as earnings of the self-employed are often not reported. Regarding regular salaried workers, earnings are more or less fixed legally and male–female differences can be ruled out. We have considered the 55th Round information on earnings as reported by the NSS surveys. Tables 4.9 and 4.10 give the respective daily wages in urban as well as rural areas for casual workers in public works as well as in other spheres.

It is observed that for male and female workers in public works, the male–female difference in the country is much wider than of the state. For casual workers not in public works, the male–female difference in the state is much less in both urban and rural areas in comparison to the country as a whole. But the difference is significant in urban areas. Male–female wage disparity is lower than the country situation. But the existing gap still needs to be eliminated.

Most of the wage disparity exists due to gender stereotyping of jobs in the state. There is also discrimination in piece-rate work in household industry enterprises.

Table 4.9
Daily Wages for Casual Workers in Public Works (1999–2000)

State/Country	Male	Female
West Bengal	37.34	34.12
India	48.14	38.06

Source: Government of India, *Employment Unemployment Survey Report*, NSSO, 55th Round, 1999–2000.

Table 4.10
Daily Wages for Casual Workers Not in Public Works (1999–2000)

State/Country	Urban male	Rural male	Urban female	Rural female
West Bengal	55.27	44.60	29.11	35.59
India	62.26	44.84	37.71	29.01

Source: Government of India, *Employment Unemployment Survey Report*, NSSO, 55th Round, 1999–2000.

Impact of Globalization

Globalization in the state has made its impact felt in many areas including female employment during the nineties. This has been mostly in the form of displacement of female labour from the agricultural sector, feminization of informal sector activities and increase in home-based production. The effects of these have been felt in West Bengal too. Displacement of female labour from agriculture is one of the major fall-outs in most districts. This is confirmed both by the NSS data as well as the census data. Referring to Table 4.4, which compares the 43rd Round and the 55th Round of the survey, the rate of displacement from agriculture is shown in Chart 4.6 by comparing the years 1993–94 to 1999–2000.

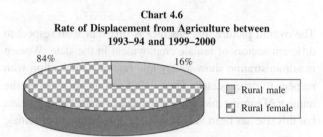

Chart 4.6
Rate of Displacement from Agriculture between 1993–94 and 1999–2000

84%   16%

Rural male
Rural female

Sources: Government of India, *Employment Unemployment Survey Report*, NSSO, 50th Round, 1993–94.
Government of India, *Employment Unemployment Survey Report*, NSSO, 55th Round, 1999–2000.

This means that the displacement of female labour from agriculture has been high in the state. This has been accompanied by more than equivalent absorption in the manufacturing sector. For the rural females in the state, the rate of absorption in manufacturing has been 84 per cent compared to 10 per cent in the country. This again speaks of extensive rural informal sector activities by women. This trend is confirmed by census reports. If we refer to the census data we can locate displacement from agriculture and its inter-district variation. The displacement is most visible in the districts of Darjeeling, Birbhum, 24 Parganas (N), 24 Parganas (S), Purulia, Medinipur, Haora and Kolkata.

Feminization of the informal sector activities is a phenomenon which has already been explained in the preceding sections. But in this state, the process is not exactly identical to what is happening in many parts of the world. This feminization here is not caused by the export-orientation of the liberal trade regime or the sub-contracted work of the multinationals. This has been more a story of safeguarding self-employment methods of survival due to rise in poverty throughout the country. The females are employed mostly in female-owned enterprises in the rural areas, which also means small self-employment units looked upon again as means of survival against global joblessness.

Home-based production has also risen as we have seen in the preceding sections. This is also linked to multinationals and sub-contracted labour of large industrial units. A rise in the percentage of earning females among the middle class is another phenomenon that needs to be taken note of. The share of female government employees stands at 14 per cent in 1999. This is high in education, health and family wel-fare and science and technology departments. More and more women from the middle class have entered the public sphere in the eighties and nineties.

Conclusion

The overall picture that emerges is different with respect to different sectors of female employment in the state. Women in administration show a very low rate of participation with respect to other states. There has been an increase in the number of earning middle class females over the last few years, but this rise has been very small. The displacement of female labour in agriculture has been significant and off-farm agricultural employment opportunities need to be created for these displaced women. For the informal sector workers, access to credit, training for new jobs, breaking of stereotype, reduction of wage disparity and occupational diversification need urgent attention. Self-employment has acted as a safeguard against joblessness and this should be encouraged as prevention against global unemployment. At the same time, gender stereotyping has become significant in all the districts. To prevent wage discrimination, stereotyping should be prevented by giving training for non-stereotypical jobs after doing a proper market survey of the demand for such non-stereotypes. However, effectiveness of a policy depends on relevant data, which is largely unavailable. Data on hours of work, entry age for work and land-size related work pattern is crucial for effective policy measures. Any noticeable job shifts in the last few years need also to be assessed. For these more area specific micro-studies need to be carried out.

Political Participation

CHAPTER 5

Vidya Munshi

Historical Background

The Constitution of free India provided for equality of all citizens irrespective of caste, creed, political affiliations, language or sex. Some people believe that Indian women did not have to fight like the suffragettes in Britain for the right to vote and therefore have not realized its value or used it to the full. However, the fact is that in India under British rule, there was no adult franchise either for men or for women. The right to vote was extremely limited on the basis of property, education or marital status. Therefore, women's participation in the freedom struggle was itself their biggest contribution towards winning adult franchise.

But the experience of the pre-independence period in India shows that though women came out in large numbers to participate in mass political actions at all critical points during the history of the freedom struggle, generally they went back to their usual role of mothers and homemakers after each such mass upsurge. Only a small section of comparatively well-to-do women stayed on in public life. They were persuaded by the predominantly male political leadership of the national movement that their role as mothers of the nation should be in the sphere of social service.

In post-independence India, the partition of the country severely intensified the pressure of population in all parts of West Bengal and caused severe economic hardship for the people. At the same time, the promises of the national leadership before independence had roused the aspirations of the ordinary people. The result was the growth of mass organizations and mass protest movements among all sections of the people, including women.

Large numbers were arrested and imprisoned without trial during these movements. Women played a big part in the movements to demand recognition of such prisoners as political prisoners and the release of those imprisoned without trial. Many of the women prisoners joined in prolonged hunger strikes in various prisons.

In June 1954, the first post-war all-India organization of women, the National Federation of Indian Women (NFIW), was formed with the objective of bringing together women of all sections of society on a common platform to tackle the impending socio-political issues. It was affiliated from its birth to the Women's International Democratic Federation, which had been formed at the end of the Second World War. The acute food crisis of 1959 resulted in mass hunger marches in many parts of the state. A huge number of women, both from rural areas and Calcutta's *bustees*, participated in these hunger marches. During the sixties, in the intense struggle for change in the balance of political power in the state, women in the students', teachers' and women's fronts again played a significant role. More than 10,000 women were arrested during the protest demonstrations against the dislodging of the first United Front government in 1968. They were also enthusiastic participants in the elections which led to the formation of the second United Front government in 1969.

Acute political disturbances marked the first half of the seventies. The Bangladesh liberation struggle brought a huge influx of uprooted humanity, both Hindus and Muslims, who needed food and shelter. Women political workers and activists played a big part in organizing relief in the refugee camps as well as solidarity actions with the liberation struggle in East Bengal. The Bangladesh Solidarity Committee published a widely circulated booklet entitled 'Opar Banglar Meyeder Pashe Epar Banglar Meyera'.

The late sixties and early seventies also saw the birth of the Naxalite movement, which considered parliamentary democracy inadequate to deal with the problems of an extremely poor undeveloped country like India and believed in armed action to eliminate 'class enemies'. This movement attracted a sizeable number of young people including young women. Many of them spent years in jails or were killed in police encounters, or were disabled due to torture in custody.

The women who joined the Naxalite movement came from different sections of society—peasant and tribal women in Naxalbari and other areas directly involved in the land struggles; urban young women, mainly students, who were ideologically drawn to the movement and women relatives of male Naxalite activists, both rural and urban. While the first two categories were often involved directly in armed actions, those in the last group mainly played a supportive role of hiding and acting as couriers of literature and arms.

In the first police firing on 22 May 1967, among the nine persons killed seven were women. Women in the movement also brought out at that time two issues of a cyclostyled magazine *Sahasi Bon* and a pamphlet entitled 'Garib Gharer Meyeder Katha'. Later, some of the women activists wrote books published in the late eighties and nineties which include *Hanyaman* by Jaya Mitra, *Jeler Bhitor Jel* by Minakshi Sen, and *Women in Indian Politics* by Kalpana Roy. Unfortunately, the Intelligence Branch and Special Branch archives in the state could not be accessed for data on women's participation in the movement as the Naxalite movement is less than 40 years old.

Just before the emergency, there was a prolonged all-India railway strike in 1974 during which women belonging to the families of railway workers in Kharagpur as well as some other centres like Kanchrapara organized themselves into Railway Women's Association for solidarity and relief to the striking families. Women of all Left parties and mass organizations led by them took out a solidarity demonstration to Writers' Buildings in defiance of ban under Section 144. A large number of them were arrested and kept at the Alipore Central Jail for four days.

International Women's Year and After

In 1973, on a proposal of Herta Kusinin, the then president of the Women's International Democratic Federation, the United Nations decided to observe the year 1975 as the 30th anniversary of the defeat of fascism and as the International Women's Year on the slogans of 'equality, development, peace'. The stated aim was 'to right a historical wrong'. At the first UN Conference for Women held at Mexico in 1975, it was felt that a single year was hardly enough to fulfil such a goal. It was, therefore, announced that the entire decade from 1976 to 1985 would be observed as the International Decade of Women.

In 1973, the UN circulated a detailed questionnaire on the conditions of women to all member nations and called for detailed answers to this questionnaire before 1975. In India, the central government headed by Prime Minister Indira Gandhi set up a broad-based Status of Women Committee, chaired by Phulrenu Guha. The committee submitted its report entitled *Towards Equality* to the Government of India in 1974. This report for the first time challenged the assumption that any rise in the general standard of living in the country would benefit all sections of society sooner or later and that any rise in the income level of any family would benefit all members of the family including women and children. Challenging this 'trickle down theory', the status report showed in great details how so many years after independence women and girls remained second class citizens with less access to nutrition, education and healthcare and were virtually unrepresented in most of the decision making processes of the state, community and family.

The committee had asked leaders of women's organizations with different political affiliations whether they wanted any reservation of seats for women in elected fora like the parliament or the state assemblies. Almost all organizations consulted felt that as women's education advanced and their opportunities for employment increased, they would come forward more and more to claim their due position in the elected bodies.

Among the recommendations made by the committee, the most important one was to set up a high-powered autonomous national commission for women with corresponding commissions at state levels. However, despite the endorsement of the report by the Indira Gandhi government and successive governments, it was not until 1992 that the National Commission for Women was set up and even then not with the extent of autonomy envisaged in the report.

In West Bengal, the NFIW, AIWC and Women's Congress Committee together set up a non-official committee for observing International Women's Year. These three organizations were also represented in the official committee set up for the same purpose by the Government of West Bengal, which had its office in the premises of the State Social Welfare Advisory Board. The non-official committee mainly popularized the aims and objectives of the International Women's Year and the contents of the proposed UN Convention for Elimination of All Forms of Discrimination Against Women (CEDAW). It also organized a broad campaign against the dowry system. The official committee organized rallies, seminars, district festivals in almost all districts culminating in a huge central rally of women at the Netaji Indoor Stadium, Calcutta in December 1975. This was the first time that the Netaji Indoor Stadium was thrown open for a mass event of this sort with tens of thousands of rural and urban housewives and working women, school and college girls and girl cadets of the NCC attending.

The official committee brought out two booklets—'Aine Apnar Ki Ki Adhikar Aache Janen Ki' and 'Shramajibi Meyeder Samashya'. It also published 2,000 sets of 13 posters for local exhibitions, projecting the main issues facing Indian women. The official committee also put together an exhibition of photographs entitled 'Indian Women in the Struggle for Independence and for Their Rights'. The State Government's Documentary Film Division prepared a documentary film on the issues facing Indian women which were shown in many cinema halls at that time.

The National Plan of Action proposed by the Status of Women Committee was approved by the central government and a working group was set up during 1977–78 to make re-commendations about women's employment. The Sixth Five Year Plan (1980–85) for the first time included a separate section on women's development. During the prime minister-ship of Rajiv Gandhi, a National Perspective Plan for Women's Development (1986–2000) was prepared in 1987 to formulate steps to realize the programme advocated in the forward-looking strategies adopted at the end of the International Women's Decade at Nairobi in 1985.

During the Seventh Plan (1985–90), a parliamentary committee headed by Ela Bhatt, Rajya Sabha member and leader of SEWA (Self-Employed Women's Association) in Ahmedabad, was set up to study the problems of self-employed women and women workers in the unorganized sector. The Eighth Plan (1992–97) saw the setting up of the National Women's Commission (1992) followed by state women's com-missions. The West Bengal Women's Commission was formed in February 1993.

Constitutional Amendments (73rd and 74th) and Women's Political Participation

The National Perspective Plan for Women created a number of administrative agencies for implementing programmes for women's development up to the year 2000. The government also proposed two amendments to the Constitution of India— Amendments 73 and 74—for one-third representation in local self-government bodies at panchayat and municipal levels. Several state governments, including West Bengal, opposed these amendments when first proposed, not because of their content but because local self-government is a state subject

and not a central responsibility, according to the Constitution. However, immediately afterwards, the West Bengal govern-ment passed its own amendment to the panchayat law intro-ducing one-third reservation for women, including SC/ST women, at all three tiers of the panchayati system. The first elections with such reservations were held in 1993.

Before 1993 and the passing of the 73rd Amendment, women were viewed only as targets or beneficiaries of devel-opment and not as its active agents. This was reflected in the Balwantrao Committee's recommendations and the elections of the first generation panchayats in free India. Based on the Ashok Mehta Committee report, the second generation pan-chayats formed in 1977 had some reservation for women in a few states like Karnataka, Andhra Pradesh, Maharashtra and Punjab. However, those elected were women from the pro-pertied sections of the rural population who had little relation-ship with the needs of the great majority of rural women.

In rural West Bengal, the participation of women in public life has been traditionally lower than the national average, which was reflected in the representation of women in the panchayats before 1993. Moreover, in the years between 1970 and the election of the Left Front government in 1977, elec-tions to local self-governing bodies had been extremely irregular and many such elected bodies had been put under bureaucratic administrators for years on end. Regular five-yearly elections of all local self-governing bodies began only after 1977. Though there was reservation for the SC/ST in the state panchayat system, there was no provision for reservation of seats for women in the West Bengal Panchayat Act. It pro-vided for a token inclusion of two women in every panchayat and if they were not elected, they could be nominated. Natur-ally such nominations were by the party having a majority in the given panchayats.

When proposing the amendment to the State Panchayat Act for 33 per cent reservation for women in general as well as in SC/ST seats at all three tiers of the panchayats, the then chief minister, Jyoti Basu, told the state legislative assembly that experience had shown that contrary to hopes even the two seats allocated for women were rarely filled through elec-tions and, therefore, it was felt that reservation was the only solution to enhancing women's participation.

Panchayati Raj and Women

The first three panchayat elections were held in West Bengal in 1978, 1983 and 1988. The first time elections were held with 33 per cent seats reserved for women was in 1993. The out-come of the 1993 elections is given in Tables 5.1, 5.2 and 5.3.

Table 5.1
Zilla Parishad Election, 1993

District	No. of zilla parishads	SC seats	ST seats	SC women	ST women	General women
Haora	28	4	–	2	–	8
24 Parganas (N)	44	9	1	4	1	10
24 Parganas (S)	58	14	–	7	1	12
Murshidabad	52	4	1	3	–	15
Nadia	34	7	–	3	1	8
Bardhaman	62	13	3	7	2	12
Bankura	44	9	3	5	2	8
Medinipur	108	11	7	7	3	26
Purulia	40	5	5	3	3	8
Birbhum	38	8	2	4	1	8
Hoogli	36	5	–	4	–	8
Jalpaiguri	26	8	2	5	1	3
Koch Bihar	24	8	–	5	–	3
Maldah	30	4	1	2	1	7
Uttar Dinajpur	18	4	–	2	–	3
Dakshin Dinajpur	14	2	2	2	–	3
Total	656	117	28	64	18	142

Source: Compiled from data provided by the State Institute for Panchayat and Rural Development (SIPRD), West Bengal.

Table 5.1 shows that out of a total of 656 zilla parishad seats, 287 were general seats and the remaining 369 or 56.25 per cent were reserved seats. Among them, 224 seats or 34.15 per cent seats were reserved for women. Table 5.2 shows that out of 9,453 total seats in panchayat samitis, 4,071 or 43.07 per cent were open and 5,382 or 56.93 per cent seats were reserved. Reserved seats for women numbered 3,182 or 33.66 per cent. Table 5.3 shows that in gram panchayats, out of a total of 61,010 seats, 36,299 or 59.49 per cent seats were reserved. Seats reserved for women numbered 21,489 or 35.22 per cent. Thus, at three levels, the total number of seats was 71,119, out of which 42,050 seats or 59.13 per cent were reserved. Out of this 24,895 seats or 35 per cent of seats were reserved for women.

This process took place in a state where land distribution to the rural poor and marginal farmers and 'Operation Barga' had shifted power, to a great extent, in favour of the rural poor. This meant that the women elected under reservation also belonged mostly to the under-privileged sections of the rural society. It has to be noted that since the 1993 elections in West Bengal had been carried out under a State Act passed before the 73rd Amendment to the Constitution, there was no provision here for women's reservation among office-bearers of panchayats at the three levels.

The election of nearly 25,000 rural women to the panchayats and the participation of about three times more in the election process led to a wave of mass enthusiasm among women throughout the state, which was reflected in a huge increase of membership of all mass organizations of women

led by different political parties. Clearly, two categories of women were being elected to the panchayats—those who came from families where women of an older generation, mothers or grandmothers, had been activists of the pre-independence era or the elected women themselves had been activists, and those who had been nominated only because they were related to the sitting male members of local panchayats. There was also a new spurt of self-confidence among the elected women members and a desire to improve their own situations by becoming literate or by learning more about the functions of the panchayats. The entry of such a huge number of women in public life also increased women's awareness about their status and rights within the family.

Table 5.2
Panchayat Samiti Election, 1993

District	No. of panchayat samiti seats	SC seats	ST seats	SC women	ST women	General women
Haora	473	62	–	37	–	121
24 Parganas (N)	629	127	16	59	8	135
24 Parganas (S)	925	212	12	126	5	181
Murshidabad	761	60	6	43	3	209
Nadia	552	165	12	56	10	121
Bardhaman	810	169	32	85	30	158
Bankura	556	177	67	61	30	98
Medinipur	1,494	159	87	90	59	356
Purulia	487	57	66	33	37	95
Birbhum	490	98	21	55	15	97
Hoogli	626	114	20	64	12	135
Jalpaiguri	354	121	17	59	18	45
Koch Bihar	375	127	–	73	1	52
Maldah	432	49	20	32	13	101
Uttar Dinajpur	294	58	9	29	8	62
Dakshin Dinajpur	192	39	21	19	16	30
Total	9,453	1,794	406	921	265	1,996

Source: Same as Table 5.1.

The West Bengal Panchayat Act also provides for holding six-monthly meetings of the gram samsad, which all voters of the gram panchayat are entitled to attend and vote. These meetings discuss the work done in the last six months, the audited account and the work plan for the next six months, and also to approve the list of beneficiaries for proposed panchayat projects. Women's organizations have been campaigning to ensure that women attend these meetings in large numbers and actively participate in them. Now this provision of gram samsad has been made compulsory in the panchayat system.

The fifth round of the three-tier panchayat elections in West Bengal was held in 1998. This was the first time that reservation for women was introduced for the office-bearers of gram panchayats, panchayat samitis and zilla parishads. It may be noted that some women who were elected from reserved seats

Table 5.3
Gram Panchayat Election, 1993

District	No. of gram panchayat election centres		Total seats in gram panchayat	Reserved seats in gram panchayat				
	Single seat	Double seat		SC	ST	SC women	ST women	General women
Haora	235	1,471	3,177	396	–	279	2	840
24 Parganas (N)	869	1,731	4,331	802	94	485	71	981
24 Parganas (S)	1,457	2,270	5,997	378	74	833	38	1,246
Murshidabad	927	2,158	5,245	428	35	320	35	1,507
Nadia	248	1,758	3,764	1,097	76	441	44	870
Bardhaman	1,230	2,090	5,410	1,107	225	615	193	1,104
Bankura	781	1,319	3,419	1,094	393	397	159	650
Medinipur	1,095	3,974	9,043	908	478	611	355	2,240
Purulia	359	1,193	2,745	332	335	181	237	550
Birbhum	500	1,246	2,992	607	110	331	109	612
Hoogli	500	1,838	4,176	738	112	430	96	942
Jalpaiguri	448	871	2,190	710	120	386	87	302
Koch Bihar	524	947	2,418	854	4	488	7	360
Maldah	447	1,183	2,813	324	117	216	79	701
Uttar Dinajpur	296	866	2,028	400	64	212	65	441
Dakshin Dinajpur	286	488	1,262	259	139	131	103	207
Total	10,204	25,403	61,010	12,434	2,676	6,256	1,680	13,553

Source: Same as Table 5.1.

in 1993 got elected again in 1998 from unreserved general seats in view of their good work as panchayat members in the previous five years. The Sabhadhipati of 24 Parganas (N) zilla parishad and the Saha-sabhadhipatis of Medinipur, 24 Parganas (N) and Haora were elected from outside the reservation quota.

Table 5.4 shows the reservation pattern of office-bearers of the three-tier panchayats in West Bengal.

Table 5.4
Reservation Pattern of Office-bearers in Three-tier Panchayats, 1998

Names of office-bearers	Total no. of posts	Total no. of women elected	Percentage of women elected
Pradhan of gram panchayats	3,226	1,081	33.5
Upa-pradhan of gram panchayats	3,226	673	20.8
Sabhadhipati of panchayat samitis	329	115	34.9
Saha-sabhadhipati of panchayat samitis	329	74	22.5
Sabhadhipati of zilla parishads	17	7	41.1
Saha-sabhadhipati of zilla parishads	17	5	29.4

Source: Same as Table 5.1.

The ground level experience of the first two years after women entered the panchayati raj in West Bengal has been captured vividly by Ashim Mukhopadhyay.[1] Through extensive interviews with women office-bearers and panchayat members, Mukhopadhyay outlines the complex negotiations that these women have to undergo. Locating patriarchal bias as the major constraint to discharging their duties, he writes,

The male members of the rural society are habituated in seeing a woman beside the cooking fire. They are now visibly annoyed or non-plussed, discovering her in a panchayat office, sitting on a chair and discussing matters like public works, relief, rehabilitation, health, literacy and funding.[2]

Many panchayat samiti members are economically dependent on the men of their families and this situation is fully exploited by the male members. Restrictions imposed by male guardians on the movements and activities of women panchayat representatives who are family members is a serious impediment to the functional success of the elected women. The most serious challenge before a female panchayat member is role conflict. These women, especially those who belong to the poorer sections of the peasant or artisan communities, have to perform multiple roles in their day-to-day existence. It is a tightrope walk for them to strike a balance between performing the different roles at home and in their place of employment on the one hand, and fulfilling their duties towards the panchayats on the other. A woman is expected to pay equal attention

[1] Mukhopadhyay, Ashim. 1996. 'Coming of Women into Panchayati Raj'. Occasional Paper No. 2. School of Women's Studies, Jadavpur University, Kolkata.
[2] Ibid.

to being a good housewife, daughter/sister, mother/wife, daughter-in-law/sister-in-law and at the same time win the bread for the family or supplement the family's income through gainful employment. In addition to performing these various roles, she has to discharge her duties as a worthy member of the panchayat. If she fails in any of the roles within the family, chances are that she gets unpopular within the household and that in turn affects her participation in the panchayat. Opposition from relatives to women's participation in non-domestic activities has intensified the role conflict of female panchayat members.

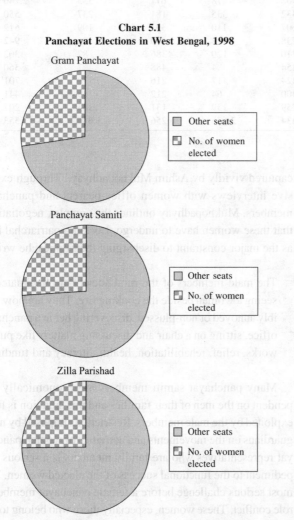

Chart 5.1
Panchayat Elections in West Bengal, 1998

Gram Panchayat

Panchayat Samiti

Zilla Parishad

Not only do these women have to fight patriarchy within the family and the rural society, but also the attitudes of male members of all political parties—most of who occupy key positions in decision making—who are a stumbling block to their real empowerment. Instances of female panchayat members forced to speak in their masters' voice are not few. Sometimes they also get caught in political rivalries and become victims of sexual politics. Wherever female panchayat members are performing well, their party's local units have been instrumental in motivating people to support women's political participation at the grassroots. Many of the women elected to panchayats are newcomers in politics and hitherto unexposed to the concept of panchayati raj. But interviews with these women and even their male colleagues indicate that all of them are serious about their roles and sincerely want to learn how to go about their business.

In spite of the enormous hurdles faced by these women in a patriarchal society, where they also have to surmount their illiteracy and lack of awareness of political rights, many of them have come up not only as sincere panchayat workers but as competent local leaders and administrators. There are at present three all-women gram panchayats in the state—Rohini, Kultikri and Belchapor. Zilla parishads, which monitor all development work in districts, are headed by women in seven districts. The panchayats also directly supervise employment and training of anganwadi workers and health workers and through them try to actively engage mothers and children in socially productive ways. The role of the self-help groups initiated by the panchayats, which are a lifeline to innumerable women, also need to be underscored. Becoming a member of a gram panchayat has meant getting a whole new identity for some women, like Hasubala Devi.[3] Hasubala, a middle-aged, part-time maid who works in five houses, said that when she got married years ago and stepped into her new home, she had first been known as 'Nitai's wife' and later as 'Bocha's mother'. It was only at the fag end of her life, when she became a gram panchayat member, that her identity as Hasubala Devi was restored and she is proud of it.

For Hasubala and her sisters, what is needed most is a regular, well-planned training programme in the form of

Table 5.5
Schedule Caste Women in Panchayat Bodies Members

Name of tier of panchayats	Total no. of members	Schedule caste members	Schedule caste women members	Schedule caste women chairpersons	Schedule tribe women chairpersons
Gram panchayat	512,000	13,465	5,254	298	94
Panchayat samiti	8,579	2,383	784	28	14
Zilla parishad (including Siliguri Mahakuma Parishad)	723	205	74	2	–

Source: Same as Table 5.1.

[3] 'Panchayat: Chena Mukher Achena Galpo', *Eksathe*, April 2003.

interactive workshops. There have been a few training camps organized by the government and a few NGOs so far, but these need to be held at regular intervals and have to be user-friendly and flexible. The workshop has to take into account the area specific problems and demands of the panchayat members and has to be structured to suit the users' requirement. Emphasis needs to be laid on the participation of male members as well in certain sessions of such workshops for gender sensitization.

Women in Urban Civic Bodies

The 74th Amendment to the Constitution provided for one-third reservation of seats for women in municipalities, notified areas and municipal corporations. In 1995, in the first elections after the amendment, the total number of women elected to the Calcutta corporation was 48, which increased to 55 in the next election in 2000. Of the 55 women councillors in the Calcutta corporation at present, 25 belong to the Trinamool Congress (TMC), 21 to the Left Front, 4 to the Congress, 2 to the BJP and 3 are independents. Three scheduled tribe women got elected from the three wards especially reserved for them. Outside Calcutta, the Baruipur Municipality, which is 125 years old, elected its first woman municipal chairperson and the Jalpaiguri Municipality elected a woman as its vice-chairperson. In the elections to the Salt Lake Municipality, there were no less than 50 women candidates. Some of the women have won from unreserved constituencies as well in Calcutta and elsewhere. There are at present 1,073 women councillors in the state. The deputy mayor of Calcutta Municipal Corporation is a woman and there are several women councillors holding important positions in the corporation. They have proved that they are second to none in their competence, skill and honesty. Before the 74th Amendment came into force, the Calcutta corporation election results show that in 1985 there were only six women councillors and in 1990 only seven. The women councillors elected in 1995 and 2000 sometimes took up issues relating to equal opportunities for women, particularly self-employment and vocational training. Apart from working for women's development, the councillors have taken up a number of civic issues like garbage disposal, waterlogging during the monsoons, shortage of drinking water, arsenic pollution of underground water, living conditions in the slums and illegal building constructions, to name a few. Many of the councillors in most civic bodies of the state are young women and quite a few of them belong to the minority communities.

Women at the State and National-level Politics

Having witnessed the encouraging presence of women in panchayats and urban civic bodies, it is our turn now to look at women's participation at the state and national level. Tables 5.6 and 5.7 speak volumes about the dismal state of affairs as far as representation of women in the legislative assembly or the parliament is concerned. Between 1971 and 1999 the number of women MPs from West Bengal in the Lok Sabha only increased from two to five. Table 5.6 also shows that in the Eighth Lok Sabha (1985–90), the number of women MPs from this state had gone up to five but plummeted in the two subsequent Lok Sabhas before going up to five again in the Twelfth (1998) and Thirteenth Lok Sabhas (1999). This matches the all-India trend during the same period. The percentage of women MPs in the Lok Sabha went up from 4.2 to 8.8 between the Fifth Lok Sabha (1971–76) to the Thirteenth Lok Sabha. In the Rajya Sabha, in 1999–2000, there were three women from West Bengal and 30 years ago (1969–70), two women represented the state in the Upper House. (For a list of women MPs from West Bengal in the Lok Sabha and the Rajya Sabha and a list of women MLAs, see Appendix E.)

Table 5.6
Representation of Women Members from First to Thirteenth Lok Sabha

Lok Sabha	Total seats	No. of women contested (all-India)	No. of women elected (all-India)	Percentage of women (all-India)	No. of women elected from West Bengal
First (1952–57)	499	not known	22	4.4	1
Second (1957–62)	500	45	27	5.4	2
Third (1962–67)	503	70	34	6.7	2
Fourth (1967–71)	523	67	31	5.9	2
Fifth (1971–76)	521	86	22	4.2	2
Sixth (1977–80)	544	70	19	3.4	2
Seventh (1980–84)	544	142	28	5.1	2
Eighth (1985–90)	544	164	44	8.1	5
Ninth (1990–91)	517	198	27	5.2	2
Tenth (1991–96)	544	325	39	7.18	3
Eleventh (1996)	544	599	40*	7.18	4
Twelfth (1998)	544	271	44*	8.8	5
Thirteenth (1999)	542	NA	48	8.86	5

Source: Press Information Bureau, Government of India.
Note: *One member nominated by the President.

Women's representation in the Legislative Assembly of West Bengal, as reflected in Table 5.7, shows that there were six women elected in 1971, and in the assembly elections held in 1996, the number of women MLAs went up to 22. Table 5.8 shows that as far as getting berths in the state ministry is concerned, the 1971 ministry did not include a single woman and from 1972 to 1996, the percentage of women ministers in the state went up from 3.5 to 8.3 per cent. But it is difficult to evaluate this increase. Table 5.8 also indicates that the percentage of women in the 1962 ministry was 13.5—much higher than the 2000 percentage of 8.3—thereby making such evaluation a very complex and tricky business. Women ministers, both during the Congress rule as well as the United Front and Left Front governments, though few in number, held portfolios which were quite important in terms of human resource development, such as, refugee relief and rehabilitation, social welfare, adult and continued education, cooperatives, agriculture marketing and tribal welfare. However, ministries like home, police or finance still remain the male bastion and have never been held by a woman.

Table 5.7
Women MLAs from West Bengal, 1971–96

Year	Total no. of seats	Total no. of women MLAs	Percentage of women MLAs in state legislative assembly
1971	280	6	2.14
1973	280	5	1.78
1977	294	4	1.36
1982	294	7	2.38
1987	294	12	4.08
1991	294	23	7.82
1996	294	22	7.40

Source: Compiled from the data available with the West Bengal legislative assembly library.

Table 5.8
Women Ministers in West Bengal Government

Year	Cabinet minister	Minister of state	Deputy minister	Total no. women	Total no. ministers	Percentage of women ministers in the state government
1952	1	–	1	2	30	6.66
1957	–	1	1	2	30	6.66
1962	2	–	3	5	37	13.51
1967	–	–	–	–	19	0
1967	–	–	–	–	3	0
1968	–	–	–	–	17	0
1969	1	1	–	2	31	6.45
1971	–	–	–	–	26	0
1972	–	–	1	1	28	3.57
1977	–	1	–	1	30	3.33
1982	–	2	–	2	45	4.44
1987	1	–	–	1	32	3.12
1991	1	3	–	4	44	9.09
1996	1	3	–	4	48	8.33

Source: Compiled from data provided by the Government of West Bengal.

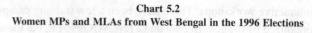

Chart 5.2
Women MPs and MLAs from West Bengal in the 1996 Elections

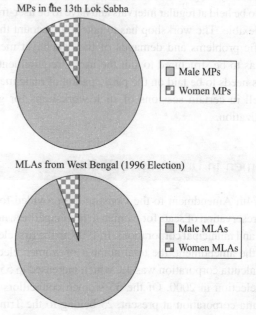

MPs in the 13th Lok Sabha

☐ Male MPs
☒ Women MPs

MLAs from West Bengal (1996 Election)

☐ Male MLAs
☒ Women MLAs

Findings of Survey among State Leaders

To ascertain the status of women vis-à-vis political participation, leaders of seven political parties and their women's wings were interviewed through a questionnaire. The leaders interviewed were Anil Biswas, Rekha Goswami and Malini Bhattacharya of the CPI (M); Nandagopal Bhattacharya and Shyamasree Das of the CPI; Gita Sengupta of the RSP; Aparajita Goppi of the Forward Bloc (FB); Phulrenu Guha and Chandrima Bhattacharya of the Indian National Congress (INC); Gouri Chowdhury and Neela Goswami of the BJP; Geeta Das of the CPI (ML); and Krishna Bose of the All India Trinamool Congress (AITMC).

In answer to a question on the trend of women's participation in politics over the last 30 years, almost all the interviewees seemed to agree that on the whole a lot more women were participating today than they were in the early seventies. The RSP leader Gita Sengupta thought that women not only are more active in politics but they are also enthusiastically spearheading health programmes and literacy drives which are no less important. At both the district and block level, women's participation has gone up steadily. Women also hold positions in the decision making bodies of other mass organizations of the RSP, like the teachers' front and the trade union front. Gita Sengupta herself is the president of the Madhyamik Siksha Sangathan. But she emphasized that patriarchal bias inherent in the Left political parties stands in the way of a large number of activists of its women's mass organization seeking to join

Table 5.9
Participation of Women in Eight Leading Political Parties

Name of the party	Total membership in West Bengal	Number of women members in West Bengal	Percentage of women members in West Bengal	Members in the highest decision making body (state-level)	Number of women in the highest decision making body (state-level)
RSP	200,000	30,000	15	15	1
FB	not available	not available	not available	12	1
CPI	70,156	10,285	14.66	9	1
BJP	560,000	168,000	30	11	1
CPI (ML)	10,000	1,000 (approx.)	10	31	2
INC	400,000 (approx.)	200,000 (approx.)	50	80	27
CPI (M)	265,000	25,440	9.6	85	8
ATMC	not available	not available	not available	not available	not available

Source: Compiled from data supplied by the respective parties. (Despite repeated efforts by the survey team no data was supplied by the ATMC).
Note: All figures are of 2000.

Table 5.10
Membership of Women's Organizations of Eight Leading Parties

Name of the party	Name of its women's organization (West Bengal)	Membership of women's organizations (West Bengal)
RSP	Nikhil Banga Mahila Sangha	85,000 (approx.)
FB	Agragami Mahila Samiti	50,000
CPI	Paschimbanga Mahila Samiti	400,000
BJP	Mahila Morcha Committee	186,675
CPI (M-L)	Pragatishil Mahila Samiti	10,000
INC	Mahila Congress	100,000
CPI (M)	Ganatantrik Mahila Samiti	3,821,946
ATMC	not available	not available

Source: Same as Table 5.9.
Note: All figures are of 2000.

the party. Not much effort is made to draw these women into the party. Besides, family and social obligations prove to be a major hindrance for women. To make women members better informed politically, regular classes are held and the weekly party magazine also helps. Earlier women's participation in the general political education programme of the party was negligible, but since the nineties women's participation has picked up considerably. The question of women's equality and women's rights is usually the responsibility of the women's organization of the party (Nikhil Banga Mahila Sangha) and not much importance is attached to the issue in the party's general propaganda.

Aparajita Goppi of the Forward Bloc was hopeful about women's participation in politics which shows a healthy trend since the eighties. They are represented in the elected committees at both the district and town levels. Women of the Forward Bloc are present in the decision making bodies of other mass organizations like the Krishi Mahila and Khet Majur Mahila Sangathan and in the students' front (Chhatra Bloc). In the Forward Bloc, members of the women's mass organization (Agragami Mahila Samiti) are accepted in the party on the basis of recommendations. Therefore, women

fail to acquire direct membership of the party and a lot of competent women get left out. Party conventions and classes are held to educate women members regularly. There is a party school in Shyamnagar. A fair number of women participate from the rural areas in the party's education programmes, especially women labourers and agricultural workers. The party focusses on women rights in its general propaganda and doesn't leave it to the women's wing only.

Nandagopal Bhattacharya of the CPI said that in 1974 there were only 3 per cent women in the state unit of his party. By 2000, this had increased to 14.66 per cent due to consistent efforts of the party and its women's organization (Paschimbanga Mahila Samiti). He said that in the seventies, women's participation was negligible in the district level and abysmal at the block level. But this had registered a steady rise and at present women's participation has been made compulsory by the party at all levels. Shyamasree Das of the same party said that more women are being voted to the elected bodies of her party. There were only four women members in elected bodies of the CPI in West Bengal till the eighties, but in the subsequent period this has increased four-fold. She also said that women don't have much say in other frontal organizations of the party. There are women members in the party's students' wing, youth and trade union fronts and the krishak sabhas. More women are required in the leadership of the party. Feudal mentality within the party and society as well as domestic responsibilities stand in the way of women activists going up the rungs in the party, which mainly uses women in organizing rallies, collecting funds and for other such purposes.

Nandagopal Bhattacharya said that most Left parties say that they make concerted efforts to recruit more women but this doesn't match the reality. It is left to the women's organization to propagate women's rights' issues though the party policy underscores the importance of such issues. The CPI holds classes for both members and sympathizers and the

Pashchimbanga Mahila Samiti takes separate classes for its women members. There are state and district level schools of the CPI where both men and women members teach different aspects of economics and politics. Compared to the seventies, when women hardly participated in these classes and workshops, 50 per cent of the women members participate in these currently.

Gita Das of the CPI (ML) thought that not too many women were coming forward to join politics and in the elected bodies of her party only one out of ten members is a woman, a trend that has not changed in the last 30 years. In the CPI (ML), women's participation is around 10 per cent at the district level and 20 per cent at the block level. Women are well-represented in the All-India Students' Association (AISA), Pashchimbanga Kisan Samiti, Gana Sanskriti Parishad and other mass organizations of the party. She felt that societal and family obligations as well as a general apathy towards politics among the younger generation are causes keeping women away. Political uncertainties in the country are also discouraging women from joining the party. The CPI (ML) organizes workshops and debates regularly to educate women members of the party. Separate classes are held for those women members who are educationally less advanced. Women come in large numbers from far off places in West Bengal to attend such classes and conventions. Women members are generally more sincere in participating in such programmes. Both the mother party and the women's wing (Pragatishil Mahila Samiti) share a symbiotic relationship regarding addressing the question of women's equality and rights.

Gouri Chowdhuri and Neela Goswami of the BJP said that from the time of the party's inception in West Bengal in 1980, the proportion of participating women has been on the rise. According to the BJP's constitution, one out of six members in all its elected bodies at all levels has to be a woman. Besides, there are Mahila Morcha Committees at all levels. The number of women party members reflects the strength of the Mahila Morcha of the BJP. However, domestic chores and feudal attitudes in society do prevent more women from participating in political activities. According to them, the deterioration of a value-based society and utter lawlessness in West Bengal are other deterrents. The Mahila Morcha holds special training camps where women members are encouraged to engage in political, economic and social issues. *Prasikkha Shibir* or training camps are also held where both men and women party members participate. At every level of the party, one-fifth of the participants are women. Issues pertaining to women are very much included by the BJP in the party's general propaganda. The BJP accords a lot of respect to its women members and treats them as mothers in a society where women are generally commodified, they said.

Chandrima Bhattacharya of the INC said that the percentage of women members has steadily risen in the last 30 years in her party and she attributed this to their growing interest in the ideology of the Congress and general political awareness among women. She felt that a good number of women were participating at the district and block levels. Women hold important positions in the Youth Congress, Chhatra Parishad and Seva Dal. Every woman member of the party by virtue of being a woman naturally becomes a member of the Mahila Congress. But more women activists are definitely needed. Threats from the ruling party (CPI [M]) in West Bengal, poor educational infrastructure and a lack of women's awareness of their rights stand in the way of women activists playing a lead role in politics.

Phulrenu Guha, ex-MP of the Congress, felt political parties do notice women who are capable and dedicated. But women workers are constrained by numerous household responsibilities, especially bringing up children. As long as the family and children remain the main responsibilities of women, they will not be able to take on additional responsibilities of their party and prove their worth. Therefore, competent women with leadership qualities are often forced to retreat after taking a few steps forward.

According to Chandrima Bhattacharya, each and every branch of all frontal organizations of the INC takes responsibility for electing women party members these days. Party conventions and conferences are held regularly to make women more politically conscious. Women are much more sincere than their male counterparts in participating in training programmes and nearly 100 per cent women members of INC come forward to attend such classes. Both the INC and the Mahila Congress cooperate with each other in propagating women's rights and the mother party is conscious of its responsibility in this regard.

Anil Biswas of the CPI (M) said that women membership in the party had increased by 60 per cent from the early seventies to 2000. In 2000, at the district level, 8 to 10 per cent members were women. In every frontal organization of the CPI (M), women's representation is adequate. He said that both at the administrative and policy making levels, women have a voice in the party. But Rekha Goswami of the same party said that the number of women members of the CPI (M) did not reflect the strength of its women's organization (Ganatantrik Mahila Samiti). Feudal attitude and the party's recruitment policy were responsible for this, she thought. Anil Biswas said that the CPI (M) had already targeted 2003 for an increase in the number of women members in every party branch. Usually each party branch has 9 to 10 per cent women members and there are 34,000 party branches in the state. He said that the party also has a special syllabus for women cadres for acquainting them with its policies. Rekha Goswami explained that district-wise separate as well as joint sessions are held for men and women. More than 60 per cent women participate regularly in these classes and women are much more serious about attending these. Male and female members equally attend the joint sessions. The party emphasizes women's equality in its general policy and sees women's rights as human rights.

Malini Bhattacharya, an ex-MP of the CPI (M), said that in parliament women are very inadequately represented. Further, they are often expected to keep themselves confined to women's issues. Besides, sometimes exigencies of party politics prevent women from highlighting issues in a united manner. In other words, there is hardly any monolithic women's constituency in politics. So far as active participation is concerned, there are inactive male MPs as well as inactive women MPs. Phulrenu Guha, too, thought that noone ever notices the large section of inactive male MPs. Women have to cross the additional barrier of lack of experience in public life too. In spite of these, there are efficient and articulate women MPs in parliament. The contribution of women politicians, activists and social workers in vital sectors like health, education, welfare and rehabilitation has never been recognized. Bhattacharya and Guha felt that 33 per cent reservation for women in parliament and legislative assemblies would not solve the question of women's inequality, but participation of women in larger numbers as candidates in electoral politics would encourage women's political participation in general. Krishna Bose, Trinamool Congress MP, said that though she was very much in favour of the 33 per cent Reservation Bill initially, the Bill needs to be modified if it has to be passed in parliament. In order to have a fare representation of women in parliament, she has suggested an amendment to the Representation of People's Act (RPA), which can be passed by a simple majority. This amendment will make it mandatory for political parties to choose not less than 40 per cent of its candidates from either males or females. This would be a step towards women's empowerment and at the same time it would be a broadening of democracy and ensure gender sensitivity within political parties.

The Autonomous Women's Movement

With the UN declaration of the International Women's Decade providing a kind of focus for activities centring on women, the late seventies heralded a new phase in the women's movement in India. In February 1980, the Bombay-based group,

Forum Against Rape (later called the Forum Against Oppression of Women) spearheaded the campaign for re-opening the Mathura Rape Case and demanded a re-trial. This was the first time that women's organizations came together across the country to coordinate a campaign.

The distinguishing features of the new women's groups were that they declared themselves to be 'feminist', despite the fact that most of their members were drawn from the Left, which saw feminism as bourgeois and divisive; that they insisted on being autonomous, though most of their members were affiliated to other political groups, and that they rapidly built networks amongst each other, ideological differences notwithstanding.[4]

Women's groups were formed all over the country including West Bengal. Some of the leading groups that came up in Calcutta in the early eighties were Sachetana, Nari Nirjatan Pratirodh Mancha, Women's Research Centre, Pratibidhan, Lahori, Mahila Pathagar and Mahila Pathachakra. These women's groups provided a mixture of legal aid and counselling and carried on sustained advocacy against dowry harassment and bride-burning; for a change in the anti-rape law; against the Muslim Women's Bill (1986), the glorification of sati and Roop Kanwar's immolation on her husband's pyre (1987). Some of these groups also functioned as consciousness-raising organizations hosting regular cultural and academic meets to focus on women's rights and demand policy changes in favour of women. Sachetana was also culturally active in staging anti-dowry and anti-Muslim Bill plays. Groups like Nari Nirjatan Pratirodh Mancha took a leading part in Niraparadh Bandini Mukti Andolan (Campaign for Release of Innocent Women Undertrials) in the state and in fighting for justice in the Archana Guha case (demanding suspension of police officer, Runu Guha Neogy, for torturing the victim in custody).

Keeping pace with the adoption of various issues like housing rights, environment, population control, child rights, focussed on by the United Nations from time to time, the women's movement, too, framed its own corresponding demands and slogans. For instance, the Child Rights' Summit convened by the UN resulted in many women's organizations campaigning with the demand 'Shishur Jadi Bhalo Chao, Ma Babader Kaj Dao' (To better children's lives, give their parents work). During the year of housing rights, Unnayan, a Calcutta-based NGO, had the responsibility of running the all-India campaign, whose main demand was recognition of housing as a fundamental right of every citizen. Several women's organizations and NGOs

[4] Kumar, Radha. 1993. *The History of Doing*. Kali for Women, New Delhi.

actively campaigned against the eviction of unauthorized slum dwellers without providing rehabilitation. Though Unnayan no longer exists, similar activities have continued and the same demand came up at the two international conferences, Habitat I and Habitat II.

Problems of environmental pollution and global warming have also been taken up increasingly by the women's movement. In particular, the movement campaigned for the punishment of the culprits of the Bhopal gas disaster and demanded compensation for the victims of the tragedy. Similarly, there has been quite a lot of support for the Narmada Bachao Andolan. On 6 and 9 August, the Hiroshima and Nagasaki Days, there is generally quite a noticeable participation of women in mass marches and rallies. The problems of population growth and measures used for controlling population are an issue of special concern to the women's organizations. In West Bengal, there have been repeated demands for enforcing a strict ban against pre-natal sex identification and selective abortion of the female foetus. Since the mid-nineties, our state has witnessed the coming together of thousands of sex workers with their own demands. The demands include legalization of their profession and recognition as workers. Not all sex workers' organizations are in favour of these demands raised by the Durbar Mahila Samanaya Samiti and there are smaller organizations who want more active support from the state and society for their economic rehabilitation as well as equal right to education for their children.

Another important development of this period, in this case at the all-India level, was the close coordination developed between seven all-India women's organizations on all issues concerning women in terms of policies and programmes. These seven organizations (often referred to collectively as the 'Seven Sisters') are: All India Democratic Women's Association, National Federation of Indian Women, All India Women's Conference, Mahila Dakshata Samiti, Joint Women's Programme, Centre for Women's Development Studies and Young Women's Christian Association of India. The Alternate Country Paper prepared by this group in preparation for the Beijing Conference was circulated and discussed in West Bengal as well as in other states and endorsed by almost a 100 NGOs and women's groups.

Since the fourth UN Conference in Beijing in 1995 and the adoption of the Beijing Programme of Action, important follow-up actions have taken place in West Bengal, which include a report-back interactive seminar at Jadavpur University, where a whole session was devoted to one-third participation of women in vidhan sabhas and Lok Sabha; a discussion organized by the West Bengal Women's Commission to collect opinions of various women's organizations on a National Policy for Women; formation of 'Maitri' as a coordinating network

for organizations and individuals concerned with women's equality, development and peace; preparation of a photographic exhibition by an ad hoc committee of historians and NGO representatives on women's participation in the struggle for India's independence; and a hand-drawn poster exhibition on women's issues commissioned by the State Women's Commission. Since the Beijing Conference in 1995, the fortnight beginning 25 November (Day of Protest Against Violence on Women) to 10 December (Anniversary of the Human Rights Charter) has been regularly observed to highlight and protest violence against women. There have been increased efforts by the West Bengal Women's Commission and various women's organizations to sensitize the judiciary and the police administration to women's problems.

Parallel to the Beijing Plus Five Conference, organized by the United Nations, there was another event of worldwide significance marking the end of the century and millennium. The World March of Women, starting in different countries in March 2000 and culminating in October of the same year at Washington and New York, was organized on the initiative of Canadian NGOs who brought together a preparatory committee with representations from 40 countries. In West Bengal, a number of women's organizations including mass organizations and NGOs formed a joint preparatory committee for this march in Calcutta and other parts of the state. Signatures were collected at different rallies including on typically Bengali saris and these were sent to the UN headquarters in New York after a national level march in Delhi. The World March declared that it was the beginning of a process which would not end until a more humane and peaceful world, free from discrimination and based on social justice could be ensured and the basic rights of women be recognized as an essential part of human rights.

While the eighties had seen women's groups come up as voluntary agencies raising their own funds, the nineties saw a proliferation of NGOs, which depended on funding agencies in India and abroad and maintained a paid staff. Some think that this proliferation of NGOs has given the government an opportunity to coopt and appropriate programmes for women's development according to its convenience. But these NGOs have also added to the rich variety of ideas, approaches and activities that form the varied spectrum of social and cultural life in our country. Growing cooperation between the NGOs and the older women's mass organizations and voluntary organizations has brought in a large number of new issues that were earlier not considered a part of the agenda of the women's movement. Such issues as price rise and communalism, which many autonomous organizations did not regard in the past as women's problems, have today become major issues for women's campaigns as a result of increasing interaction between feminist organizations and mass women's organizations led by political parties. On the other hand, Left-oriented mass organizations of women have also come to realize that participation in economic production or legal changes cannot by themselves empower women unless there is a conscious and continuous struggle against the dominance of patriarchal ideas in society.

Women in the Trade Union Movement

During the three decades covered in this report, the pattern of women's participation in remunerative work, whether in or outside their homes, has changed to a very great extent. In the early seventies, the main areas of women's employment in the formal sector were jute and cotton textiles, mines and the tea gardens. In all these, the workforce, both male and female, consisted largely of people from outside Bengal, especially Uttar Pradesh and Bihar. In the case of tea gardens, the workforce in the Duars consisted mainly of tribal men and women brought from outside Bengal through recruiting agents, while in the hills it was mainly the Nepalis. The level of participation of Bengali women was relatively low compared to such states as Maharashtra and Punjab. The absence of gender-differentiated statistical data on such sectors as agriculture, pottery, handloom industry and other cottage industries veiled a large amount of women's economic contribution to their family incomes since they were not the main producers in such occupations.

Among educated middle class women, the main areas of employment were clerical jobs in government offices and private firms, teaching at different levels, nursing etc. Women engaged in these occupations were enrolled in trade unions in large numbers and played an active part in the of economic struggle. However, only a few of them occupied leading positions in the unions as the main burden of housework and childcare fell on them. A few outstanding women leaders have found a place in Bengal's trade union history—Santosh Kumari Devi was a pioneer in organizing the jute workers. Prabhabati Dasgupta was president of the jute workers union at the time of the first general strike in Bengal's jute industry. Begum Sakina was an organizer of the sweepers and scavengers of the Calcutta Municipal Corporation. Maitreyee Bose and Sudha Roy built powerful trade unions amongst an almost exclusively male workforce like the dock workers. There were also some women leaders like Dukhmat Didi in Baranagar, Comrade Jamuna and others in the tea gardens of Duars, who rose from the ranks to become recognized leaders. But these were exceptional individuals whose existence did not negate overwhelming male dominance in the trade union leadership of West Bengal.

There has been a sea change in the composition of the working class in the state not just quantitatively but also qualitatively in the three decades under discussion here. Women workers have been almost totally eliminated from such organized sectors as jute and cotton textiles mainly because of the unwillingness of the employers to implement maternity benefit laws, ban night shift work for women and provide childcare facilities provided under ILO conventions or acquired through trade union struggles and the women's movement. On the other hand, increased unemployment among male family members combined with increased literacy and education among women has led to large number of women, particularly in urban and suburban areas, to seek employment in small-scale industrial units in the unorganized sector. In addition to the organized readymade garments, industry, the unorganized sector produces handbags and other items out of scrap leather, plastic goods, toys, hairbands, costume jewellery and innumerable other items of daily use. Packaging of medicines, biscuits and other goods also provides employment to a large number of women in the unorganized sector.

The strength of unions in this sector has always been very limited. First, employers restrict the total employment to a number just below the stipulated minimum required for registration under the Factory Act. This is to avoid giving trade union rights to employees or minimum legal benefits under existing laws. Next, there is always a huge pool of job-hungry women available to replace troublemakers the moment any attempt is made by the workers to organize. Most of the workers in the readymade garments' and handicrafts' industry work from home and receive payment in cash on delivery of finished goods. Suppliers of raw materials very often provide garments already cut out or ready with designs. Also, a whole family sometimes works to complete the order and the bulk of the income goes to the middlemen.

In rural areas and small towns, *bidi* is another major industry employing women working from homes. The benefits available under the Welfare Act, which include healthcare and help for schoolgoing children in the form of free textbooks and uniforms, can only be available if a *bidi* worker has an identity card with his or her photograph. The employer usually does not want to recognize home-based women workers. Since most unions do not have women organizers, women *bidi* workers usually get their identity cards only if leading women activists of political parties or its mass organizations take this up. Similarly, women agricultural workers and self-employed women in the unorganized sector can get benefits, loans or other facilities under various welfare schemes only when women's organizations or NGOs or mass organizations dare to act on their behalf. Very large number of women, often illiterate and with no occupational training, only have the option to work as domestic help. As their employers are in most cases middle class housewives, they are averse to unionizing this section of women workers.

Organizing women workers in diverse occupations is in any case a formidable task. The teachers' organizations at various levels have a few women leaders. An outstanding personality like Anila Devi was for many years the general secretary of All Bengal Teachers' Association (ABTA), the biggest teacher's organization in the state. In West Bengal, women bank employees are one of the very few who have a coordinating machinery of their own. The banking industry was almost forbidden to women till the sixties. After nationalization in 1969, the banks opened their doors to women, when a common process of recruitment through competitive tests was introduced. By the eighties, the number of women bank employees reached 100,000 constituting 15 per cent of the total workforce in the industry.

The All-India Bank Employees' Association (AIBEA) is first amongst all trade unions of the industry, and that of other sectors as well, that took some concrete and positive steps to organize and mobilize the female workforce since the eighties. A series of steps were taken for greater and increasing involvement of women from the branch level to the top leadership of AIBEA paving the way for women's entry into the decision making bodies. In 1995, AIBEA issued some guidelines to all its affiliated units instructing them to make a special drive to involve women employees a lot more in trade union activities and in leadership positions as well.

The first ever All-India Women Bank Employees' Convention was held in Mumbai 1995. In West Bengal, the Ladies' Cell of AIBEA was formed in the same year from a state level women employees' convention. The holding of separate all-India meetings or conventions, open to only women bank employees, since 1995 and the formation of Ladies Cell of the state AIBEA has encouraged women to put forth their views in all matters vis-à-vis the management of the banks as well as the unions, pointing out specifically the obstacles and hindrances in the way of playing their proper roles in the unions.

At the state level, none of the major trade union federations, irrespective of their political affiliations, have any woman as an elected office-bearer or executive committee member. At the most there is a token representation of one or two women in their executive committees. Although in their annual conferences all these unions adopt resolutions in support of demands of women workers, when any negotiations take place between trade union representatives and employers, women's specific demands, even such an elementary one as a separate toilet, get pushed to the background. Little has been done by any major union to ensure proper implementation of the law on equal pay for equal work passed in 1976 or the Supreme Court directive on sexual harassment of women at their workplace. Thus, women's work participation and their presence in trade unions have increased enormously in the last three decades but their role as organizers and leaders in unions has remained negligible, except in rare instances like the women bank employees' union.

Conclusion

In 1974, at the time of the publication of the report *Towards Equality,* women leaders of practically all all-India organizations and political parties had believed that with the equality provided in the Constitution and increasing access to education and employment, there would be a gradual increase in the number of women MPs and MLAs elected through open competition. This, however, has not happened. On the other hand, it has been seen that elected decision making fora can never find the necessary time to discuss urgent issues facing women and such debates usually get pushed to the very last day of any session of the parliament. A substantially increased presence of women in the elected decision making fora would force members to discuss such issues with more time and seriousness, since on the whole there is a wide consensus among women of different political parties on urgent issues facing almost half of the country's population. Even after the introduction of the 81st Constitution Amendment Bill in the Lok Sabha, voting has been postponed again and again either through disturbances on the floor of the House by its opponents or the insistence of the ruling party at the Centre that it cannot be passed unless there is a consensus arrived at among all the parties in the Lok Sabha because a two-thirds majority is required for such an amendment.

Now a new proposal has come up according to which all political parties would be required under the electoral law to nominate a certain fixed percentage of their election candidates from among women. This, however, will not guarantee any increase in the number of women elected since in our country election is not carried out under a proportional representation system. There is also another proposal that three parliamentary constituencies may be combined together and should have two men and one woman as candidates. The size of the total electorate in India has increased manifold since 1951. However, the number of Lok Sabha seats during this period increased only from 499 to 544. It would be impossible for any candidate, let alone a woman candidate, entering the fray for the first time, to cover such large constituencies and huge number of voters during their electoral campaign.

Women's organizations in West Bengal have continued to demand that the 81st Amendment Bill for women's reservation be voted on immediately as it stands and that all political parties in the state which had earlier supported this Bill insist in the Lok Sabha and with their respective all-India party leadership to get it passed without further delay.

It is to be noted that almost three decades after the International Women's Year, demand for one-third reservation of seats for women in national and state legislatures is central to the major issues for advocacy and campaign, which also include revision of existing laws to eliminate traces of discrimination against women including the law about rape; revision of the law against domestic violence; and proper implementation of the Supreme Court directive for elimination of sexual harassment at places of work.

seats for women in national and state legislatures is central to
the major issues for advocacy and campaign, which also include revision of existing laws to eliminate traces of discrimination against women including the law about rape, revision of

Bengal have continued to
to raise women's reservation
and that all political par-
ported this Bill in list in

Culture

CHAPTER 6

Malini Bhattacharya

Methodology

It is difficult, perhaps impossible, to quantify cultural status.
Culture has many different aspects. When we look at culture
as a production, we find that it is associated with the production
of exchange-values as well as use-values. The decorative design on the wall of a tribal house is a use-value produced through
an aesthetic exercise. The production of certain kinds of human
relationships—certain kinds of hospitality, for instance—em-
body such use-values. The way in which one serves food to a
guest and the way in which the mother dresses up her child
are also embodiments of culture generating use-value. The
production of an earthen pot by a village potter is also a cultural
activity, but when he takes it to the market it generates
exchange-value just as a Hindi blockbuster or a new novel by
Vikram Seth does. In other words, it is not just singers, playwrights, film directors, poets, visual artists, but all ordinary
men and women who are engaged in the production of culture.
Some cultural products are sold, others are used by the producers themselves.

Again, culture is not monolithic. Within a particular social
formation there may be a multiplicity of sometimes contesting
cultural codes. Accessibility to these cultural codes is restricted
by social training that operates within hegemonic structures.
Poor and illiterate persons, members of the so-called lower
castes, as also women, are excluded from cultural codes to
which the literate elite with 'upper caste' pedigree alone have
access. Thus, Shudras and women have been excluded from
the study of the Vedas and today access to the internet is limited
to the elite in our country. On the other hand, an elite consumer
of culture, if he so wishes, can find access to taped music ap-
propriated from its tribal or 'lower caste' producers. The
language of science and technology is often accepted to be a

male preserve, whereas 'humanities' is considered to be an
area where anyone can enter without any preparation. Thus,
culture is not without its underpinning of politics.

The discourse of man–woman relationship is itself a part
of cultural ideology, and its presence, visible or invisible, may
be detected in all kinds of cultural formations and the texts
they generate. The cultural status of women in a particular
society can be inferred from our reading of such cultural texts,
whether it is a novel, a film, a play or a particular kind of architecture. But it may also be derived from our study of the boundaries within which women operate both as practitioners and
consumers of culture. These boundaries are not static, but may
be found to be continually redefined within the historical situation. Women's power of access to a cultural code, which may
be a major determinant in understanding her cultural status,
has to be studied simultaneously. Thus, we may perhaps have
certain indications of cultural status, but it would not be possible within the scope of this study to capture its multiple
nuances in their entirety.

Cultural life in West Bengal is rich and multifaceted. Bangla
is the main language, but there are other languages like Nepali,
Saontali, Urdu and Hindi that are spoken by different groups
within the state. Urban culture, centring around Kolkata, has
rich traditions, but there are also vibrant cultural forms to be
found in the rural areas of West Bengal. Apart from this, a
number of suburban towns are also centres of various cultural
activities. There are highly literate cultural forms, as well as
oral transmission of culture among the very poor. Our aim is
to find out certain major trends, in the last 30 years, in the
gendering of these different, sometimes contesting, cultural
codes.

We have tried to look at the representation of women and
women's issues in different cultural forms. Changes in the
cultural milieu in the state must be reflected in the cultural

products, perhaps not in obvious ways, but at least in indirect, mediated forms. The market for cultural productions has expanded tremendously with the commercialization of cultural activities in recent years. We have tried to find out how the gender equations within cultural ideology are affected by all this. Apart from women's images that different cultural codes use as icons, women themselves produce culture. How has her role as producer of culture changed? We have also looked at women's role as consumers of culture. A micro study done by us on rural women artists of West Bengal is enclosed towards the end of this report as Appendix F. This study tries to understand how women's presence is felt in the sphere of cultural production and thinking in West Bengal from a study of cultural spaces from all three angles.

Considering the enormous area that falls under 'culture', we have had to limit our scope severely and look only at the tip of the iceberg. We have, for instance, concentrated almost exclusively on material in Bangla although we know that cultural activities in other languages are not negligible in the state. Again, many of the groups and individuals that we have approached are located in and around Kolkata. This report, however, does not reflect the cultural scenario in the suburban towns of West Bengal.

In conducting the survey, we have focussed on certain quantitative data. These are based on materials like publications, cassettes, institutional records, and other such things. Since quantitative data do not necessarily provide us with a clear picture of the scenario, we have also taken qualitative data into account. This includes interviews and analysis of texts. In the case of plays which are no longer being staged, we have looked at videotapes when available, consulted scripts or the directors or those involved in the production as well as contemporary reviews. We have watched a number of films, studied literary texts and newspapers and magazines. The areas covered are literature, print media, theatre, film, television, advertisements, music, dance, radio, educational material and visual arts.

Literature

To give an overview of literary representation of women and by women before the seventies in Bengali, one can only say that while on the one hand, gender relationship had been problematized and made visible by many writers, on the other hand, there were some eminent women writers in the fictional and non-fictional genres. For instance, in the writings of Manik Bandyopadhyay, Samaresh Basu, Narendranath Mitra and others, who were continuing the realistic trend in the Bangla novel, the problems of man–woman relationship were constantly foregrounded and intricate constructions of the 'women's point of view' did sometimes come through. The most important woman writer of this period was Ashapurna Devi. But there were some other popular women writers too. In writings by women, women's issues were highlighted and efforts to break stereotypes were sometimes found. Ashapurna Devi herself tried this in her novels.

The period from the mid-sixties to the mid-seventies was of social and political turbulence. A new group of writers like Sunil Gangopadhyay, Sirshendu Mukhopadhyay, Shyamal Gangopadhyay and Moti Nandy emerged during this time. Kavita Sinha was their contemporary, as is Nabaneeta Dev Sen. In the writings of this period, we observe the emergence of the spirit of individualistic rebellion against established social norms. However, while narrative experiments and experiments with poetry characterized this period, we do not really observe the introduction of new dimensions in the area of gender relationship. The prevalence of internal monologues in the fiction of the time is generally male-centric. From our point of view, a more interesting development may be traced in the writings of Mahasweta Devi. Her *Hajar Churashir Ma* seeks to explore the alienation of a woman from the elite classes vis-à-vis her own society, as a result of her coincidental involvement in the Naxalite movement through her son's death. In Mahasweta Devi, we also find, from this time onwards, explorations of gender relationships in the context of subalternity.

While it is difficult to mark transitions in literary trends from one particular point of time to another, we can definitely say that as compared to the earlier period, there has been an increase in the numbers and the visibility of women writers in the period being studied by us. For instance, if one looks at the successive issues of *Desh*, a fortnightly brought out by the Ananda Bazaar Group, one finds that a number of novels being serialized since the late eighties are by women. Women authors like Bani Basu and Suchitra Bhattacharya were introduced to the community of readers by *Desh*, whereas in the earlier period, we do not find a single novel by a women being serialized in this periodical. This shows that women's writings have found a niche in the literary market today.

However, it may also be noticed that in the dominant literature within our period, the critical realism of the forties and the fifties and even the individualistic iconoclasm of the sixties seem to have given way to a more moralistic vein, when the novelist whether male or female is expected to uphold and corroborate a set of social values for which consent may be found in some level of the readership and which the characters stereotypically represent. At their best, these values may represent a somewhat vague 'apolitical' humanism and at their worst, one sees in them a retrograde pull towards a reinforcement of traditionalism and conservatism which can be exemplified from the writings of some of the male authors like Shirshendu Mukhopadhyay and Sanjib Chattopadhyay. Within this world-view, the configuration of the modern 'aggressive' woman looms large and comes to be seen as the source of all social disruption.

Trends in the Representation of Women in Fiction

We have looked at 450 books—novels, short stories and bio-graphies—written by women between 1975 and 2000. In the period 1975 to 1985, 10 women writers were considered and a much larger number of women writers, about 50, were con-sidered between 1990 and 2000. In the first case, most of the writers dealt with a middle class setting and the principal women characters were in the 25–40 age group. There was very little representation of women working outside the home. In the later period, while the majority of the characters were middle-class housewives, 10 per cent of the characters happen to be from the working class and 25 per cent of the women are shown as working outside the home. Depiction of women from religious, linguistic and other minorities also show a slight rise. Of the 450 texts studied, 80 per cent may be described as women-centred. The specifically gender-related problems which are tackled are dowry (2 per cent), violence against women and problems of working women (25 per cent), family problems and marital disharmony (48 per cent).

Autobiographies and Academic Books

Apart from works of fiction, the eighties and nineties have witnessed a remarkable retrieval of many lost autobiographies by women from the nineteenth and early twentieth centuries. The journal, *Ekshan*, took a leading role in publishing such autobiographies. Subsequently in the nineties, the School of Women's Studies, Jadavpur University, came up with a project of publishing these forgotten autobiographies and other writ-ings by women belonging to this period. Quite a few recent memoirs by women have also appeared in the last 10 to 15 years. These include writings of academics like Kalyani Dutta, littérateurs like Nabaneeta Dev Sen, performing artists like Reba Roy Chowdhury and Nihar Barua, political activists like Manikuntala Sen, Jaya Mitra and Minakshi Sen.

Academic books in Bengali, which may be broadly clas-sified as 'Women's Studies', have also seen a spurt in the same period. Such books deal with a variety of issues like female foeticide or dowry and bride-burning. Bengali books on social history, feminist literary theory and criticism are also on the rise. These, however, are small in number when compared to the range and number of cookery books or books on embroi-dery and sewing. There are very few books in Bangla by women on economics, science and technology or politics.

Changing Social Status of Women Writers

Five writers from different age groups were interviewed for the purpose. The eldest was 85 and the youngest 28. All of them belonged to the middle class. Two of them were full-time writers and the other three were professionals. Two were writers of non-fiction, one wrote fiction as well as non-fiction, one was a poet and one wrote only fiction. Of the three pro-fessional women, two were professors and one an IAS officer —all belonging to the high income group. Their income was not less than their husbands. It is interesting that the seniormost writer earned enough from her writings to maintain her own household. The youngest, a poet, said she earned very little from her writings. The seniormost author carries on the earlier trend of the housewife saving time from her housework for writing. This was largely true of the generation to which Ashapurna Devi, for example, belonged. For this author, writ-ing is not only a source of creativity but it is her only source of independent income. The other three who belong to the next generation are employed in responsible positions and for them the income from writing is only a supplement. They are not really interested in making money from it.

Three of them are married. The eldest is a widow and the youngest a divorcee. None of them believe in any religion. When asked whether they had any specific time of the day earmarked for writing, all of them apart from the seniormost replied in the negative. The seniormost author specified evening as the time when she wrote. The fact that four of the respondents could not specify any time for writing compares curiously with the response of women rural artists in our micro study. When asked how they found time to practice their art, most of them were unable to specify any time. A few said that they do it in the evenings when all other work is over. This seemed to indicate that while for a housewife writing could be taken up only when she finished housework, for professional women writing was to be taken up in the time that they could spare. Questioned on the attitude of the family and of society in general towards them as writers, the majority gave a positive answer. The seniormost writer, while asserting that the family was supportive, described the attitude of society as 'partly negative'. Another respondent said that while the family did not object to her writing, they were not very encouraging either. A point to be noted is that except for one, the others did not wish to be branded as feminists or dealing with women's issues. Two of them specifically referred to 'human issues' as their main concern rather than gender issues. Only one said that the economic and social position of women and women's movements were her main concern.

Trends in Readership

Our survey findings indicate that it is not invariably true that women read books by women writers and men read books by male writers only. However, generally, women readers do seem to have a preference for women writers. It is interesting to note that women readers read poetry and writings on social issues, apart from fiction. In answer to a question on whether the number of women writers has increased over the years and whether these writers limit themselves to women's problems, there was a variety of responses. Most of them thought that the number of women writers has gone up and that women write on a variety of issues. Out of 11 respondents who said that women are not limited to women's issues, 3 were men. There was another man who said that women are limited as writers. Regarding representation of women in literature, some felt that women are being portrayed as more arrogant or they were being commodified. The others felt that a positive change had occurred in the portrayal of women in literature.

Theatre

Group theatre of Kolkata, which has emerged as a major theatre movement in the last 50 years, is an offshoot of the Indian People's Theatre Association (IPTA). It made a humble beginning with the formation of Bohurupee in 1948 which vowed to produce 'honest theatre' as opposed to the melodramatic excesses that commercial theatre was prone to. Over the years, it has emerged as a theatre movement reflecting life as it is. This study has confined itself to focussing on women in Kolkata's group theatre and has not been able to include the popular *jatra* tradition of Bengal. However, it must be noted that women are playing significant roles in the *jatra* groups operating from Kolkata. They are heading groups besides playing the role of protagonists in most *palas* or plays. Women-

oriented plays, progressive or regressive, remain the staple food of the *jatra* tradition. Since commercial theatre of north Kolkata died a natural death in the eighties, we had chosen only a single representative of this form, Ketaki Dutta, who has been in this profession since her childhood and has lately made her mark in group theatre as well.

As opposed to commercial theatre, group theatre has no profit-making agenda. Working part-time or full-time, the group theatre activists use the proscenium stage as an effective mode to impart messages relevant to society. There are several such groups not only in Kolkata, but also in the district towns. There are many women actresses for whom this is a part-time or full-time occupation.

Among our 27 respondents, there were two groups of women—those hailing from theatre families and those who joined as outsiders. Coming to theatre was a conscious choice for all of them. Though the percentage of women in the theatre groups of Kolkata is still roughly 20, women have gradually increased in number since the seventies. These women are mostly from educated middle-class families and are literate. Few among the senior actresses studied beyond the high school level. But the new generation of theatre women are at least graduates; some of them hold postgraduate degrees as well and at least three of our respondents were doctorates. Most of them have a regular source of income. Hence, the number of those financially dependent on others is small. These days a few theatre women working in different groups are being paid for their performances. When a payment is made there is no gender discrimination as such. A few of them earn their living through different theatre-related activities like conducting workshops, writing books, doing research projects and the like. At least half of them take part in choreography, costume designing, music and lights. But only a few of them take active part in organizational activities. A handful (except the groups run by women) are 'executive members' of their groups. Women playwrights and directors are few and far between.

Those who belonged to theatre families or were married to theatre-persons usually had family support. They often went to rehearsals with toddlers in tow. For many others, theatre had to take a backseat after they got married and had children. Some of them made a return after domestic responsibilities became manageable and they had some time for themselves. On the other hand, a few women from lower middle class families were inspired to join theatre so that they could contribute to the family income. The younger respondents in our survey definitely indicated positive changes in the attitude of their families and society towards theatre women.

The survey shows that gender discrimination operates both overtly and otherwise. For example, there were instances of marginalizing talented actresses when they became better known than their male colleagues, which ultimately forced the actresses to leave their respective groups. Again, there were instances of a husband and wife duo working in the same group where the husband deliberately tried to suppress the wife's talents. Besides, there were instances where husbands tried to put pressure on wives by harping on family responsibilities and children. Our respondents were mostly well-known and established. If they had to face discrimination both within the family and the group, those who came from lower middle class families and depended on their income from performances must be in an even more disadvantageous position.

In the public sphere, for example in the case of organizing and speaking at seminars and colloquiums on different aspects of theatre, senior actresses felt that until recently these were almost exclusively reserved for male theatre personalities. Even in March 2000, when the theatre group Rangakarmee organized 'Samanvay: A National Convention of Performing Women', as part of their silver jubilee celebrations, not a single man from the Calcutta group theatre scene was present though many of them were invited personally by the group's director, Usha Ganguly. The late-nineties also saw a few such seminars

and workshops focussing on women's contribution to Bengali theatre and bringing together women actresses/directors of two/three generations in an attempt to voice the usual unheard voices. However, these platforms are still not able to bring together thespians of both sexes to engage in a dialogue.

It is encouraging to note that many senior actresses have written plays, published their memoirs, translated plays from other Indian languages and penned theoretical pieces, especially in the last 20 years, thus making a significant intellectual contribution. Commemorative volumes were also published after the death of two leading actresses, Keya Chakraborty and Tripti Mitra. A couple of journals, notable among them, *Seagull Theatre Quarterly* and *Group Theatre*, brought out special issues on women in theatre. Sachetana, a voluntary women's group, produced a booklet containing two anti-dowry plays in 1984, one of which was widely performed in the mid-eighties by the woman's group.

Women are represented more positively these days on stage and there are many more plays addressing women's issues. This has increased the visibility of women theatre artists greatly. Table 6.1 enlists 18 such productions staged between 1975 and 1999, which, by no means, is an exhaustive list.

Table 6.1

Productions that have Increased Women's Visibility in Theatre, 1975–99

Year	Title	Written/produced/directed by a woman*	Theme
1972	*Baarbodhu*	No/No/No	Ketaki Dutta's interpretation of Lata, a prostitute who becomes a victim of middle class hypocrisy.
1981	*Tapaswi O Tarangini*	No/No/No	Based on a myth from the *Ramayana*, portrays a woman's search for her true self.
1983	*Nathabati Anaathbath*	Yes/Yes/Yes	A reinterpretation of the *Mahabharat* from Draupadi's point of view.
1987	*Sati*	Yes/No/No	The continuing oppression of a woman in her marital home and her protests against the double standards of the middle class 'progressive' male.
1988	*Madhab Malanchi Kanya*	No/No/No	A reworking of a mythical story which centres around a woman and where the princess rescues the prince.
1989	*Uttaradhikar*	No/Yes/No	Crumbling of a rural joint family and the predicaments of the women therein.
1989	*Alakanandar Putra Kanya*	No/No/No	Alakananda, the middle-aged heroine, goes on adopting orphans, bearing the burden of all the mishaps and problems that accost her.
1992	*Darpaney Sharatshashi*	No/No/ No	Interesting study of the female performer of the nineteenth century.
1992	*My Story/Our Story*	Yes/No/Yes	A woman protests against domestic violence.
1993	*Care Kori Naa*	Yes/Yes/Yes	Problems of children with an over-protective, single mother.
1993	*Rudali*	Yes/Yes/Yes	Two impoverished lower caste women adopt a strange profession, that of mourners at funerals.
1993	*Kamalkamini*	Yes/Yes/Yes	Theatre anecdotes and real life incidents from Ketaki Dutta's life and career in theatre.
1994	*Je Jan Ache Majhkhaney*	Yes/Yes/No	A woman who has broken conventional boundaries herself cannot accept when her son falls in love with a girl from another community.
1996	*Karnabati*	No/No/No	A woman's search for the ideal man is frustrated and she decides to become both father and mother to the child she has conceived.
1997	*Jara Bristite Bhijechhilo*	No/No/Yes	The oppressive life of a middle class woman until she breaks free.
1998	*Shanu Roy Choudhury*	No/No/Yes	A middle class house wife's search for liberation.
1998	*Nija Bhumey*	No/Yes/No	An actress of yesteryears dies during the shooting of a film based on her life.
1998	*Shudrayan*	No/No/No	A reinterpretation of the myth of Shurpanakha as a betrayed non-Aryan woman.
1999	*Apoorba Golap*	Yes/Yes/Yes	Dramatization of the tragic life of Golapsundari, an exceptional actress of the nineteenth century.

Note: *Ketaki Dutta put in all her savings for *Baarbodhu* but it went in the name of the group. In the case of plays where production credits are ascribed to the group, it is difficult to say (except in a few obvious cases) who produced it.

Critics and reviewers have not always been very receptive to these changes. There has been a fear among critics that 'feminist issues' may take over the stage. However, since the mid-nineties, women's issues have found some space in the critical discourse on Bangla theatre. Certain groups have specialized in producing women-oriented plays, a thing unthinkable in the seventies. Audience reception is enthusiastic, prompting more such productions. On the whole, more women are coming to the forefront, writing plays on gynocentric themes and donning the director's cap, besides running theatre groups.

Film

Bengali cinema has undergone major changes in the last 30 years or so. In order to analyse such a modified image of Bangla cinema, it is essential to understand that the seventies marked a departure from the cinematic practice of the previous decades. Bangla cinema, during the earlier period, drew its sustenance primarily from literature and mythology; the result was that the representation of women in films was stereotypical (altruistic mother, wife, etc.) yet at the same time made some bold departures, such as in *Mukti*, *Shesh Uttar* and *Udayer Pathe*. In the golden decade of the fifties with the glorious matinee idols, Uttam–Suchitra, dominating the Bangla screen, the image of the woman in all these overtly romantic melodramas seems to be shimmering with the 'desire for modernity', reflecting the zeitgeist of a country throbbing with a collective dream of the possibility of a new, modern India. Hence, we see women stars of the time in a variety of roles ascribed to the urban, modern woman as conceived in the fifties and sixties—doctors, nurses, artists, teachers, journalists, office assistants—all educated, urban, active, accomplished women who do not sit at home and pine for their lovers/husbands. Most often than not, these characters were not deprived of 'agency' within the narrative and they actually precipitated action that led to the complication or denouement of the plot.

Bangla films in the seventies moved away from some of these trends set in the fifties and sixties. The seventies had been a time when the demarcation between the so-called commercial/mainstream cinema and art/parallel cinema started becoming rather pronounced. Cinema was increasingly moving away from literature and Bangla films started 'manufacturing' stories for its content in the Bombay style. During the period under discussion, that is from the seventies to the nineties, the gap between commercial cinema and parallel cinema grew wider. Thus, Bangla film industry went on producing operatic melodramas on the one hand, with a strikingly different serious cinema by Satyajit Ray, Mrinal Sen and Tapan Sinha, on the other. The representation of women, too, significantly differed in these two kinds of films, particularly in the seventies and eighties.

In the former, the woman is typically represented as mother, sister, wife and lover—upholding the status quo. Significantly, till the seventies, unlike the mainstream Hindi films, representation of overt sexuality even in the form of song and dance sequences was somewhat prohibited in Bangla films. The films during this period that were concerned with women's issues primarily centred around the theme of 'virtue rewarded', that is, they were about women who suffered a lot in life but ultimately their moral uprightness reformed their male persecutors who came back to them and offered to re-instate the heroines in family and in society. Almost all the so-called women-centric films revolved around such themes, thereby diluting, simplifying and reducing the monstrosity of such issues as bride-burning, domestic violence, trafficking, rape and other kinds of sexual violence. Protesting against tyrannical husbands or in-laws or any attempt at self-assertion on the part of women were relegated to the binary pole of the 'negative' within the moral economy. Such acts were considered acts of violation and were punished accordingly within the story world.

The parallel cinema of Ray, Sen, Sinha et al., on the other hand, concerned itself with the recognition of women's oppressed and marginalized predicament. In this 'other' cinema, women were represented as products of diverse social formations, seeking to transcend their difficult circumstances, caught in the contradictory pulls of tradition and modernity, past and present, individuality and communality.

Yet another trend emerged in the nineties where serious issues similar to those taken up by parallel cinema were evoked, particularly gender issues, but essentially within the structure of mainstream melodrama, where binary polarization is still dominant. This neo-melodramatic tradition in Bangla cinema in the nineties may primarily be attributed to Aparna Sen and Rituparno Ghosh and partly to Prabhat Roy. These films lack serious exploration as they subtly pose problems which are simplified and, to a certain extent, diluted by their inherent ambiguity so far as the binaries of the commercial and the artistic are concerned. But, at the same time, these films mirror a definite positive image of the woman—professional and successful, confident and liberated, as opposed to the passive stereotypes of patriarchy.

At a time when this new wave of films is depicting professional women rather positively on screen, a survey among 25 film personalities of Tollygunge indicate that working conditions in the film industry have deteriorated substantially for women in the last two decades of the twentieth century. This

Table 6.2
Representation of Women's Issues in Bengali Films, 1975–2000

Year	Name of film	Theme
1975	*Swayamsiddha/Sister/Pranay Pasha*	Protest/violence against women/marital problems and violence against women
1976	*Kabita/Jana Aranya*	Working women/prostitution
1978	*Tilottama/Baarbodhu*	Marital problems/prostitution
1979	*Nabadiganta*	Dowry and violence against women
1980	*Bhagyachakra/Ekdin Pratidin*	Marital problems/problems of working women
1981	*Duratwa/Ogo Bodhu Sundari/ Kalankini/36 Chowringhee Lane*	Marital problems/marital problems/prostitution/exploitation and old age
1982	*Adalat O Ekti Meye*	Rape and the law
1983	*Koni/Ashlilatar Daye/Chena Achena/Tanaya/Khelar Putul*	Women in sports/violence against women/working women/working women and violence against them/dowry and violence against women
1984	*Grihayuddha/Amargeet/Deepar Prem/Mohonar Dike/Parabat Priya/Ghare Bairey*	Marital problems/prostitution/protest/violence against women/marital problems/women stepping out in the public sphere during the Swadeshi Movement
1985	*Parama*	Women's sexual relationships outside marriage
1986	*Daktar Bou/Atanka*	Working women/violence against women
1988	*Boba Sanai/Chhoto Bou*	Marital problems/dowry
1989	*Antarjali Yatra/Sati*	Problematizing the practice of child marriage/polygamy and Sati in nineteenth century Bengal
1992	*Swet Patharer Thala/Ananya/ Antardhan/Nabarupa*	Widowhood and protest/prostitution/violence against women/working women
1994	*Wheel Chair*	Violence against women
1995	*Lady Daktar/Mejo Bou*	Working women/marital problems, dowry and working women
1996	*Unishe April/Yuganta*	Mother–daughter relationship/protest
1998	*Lathi/Dahan*	Problems of old age/violence against women
1999	*Anu*	Protest
2000	*Sasurbari Zindabad/Bastir Meye Radha/Paromitar Ekdin*	Violence against women/working women and violence against women/ working women, marital problems and protest

was emphatically suggested by those who had been with the industry for a very long time. Some veteran artists attributed this to the fact that cinema is increasingly emerging as a lucrative business for easy and quick money, thereby inviting all and sundry hitherto unacquainted with any artistic pursuit.

Exploitation is both at the sexual and non-sexual levels. Two very eminent actresses of the past complained that many times they were not given full payments according to their contracts on flimsy grounds. As far as sexual exploitation is concerned, some felt that the victims are usually helpless while others said that it completely depended on the woman's attitude. Strangely enough, one of the most eminent and progressive filmmakers noted for her gender-sensitive films denied any possibility of sexual exploitation or gender discrimination taking place in the industry. On the other hand, a veterinary surgeon-turned-filmmaker came out with her tales of discrimination and how she faced technical difficulties in the pre-production and post-production phases of her first film.

In the ultimate analysis, one may conclude that the most unfortunate part of the story is that women themselves are more often than not unaware of their exploitation and end up internalizing patriarchal violence and prejudices and, even propagating and justifying these themselves.

Print Media

Newspapers

During the period under consideration, several newspapers, both English and Bengali, were launched in the state. These include *The Telegraph*, *Aajkaal*, *Bartaman* and *Pratidin*. *Ganashakti* became a morning daily from being an eveninger. This period also saw the closure of old ventures such as *Jugantar* and *Amrita Bazaar Patrika*. A few important trends emerged from a random sampling of some of the important and popular newspapers in the state that are of relevance to the terms of reference of this study. The change in the perception regarding the importance of women readership is reflected in the fact that almost all newspapers, Bengali and English, introduced 'Women's Pages'. The phenomenal growth in female readership made the newspapers introduce such pages in order to boost circulation and remain relevant. But these women's pages are usually weekly supplements to the main paper. Fashion, cookery, interior decoration and the like usually take up the lion's share of such supplements. A couple of serious articles are squeezed in and there are weekly columns on legal advice or diet and yoga therapy which serve as added attractions. However, there are exceptions to this general rule, as in the case of an English daily from Kolkata which carries a women's page every Sunday without beauty tips or food recipes. Among Bengali newspapers, *Ganashakti* and *Kalantar* have weekly or fort-nightly women's pages, where serious issues are discussed.

The coverage of women's issues in newspapers also show a few changes from the past. Though these stories continue to be generally placed in inconspicuous positions in the inside pages, there has been a shift from the earlier tendency to only portray women as victims of crime. From the eighties, gradually one notices a more varied coverage of gender issues, where the activities of women's organizations, including their advocacy and protests, get reported. Achievements of women also get the spotlight. Some newspapers also show a trend towards placing gender issues within a broader socio-political context. These papers carry editorials and edit-page articles on hotly-debated issues like the rights of sex workers or the Women's Reservation Bill.

The eighties and nineties was also a period when the number of women working in the press at various levels rose sharply. Women gained importance not only in numbers, but some of them also rose to important positions in several departments. Our survey among women in the print media show that they are still working primarily at the desk—subediting and feature-writing being their mainstay. Women journalists are usually discouraged from working as reporters and not until the nineties did the news bureaus of most newspapers open their doors to women. Till the end of the nineties, only very few women journalists were in key positions. Most of the journalists interviewed for the survey mentioned that men did not like working for female superiors and this led to much tension. Very few women were found to be employed in the marketing or circulation departments of newspaper houses.

Periodicals and Women's Magazines

A survey of two most widely-read periodicals (one English and one Bengali) published from Kolkata in the period under consideration show interesting results. The weekly English magazine *Sunday* (which folded up a few years ago) demonstrates an unusually high number of women journalists employed in the eighties and nineties. In 1979, women journalists contributed to about half of the issues published during that year. By 1985, women journalists were contributing to 62.5 per cent of the cover stories, of which about 90 per cent were on political issues. In the early nineties, they were contributing to two-thirds of the cover stories and more regularly to the other sections, especially the business columns.

Till the late seventies, most stories concerning women were about violence against them and tended to represent women as helpless victims. Gradually, this gave away to a few serious articles on issues like child marriage, exploitation of the girl child, dowry and the rights of sex workers. However, women were subjects of cover stories usually when there was a political slant or when there was room for sensationalism. Thus, Phoolan Devi, Naina Sahni and Rupan Deol Bajaj became cover stories because salacious headlines and sensational photographs were possible.

In the case of the Bengali periodical *Desh*, during the early part of the period under consideration, there are remarkably few essays on gender issues. Columns targeted at women were full of household tips. Articles on women's issues were full of sarcasm about the women's movement or women's rights. The coverage of the Mexico Conference of Women Journalists, for example, takes delight in the political disagreement among the participants, with the attitude 'see how the women squabble amongst themselves.' Later, a change in this attitude is perhaps reflected in the increase in the number of letters published which were written by women. By the nineties, 50 per cent of the letters published in *Desh* were written by women. It is true that an influential periodical like *Desh* also sponsors long articles by women authors on the construction of gender where a more obviously radical view is taken. But what is interesting is the mix and the allocation of specific roles to women writers, while male authors are expected to cater to a more conventional taste, which constitutes an important part of the literary market.

Three Bengali women's magazine surveyed during the period under consideration show them focussing on women's role in the family and functioning as advisors to 'modern' women on a range of topics like health, family planning, marital discord, home décor, career options and the like. However, the construction of this 'modernity' is firmly within the patriarchal structures of society and urban and upper class in outlook. This 'modernity' may be redefined periodically, for example, in the withdrawal of the section called 'Sahabat' in one of the women's magazines which instructed readers on how to lay the table, table manners etc. Successful women in various walks of life are interviewed and profiled from time to time in these magazines, but the focus is on the woman at home.

In West Bengal, there are also numerous little magazines which accommodate a whole variety of authorship. In contrast to women's magazines, it was found that gender issues have been finding greater importance over the last few years in some little magazines. Many have come up with special issues on women in the nineties, especially focussing on women's writing. A couple of magazines were found which were not entirely devoted to women's issues such as *Khoj*. These magazines debate on topics like human rights and women or give space to marginalized sections of society, like women in tribal communities. But it is noticeable that in these magazines, women authors generally write in non-fictional genres; sometimes they write poetry, but very rarely does one find instances of women fiction-writers.

Electronic Media

The one medium that has changed very drastically over the period under consideration is television. In the seventies, television was still a luxury and not many households could afford it. By the end of the last century, television had changed the way in which households gain access to information and entertainment. The introduction of private satellite channels and the growth of regional language television channels have also contributed significantly to the changed scenario. This has especially affected women as in Bengal, adult women constitute the group that watches the longest hours of television. For many women who were traditionally house-bound and who did not have the means or the opportunity to leave the confines of their home, television brought in a whole new world. At the same time, our survey shows that while television has played a positive role in allowing access to information to otherwise information-poor households, this use of television as a source of news, information and opinion is not the one that women have adapted to. Serials and films remain the overwhelming favourites for women viewers. It is also interesting that these women are more attracted to programmes in Bengali than in any other language.

In terms of programming, there is a rise in the number of programmes aimed at women, which usually, like the 'women's pages' in newspapers, concentrate on cookery and fashion, sometimes also including interviews with 'successful women'. This construction of the 'successful woman' is interesting. The interviews typically bring out the successful combination of the roles of wife, mother and business/professional person. The fact that these women succeeded is interpreted as a reflection of the fact that women can 'make it' if they try hard enough, that there are no 'prejudices' or 'patriarchies' at work; if other women have not 'made it' it is their fault, not the system's or the society's.

In general, the programmes serve to reinforce stereotypes of women's role in society. More recently, there has been a move away from woman as mother to woman as wife and lover. In these serials, women do get some airtime in terms of visibility. However, most serials still typically present the working woman as evil, selfish and insensitive in contrast to the woman who is wifely, that is, sacrificing, sensitive and nurturing the males.

While there are individual attempts at breaking the stereotype and producing more interesting programmes for women, these do not seem to be as popular as the more typical fare. There are a few programmes which take up gender issues but these too are rare interventions in an otherwise bleak scenario. Over the last 10 years or so, there has also been a trend towards producing serials set in the past, which seem to be creating a kind of 'ideal Bengali past' that is pre-capitalist, pre-globalized and pre-modern. Gender roles are very well-defined here. These serials are quite popular and are screened during the day, clearly aimed at non-working women.

That domestic power equations remain unchanged in spite of increased television viewing is clear from the fact that many women mentioned the television set as a source of family conflict. Because programme choices differed widely, there would be tussles over what programmes could be watched. In these tussles, inevitably the women would concede to the male members of the family, and also to the children if there were any.

It is worthwhile to note that the electronic media has thrown up many women in responsible positions in the industry as directors or producers. Studies of the comparative representation of women in Indian and American television channels also reveal that women and men get almost equal time on air in India as in the US. However, this does not translate into a more 'progressive' representation of women. Because of the need to attract large audiences and therefore advertisers, producers prefer to 'play safe' and serve to reinforce social stereotypes rather than attempt to evolve anything new.

Advertisements

The print advertisements in the seventies, eigties and nineties reflect the tremendous rise in consumption-oriented spending and a gradual but significant change towards targeting women as consumers to a large extent. Earlier, the advertisements were almost exclusively addressed to the male as the decision making consumer, even in the case of products like jewellery. Later, we find that advertisements for some products are targeted towards women who are now perceived as decision makers in a few areas. The more contemporary jewellery advertisements, for example, suggest that women can and should buy jewellery for themselves. However, for several products, the impression still is that male members usually make the decisions. So, in advertising for products like electronic equipment, advertisers either show women in secondary roles or they are entirely absent.

In the area of representation, we find that while stereotypes still dominate, there are some changes very consciously worked into the brand image of certain products. Earlier, women were almost always shown as passive or overtly commodified. Male models, too, were always depicted in very 'masculine' postures. In more recent advertisements, we find that women are shown in varied roles. More working women are shown at work and men are shown playing the role of fathers or sons.

More specifically, surveying products manufactured in and aimed at the regional consumers of Bengal, we found that the advertisements were appealing to a notion of 'traditionalism' in which the woman was represented in much more traditional roles than in the advertisements for similar products aimed at national markets or goods produced by multinational firms. Spices is one such product where advertisements would stress the role of the woman as the cook for the entire household. Local jewellery firms stressed on jewellery being given as dowry rather than jewellery being bought for fashion. It seems that there is a relationship between 'regionalism' and 'tradition' in which the emphasis is on the continuation of stereotyped roles as against the more 'modern' or 'global' roles for women. These roles hold true for children too. Girls are shown more in tune with traditions. This is also true for advertisements for wider markets. Products like Iodex, which are shown as relieving pain and are sports-related, inevitably show boys or men, ignoring women or girls almost entirely, unless depicted as part of the caring mother's necessary first-aid kit.

With a lot more sophistication in advertising, representation of women has also become more varied and less obviously objectionable in many cases. Crude eye-catching techniques have been replaced with more subtle ways of using women. Yet the commodification of women continues. There are many advertisements which transform the notion of women's freedom into the freedom to choose between particular brand products. A person's freedom is redefined in these ways so that the woman as citizen gets replaced by the woman as consumer. Advertisements for household consumer products like refrigerators, washing machines, etc., allow more time for the woman to 'be free'. Even soap powders and detergents often make similar claims. In some, it is quite specifically mentioned that the free time is to be used for entertaining the husband once he is home from office.

Music

In the fifties, women artistes were required to show their marriage certificates before they were allowed to sing on the radio. Though we have come a long way from there, many differences still exist in the way in which girls are trained for music compared to boys. A cursory look at the list of releases of various companies does not suggest any gender bias in the number of overall recordings by male and female artists. But on close examination it is obvious that in a field where female students far outnumber male students on the whole, the range of genres in which they train and perform is still very limited.

Girls are trained in music mainly as an additional qualification to enable their families to find the right grooms. Once a girl is married, however, she is expected in most cases to devote time to home-making rather than continue in her training and performance. Most of them, therefore, give up music. Music is still considered a desirable quality in a 'feminine' woman, not as an expression of the woman's creativity. Then there exists a hierarchy of forms, for example, in classical music, *khayal* is considered superior to *thumri* and *kajri*. It is, of course, the latter forms which are associated with women and in which women are mostly trained. In the case of instruments too, women are generally trained to play the *tanpura* or the *violin* or *sitar*. Women *tabla* players or flutists are still rarely found, though towards the end of the last century Bengal has discovered a couple of gifted *tabla* players who are being recognized for their talent.

The new wave of Bangla 'jibonmukhi' songs of the nineties which address contemporary social issues do occasionally deal with women. This wave has thrown up a handful of very talented women composers and singers who compose sing their own songs. But the bulk of the songs are written and sung by men, who echo the frustration of the urban male youth of today. Bengal has a rich tradition of 'ganasangeets'. However, even here the male voice is predominant.

Dance

Two distinct phases can be identified based on a survey of dance reviews in the major newspapers and magazines from the mid-seventies to nineties. The first phase, from 1975–85, shows that the emphasis was clearly on conformity to the classical traditions and on technical skill. Innovations were limited to those within the classical framework. The number of women dancers far outnumbered the male and many women had started their dance schools. However, the position of the male gurus was supreme. Not so well-known male dancers were, on the other hand, looked upon as somewhat deviant. During this time a very important change was taking place, which was a tendency to increasingly relocate dance from the zone of high culture to a zone of cultural democratization. More and more middle and lower middle class women began to learn, practice and create their own performances.

In the next phase, between 1986–2000, there was a sudden spurt in experimentation of all kinds. This led to a wide range of unusual compositions. In the earlier period, an analysis of the records of Rabindra Sadan shows that the most popular performances were the woman-centred dance-dramas of Tagore—*Shyama, Chitrangada and Chandalika*. Later, there were a number of performances where the classical forms and Indian mythology were used to explore contemporary issues. Dancers' Guild, under the guidance of the late Manjushree Chaki Sircar, made a pioneering contribution to exploring a new vocabulary for dance and producing a number of performances centring around the woman. Their production, *Tomari Matir Kanya* (1984), based on Tagores's *Chandalika*, is a particularly significant one.

The number of dance institutes, most of them established by women, offering diploma or special courses affiliated to various boards around the country, proliferated. Interestingly, the number of male dancers also increased during this period. A survey among the male students of Viswa Bharati University's dance department showed the increased possibility of securing teaching jobs as one reason for their choice of taking formal degrees in dance.

Interviews with senior and junior dancers indicated the fact that the social status of women dancers has changed significantly in the last three decades of the twentieth century. Senior dancers recalled how they were looked upon as *baijis* even in the fifties and the sixties and had to fight for social acceptance. In response, some of them, like the noted Kathak dancer Bandana Sen, tried to spiritualize traditional forms and choreographed pieces like *Mirabai* or *Mahajiboner Pathe*. But the senior dancers felt that with dance gaining a lot of respectability these days, young dancers keep performing and teaching dance after marriage and even after having children. Family support is a lot more forthcoming. On the contrary, earlier, dancers serious about pursuing dance as a career would generally choose to remain single.

In the nineties, in Bengali middle class homes, dance was seen as a desirable accomplishment in women. But for most parents and many students dance is not yet a feasible career option. There are very few avenues open for earning,

performers are in general badly paid and to establish a dance school is also difficult. Though running a school is an option that many women have exercised, but that too is not lucrative. There are a few exceptions to these typical cases. In the mid-nineties, a young and talented girl was taken out of her school, with the encouragement of her parents (who are well-off) and teachers, and was given training at home in subjects that helped her develop as a dancer.

Even in changing times, the audiences' attitudes to older women dancers have remained largely unchanged. The general perception that female dancers ought to be young and beautiful while male gurus can continue to be acclaimed as long as they perform well is a serious deterrent to senior women dancers getting the recognition that is due to them.

Radio Programmes

Of all the programmes broadcast by the Kolkata station of All India Radio, *Mahila Mahal* is the most popular programme specially targeted at women. The evolution of *Mahila Mahal* from the seventies to 2000 is interesting and shows certain trends that reflect the changing position of women in society. The timing of the programme is significant—it is broadcast at 1:40 p.m. on Mondays, Wednesdays and Fridays and has remained so from the beginning. Obviously this excludes most women who work, whether urban or rural, white-collar or working class. But over the years, the orientation of this programme has evolved from being pure entertainment for middle class housewives (providing them with recipes and other typical household tips) into an informative programme which tries to address a range of issues relating to socially and economically disadvantaged women. *Mahila Mahal* now focusses on women in unusual professions, highlights development work by NGOs, and hosts discussions on numerous socio-cultural issues. There are of course regular slots on information regarding legal rights of women or health advice. Hand in hand with these changes, some earlier slots continue as part of the programme; for example, 'Ranna Banna Ghar Grihasthali' (The kitchen and the household) or 'Pujar Kenakata' (Puja shopping). Listeners' responses also indicate that more men were calling in or writing in the nineties, which is probably a result of the fact that *Mahila Mahal* is no longer confined to offering only household tips. There were even reports of male listeners calling in to demand that the programme be taken off the air when it had highlighted the work of organizations fighting sexual abuse of women and children or discussed AIDS.

Apart from *Mahila Mahal*, there is another programme called *Sri-Bhavan* exclusively for rural women. This programme invites government officials and experts to speak on subjects like small savings, literacy and family welfare schemes for rural women. Radio FM has also started hosting a programme, *Suchetana* (later renamed *Darpan*) of late. This is meant to be a phone-in talk show hosted by two women on women's issues.

A survey among the women employees of AIR's Kolkata station indicated that there were very few women in decision making positions in the year 2000. The employees attributed this to the recruitment policy in recent years. But the fact that very few women were in sections like news, sports and drama (in the drama section, there was no female staff during the time of the survey) was put down to the fact that women themselves preferred to work with women's programmes or music or youth programmes rather than news or sports. The women employees agreed unanimously that there was no overt discrimination at the workplace. Most of them agreed that when they made suggestions regarding changing the focus of programmes, their suggestions were dealt with sympathetically. A woman who had joined as programme executive in the sports' section, for example, said that during her tenure, she had tried to focus equally on women's sports, and had tried to include more female commentators and sports journalists. She did not face any problems while trying to implement these changes. But since her transfer to another department, these innovations have been discontinued. Most of the women employees said that they had introduced new concepts in the women's, youth and FM programmes. However, many of them said that there was a great demand for programmes on beauty and cookery and that sometimes men would write objecting to radical programmes on womens' issues.

Educational Material

A survey of some of the school and college texts to determine the depiction and representation of women in textbooks was undertaken and the results are not in the least encouraging. The findings point out that history texts in school, in general, give the impression that women have had very little or no role to play in the history of India; the sums in the maths textbooks usually centre around men or boys or project women or girls in gender stereotypes; the literature texts, both Bengali and English, hardly include writings by women or pieces which focus on issues concerning women. At the college level, the Bengali Honours syllabus of Calcutta University has no mention of any women writers in the paper on the history of Bengali literature. The English Honours syllabus of the same university includes only 2 women poets among the 18 selected. None of the essays selected in any of the papers are written by women or focus on women's issues.

Interviews with teachers and academics teaching in various schools, colleges and universities of the state point to the fact that a radical syllabus revision is overdue. The teachers feel that the style and content of textbooks is severely dictated by the demands of the syllabus. As the syllabus does not mention women separately, the textbooks reflect this omission, though 60–70 per cent school textbooks are written by women. The teachers felt that most students are not aware of the role of women in history or society, because they are not encouraged to think beyond the confines of the syllabus. Though a few teachers said that in recent years some texts may have changed, but the orientation of the syllabus is far from being free of gender stereotypes. Academics teaching in colleges also felt that framers of the syllabi and writers of textbooks are not conscious of gender bias or omission of women writers. All the secondary material that the students consult are also mostly written by male authors and students are hardly conscious of the gender bias of syllabi.

An interview with the secretary of the Board of Primary Education, Shri Ujjal Kumar Bose, revealed that syllabus revisions were underway keeping in mind four important areas: illustrations are being revised and care is being taken to show girls in active roles; in all textbooks in Bengali the word '*shikshak*' (mlae teacher) is being replaced by '*shikshika* (female teacher)/*shikshak*'. Then, care is being taken to introduce non-Hindu names of characters alongside Hindu names and the content of the selections is being revised to prevent the current excessive focus on boys. For example, mathematics textbook writers are being asked to avoid examples that reinforce gender stereotypes—for example, sums will no longer say that the same work is done in two days by a man and five days by a woman.

However, the setting up of Centres of Women's Studies at the university level and introduction of special papers on women's issues in some departments at the postgraduate level has led to a greater emphasis on the anthologization and publication of educational materials addressing gender issues. The School of Women's Studies, Jadavpur University, has also produced audiovisual materials on issues like dowry and the PNDT Act. Some undergraduate colleges are now introducing extramural courses on subjects like 'women and law'. This is also generating some new educational materials.

Visual Arts

The case of visual arts is particularly interesting as traditionally drawing and painting has always been pigeonholed as 'feminine' skills whereas the 'artist' is always characteristically male. Like music, painting is seen as a desirable accomplishment in 'refined' young ladies, yet it is not supposed to be a serious profession for women to pursue. Unlike music, which has opened up for women artists, the field of visual arts has still largely remained a male preserve. The Table 6.3 illustrates the break-up of male and female enrolement in the Government Art College, Calcutta, where the percentage of female students has remained very low over the last 20 years.

The table makes it quite clear that even in the subjects chosen by students there is a definite pattern. Certain specializations is regarded as 'masculine', of which sculpture and wood are the most unsuitable for women, while textile has attracted a number of female students. Commercial or graphic art, which has more immediate career prospects, has also not been a popular choice for female students.

The Kala Bhavan of Viswa Bharati University consciously tries to maintain a more balanced gender-ratio, and thus, a larger percentage of the students there are female. However, this is true for the undergraduate course only, and not for some of the other courses like the Advanced Diploma for the postgraduates. Interestingly, there is no female faculty member at present in Kala Bhavan and only a few women have taught since the inception of the department.

There is also a huge difference in the gender-ratio of practising artists in the public sphere evident from the data collected from some of the major art galleries of Kolkata. Tables 6.4 and 6.5 record the participation of male and female artists in exhibitions held in the Academy of Fine Arts and Birla Academy of Art and Culture from 1975 to 1999. Figures for some years were not available due to loss of records.

What is interesting in these figures is that the participation of female artists has not grown in the period under scrutiny. This contradicts the findings in many of the other cultural spheres and is perhaps connected with the idea that women train in the arts as a hobby and not as a profession. Besides, when women artists are discussed in press reviews, most often the discussion centres around whether they are stylistically 'feminine' or not. The reviewers tend to evaluate women artists as a distinct category. There are almost no reviews of women sculptors.

A couple of issues that emerged from an interview-based survey of women artists are their problems of having to balance household and family responsibilities with creative work as well as constraints on physical space to follow their vocation. Kamala Ray Choudhury, one of the pioneers of the modernist art movement in Bengal, spoke of the studio that she and another fellow artist created to enable any artist, women or men, constricted by space, to paint. The survey shows that quite a number of trained artists, who are middle-aged or elderly, have chosen not to continue art as a profession and are housewives. Several extremely talented artists gave up their careers once they were married and became mothers. Some of them

Table 6.3
Enrolment in the Government Art College, Calcutta (1981–2000)

Academic year	Total students	Female students	Indian style	Western style	Commercial	Sculpture	Textile	Wood	Ceramic
1981–82	89	7	3	3	–	1	–	–	–
1982–83	61	5	2	2	–	–	1	–	–
1983–84	51	7	3	–	2	–	2	–	–
1984–85	69	11	2	1	4	–	3	1	–
1985–86	69	9	3	2	1	–	3	–	–
1986–87	63	9	4	1	–	–	3	–	–
1987–88	63	7	1	–	2	–	3	–	–
1988–89	75	7	1	2	2	1	1	–	1
1989–90	72	11	4	1	1	–	3	–	2
1990–91	73	12	3	2	1	–	4	1	3
1991–92	80	16	2	2	3	–	5	–	1
1992–93	72	11	2	3	2	1	2	–	1
1993–94	77	15	5	1	1	–	6	–	1
1994–95	27	3	–	1	–	–	1	–	2
1995–96	67	13	2	1	–	–	5	–	2
1996–97	48	7	1	–	–	–	3	–	1
1997–98	50	9	3	–	–	–	4	–	3
1998–99	88	15	4	4	1	–	3	–	3
1999–2000	88	24	6	5	1	1	7	–	–

Table 6.4
Record of Exhibitions Held at the Academy of Fine Arts (1975–99)

Year	Total number of participating artists	Number of female artists
1975	223	30
1976	286	34
1977	–	–
1978	185	18
1979	231	23
1980	217	28
1981	262	35
1982	231	20
1983	209	32
1984	172	21
1985	227	25
1986	265	37
1987	–	–
1988	–	–
1989	211	26
1990	249	33
1991	204	28
1992	175	21
1993	–	–
1994	–	–
1995	150	18
1996	116	10
1997	–	–
1998	130	25
1999	152	22

Table 6.5
Record of Exhibitions Held at the Birla Academy (1975–99)

Year	Total number of participating artists	Number of female artists
1975	133	22
1976	–	–
1977	150	18
1978	175	29
1979	–	–
1980	199	31
1981	172	32
1982	181	31
1983	165	23
1984	164	24
1985	145	27
1986	–	–
1987	–	–
1988	128	15
1989	156	27
1990	228	32
1991	176	25
1992	50	9
1993	209	26
1994	167	25
1995	185	21
1996	214	25
1997	217	30
1998	266	45
1999	238	23

opted as teachers. Those who try to combine the roles of home-maker and artist usually have very little time of their own to pursue art. They do not have regular incomes from selling their art and are dependant on their spouses financially.

Barring one or two, almost all the artists said that they had not faced gender discrimination at home or in the professional arena. Among the younger artists, most have chosen art as a career but they are not financially independent either. Their output and income from selling art is irregular and here again they depend on their spouses who have regular jobs. Most of them said that they had very supportive families and had never faced any opposition from in-laws. Majority of the artists, young or old, said that they were unaware of any 'feminine' quality in their work. They were also unsure of what critics meant by such qualities.

Conclusion

This report has tried to indicate some of the changes that have taken place in the cultural life of West Bengal that have bearings on the status of women. But of course there are a few serious gaps. For instance, we were unable to focus on a few publishing houses in the state which are run by women or where women have an important role to play. In these houses, there is a distinct emphasis on publishing women's writings and writings on women's issues. Another area which has remained unaddressed in this report is the impact of literacy on reading habits of women. In theatre, we could only study the group theatre scenario of Kolkata and had to leave out the popular *jatra* tradition. In dance and visual arts, our survey was limited to artists who have made these their profession. In some areas where no data could be obtained from official sources, we had to do with whatever secondary data was available to us. Our study of radio broadcasting is one such area.

On the other hand, in our study of films, advertisements, the print and the electronic media, where more data was available to us, there have been such rapid changes between the time we collected the data and wrote the report that many new elements have been left out. As our introduction emphasizes, culture does not merely mean literature, music, dance, films or visual arts, but it manifests itself in ways of life, ways of thinking, habits and customs. It is obvious that these aspects have been left largely untouched in our survey.

In spite of these gaps, our general impression is that women artists have increased both in number and in importance. So far as the content of the artistic product is concerned, women's issues have gained a greater visibility. Several women have made interesting experiments with forms in literature, theatre, films and the visual arts. But gender stereotypes still persist everywhere, ranging from the media to school textbooks.

In our study of readership/audience, we have found a growing interest in women's issues. On the whole, we can say that in the last 30 years women of West Bengal have become culturally more articulate than before. Our cultural life is witnessing radical changes as a result of globalization. Identity politics—religious, ethnic and linguistic—is on the rise. These are shaking up familiar and traditional cultural norms. Women both as producers and consumers of culture have a growing awareness of this.

Law and Violence against Women — CHAPTER 7

Manjari Gupta and Ratnabali Chattopadhyay

Historical Perspective

The acceptance of gender equality in the Constitution of independent India provided women with a basis for a new identity, as full citizens of the republic and a source of their rights to equality, dignity and justice in other spheres of life. But long before such constitutional guarantee came through, the struggle for legal reforms has always been central to organized efforts in improving women's status in India. The social reformers of the nineteenth century, women in the independence movement and women in the contemporary women's movement turned to law as a vehicle for improving women's social, economic, political and cultural status, though the focus and objective of legal reform varied in important ways in the three successive phases.[1]

Nineteenth century reformers like Raja Rammohan Roy campaigned for the abolition of Sati, Iswar Chandra Vidyasagar fought for widow remarriage and the issue of child marriage was taken up in the latter half of the century by Behram Malabari and Ranade. These reformers sought protective forms of legislation in trying to eliminate evil customs and practices perpetrated on women. In the latter part of the century, women came to the forefront and campaigned mainly for their education and public participation. Women's organizations at the all-India level began emerging in the early part of the twentieth century and their agenda included advocacy of women's suffrage, the issue of child marriage and campaign for reforming the personal laws.

The Hindu personal law underwent a major reform with the passing of the Child Marriage Restraint Act in 1928 and since the early thirties, women's organizations like AIWC and Women's Indian Association began pressing for a Hindu Code that would remove all legal disabilities of women in marriage and inheritance. The Hindu Code Bill, defeated in the Indian Legislative Assembly in 1945, was finally passed as late as 1955, when four separate pieces of legislation were enacted that significantly improved the legal status of women under the Hindu personal law. Meanwhile, demands for equal rights and political representation by women, which also gained momentum in the thirties, found a valediction in the Fundamental Rights of the Constitution drafted by the Constituent Assembly (1946).

While Indian women achieved formal political and economic equality, their role in the private sphere was left fundamentally unchallenged until the autonomous women's movement of the late seventies and eighties. This phase saw nation-wide campaigns to reform rape and dowry laws, implement a uniform civil code, amend the legislation prohibiting sati, ban sex-determination tests and seek amendments to sexual assault laws. In 1983, the rape law was finally amended to include the recognition of custodial rape in which consent was not relevant and stipulated mandatory minimum sentences for rape. The Dowry Prohibition Act was amended in the following year enhancing punishment and fine. Shortly afterwards, the Shah Bano (Muslim Women's Act, 1986) and the Roop Kanwar (Commission of Sati Prevention Act, 1988) controversies challenged issues of family, religion, tradition and gender. These campaigns and the earlier ones against dowry and female sex-selections

have been important in the struggle over the social and cultural meaning of violence against women.... These issues have been brought into the public arena.... Legal provisions

---

[1] Kapur, Ratna and Brenda Cossman, *Subversive Sites: Feminist Engagements with Law in India.* Sage Publications, New Delhi, 1996.

may not have been able to stem the violence ... but legal discourse has been central in the very naming of these issues as social practices which need to be eliminated.[2]

The nineties witnessed the historic passing of the 73rd and 74th Amendments to the Constitution (1993) conferring constitutional status on local self-government bodies as integral parts of India's democratic governance structure and mandating one-third reservation for women in all these bodies, with in-built quotas for scheduled caste and scheduled tribe women. These two, along with the pending 81st Amendment Bill (1996) seeking to reserve one-third seats for women (including within the two already reserved categories for scheduled castes and scheduled tribes), are bound to have long-term implications on the future of India's democracy and governance.

International Covenants and Women's Rights

Internationally too, certain important covenants pertaining to women's rights were ratified during the International Women's Decade. The most significant of these is the Convention on the Elimination of all Forms of Discrimination Against Women (CEDAW), which was adopted by the United Nations in 1979 and became a legally binding agreement in 1981. Prior to the CEDAW, the International Covenant of Economic, Social and Cultural Rights (1966) recognized the right of every individual to just and favourable conditions, which included fair wages and equal remuneration for work of equal value without distinction of any kind. It laid stress on children and young person's need for protection from economic and social exploitation and urged the states to set age limits below which the paid employment of child labour should be prohibited and punishable by law.

CEDAW laid down the condition that continuation of discrimination against women, denying or limiting their equal rights with men is fundamentally unjust and constitutes an offence against human dignity. Therefore, all appropriate measures should be taken to abolish existing laws, customs, regulations and practices which are discriminatory against women and to establish adequate legal protection for equality between men and women. CEDAW emphasized equal remuneration for equal work and working conditions for women not inferior to those enjoyed by men. The necessity of special protection to working mothers before and after child birth was underscored and particular stress was laid on maternity benefits, paid leave and special benefits for children of working women. Provisions

were included to ensure protection and assistance for all children and young persons without any discrimination being made for reasons of parentage or otherwise. The Convention went into details about providing legal protection to children born in or out of lawful wedlock and of children born after dissolution of marriage etc. The Convention called upon the state to take appropriate measures to eliminate discrimination against women in political and public life and to make it possible for women to participate in the formation of government policy and the implementation thereof and to hold public office and perform functions at all levels of the government. CEDAW deliberated on the problems of rural women and asked the state to ensure their access to all agricultural credit and loans, marketing facilities, appropriate technology and equal treatment in land and agrarian reforms as well as in land settlement schemes. It also urged formation of self-help groups and co-operatives in order to obtain equal access to economic opportunities through employment. CEDAW was ratified by 155 countries including India in 1993.

Social Justice, Human Rights and Legal Provisions in India

The concept of 'social justice', which the Constitution of India engrafted, consists of diverse principles that are essential for the orderly growth and development of the personality of all citizens. It is thus an integral part of justice in the generic sense. Justice is the genus and social justice is one of the species. Social justice is a dynamic device to mitigate the sufferings of the poor, weak, dalits, tribals and deprived sections of the society. The concept acknowledges the right of every human being to live with dignity.

Social justice is not a simple or single idea of society but is an essential part of complex social changes to relieve the poor, to ward off distress and to make their lives livable for the greater good of society at large. Social justice and equality are complementary to each other. In accordance with this concept of social justice, Section 376 of the Indian Penal Code declares that socio-economic status, prestige, race, caste or creed of the accused or the victim are irrelevant considerations in the sentencing policy.

Human rights are derived from the dignity and worth inherent in human beings. Human rights as fundamental freedoms have been reiterated in the Universal Declaration of Human Rights. Democracy, development and respect for human rights and fundamental freedom are interdependent and have mutual reinforcement. Human rights for women including

[2] Ibid.

Table 7.1
Laws Relating to Women Enacted since 1947

Family laws	Laws relating to termination of pregnancy	Laws relating to violence against women	Laws relating to property	Laws for working women	Laws for empowerment	Procedural laws
Special Marriages Act (1954)	Medical Termination of Pregnancy Act (1971)	Section 304B and 498A of the Indian Penal Code	West Bengal Land Reforms Act (1955)	Factories Act (1948)	Constitution (73rd) Amendment Act (1992)	The Family Courts Act (1984)
Hindu Adoption and Maintenance Act (1956)	Pre-natal Diagnostic Techniques (Prevention and Misuse) Act (1994)	Section 376A, 376B, 376C, 376D of the Indian Penal Code	West Bengal Land Reforms Manual	Mines Act	Constitution (74th) Amendment Act (1993)	The Legal Aid Services Authority Act (1987)
Dowry Prohibition Act (1961) (amended in 1984, 1986)		Section 113A, 114A of the Indian Evidence Act		Plantation Labour Act (1951)	West Bengal Panchayat Amendment Act (1993)	The West Bengal State Commission for Women Act (1992)
Section 125–128 of the Criminal Procedure Code 1973				Maternity Benefit Act (1961)	West Bengal Municipal Election Act (1994)	
Child Marriage Restraint (Amendment) Act (1978)				Equal Remuneration Act (1976)		
Muslim Women (Protection of Rights After Divorce) Act (1986)						
Parsi Marriage (Amendment) Act (1988)						
Indian Divorce (Amendment) Act 2001						

girl children are, therefore, an inalienable, integral and individual part of the universal human rights. Equal participation by women in political, social, economic and cultural fields are concomitants for their natural development, social and family stability and for the country's cultural, social and economic growth. All forms of discrimination on grounds of gender are violative of fundamental freedoms and human rights.

There are aspects to the legal provisions in the Indian Constitution meant to further gender equality. The laws provide certain directions which need to be followed and the violation of which has penal consequences. Apart from this the other important aspect of these laws is to create social awareness. Laws want to involve administration as well as various social welfare organizations including women's organizations to make social justice not a constitutional clap-trap but a fighting faith which enlivens legislative text with militant meaning.

A recent judgement of the Supreme Court of India must be mentioned in this context. The sexual harassment guidelines promulgated by the Supreme Court in August 1997 aims at preventing violation of women's rights and freedom and was issued in response to a writ petition filed by women's organizations for the enforcement of fundamental rights of working women. This landmark judgement brings sexual harassment within the purview of human rights' violation and has thereby expanded the arena of women's human rights. It has emphasized that the guidelines are to be treated as law under Article 141 of the Constitution. The judgement also includes duty of the employer or other responsible persons in workplaces and other institutions.[3]

Legal Reforms in West Bengal

Certain significant legislations came into force in West Bengal in the period under discussion to empower women and protect their human rights. Three of these measures are discussed here.

[3] Mukherjee, Mukul, *Human Rights and Gender Issues*. Institute of Social Sciences, New Delhi, 2003.

Establishment of Family Court

The Family Court Act, 1984, was enacted with a view to promote conciliation in and secure speedy settlement of disputes relating to marriage and family affairs and for matters connected therewith. According to this Act, a family court is to be established for every area in the state comprising a city or town, where the population exceeds one million, and also in other areas as it may deem necessary.

The Kolkata Family Court was established in September 1994. This court looks into cases of nullity of marriage, validity of marriage, reinstitution of conjugal rights, dissolution of marriage, maintenance and guardianship and custody of minors. According to the Family Court Act, no other court can exercise jurisdiction regarding the above matters where there is a family court in existence. If a husband or wife or both happen to reside within the 14 police stations under Kolkata Police or have been married within the limits of the said police stations, they are eligible to apply to the Kolkata Family Court for settlement. The Court was set up with one sitting judge and 36 counsellors. The counsellors included 14 members of different voluntary organizations, with the approval of the Calcutta High Court.

According to Shipra Raha and Ranju Ghosh, counsellors of the Kolkata Family Court, cases pending for 10 to 20 years have been settled within six months of the establishment of this court. Between 1995–96, 734 out of 1,293 cases filed for settlement of marital discord had been resolved and at least 356 out of 515 cases pertaining to guardianship of children were settled. Women have received a one-time maintenance in cases of divorce ranging from Rs 70,000 to Rs 100,000 and it has also been possible to retrieve their *streedhan* on several occasions. The Court has also found a solution to sensitive cases pertaining to custody and maintenance of children of separated couples. Reconciliation has been possible in a number of instances. The experience of these few years since 1994 has made both the women's organizations and the judiciary realize the importance of establishing more such courts in West Bengal.

Legal Aid

Pursuant to Article 39A (equal justice and free legal aid), a Legal Aid and Advice Scheme was framed in 1980 by the Government of West Bengal. Under this scheme, a State Legal Aid and Advisory Board, and several District Legal Aid and Advisory Boards were formed.

Legal aid panels of advocates were formed in the high court and district courts so that people of low income groups could get free legal aid. Persons entitled to free legal services include members of scheduled castes/scheduled tribes, victims of trafficking, beggers, women or children and mentally ill or otherwise disabled persons. But it was found through discussions

that for the purpose of equal legal rights or equal protection of law, only free legal aid was not enough, the disadvantaged groups, particularly women, had to be made aware of their legal rights. Steps had to be taken for deciding disputes out of courts so that delay would not stand in the way of getting justice. It was decided that a discourse would be generated for creating legal awareness amongst people up to the village level. This would make it easier for them to get justice. Lok Adalats were organized in the districts and legal aid centres for women were also opened by different women's organizations and the State Social Welfare Advisory Board. The Legal Service Authorities Act, 1987, was enacted with a view to provide free and competent legal services to the weaker sections of the society and to organize Lok Adalats. Under the Act, there is now a State Legal Services Authority which is empowered to provide legal service to eligible persons, conduct Lok Adalats, undertake preventive and strategic legal aid programmes and the like. It also coordinates with other governmental and non-governmental voluntary organizations, universities and others engaged in providing legal aid to the poor.

West Bengal Commission for Women

The West Bengal Commission for Women was established in 1992. Its functions and duties inter *alia* are to review the existing provisions of the Constitution and other laws affecting women and recommend amendments to them as also suggest remedial legislative measures to meet any lacunae, inadequacies or shortcomings in such legislation, and evaluate the progress of advancement of women in the state. Besides, the Commission is also duty-bound to call for special studies or investigations into specific problems or situations arising out of discrimination and atrocities against women and identify the constraints so as to recommend strategies for their removal. It is supposed to visit jails, destitute girls' home, women's institutions or other places where women are kept as prisoners or otherwise and take up with the concerned authorities such matters for remedial action as may be necessary. For the above purpose, the Commission has been given powers of a civil court under CrPC in respect of summoning and enforcing attendance of any person from any part of India, examining him/her on death, requiring the discovery and production of any document, and receiving evidence on affidavits.

Since 1992, the Commission, amongst other things, has held legal literacy workshops in a number of districts with panchayat members, women's organizations and district administrative officers. It also runs a pre-litigation counselling centre and holds meetings with police personnel and NGOs. Several sensitization programmes in various police camps and police training centres have also been organized. In some districts, pre-litigation centres or counselling centres have been opened by the police outside the precincts of police stations. In Nadia, a pre-litigation centre was opened by the Chakdaha Police Station to be followed by several others in the same districts. In Kolkata, there is a pre-litigation centre in Lalbazar and one at Bhabani Bhavan in Alipore. Besides, there is a women's grievance committee headed by the district magistrate in each district. Thus there is an endeavour to redress women's grievances at all levels.

Violence against Women: Concept and Definition

Throughout written history, violence has been considered to be a part of girls' and women's lived experience, yet there is no single agreed definition of violence against women. Till the mid-seventies, a range of concepts were used and these varied according to culture and class. Since the mid-seventies, pro-women authors, researchers and activists have put the issue of gender violence on local, national and international agendas. This also led to the United Nation's adopting CEDAW in 1979.

Originally, CEDAW did not make explicit reference to violence against women. This hindered the application of a human rights' perspective to the issue and prompted the formation of a global coalition of 900 women's organizations, which successfully lobbied for recognition of gender violence as a fundamental violation of women's human rights. At the 1993 UN World Conference on Human Rights, gender violence was defined as violence which jeopardizes fundamental rights, individual freedom and women's physical integrity. Articles 1 and 2 of the declaration on the elimination of violence against women expanded this further to include a number of details. The broader sub-sections like the one on domestic violence included physical, sexual and psychological violence occurring within the family. It included certain general terms, like battering, along with specific cultural forms of abusing women, like dowry harassment and bride-burning, found mainly in India, Pakistan and Bangladesh. Physical and psychological violence occurring within the community covered rape, sexual abuse as well as sexual harassment at work, in educational institutions, and also in places like hospitals and lawyers' chambers. These broke the boundaries of public and private spaces where crimes against women were recorded. Trafficking in women and forced prostitution were specially mentioned in this document.

Table 7.2
Types of Violence against Women

Phase	Type of Violence
Pre-birth	Sex-selective abortion; effects of battering during pregnancy on birth outcomes
Infancy	Female infanticide; physical, sexual and psychological abuse
Girlhood	Child marriage; female genital mutilation; physical, sexual, psychological abuse; incest; child prostitution and pornography
Adolescence and adulthood	Dating and courtship violence (e.g., acid throwing and date rape); economically coerced sex (e.g., school girls having sex with 'sugar daddies' in return for school fees); incest; sexual abuse in the workplace; rape; sexual harassment; forced prostitution and pornography; trafficking in women; partner violence; marital rape; dowry abuse and murders; partner homicide; psychological abuse; abuse of women with disabilities; forced pregnancy
Elderly	Forced 'suicide' or homicide of widows for economic reasons; sexual, physical and psychological abuse

Source: WHO Violence against Women Information Pack from Mukhopadhyay, Ishita (ed.), *Violence against Women: A Popular Intervention.* Vyas Prakashan, Calcutta, 2002.

An important aspect of the UN document was to stress on the responsibilities of the state not only to punish the perpetrators of crimes against women but to ensure that the victims were protected and rehabilitated. A UN special rapporteur on 'Violence against Women, its Causes and Consequences' was appointed in 1994 to document and analyse the causes and results of violence inflicted on women at a global level.[4] The Beijing Plan of Action from the Fourth UN World Conference on Women especially demanded that governments of all countries take up integrated measures to prevent and eliminate crimes against women. In addition, some regions have developed international contacts to put pressure on their respective governments to bring about reforms and rethink their policies about women. All forms of sexual assault are under-reported. Either the victims themselves do not confide in those whom they are supposed to report to or the police do not record these as crimes. Official records are therefore never really available to policy makers to formulate designs of intervention at national and international levels.

Violence has profound effects on women throughout their lives and can be divided into phases. In developing countries like India, violence is recorded even before birth in the form of sex-selective abortions and killing of just-born females by parents desperate for a son. It continues throughout adolescence as girls are more likely to be raped than their brothers.

---

[4] Kelly Liz, *Violence against Women* (A briefing document on international issues and responses). The British Council Gender Team, UK, 1999.

In some cases, women and girls have been forced to marry their attackers or may be imprisoned accused of committing a criminal act. When women become pregnant before marriage, grow old or suffer from mental or physical disabilities, they may be ostracized by the community they belong to. Women who are displaced, imprisoned or isolated in any way become prone to more attacks than others. During armed conflict, assaults on women escalate including those committed by both the enemy and indigenous armies. These are general assumptions based on information received at the global level.

As discussed in the introduction to this chapter, the seventies were marked in India by a strong women's movement launched to protest against the violation of constitutional rights. It was triggered off by successive reports of rape and rising tolls of dowry deaths all over the country. It proved that rape could not be defined as a personal and biological desire of a man for a woman. It had to be placed in the context of social, economic and political tensions operating in the country. Laws too reflected the ideological beliefs of the perpetrators who were mostly men. These laws, therefore, needed to be changed and the contemporary women's movement galvanized towards bringing about amendments to such laws. A major women's conference was organized in Patna in February 1988 by a wide coalition of women's groups ranging from those who called themselves 'autonomous feminist' to women's organizations connected with radical mass movements. One of the major issues was violence against women. The deliberations pinpointed the state as the major support for and source of violence. It also asserted the autonomy of violence as a factor behind economic exploitation.

Though the Indian Constitution in theory upholds the right to equality before law of all its citizens and prohibits discrimination on the grounds of religion, race, caste and sex, it is clear from the discussions which follow that the actual situation does not reflect this.

Violence against Women in West Bengal

In trying to get empirical evidence for the way women are harassed and tortured, we had to depend mainly on crime records provided by the police and the National Crime Records Bureau (NCRB). Important sources of the study have been the reports and research works by scholars and activists who have worked in related areas. According to NCRB data,[5] the proportion of IPC crimes committed against women towards total IPC crimes increased 7.2 per cent during 2000 at the all-India level from 7.0 per cent in 1999 and 6.7 per cent in 1998. Rape cases registered a 6.6 per cent increase from 1999 to 2000 and cases of dowry deaths registered a 4.4 per cent increase in the same period. Torture cases rose by 4.5 per cent from 1999–2000. As far as crimes against women in cities are concerned, 23 mega cities shared 11.9 per cent of such cases reported at the national level in 2000—Chennai shared 24.0 per cent of these cases followed by Delhi (12.7 per cent).

In an overview of gender-based violence in West Bengal, Anuradha Talwar, an activist, writes,

A report placed by the Home Minister in the state Assembly showed that though there has been a decline in crimes on the whole in West Bengal, crimes against women have increased from 3,937 in 1990 to 7,489 in 1998.... The district-wise data of crimes reported against women in West Bengal show that South 24 Parganas has the highest percentage of crimes against women at 938 for the year 1999 [see Table 7.3] and is much ahead of the other districts. In fact 70 per cent of the crimes against women occur in the south Bengal districts of North and South 24 Parganas, Medinipur, Barddhaman, Hoogli, Haora and Nadia, along with Kolkata. The northern and western parts of the state, on the other hand, show smaller incidence of crimes against women.[6]

Table 7.3
Ranking of Districts According to Incidence of Crimes against Women in 1999

District	Incidence of crimes
24 Parganas (S)	938
24 Parganas (N)	772
Medinipur	734
Bardhaman	566
Hoogli	528
Kolkata	509
Nadia	499
Murshidabad	363
Jalpaiguri	270
Koch Bihar	265
Birbhum	256
Haora	213
Uttar Dinajpur	200
Maldah	188
Dakshin Dinajpur	171
Bankura	170
Purulia	149
Darjeeling	86

Source: *Crime in India 1999.* NCRB, New Delhi, 1999.

---

[5] *Crime in India 2000.* NCRB, New Delhi, 2000.
[6] Talwar, Anuradha, 'Gender Based Violence in West Bengal', in *Support Services to Counter Violence against Women in West Bengal: A Resource Directory.* Sanhita, Kolkata, 2002.

Table 7.4 covers crimes against women in West Bengal excluding Kolkata from 1995 to 2000 and Table 7.5 covers such crimes reported in Kolkata between 1997 and 2000. Table 7.4 demonstrates that cases registered under the head 'cruelty by husband and other relatives' rose steadily from 3,208 in 1995 to 3,829 in 2000 in the state barring Kolkata. Similarly, cases under 'torture on housewives' rose from 134 in 1997 to 196 in 2000 in Kolkata. It is noticeable that cases of caste-based rape are significantly less in West Bengal that in other states, but on the whole rape cases rose sharply from 733 in 1995 to 826 in 1996, then dipped to 730 in 1998 to climb to 779 in 2000 in the state. In the state capital, rape cases registered were 28 in 1997 and stood at 35 in 2000. Cases of molestation in Kolkata were 119 in 1997 and having gone up to 199 in 1999, came down to 152 in 2000. Molestation cases in West Bengal excluding Kolkata, too, followed a similar pattern, recording 1,174 in 1995 and coming down gradually to 905 in 2000.

Table 7.4
Crimes against Women in West Bengal (Excluding Kolkata)

Crime heads	No. of cases registered					
	1995	1996	1997	1998	1999	2000
Dowry murder	5	3	16	8	6	9
Dowry deaths	80	69	241	239	252	269
Bride murder	148	149	145	156	131	135
Death other than dowry deaths	1,249	1,196	1,030	1,027	1,080	957
Cruelty by husband and other relatives	3,208	3,288	3,594	3,535	3,618	3,829
Kidnapping of women and girls	729	699	788	700	711	701
Rape	733	826	796	730	795	779
Molestation of women	1,174	1,117	1,158	1,076	1,001	905
Eve-teasing	13	11	10	5	5	9

Source: The Additional Director General of Police, State Crime Records Bureau, Kolkata.

Table 7.5
Crimes against Women in Kolkata

Heads of crime	1997	1998	1999	2000
Rape	28	27	24	35
Dowry death (U/S. 304B IPC)	6	10	5	15
Abetment of women to commit suicide (U/S. 306 IPC)	27	26	31	25
Torture on housewives (U/S. 498A IPC)	134	169	159	196
Molestation (U/S. 354 IPC)	119	167	199	152
Eve-teasing (U/S. 294 IPC/509 IPC)	53	22	28	46

Source: Crime Record Section, Detective Department, Kolkata Police.

[7] Talwar, *Gender Based Violence.*

The share of dowry death cases reported in the cities was 7.3 per cent of the total such cases reported in the country in 2000. The share of Delhi was highest (19.9 per cent) in this category. Kolkata reported a 200 per cent increase in such cases from 1999 to 2000.

Dowry Harassment and Death

Records show that (in West Bengal excluding Kolkata) dowry murder increased from 5 in 1995 to 16 in 1997 and though it dipped to 9 in 2000 (see Chart 7.1), dowry deaths went up from 80 in 1995 to 269 in 2000 (see Chart 7.2), all the while showing a steady rise in the rate of the crime. Registered cases of dowry death in Kolkata rose from 9 in 1995 to 15 in 2000 (see Chart 7.3). 'In 1999–2000, the vidhan sabha's Estimates Committee for Police Matters reported that in the preceding eight years, reports of dowry deaths and cruelty by husband and relatives had increased a great deal, especially in the village areas. The Committee felt that this was a result of greater awareness of rights among women.'[7]

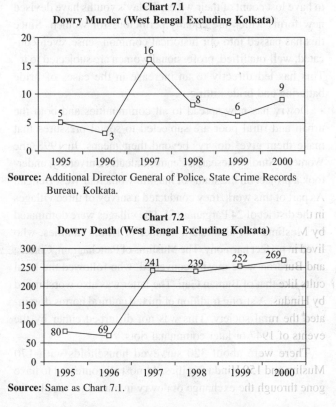

Chart 7.1
Dowry Murder (West Bengal Excluding Kolkata)

Source: Additional Director General of Police, State Crime Records Bureau, Kolkata.

Chart 7.2
Dowry Death (West Bengal Excluding Kolkata)

Source: Same as Chart 7.1.

Together, the dowry related cases of suicide and homicide show an alarming rise in the violence women face in their own homes. Unfortunately, though more and more cases of

Chart 7.3
Dowry Death (Kolkata)

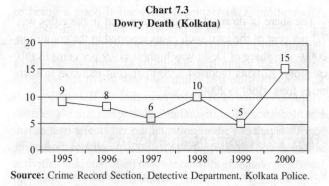

Source: Crime Record Section, Detective Department, Kolkata Police.

dowry harassment and death are continuing, there seems to be a strange apathy among people who have now taken it for granted that this is in-built into the customs of marriage of all communities. Among the middle classes, the increased desire of young men for recognition of their 'worth' have made matters more complex, which has resulted in the desire for hypergamy getting further entrenched among the educated and affluent families. The new educated youths have dispensed with the older forms of hypergamy prevalent in nineteenth century Bengal when marriage had become a lucrative source of income for Kulin Brahman males and they were supposed to have lost count of their wives. Today's youths have devised new forms which are equally pernicious for women. Since this has passed into our historical common sense, even educated, well-qualified, professional women are subjected to it.[8] This has led directly to an increase in the cases of bride battering and bride killing.

Dowry has now spread to all communities and both the urban and rural poor are subjected to social pressures that make them give 'dowry' beyond their means. In 1998, the Women's Studies Research Centre, Calcutta University, undertook a project on the status of muslim women in West Bengal. As part of this work, they conducted a survey of three villages in the district of 24 Parganas (S). The villages were dominated by Muslims, but also had a number of Hindu families, who lived in perfect harmony. The Muslims of Panchagram, Chanda and Burdron were mostly converted, who followed the local cults like that of Baman Gaji. The latter was also worshipped by Hindus. A strong tradition of mixed cultural norms dominated the rural society. This was not disturbed either by the events of 1947 or later communal riots.

There were about 320 surveyed households with 170 Muslim and 150 Hindu families. Almost all confessed to have gone through the exchange of dowry in marriage, whether in cash or kind and sometimes both. This is considered to be a big change in attitude within the community. Elderly women (above the age of 70) said that they had never heard of groom's price in their youth. Yet they also confessed to accepting it as a custom and felt there was no way of combating it. Acknowledging the consequences of such an evil custom they were willing to participate in it in order to give their daughters a better chance in life.

An interesting development emerges when dowry is compared to *mehr*. While dowry is accepted as price for the groom, *mehr* is still considered marriage settlement for the bride. In the survey report, around 170 Muslim women were questioned. Among them, 84 were paid *mehr* in some form, while 96 women denied getting anything except a token coin. Thus, a definite deterioration now occurs in the property rights of Muslim women as compared to the privileges that they enjoyed even 20 years ago. Also, with the increase in dowry harassment and deaths in the community, Muslim women are now more marginalized than their Hindu neighbours. It is this transformation in the traditional practice of most communities that points to the necessity of building up a wider network to bring about a change not only in the law, but also in socialization.

In order to understand and contextualize the rising trend in dowry related crimes, some of the questions raised by women activists and researchers need to be addressed. The first question relates to women's labour and the way it is situated within social, economic and ideological locations. In the earlier bride price regime, women's contribution, both in the deployment of her labour and reproductive labour, was considered equal to or even greater than that of the man. Now women are getting more and more confined to domestic labour, which also mediates their choice of and control over paid labour.[9] Thus, while the area of women's job options is shrinking, the institutional operatives under which women's socializations take place remain unchanged. Also, most families place great importance in containing a girl's sexuality within marriage. Girls are therefore married off as early as possible after puberty. It is also stated that one pays less dowry if the girl is married off young. This leads to a definite increase in child marriage, most of which go unreported. Another evil effect of dowry is the way families build up strong resistance to allocating property to daughters, especially land or house. Yet, Jayati Gupta's study has shown land acquired from the government, particularly after 'operation-barga' changed hands, being sold to fulfil dowry requirements.[10] This has also affected the schedule

[8] Blei, Tone, 'Dowry and Bride Wealth Presentations in Rural Bangladesh: Commodities, Gifts or Hybrid Forms?' Working Paper. Michelsen Institute, Bergen, 1990.

[9] Banerjee, Nirmala, 'Work, Poverty and Gender'. Occasional Paper No. 133. Centre for Studies in Social Sciences, Kolkata, 1992.

[10] Gupta, Jayati, *Women, Land and Law: Dispute Resolution at the Village Level*. Sachetana Information Centre, Kolkata, 2000.

castes and tribes, who face dowry demands during marriage of each daughter and that is the main reason why land is getting alienated from small and marginal farmers and sharecroppers.

Domestic Violence

The term 'domestic violence' refers to the violence and abuse women suffer at the hands of husbands or partners. It is not the same as family violence—a broader term, which refers to all forms of violence within families. Though violence against women has been recognized internationally during the nineties, many policy makers and policy documents, while acknowledging the wider meaning of violence against women, focus almost entirely on domestic violence in terms of policy and intervention. Both tolerance and experience of domestic violence are significant barriers to the empowerment of women, with consequences on women's health, their health seeking behaviour, their adoption of a small family norm, and the health of their children.

In every country where large scale studies have been conducted results indicate that between 16 and 52 per cent women have been assaulted by an intimate partner.[11] Although national data are scarce, there are a growing number of community-based and small scale studies which indicate widespread violence against women as an important cause of morbidity and mortality. There has been a failure in most countries to identify and provide support to women suffering from domestic violence, mostly because women seek help from neighbours or family members rather than the police or other public agencies. A number of studies have shown that shame or fear of reprisal often prevents women from reporting a sexual attack to authorities. The authorities such as police or those in healthcare often cannot identify the problems, or they are not properly equipped to deal with the complex situation. Unless it

it is recorded as crime, the authorities are unwilling to recognize domestic violence against women as a punishable offence.

The bulk of the crimes reported against women in West Bengal are those of by husbands and relatives, which accounts for 55 per cent of the crimes. Domestic cruelty by husbands and relatives at the all-India level, however, form only 36 per cent of the total crimes against women. If the ratio of domestic violence in West Bengal is related to the districts, 24 Parganas (N), 24 Parganas (S) and Medinipur report very high number of crimes.[12] Chart 7.4 graphically represents the rise in crimes registered under cruelty by husbands and other relatives in West Bengal (excluding Kolkata) from 1995 to 2000. Chart 7.5 similarly shows the rise in torture on housewives in Kolkata from 1997 to 2000.

Chart 7.5
Torture on Housewives (Kolkata) (under Section 498A IPC)

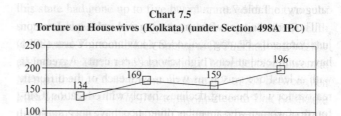

Source: Criminal Record Section, Detective Department, Kolkata Police.

In NFHS-2,[13] an attempt was made to assess whether women view wife-beating as justified, and to measure the prevalence of violence against women including, but not limited to, violence committed by husbands. In order to assess women's attitude towards wife-beating, before asking about personal experiences with domestic violence, the survey asked the respondents whether they thought that a husband was justified in beating his wife.

The survey indicates that almost one out of four women (23 per cent) in West Bengal accept at least one reason as justification for wife-beating (much lower than the estimate of 56 per cent for India as a whole). Women are most likely to agree that wife-beating is justified if the wife neglects the house or children (16 per cent) and least likely to agree that wife-beating is justified if her natal family does not give expected money or other items (3 per cent). If a wife goes out without telling her husband, 14 per cent women say that the husband would be justified in beating her. If the wife shows disrespect towards her in-laws, 11 per cent women agree that wife-beating is justified and 7 per cent believe it is justified if she does not cook properly.

Chart 7.4
Cruelty by Husband and Other Relatives against Women in West Bengal (Excluding Kolkata)

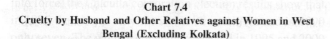
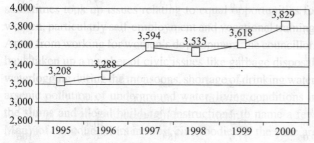

Source: Additional DG of Police, West Bengal.

[11] Mukhopadhyay, Ishita (ed.). *Violence against Women: A Popular Intervention*. Vyas Prokashan, Calcutta, 2002.

[12] Talwar, *Gender Based Violence*.

[13] NFHS-2 (1998–99), India, IIPS, Mumbai, 2000.

Women who are neither Hindu nor Muslim are more likely to agree with at least one reason for wife-beating than any other population group shown in Table 7.6. There are no sharp differences in terms of age or marital duration in women's attitudes towards wife-beating, although the percentage justifying wife-beating are somewhat lower than average for women aged 40–49 and for women who are not currently married. There are notable urban–rural differences in these attitudes. Not only do a higher proportion of rural women (26 per cent) than urban women (11 per cent) agree to at least one reason justifying wife-beating, but rural women are also more likely than urban women to agree with each specific reason. A lower percentage of women in Kolkata (7 per cent) agree with at least one reason justifying wife-beating than any other category in Table 7.6.

The percentage of women agreeing with at least one reason justifying wife-beating is also very low among women who have completed at least high school (9 per cent). Agreement with at least one reason, as well as with each of the different reasons for wife-beating, declines sharply with education. One-fourth of women who are either illiterate or have not completed middle school agree with at least one reason justifying wife-beating, compared with 15 per cent of women who have completed middle school and 9 per cent of women who have completed high school.

In order to assess the prevalence of domestic violence, NFHS-2 asked women if they had been beaten or mistreated since age 15. Women who reported being beaten or physically mistreated were asked about who beat or physically mistreated them. According to the reports (Table 7.7), 18 per cent women in West Bengal have experienced violence (lower that the national average of 21 per cent), and 16 per cent have been beaten or physically mistreated by their husbands, 2 per cent have been beaten or physically mistreated by in-laws and 2 per cent by other people. This implies that among women who were beaten, almost 9 out of 10 (89 per cent) have been beaten by their husbands and 1 out of 10 have been beaten by their in-laws.

Women aged 15–19 are less likely than older women to have been beaten, but because of their young age they have had less time to be exposed to the risk of being beaten. Urban women (11 per cent) are less likely than rural women (20 per cent) to experience violence. In Kolkata, 9 per cent of women have been beaten or physically mistreated. Illiterate women

Table 7.6
Percentage of Women Who Agree with the Reasons Given for Justifying a Husband Beating His Wife in West Bengal, 1998–99

Background characteristics	Percentage who agree with at least one reason	Husband suspects wife is unfaithful	Natal family does not give expected money or other item	Wife shows disrespect towards in-laws	Wife goes out without telling husband	Wife neglects house or children	Wife does not cook properly	Number of women
				Percentage who agree with specific reasons				
Age								
15–19	26.9	13.0	3.6	16.6	17.7	20.3	8.7	383
20–29	24.7	10.6	2.6	12.4	16.2	17.8	8.2	1,706
30–39	22.5	11.1	2.8	11.6	13.8	14.9	6.1	1,430
40–49	17.1	7.2	1.5	6.5	10.0	11.2	3.7	889
Residence								
Urban	11.1	4.4	0.8	5.0	4.5	7.6	2.8	1,049
Rural	26.3	12.1	3.0	13.3	17.4	18.3	7.9	3,359
Kolkata	6.8	1.6	0.2	3.6	3.8	5.5	1.6	242
Education								
Illiterate	25.7	12.1	3.9	12.8	17.6	17.9	7.9	2,202
Literate, <middle school complete	25.2	10.8	1.7	12.6	15.1	17.6	8.0	1,289
Middle school complete	15.2	7.0	0.5	7.1	6.7	9.3	2.4	443
High school complete and above	8.8	3.7	0.1	5.0	4.2	6.4	1.5	469
Religion								
Hindu	20.3	8.6	2.0	10.1	11.8	13.8	5.5	3,285
Muslim	29.3	14.9	4.4	15.6	22.9	21.8	10.4	1,007
Other	33.5	18.0	1.2	9.0	11.6	18.0	6.4	106
Caste/tribe								
Scheduled caste	23.8	9.7	2.2	10.5	14.7	16.7	7.9	1,038
Scheduled tribe	23.6	11.2	3.0	11.7	14.2	13.5	7.2	319
Other backward class	22.5	11.1	1.1	9.2	10.1	10.2	3.6	196
Other	22.1	10.3	2.7	11.7	14.5	16.0	6.3	2,834

(23 per cent) are almost nine times as likely to experience violence as women who have completed high school (3 per cent). The prevalence of domestic violence decreases substantially as the standard of living increases. Largely due to the inherent tendency for underreporting of domestic violence, these results need to be interpreted with caution. Nevertheless, the NFHS-2 estimates set a lower limit on the proportion of women experiencing domestic violence in West Bengal: at least 1 in 6 ever-married women in West Bengal experience domestic violence since age 15, and at least 1 in 11 has experienced domestic violence in the past 12 months.

Table 7.7
Percentage of Ever-married Women Who Have Been Beaten or Physically Mistreated by Their Husbands, In-Laws, or Other Persons since Age 15 in West Bengal, 1998–99

Background characteristics	Beaten or physically mistreated since age 15	Beaten or physically mistreated since age 15 by			Number of women
		Husband	In-laws	Other persons	
Age					
15–19	12.5	10.6	0.4	2.6	383
20–29	17.5	15.4	1.7	2.4	1,706
30–39	20.2	18.0	2.4	3.0	1,430
40–49	15.7	14.7	1.2	1.2	889
Residence					
Urban	11.0	9.1	0.9	2.1	1,049
Rural	19.6	17.7	2.0	2.4	3,359
Kolkata	8.9	7.6	0.6	1.6	242
Education					
Illiterate	22.9	21.0	2.0	2.6	2,202
Literate, <middle school complete	17.0	14.7	1.8	2.8	1,289
Middle school complete	8.5	6.6	1.5	1.5	443
High school complete and above	2.6	1.6	0.2	0.9	469
Religion					
Hindu	15.9	13.9	1.6	2.5	3,284
Muslim	23.4	22.0	2.0	1.7	1,007
Other	10.3	10.3	0.0	1.3	106
Caste/tribe					
Scheduled caste	18.5	16.0	1.8	3.1	1,038
Scheduled tribe	17.8	16.5	0.4	2.2	319
Other backward class	14.7	12.8	0.4	1.5	196
Other	17.4	15.6	1.9	2.2	2,834

What is interesting to note, however, is the increasing reportage of such crimes in recent years. This could be attributed to a growing awareness of the issue of violence against women in families, spearheaded by the efforts of women's organizations, resulting in a range of initiatives dealing with the problem at almost every level of society. Besides, the result of reduction in barriers to women participating in public life, especially with reservation of seats for women in the panchayats, have made women more visible. Thus, more and more women are wanting to share their experiences of violence and looking for suitable platforms to do so.

Sexual Assault and Rape

Women who are the victims of sexual violence are often reluctant to report the crime to members of the family, police or other authorities due to personal trauma attached to the incidents. In countries like India, where a woman's virginity is associated with family honour, unmarried women who report a rape may be forced to marry their attacker. They could also be killed by their shamed fathers or brothers as a way of restoring family honour. Instances of women being imprisoned and prosecuted for not being able to prove that the sexual assault on her was actually a rape has been found in several countries other than India. Women who do disclose abuses are often advised to restrict their movements or adapt their clothes so as to avoid tempting men to attack them. This puts the blame entirely on women, projecting them as sexual objects who arouse male desire. It also ignores the fact that many rapes take place by people they trust and are often an assertion of male authority.

Armed conflict also unleashes violence against women. The general breakdown in law and order situation which occurs during conflicts leads to an increase in all forms of violence. These can include random acts of sexual assault by both enemy and friendly forces or mass rape as a deliberate strategy of genocide. Some groups of women and girls are particularly vulnerable in conflict and displacement situations. These include targeted ethnic groups, where there is an official and unofficial policy to use rape as a weapon of genocide. The situation is compounded by the fact that women are symbolized as the bearers of a cultural identity and their bodies perceived as territory to be conquered.

In the all-India context, in 1998, the highest reported cases of rape were from Madhya Pradesh followed by Uttar Pradesh and Bihar. For molestation cases too, Madhya Pradesh took the lead followed by Andhra Pradesh and Maharashtra.[14] West Bengal ranks seventh according to the number of rape cases registered and tenth according to the number of molestation cases registered. According to the National Crime Records Bureau (NCRB) figures of 1999, rape accounts for 12 per cent of the crimes against women reported in West Bengal and molestation accounts for 17 per cent. Table 7.8 contains

---

[14] *Crime in India 1999*. National Crime Records Bureau, 2001. New Delhi.

Table 7.8
District-wise Incidence and Rate of Sexual Assaults against Women in West Bengal in 2000

District	Rape										Molestation		Eve-teasing		Total	
	Custodial		Gang		Others											
	Cases	Persons arrested	Cases	Persons arrested	Cases	Persons arrested	Cases	Persons arrested	Cases	Persons arrested	Cases	Persons arrested				
Bankura	1	4	8	14	31	28	–	–	40	46						
Birbhum	5	3	44	21	44	17	1	4	94	45						
Bardhaman	6	18	34	44	96	113	3	9	139	184						
Koch Bihar	5	2	43	22	52	33	–	–	100	57						
Darjeeling	3	12	20	18	29	30	1	1	53	61						
Hoogli	7	6	33	24	43	26	1	3	84	59						
				1*	1											
Haora	2	2	15	11	30	33	–	–	47	47						
Jalpaiguri	6	8	47	30	54	32	–	–	107	70						
Medinipur	7	2	63	40	56	44	1	–	127	86						
Murshidabad	7	18	61	53	64	43	–	–	132	114						
Maldah	4	11	35	37	40	43	1	5	80	96						
			2*	1												
Nadia	5	13	60	64	69	63	1	1	135	141						
24 Parganas (N)	6	9	67	48	75	59	–	–	148	116						
24 Parganas (S)	11	13	54	41	73	52	–	–	138	106						
Purulia	3	6	30	32	59	75	–	–	92	113						
Uttar Dinajpur	3	5	43	26	26	14	–	–	72	45						
Dakshin Dinajpur	1	2	26	15	48	28	–	–	75	45						
Total	82	136	697	543	905	753	9	23	1,693	1,455						

Source: *Sexual Violence and the Law*. West Bengal Commission for Women, Kolkata, 2002.
Note: *Rape with Murder

district-wise data relating to sexual assault and rapes of women in 2000. It records the cases registered as well as the number of persons arrested. The districts where the rates of crimes are highest are Bardhaman, 24 Parganas (N) and 24 Parganas (S). Though it is not clear from this numerical data as to why sexual assaults against women are higher in some districts as compared to others, it seems that in certain districts, where there are generally more reported cases of crimes against women, reports of sexual assaults also tend to be high, because larger number of women are coming forward to record their grievance.

In West Bengal, civil rights' groups and women's organizations brought before the public a number of cases where the police were held directly responsible for rapes in custody. In 1992, Nehar Banu was raped in the Phulbagan police station in Kolkata. The court condemned one of the accused to life imprisonment while the other two were sentenced to rigorous imprisonment for six years each. It marked a victory for the women's organizations as well because the state was forced to take notice of the way the police and other officials were abusing their powers. Special provisions were made for custodial rape and certain procedural issues were also raised about rapes in police lock-ups and jails. In recent years, not only the Law Commission, but also the National Commission for Women, NGOs and lawyer's groups have engaged in the exercise of providing better laws against rape. The West

Bengal Commission for Women also took up this exercise in 1998–99 and has conducted two workshops with experts and representatives of NGOs to determine the parameters within which certain recommendations may be made. A bilingual book called *Sexual Violence and the Law* is the outcome of that intervention.

Trafficking of Girls and Women

Trafficking is defined as systematic buying and selling of women and girls by means of violence, threats, abuse of actual and perceived authority arising from a relationship, or deception, in order to subject them to the actual and unlawful power of other persons. An individual may be trafficked for various purposes, invariably ending up captive in coercive and exploitative situations, for example, forced labour in domestic, industrial or commercial sex sectors. It has been made illegal under the Indian Penal Code (IPC) and the Immoral Traffic in Persons Prevention Act (ITPA). In spite of this, trafficking operates both within the country and internationally through an expanding network of supply, demand and transit of women and girls for commercial sex.

Information about trafficking is hard to acquire. Our main data is from police sources. Figures for kidnapping of women and girls for the years 1995–2000 (vide Table 7.4) show kidnapping of women and girls to be 729 in West Bengal in 1995, which increases to 788 in 1997 and takes a dip in 2000 by coming down to 701. These numbers, however, have to be matched with the information received from the trafficked persons. The largest group is the commercial sex workers in Bengal. Women between 5 and 50 years of age are being abducted and sold all over the world mainly for prostitution and for begging. A survey done by Sanlaap (an organization working mainly for rehabilitation of minor prostitutes) showed that traffickers used the following methods—kidnapping, promises of better jobs and procuring, and through marriages (quite often these are fake marriages). Very often women and girls are sold by their own kin—parents, guardians, husbands and lovers. Rape victims, ironically, are also sold into prostitution as they are considered unfit to lead a normal social life.

In India, a 1986 study by the Joint Women's Programme documented that parents were selling unborn female children. The study is said to be the most important report on prostitution to date. It covers the situation in 12 states and 2 union territories. The study claims that some deals are made when foetuses are three months old, commanding a price of Rs 3,500. After birth, most of these girl children are sold into prostitution. The study also reports that among those who are sold, 33 per cent are sold by parents and relatives, 19 per cent by gangs, and 10 per cent by strangers.[15]

Since trafficking of women and girls is a multi-billion dollar business, it has become as important as dealings in drugs and ornaments. India falls within this wide criminal network since it serves not only as a sending but as a receiving and transit country as well. Women and girls from Nepal and Bangladesh are sold to brothel-keepers in India. A large number are also to be found in Kolkata's red light areas, though their exact number has never been estimated.

The conditions under which trafficked women and girls operate in West Bengal verge on white slavery. Most of them work under the Aadhya or the Chhukri System. Under the Aadhya System (meaning half-payment), women give half of their earning from each client to the madam of the brothel. The rest of her earnings are spent on personal expenses (food, clothing and medicines) and financial support to other members of her family including small children, who are generally left behind at home. This system is widely practiced in Kolkata's red light areas such as Sonagachi, Khidirpur and Bowbazar.[16] Under the Chhukri System, women, mainly girls, virtually work like bonded labourers. The madams or pimps who buy a new girl keep all her earnings until the girl has paid her debt, which

means the money spent to buy her and maintain her. The girl's daily expenses are added up to keep her in bondage as long as possible. When she is finally released, the woman tends to move into another locality where she can operate independently by renting a room for herself.

The legislative framework which makes trafficking a crime against women and girls consist mainly of the ITPA of 1986. The underlying philosophy of the ITPA is a carry-over from that of the Suppression of Immoral Traffic in Women and Girls Act 1956 (SITA), which was originally passed as a result of the United Nations International Convention in New York in 1950 for the suppression of traffic in persons and of the exploitation of women, to which India is a signatory. The Act was amended twice. It was first amended in 1978, and then amended and renamed as the ITPA in 1986. ITPA merely extends the SITA application to both women and men and increases the punishment for certain offences. In West Bengal, from a study made of police records by Sanlaap, persons arrested under ITPA in 1989 showed women sex workers to be 80 per cent of the total. Hence, sex workers in India feel that, contrary to its declared objectives, the Act has made the prostitute the chief target for penalization through its operation.[17]

Both trafficking and prostitution emerged on the scene of public debate only after the detection of the first Indian case of HIV infection in a sex worker from Chennai in 1986. The AIDS epidemic attracted the attention of researchers, social workers and the media. The Government of India took an extremist approach and the AIDS Prevention Bill was drafted in 1989 which targeted the members of so-called 'high-risk' groups. It also provided the health authorities with invasive policies in the form of testing and isolating individuals who belonged to the group of potential contractors of the disease. The sex workers now complained that forced medical tests were imposed on them, treating them as human guinea pigs. The proposed Bill was dropped once the National AIDS Control Organization (NACO) drafted a National AIDS Policy that reflected a more progressive response by the government to the AIDS epidemic.

As per a survey report on Sonagachi, the best known red light area in Kolkata, published in 1998 by the All India Institute of Hygiene and Public Health under the aegis of WHO, the number of minor girls in sex trade in 1992 was 25.29 per cent but this had significantly dropped to 3.56 per cent by 1998 due to constant advocacy and social service campaigns from the ends of both government and NGOs.

---

[15] *Reproductive and Genetic Engineering*. Vol. 2. No. 1.

[16] Sleightholme, Carolyne and Indrani Sinha, *Guilty without Trial*. Stree, Kolkata, 1996.

[17] Ibid.

Chart 7.6 represents the declining trend in the percentage of minor girls in sex trade in Sonagachi.

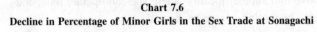

Chart 7.6

Decline in Percentage of Minor Girls in the Sex Trade at Sonagachi

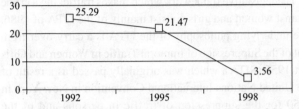

Source: *The Status of Sex-workers in Kolkata and the Social Services Available to them.* Department of Women and Child Development and Social Welfare, Government of West Bengal, 2001.

A new chapter opened in the lives of sex workers when the HIV intervention programme started functioning all over the country. In Kolkata, it was begun by the Institute of Hygiene and Public Health. A team of peer educators was formed, who were recruited from amongst the sex workers themselves and given requisite training. Another institution which was a direct product of the HIV intervention programme was the Mahila Samanwaya Committee consisting of members who were mainly sex workers. From 1995, the Mahila Samanwaya Committee was renamed Durbar Mahila Samanwaya Committee. The organization's membership and aims remained the same. They held their first conference on 29–30 April 1996 in Kolkata. One of their main demands was that 'the PITA should be scrapped. Will you support a legislation that legalizes female torture?' they asked. As an alternative they put forward what they felt was a cogent suggestion: 'As the first step towards self-regulation we would like to form a Board ... which will make rules and regulations of the trade and regulate the entry of new girls.[18] In India, a national level networking of prostitutes is taking place now, who demand that ITPA should be abolished and prostitutes be legally recognized as sex workers.

The issue of trafficking in women and children remains a crime which will lead to the punishments laid down by IPTA and the IPC. It is leading to the criminalizing of women who are mainly victims. Also, since all these police measures are not free from class prejudice, the women who are usually picked up for selecting or trafficking belong to the poorest group of sex workers. On 30 August 1997, Shyamali Sarkar, a sex worker from Sonagachi, was brutally murdered because she tried to protest against the way trafficking was being carried on by the landladies, the madams, the local touts and men who had invested a great deal of money in maintaining minor prostitution as a lucrative business. She was shot dead in broad daylight. In some ways it pointed at the way sex workers were caught in a vicious circle by traffickers, from which the present law offered them no way out.

Survey on Impact of Legal Reforms on Women

A sample survey was conducted among women spread over 10 districts of the state to find out the impact of constitutional and legal provisions in their lives. The districts were 24 Parganas (N), 24 Parganas (S), Kolkata, Purulia, Nadia, Murshidabad, Bardhaman, Malda, Jalpaiguri and Darjeeling. The districts have been clubbed into four zones here: Zone I being Kolkata, 24 Parganas (N) and 24 Parganas (S); Zone II being Nadia and Murshidabad; Zone III comprising Medinipur and Purulia; and Zone IV including Malda, Darjeeling and Jalpaiguri. The responses of Muslim respondents of all four zones were grouped to form Zone V. The number of respondents were 35 each in Zone I and Zone II and 25 each in Zones III, IV and V. Tables 7.9 to 7.17c reveal their responses which in turn reflect their awareness in each area.

Of the 145 respondents, 98 were between 15–39 years and 105 hailed from the lower income group. Most of the respondents had studied up to the secondary level but there were about 10 illiterate respondents as well (vide Table 7.9). In the first place, the survey tried to assess a woman's position in the family, her role in the decision making process and any assistance in household work that she received without which it was difficult for a woman to contribute to different spheres of life other than the family. Even though majority of the respondents spread over all the zones were housewives, Table 7.10 reveals their diverse vocations as teachers, nurses, midwives, domestic help, cultivators and employed in other capacities. Though husbands still play the main role in the decision making process, the incidence of the women making decisions or both spouses jointly doing it have proved to be very encouraging. Household work, too, is being shared by the husband as well as by the son. Quite a few respondents of Zones I, III and V have reported getting help from husbands in doing household chores. Such a development is encouraging as it is a step towards breaking stereotypes for men and women.

---

[18] 'Sex Workers' Manifesto'. Theme paper of the first National Conference of Sex Workers organized by Durbar Mahila Samanwaya Committee at Salt Lake Stadium, Kolkata, November 1997.

Table 7.9
Introduction of the Respondents

Zone	Age group							Income group					Educational qualification							Literacy camps	Training	Language			Caste/Religion		
	154-84	19-29	30-39	40-49	50-59	60-69	70+	Rs 500-1,000	Rs 150-5,000	Rs 500-10,000	Rs 10,000-20,000	Above 20,000	Illiterate	Primary +	Secondary	H.S.	Others	Graduate	Postgraduate			Bangla	Urdu	Hindi	SC	ST	Christians
I/35	1	6	18	4	6	X	X	15	9	10	X	X	X	10	5	8	3	1	13	X	1	32	2	1	X	1	1
II/35	X	22	16	12	2	X	1	21	7	4	1	X	2	19	4	4	2	1	4	3	5	35	X	X	5	2	X
III/25	X	7	8	5	3	X	X	12	6	5	X	X	6	1	3	8	3	5	1	5	1	25	X	X	8	X	X
IV/25	2	14	9	5	1	X	X	8	12	4	1	1	X	6	8	2	X	5	4	5	X	24	X	1	2	X	X
V/25	1	10	13	4	1	X	X	20	5	X	X	X	2	11	X	6	1	X	X	X	X	18	3	1	X	X	X

Table 7.10
Occupation/Role in Decision Making/Assistance in Houshold Work

Zone	Occupation							Role in decision making				Assistance in housework					
	Housewife	Teacher	Nurse	Employed in other capacities	Cultivator (labourer)	Domestic help	Midwife	Self	Husband	Both	Others	Husband	Son	Daughter	Mother-in-law	Others	Servants
I/35	16	4	1	6	2	6	X	12	10	10	3	8	5	7	5	8	2
II/35	22	3	1	4	X	5	X	3	12	18	2	5	2	8	15	X	5
III/25	7	2	7	X	2	1	6	5	9	8	3	10	X	3	2	3	4
IV/25	14	1	7	2	2	X	X	5	7	10	1	5	8	5	5	2	4
V/25	10	3	X	2	6	3	X	9	10	7	X	8	X	5	3	5	4

Table 7.11
Exposure to Violence

Zone	Domestic violence		Due to birth of girl child		Violence in the vicinity dealth by					
					Aware of it	Neighbours	Police	Women's oganization	Panchayat	Others
	Yes	No	Yes	No						
I	20	15	12	10	16	8	8	2	3	5
II	7	18	10	15	9	4	5	1	1	2
III	11	17	8	17	13	12	4	7	8	6
IV	9	17	10	15	17	17	4	5	4	X
V	3	4	3	14	6	5	5	2	3	1

Next, the survey wanted to probe women's exposure to/experience of domestic violence. About 50 respondents said they had faced some form of domestic violence (vide Table 7.11) and 43 said they had encountered violence at the birth of a girl child in the family. About 61 of those surveyed showed an awareness of violence on women living in the vicinity and were also quite clear about the agencies that intervened. This awareness exposes the fact that general awareness about domestic violence has gone up that it is a force to reckon with and not a result of one's fate.

The query regarding earning of equal wages with men have evoked an emphatic 'no' from the respondents (vide Table 7.12). However, most women have also categorically stated that they faced no difficulty in working with men. The respondents from Zone I who hailed from an urban background took a contrary view on this. In answer to questions relating to implementation of various acts affecting working women, especially relating to creche facilities in workplaces, most women felt it was still a dream. The respondents from Zones III and IV were not aware as to what a crèche was. This inevitably leads us to the conclusion that welfare legislations have languished in the statute books and their implementation, if any, has left no mark on the status of women.

Table 7.12
Working Outside Home—Wages and Other Facilities

Zone	Earn equal wages with men		Experience any difficulty in working with men		Availability of creche facilities for children	
	Yes	No	Yes	No	Yes	No
I	6	19	20	15	1	10
II	3	4	1	14	1	9
III	11	14	2	15	X	20
IV	7	10	3	15	X	X
V	6	12	2	16	X	2

Majority of the respondents were married. It is distressing to note that the number of deserted wives was disturbingly high particularly among the Hindu respondents (vide Table 7.13). It is evident that the wife played a key role in decision making regarding family planning in most zones. The response in Zone I, where the respondents hailed mainly from urban areas, reveals that the husband had the main role in decision making. The number of children of the respondents mainly ranged from one to three, but they thought the ideal number of children should be two.

The table relating to litigation arising out of marriage (Table 7.14) show only four respondents, two each from Zones I and II, who have been divorced pursuant to an application and alimony has been received by only one of them. Zone I has six respondents whose spouse got married while the first wife was still around, while one had a live-in extra marital relationship. The queries relating to custody of children reveal that the mother usually had the custody of the child.

The law requires that men as well as women maintain their dependents. The personal laws and Section 125 of CrPC lay down provisions for maintenance. The survey had questions relating to the respondents being maintained by someone/on maintaining others. Table 7.15 shows that in most cases the husband maintained the wife. Only one respondent in Zone I and another in Zone III said they were being maintained by their sons and father-in-law respectively. The question on how the respondents maintained others extracted mixed responses from each group. On the whole, in some form or the other, the parents of both spouses are being taken care of financially or otherwise. This sense of responsibility towards the elderly manifests the success of Section 125 CrPC.

Out of the respondents who had inherited some property, majority happened to be from Zones I and IV. It appears that most of them had inherited from their fathers or husbands. Again, the respondents of Zones I and IV were highest in number with regard to receiving an equal share of property with their brothers (vide Table 7.16). The respondents in Zone V did not respond to this question as according to their 'faraz' in Shariat, a sister inherits half of the brothers' share.

Regarding awareness of laws, the survey chose to focus on three laws—laws on prevention of child marriage and prohibition of dowry; land laws; and the 73rd Amendment and the role of the panchayats. Since 1929, child marriages in this country are considered an offence and at present the minimum

Table 7.13
Marital Status and Family Planning

Zone	Marital status				Number of children					Family planning decision		Ideal no. of children			
	Unmarried	Married	Abandoned	Divorce	1	2	3	4	5	Self	Husband	1	2	3	4
I	4	20	11	2	3	6	4	1	1	5	19	X	25	4	1
II	4	25	16	X	3	20	2	3	X	20	3	3	22	1	X
III	5	17	3	X	9	5	1	3	X	4	13	8	12	1	X
IV	4	20	1	X	2	5	5	X	X	6	14	1	15	5	X
V	5	14	1	5	3	1	5	X	2	3	11	X	13	5	1

Table 7.14
Litigation Arising Out of Marriage

Zone	Divorcee		Alimony		Marriage during existence of a wife	Extra-marital affair	Custody of children	
	Mutual	On application	Received	Not received			Father	Mother
I	X	2	1	1	6	1	2	14
II	X	2	X	2	1	X	7	10
III	X	X	X	X	X	X	1	2
IV	X	X	X	X	X	X	X	1
V	X	X	X	X	X	X	2	3

Table 7.15
On Maintenance and on Maintaining Others

Zone	Maintenance case filed	Case not continuing	Received	Being maintained by				Maintaining others							
								Father		Mother		Father-in-law		Mother-in-law	
				Husband	Father	Son	Father-in-law	Financial	Otherwise	Financial	Otherwise	Financial	Otherwise	Financial	Otherwise
I	8	1	7	15	2	1	X	2	1	8	1	4	1	5	2
II	2	1	3	17	1	X	X	X	1	1	4	2	3	X	6
III	1	X	5	5	2	X	1	1	1	5	1	2	X	2	2
IV	X	1	X	17	2	X	X	X	X	6	3	11	2	11	2
V	1	1	2	15	X	X	X	X	1	9	1	2	X	X	3

Table 7.16
Property Laws

Zone	Inherited property	Husband	Father	Mother	Father-in-law	Mother-in-law	Child	Obtained equal share with brother		Relinquished share	Compelled to do so	Brother's plight main consideration
								Yes	No			
I	17	6	11	X	X	X	X	15	4	2	X	8
II	10	1	7	X	3	X	X	1	2	X	3	2
III	7	3	X	X	4	X	X	1	6	5	X	X
IV	18	3	10	5	X	X	X	12	2	3	X	1
V	13											

age of marriage for the groom is 21 years and for the bride 18 years. It appears (vide Table 7.17a) that boys and girls are married off far below the statutory age. Zone V or the Muslim respondents did not respond to this query about when they married off their children. The reason being that 20 out of 25 respondents were aged below 30–39 years and, therefore, presumably have not yet got their children married. Though the Dowry Prohibition Act was passed in 1961 and amended in 1983, it seems that giving and taking of dowry has increased and the dowry menace has spread to communities where women traditionally had property rights, like among the Muslims. This corroborates with what we have studied in the section on dowry harassment and death in West Bengal, where we have seen a steady rise in dowry-related crimes and a definite deterioration in the property rights of Muslim women. Some respondents also said that they were 'unaware' that giving and taking of dowry was an offence, which shows that much needs to be done to raise awareness against dowry.

Table 7.17a
Awareness of Laws on Child Marriage and Dowry Prohibition

| Zone | Age of marriage of children | | | | | Aware of dowry being an offence | |
	Son below 21	Daughter below 18	Received dowry	Paid dowry	No demand for dowry	Yes	No
I	X	1	X	1	2	4	2
II	X	2	X	1	X	1	2
III	4	1	1	1	X	4	1
IV	3	4	X	2	X	4	5
V	X	X	X	1	X	1	X

Table 7.17b
Awareness of Land Laws

| Zone | Whether from landless family | | Applied for *patta* | | Obtained joint *patta* | | Knowledge of co-wives being counted as one wife | | Recorded as bargadar | |
	Yes	No	Yes	No	Yes	No	Yes	No	Yes	No
I	5	2	X	2	X	4	1	1	X	3
II	7	14	X	10	1	5	4	1	2	4
III	10	6	X	7	1	4	6	3	X	7
IV	13	10	3	4	1	2	1	1	1	3
V	8	8	X	4	1	2	2	3	X	6

Table 7.17c
Awareness of Law—On Panchayat and Other Activities

Zone	No. of respondents who are members of the panchayat	Gram sabha held	Attends gram sabha	Receives financial assistance through panchayat scheme	Earns through a co-op. society	Obtained assistance from co-op. bank
I	X	1	1	2	4	5
II	8	13	13	1	X	6
III	4	19	16	X	X	X
IV	3	4	3	X	1	3
V	2	4	4	1	2	X

The land reforms movement of the Left Front government in the state has succeeded in vesting of lands with the rural poor and in securing the rights of the *bargadar*. Vested lands are settled by granting *pattas* (ownership deeds) and joint *pattas* are issued to the spouses. However, it is apparent from Table 7.17b that agriculture is considered a 'man's job' since the majority of the respondents have not applied for *patta*. Joint *pattas* have also been received by only a few. Only three respondents said they had their names recorded as *bargadars*. All these responses reflect that much needs to be done in addressing these imbalances regarding land rights. *Pattas* are issued in the name of women when they are heads of families. Usually the master or the head of the family applies for settlement of vested land and *pattas* are actually issued in his name and the wife's name is merely included on the deed. The state government issues joint *pattas* to landless families so that both the husband and the wife feel they are owners of a joint property. Only if both the husband and the wife apply for settlement of vested land that *patta* is issued in both their names. In the case of a Muslim applicant of joint *pattas*, the name of only one wife is included even if a man has more than one wife. Women's organizations and NGOs need to come forward to address these problems.

The 73rd Amendment to the Constitution ushered in a new era in women's empowerment by reserving one-third of the seats for women in the three-tier panchayati system. Except Zone I (urban area), respondents of all other zones included members of the three-tier panchayati raj (vide Table 7.17c). Under Section 16B of the Panchayat Act, a gram sabha comprises all persons in the panchayat area whose names appear on the electoral rolls. The responses indicate a moderate incidence of participation in gram sabhas thereby showing the success of decentralization of power.

Conclusion

From the survey report, it appears that in West Bengal the legal status of women is slowly changing for the better. Women are now being educated, employed, doing social work and engaged in other productive activities in society. Mothers are seriously planning their families as they are aware of the responsibility of bringing up children. It is really heartening to find that daughters and daughters-in-law are coming forward to maintain their parents or in-laws with financial and other kinds of assistance. Women are now working in panchayats and municipalities and are taking part in planning and implementation of development activities. These engagements are making them aware of their constitutional and legal rights as citizens. Most women face violence at home and in the outer world. But violence on women does not go unnoticed these days. People have begun to react, at least women's organizations, panchayats, and the police are there when women themselves decide to take recourse to law.

Nevertheless, it is very disturbing to note that many of our women are still illiterate or semi-literate. A vast number of them are employed either in the unorganized sector or in home-based industries and are thereby deprived of the benefits of working women, and at the same time face tremendous occupational hazards. The fact that the concept of equal wages with men is an alien one for most women workers should be an eye-opener for the women's movement and it has to make concerted efforts to correct this imbalance. It is also distressing to note that child marriage is still rampant and mothers are not always aware that giving or taking of dowry is a punishable offence. In this connection, another important aspect needs to be highlighted. Often we hear of girls or women being harassed for having 'illicit' relationships, which are prohibited on the basis of caste or religion. To combat all these obscurantist and fundamentalist forces, an all-round social awareness based on legal rights is to be advocated relentlessly. The social aspect of law needs more sustained campaigns, failing which women can never be expected to improve their legal status.

Tribal Women

CHAPTER 8

Anuradha Chanda

Introduction

The tribals are the original inhabitants of India and numerically form a significant part of the total population. They signify various races with different cultural traits living in varied ecological zones. In India there are about 426 scheduled tribe groups. Culturally hit by the steady process of sanskritization and deprived of their land settlements by colonialism, the tribals formed an acutely marginalized section in independent India. Since independence, various strategies have been adopted at the national level for safeguarding the interests of the scheduled tribes of the country and special attention was paid to tribal development in the successive plan periods. While initially the policy was based on tribal welfare, from the seventies the emphasis has shifted to development. In the context of development it was noticed that different tribal groups were at different stages of development (according to the Dhebar Commission appointed during the Fourth Five Year Plan) and on the basis of several studies a sub-category was demarcated within the category 'tribal'. This was the 'Primitive Tribal Group' which included groups that were in the pre-agricultural level of technology (i.e., at the hunting and gathering stage), and that had a stagnant or diminishing population. The state governments were empowered to identify the tribal groups who may be categorized under 'Primitive Tribes'. Based on the recommendations of the state governments, the Government of India identified 52 scheduled tribe communities as Primitive Tribes. In the Fifth Plan (1975–80), emphasis was given to the Primitive Tribes and a sub-plan was brought into effect, wherein an 'area development approach'

was adopted which allocated special funds only for areas with more than 50 per cent tribal population. During the Fifth Plan, an Integrated Tribal Development Project was undertaken to focus on the development of tribal-dominated areas. At the end of the Sixth Plan, thorough assessments were made and before entering the Seventh Plan, development of the primitive tribal groups was prioritized. From the Seventh Plan, a special emphasis was laid on tribal women and children. The Government of India also took a policy decision that only sensitive and competent government servants were to be given posting in tribal areas. Competent NGOs and voluntary organizations were given opportunities to work with the tribals. The changing status of tribal women in West Bengal needs to be studied keeping in mind this historical background.

Tribes of West Bengal

The total tribal population of the state as per the 1991 Census is 3,808,760. It is a sizeable number forming 5.59 per cent of the total population of West Bengal and 5.62 per cent of the total scheduled tribe population of India. Of this 1,938,955 are men (50.91 per cent) and 1,869,805 (49.09 per cent) are women. Tribal women in West Bengal form 6 per cent of the total population of the state. By sheer number, they form a significant segment of the state's population and their changing status reflects upon the overall well-being of the state.[1]

In West Bengal there are 38 tribal groups, 3 of which are Primitive Tribes. The district-wise distribution pattern of the 38 tribes of West Bengal are given in Table 8.1.[2]

---

[1] Gupta, R. 'Socio-Economic Status of Tribal Women in West Bengal', *Bulletin of the Cultural Research Institute* (CRI), 20(1), 1998.
[2] Baske, Dhirendranath, *Paschim Banger Adivasi Samaj*, Vol. 1. Subarnarekha, Calcutta, 1987, pp. 30–32.

Table 8.1
District-wise Distribution Pattern of the Tribes of West Bengal

Tribes	Districts
Asur	West Dinajpur
Baiga, Bedia	West Dinajpur, Purulia
Bhumij	Kolkata, Koch Bihar, 24-Parganas, Jalpaiguri, Nadia, W. Dinajpur, Bardhaman, Maldah, Murshidabad, Medinipur, Haora, Hoogli
Bhutia	Kolkata, Koch Bihar, 24-Parganas, Jalpaiguri, Nadia, W. Dinajpur, Bardhaman, Maldah, Murshidabad, Medinipur, Haora, Hoogli
Birhor	Purulia
Birjia	W. Dinajpur
Chakma	Kolkata, 24-Parganas, Darjeeling, Nadia, Bardhaman, Birbhum, Maldah
Chero	W. Dinajpur
Chik Baraik	Darjeeling, W. Dinajpur
Garo	Kolkata, Koch Bihar, 24-Parganas, Jalpaiguri, Darjeeling, Nadia, W. Dinajpur, Bardhaman, Murshidabad, Medinipur, Haora, Hoogli
Gond	W. Dinajpur
Gorait	W. Dinajpur, Purulia
Hajang	Kolkata, 24-Parganas, Jalpaiguri, Darjeeling, W. Dinajpur, Bardhaman, Haora, Hoogli
Ho	Kolkata, 24-Parganas, Jalpaiguri, W. Dinajpur, Purulia, Bardhaman, Birbhum, Murshidabad, Medinipur, Haora, Hoogli
Karmali	W. Dinajpur, Purulia
Kharwar	W. Dinajpur
Kisan	Darjeeling, Purulia
Kora	Kolkata, Koch Bihar, 24-Parganas, Jalpaiguri, Nadia, W. Dinajpur, Purulia, Bardhaman, Bankura, Birbhum, Maldah, Murshidabad, Medinipur, Haora, Hoogli
Korwa	W. Dinajpur, Purulia
Lepcha	Kolkata, Koch Bihar, 24-Parganas, Jalpaiguri, Darjeeling, Nadia, Purulia, Bardhaman, Murshidabad, Medinipur, Haora, Hoogli
Lodha, Kharia	Kolkata, Koch Bihar, 24-Parganas, Jalpaiguri, Darjeeling, Nadia, W. Dinajpur, Purulia, Bardhaman, Birbhum, Murshidabad, Medinipur, Haora, Hoogli
Lohara	W. Dinajpur, Purulia, Bankura
Magh	Kolkata, 24-Parganas, Jalpaiguri, Darjeeling, Nadia, W. Dinajpur, Bardhaman, Birbhum, Murshidabad, Medinipur, Haora, Hoogli
Mahali	Kolkata, Koch Bihar, 24-Parganas, Jalpaiguri, Darjeeling, Nadia, W. Dinajpur, Purulia, Bardhaman, Bankura, Birbhum, Maldah, Murshidabad, Medinipur, Haora, Hoogli
Mahli	Purulia
Mal Paharia	Kolkata, 24-Parganas, Jalpaiguri, Darjeeling, Nadia, W. Dinajpur, Purulia, Bardhaman, Birbhum, Maldah, Murshidabad, Medinipur, Haora, Hoogli
Mech	Kolkata, Koch Bihar, 24-Parganas, Jalpaiguri, Darjeeling, W. Dinajpur, Medinipur, Haora
MRU	24-Parganas, Jalpaiguri, Darjeeling, Nadia, W. Dinajpur, Purulia, Medinipur, Haora
Munda	Kolkata, Koch Bihar, 24-Parganas, Jalpaiguri, Darjeeling, Nadia, W. Dinajpur, Purulia, Bardhaman, Bankura, Birbhum, Maldah, Murshidabad, Medinipur, Haora, Hoogli
Nagesia	Kolkata, 24-Parganas, Jalpaiguri, Darjeeling, Nadia, W. Dinajpur, Haora
Oraon	Kolkata, Koch Bihar, 24-Parganas, Jalpaiguri, Darjeeling, Nadia, W. Dinajpur, Purulia, Bardhaman, Bankura, Birbhum, Maldah, Murshidabad, Medinipur, Haora, Hoogli
Parhaiya	W. Dinajpur
Rabha	Kolkata, Koch Bihar, 24-Parganas, Jalpaiguri, Darjeeling, Nadia, Purulia, Bardhaman, Murshidabad, Medinipur, Haora, Hoogli
Santhal	Kolkata, Koch Bihar, 24-Parganas, Jalpaiguri, Darjeeling, Nadia, W. Dinajpur, Purulia, Bardhaman, Bankura, Birbhum, Maldah, Murshidabad, Medinipur, Haora, Hoogli
Sauria Paharia	Purulia
Savar	Purulia

The settlement pattern of the tribes of West Bengal show that they live interspersed with others. This is quite distinct from the settlement pattern one finds in states like Bihar, Orissa and Madhya Pradesh. During the colonial period, different tribal groups of neighbouring states migrated to the mineral-rich areas as labourers and also to the hilly areas of West Bengal. Racially, linguistically and culturally these tribals may be categorized into two broad groups—the plain tribes and the hill tribes residing in the Himalayan and sub-Himalayan regions. The tribes living in the plains belong to the Pre-Dravidian or Proto-Austroloid racial stock. The Santhal, Oraon, Munda, Mal, Bhumij, Lodha, Kora, Birhor, and some others come under this category. The languages that they speak belong to the Austric-Dravidian family of languages. Most of them migrated from the neighbouring states of Bihar and Orissa and settled in the districts of Medinipur, Purulia, Bankura and Birbhum. The tribal groups of the hilly regions of north Bengal (Darjeeling, Jalpaiguri, Dakshin and Uttar Dinajpur) belong to the Mongoloid racial stock. The dialects of the Lepchas and Bhutias belong to the Tibeto-Chinese family of the Tibeto-Himalayan group. The dialects of Mechs, Garos and Rabhas belong to the Assam-Burmese group and the dialects of the Chakmas, Hajangs, Maghs belong to the Assam group. Majority of these communities have migrated from Sikkim, Bhutan, Assam and Nepal. Matrilineal system still exists among the Rabhas.[3]

According to the size of the population, the 38 groups may be classified under five heads—very large, large, medium, small and very small. The Santhals are the only community which can be called 'very large', covering more than 50 per cent of the total tribal population of the state. It is also the most advanced among the tribes. The Oraon community, which forms more than 14 per cent of the state's tribal population, can be termed as a 'large' community. Two other communities—Bhumij and Munda may be categorized as 'medium-sized'. Under the 'small' sized communities there are the Koras,

Lodhas, Kherias, Mahalis, Bhutias and Savars. The remaining 29 communities with a population below 1 per cent of the whole may be termed as 'very-small'. It must be noted that the first nine communities constitute 93 per cent of the total scheduled tribe population of the state. Of the 18 districts in West Bengal, according to the 1991 Census, maximum tribal concentration has been recorded in the district of Medinipur (18.11 per cent). On the other hand, in relation to the total population of the district, Jalpaiguri registered the highest percentage of tribal population (21.04 per cent). The combined tribal population of Medinipur and Jalpaiguri make up one-third of the total tribal population of the state. Out of the 339 blocks of all the districts of West Bengal, there are only 4 blocks (2 each in Purulia and Jalpaiguri districts) which have more than 50 per cent tribal population and hence come under the Tribal Sub-Plan.[4] With the exception of a very few gatherers, most tribes in West Bengal grow crops, some are craftsmen and others are labourers in collieries, industries and tea plantations. Only a very small number are engaged in trade, commerce and other services.

The seventies, eighties and nineties witnessed significant changes in the life of the tribals of West Bengal. The state government of West Bengal instituted the Departmentof Tribal Welfare as a separate entity in 1952. In 1967, this department was renamed as the Scheduled Castes and Tribes Welfare Department. Since the welfare and development of backward classes also came to be included under the ambit of this department, it was once again renamed in 1998 as the Department of Backward Classes Welfare. An institute called the Cultural Research Institute is run by this department which has made a significant contribution towards the understanding of changes in tribal society. Apart from these, informed NGO activities in the nineties, along with the implementation of the three-tier panchayati raj and the Joint Forest Management (JFM) programme, have affected several shifts, positive as well as negative, in the status of tribal women. The changing status of these women has been studied here in relation to demographic data, literacy and educational trends, economic empowerment and socio-cultural aspects in the last 30 years.

Demographic Trends

Among the tribals, the growth rate of females vis-à-vis males is proportionately higher than in the general category. The female–male ratio per 1,000 males among the tribals in the state was 969 in 1961, 956 in 1971, 970 in 1981 and 964 in 1991 (census figures). The female–male ratio for the general category in West Bengal was 891 in 1971, 911 in 1981, 917 in 1991 and 934 in 2001. Chart 8.1 shows the percentage of scheduled tribe females in the total female population in 12 states of India in 1993.

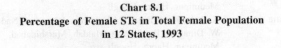

Chart 8.1
Percentage of Female STs in Total Female Population in 12 States, 1993

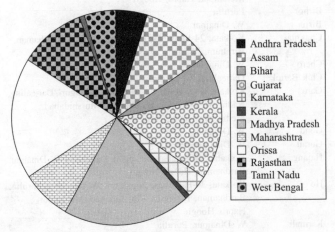

- ■ Andhra Pradesh
- ▨ Assam
- ▣ Bihar
- ▢ Gujarat
- ▦ Karnataka
- ■ Kerala
- ▨ Madhya Pradesh
- ▨ Maharashtra
- ▢ Orissa
- ▨ Rajasthan
- ▨ Tamil Nadu
- ◉ West Bengal

Source: *6th All-India Educational Survey Report*, NCERT, New Delhi, September 1993.

A recent study of three tribal mouzas—Amgachhi, Uporjole and Moubelia, comprising six villages located under the Integrated Tribal Development Project areas of Birbhum district, reveals interesting demographic facts. A comparative study of population of the three mouzas in 1978 and 1993 is reflected in Table 8.2.

From Table 8.2 it is clear that in comparison to other categories the increase in population among the scheduled tribe communities in West Bengal has been the least. The growth rate of females is higher than the males among the tribes. This may be related to the cultural specificities of a tribal society where girls are not looked upon as burdens but valued for their work participation. For a better understanding of the situation among the scheduled tribes, a community analyses has been made in Table 8.3.

Table 8.3 shows that the number of families among the Oraons and the Santhals has increased during these 15 years whereas the number of Kora families has decreased. The reason is that a few Kora families have migrated to some other villages during this period. Among these three tribal communities, both male and female population among the Santhals shows a higher rate of increase.[5] The normal tribal family

[4] Ibid.

[5] Chowdhuri, M.K., S. Das and A. De, 'Tribal Villages Revisited—A Study in Birbhum District, West Bengal', *Bulletin of Cultural Research Institute*, 19(2): 1–33, 1997.

Table 8.2
Distribution of Families and Population in 1978 and 1993

Section	No. of families		Increased by per cent	Number of members						
				Male		Female		Total		Increase
	1978	1993		1978	1993	1978	1993	1978	1993	by per cent
ST	157	192	22.29	358	468	298	417	656	885	34.91
SC	12	16	33.33	25	33	23	33	48	66	37.50
Others	23	37	60.87	72	83	63	72	135	160	18.52
Total	192	245	27.60	455	589	384	522	839	1,111	32.40

Source: M.K. Chowdhuri, S. Das and A. De, 'Tribal Villages Revisited—A Study in Birbhum District, West Bengal', *Bulletin of Cultural Research Institute*, 19(2): 1–33, 1997.

Table 8.3
Distribution of Tribal Families and Population

Community	No. of families		Increased by per cent	Number of members						
				Male		Female		Total		Increased
	1978	1993		1978	1993	1978	1993	1978	1993	by per cent
Santhal	118	115	31.36	274	379	209	320	483	699	44.72
Oraon	11	15	36.36	32	38	37	45	69	83	20.29
Kora	28	22	21.43	52	51	52	52	104	103	–0.96
Total	157	192	22.29	358	468	298	417	656	885	34.19

Source: Same as Table 8.2.

consists of an average of three to five members as tribals generally live in nuclear families.

A study of the three tribal groups—Santhals, Mahalis, Lodhas—of Purulia, Bankura and Medinipur shows that in Medinipur and Purulia, the girl child population is higher than the boy child, whereas in Bankura it is the reverse. In this context, it is worthwhile to note that the growth rate of female children can be related to cultural specificities.[6] Low growth rate of female children is also an indicator of low growth rate of the community.[7]

The change is not uniform among the non-Mongoloid tribes according to the census figures. Tribes like Bhumij, Kora, Mal Paharia, Bedia, Savar, Lohra and Magh have a high female population whereas the Lodha, Mahali, Munda, Santhal, Ho, Korwa and Chakma show a decrease.

Literacy and Education

Between 1961–91, the literacy rate among scheduled tribes showed an increase of 21.23 percentage points against 28.63 for the scheduled castes and 29.74 for other communities. The 1991 Census further reveals that the scheduled tribes are 14.43 percentage points behind the scheduled castes and 37.20 points behind other communities in literacy. However, during the period 1961–91, the scheduled tribe females recorded only 19.18 per cent increase in literacy against 24.26 and 33.21 per cent increase among the scheduled castes and other communities, respectively. In 1991, percentage of literacy among schedule tribe women was 14.98. This is a very low percentage and shows that much remains to be achieved in this field.[8]

From Table 8.4 it is obvious that the situation is miserable as far as education of scheduled tribe females in West Bengal is concerned as the percentage of such girls enrolled is just 4.4 at the primary level, 2.1 at the upper-primary level, 1.6 at the secondary level and 1.7 at the higher-secondary level even in 1993. However, the proportion of scheduled tribe girl students has increased steadily between 1973–74 and 1985–86 as the Table 8.5 will show. The gender gap between tribal boys and girls enrolled at the primary level also went down quite a bit by 1985–86. With the increase in the number of girl students enrolled, the proportion of boys enrolled went down.

[6] See Agnihotri, Satish, *Sex-Ratio Patterns in the Indian Population: A Fresh Exploration*. Sage Publications, New Delhi, 2000.
[7] Chowdhuri, M.K. and Swapan Kumar Kolay, 'Tribal Development—A Micro Level Study in West Bengal.' *Bulletin of the Cultural Research Institute*, 20 (3): 4–5, 1999.
[8] Das, Amal Kumar, 'Glimpses of Development of the Scheduled Castes and Tribes through Decades', in *Fifty Years of Independence*, Government of West Bengal, 1997.

Table 8.4
Percentage of ST Girl Students Enrolled in Different Stages of School (1973–93)

	Percentage of ST girls among total girl students															
	Class I–V				Class VI–VIII				Class IX–X				Class XI–XII			
	1973	1978	1986	1993	1973	1978	1986	1993	1973	1978	1986	1993	1973	1978	1986	1993
Andhra Pradesh	2.6	3.9	4.9	6.4	0.8	1.0	2.4	2.5	0.5	0.8	2.1	1.8	0.3	0.7	1.5	1.8
Assam	13.7	14.0	15.2	19.6	7.7	10.5	13.4	17.9	6.6	9.7	11.7	17.7	2.5	5.8	5.9	13.4
Bihar	9.3	9.8	8.8	9.5	8.8	7.7	7.2	7.4	7.4	9.7	7.4	6.8	6.9	0.0	9.7	4.0
Gujarat	9.7	11.2	14.0	15.8	4.3	5.3	10.4	10.8	2.5	4.4	8.8	10.0	2.2	3.2	8.0	9.2
Haryana	0.4	0.0	0.0	0.0	0.6	0.0	0.0	0.0	0.8	0.0	0.0	0.0	1.3	0.0	0.0	0.0
Karnataka	0.8	1.6	3.3	5.6	0.8	1.1	2.6	3.7	0.6	1.1	2.3	3.2	0.3	1.3	2.8	3.2
Kerala	0.5	0.6	1.1	1.3	0.4	0.3	0.7	0.9	0.4	0.3	0.5	0.7	0.3	0.5	0.6	0.4
Madhya Pradesh	14.0	11.3	16.6	18.0	4.5	5.0	9.0	11.7	3.2	3.1	7.5	8.6	3.2	3.2	5.2	5.9
Maharashtra	4.0	4.9	8.3	10.3	2.1	2.7	4.6	6.2	1.7	2.5	3.9	5.5	1.4	1.9	1.3	4.5
Orissa	14.2	15.1	16.0	18.0	6.0	5.4	7.4	8.6	6.6	4.3	6.1	6.9	6.1	3.6	1.4	5.3
Punjab	0.0	0.0	0.0	0.0	0.0	0.0	0.0	0.0	0.0	0.0	0.0	0.0	0.1	0.0	0.0	0.0
Rajasthan	2.9	3.9	8.2	16.0	1.2	0.9	3.6	4.7	3.0	0.8	2.2	3.8	3.3	0.6	1.5	2.0
Tamil Nadu	0.6	0.4	0.9	1.2	0.3	0.2	0.6	0.5	0.4	0.3	0.7	0.6	0.5	0.1	0.5	0.4
Uttar Pradesh	0.4	0.1	0.2	0.3	0.7	0.1	0.1	0.3	0.4	0.1	0.1	0.3	0.4	0.1	0.1	0.3
West Bengal	2.8	3.1	4.3	4.4	1.9	1.6	2.1	2.1	2.4	1.6	1.4	1.6	1.5	2.2	0.7	1.7
India	4.9	5.4	7.3	8.7	2.6	2.7	4.3	5.2	2.2	2.5	3.7	4.6	2.5	1.4	2.5	3.1

Source: Compiled from various tables from the *3rd, 4th, 5th* and *6th All-India Educational Survey Reports*, NCERT, India, 1973, 1978, 1986, 1999 and *Census of India.*

Table 8.5
Sex-wise Enrolment to Total Enrolment in West Bengal

	1973–74		1979–80		1985–86	
	Boys	Girls	Boys	Girls	Boys	Girls
ST	76.10	23.90	68.19	31.81	59.13	40.87
SC	69.84	30.16	66.87	33.13	63.00	37.00
Non-SC/ST	67.99	32.01	57.14	42.88	57.24	42.76
All communities	61.56	38.44	58.98	41.02	58.23	41.77

Source: Das, Amal Kumar, 'Assessment of Achievement of Scheduled Tribe Females', in R. Gupta (ed.), *Profiles of Tribal Women in West Bengal*, p. 159.

Table 8.6
State-wise Percentage of ST Girls Enrolled at Various School Stages in West Bengal

	Percentage of ST girls enrolled				
Area	I–V	VI–VIII	IX–X	XI–XII	I–XII
Rural	40.16	28.26	21.18	33.39	37.71
Urban	42.56	38.92	36.74	44.96	41.35
Total	40.33	29.78	23.63	37.51	38.04

Source: *6th All-India Education Survey Report*, West Bengal, NCERT, New Delhi, 1998, pp. 209, 213, 217, 221, 225.

Table 8.6, based on the *6th All-India Educational Survey Report* of West Bengal (1993), demonstrates quite a high percentage of scheduled tribe girls enrolled in school from Classes I to XII in the rural and urban areas separately, as well as in the rural and urban regions of the state taken together. The enrolment of tribal girls in the primary classes is quite high: 40.16 per cent in rural areas, 42.56 per cent in urban areas and 40.33 per cent in both these areas taken together, which reflects a lot of enthusiasm on their part to learn and educate themselves. But this gradually seems to die out as the percentage of enrolment drops in the secondary classes to 21.18 per cent in rural areas, 36.74 per cent in urban areas and 23.63 per cent in both the areas. There is a sharp decline in the actual number of tribal girls taking admission at the upper-primary stage. However, there seems to be a rise in the enrolment of tribal girls again at the higher-secondary stage. These figures show that there is not much consistency in the pattern of enrolment of scheduled tribe girls at the different stages of school.

During the Eighth Plan period, a special merit scholarship scheme was introduced among the scheduled caste and scheduled tribe girl students enrolled at the secondary stage to check drop-outs at this stage. The annual report of the Backward Classes Welfare Department, Government of West Bengal, 2001, shows that out of 165 ashram schools with hostels for STs, only 15 are for ST girls exclusively and 3 for both SC and ST girl students. A residential higher-secondary girls' school has been established at Belpahari in the Jhargram subdivision of Medinipur district. The school can accommodate 360 scheduled tribe girls. Another Adivasi Chhatri Nivas for 45 girl students is being built at Jhargram, Medinipur. But the total number of such schools is really few compared to the state's total tribal population.[9] The state's literacy programme has made an impact on the tribal women but it has so far failed to provide a suitable and effective primary education system in the tribal regions. One noticeable change in the tribal women of Bankura and Medinipur is their consciousness about

[9] *Annual Report*. Backward Classes Welfare Department, Government of West Bengal, 2001.

the need to educate their children. Perhaps a more tribal-friendly delivery system could bridge the gaps in literacy and education.

Health

There is acute paucity of information regarding the health status of tribal women in West Bengal. Although it is one of the few states where much research has been undertaken on tribals, most of these studies focus on specific communities and do not provide any qualitative or quantitative analyses of tribal women's health in the state.

The ailments among tribals are often region-specific. For example, in the arid climate of Purulia, leprosy is a predominant disease. The other two are tuberculosis and malaria. A survey conducted in four blocks of Purulia in 1979–81[10] revealed that of the 6,705 leprosy cases reported in the district, 1,580 were tribals. Of these, 907 were males and 673 females. The survey showed that women suffer from leprosy mostly in the age group of 30–44 years whereas most cases for men have been reported much earlier, in the 13–29 age group. For tuberculosis too, women in the 30–44 age group tend to suffer most, according to the survey.

A comparative study of Santhal and Mahali women living in the Medinipur district of West Bengal throws up interesting facts.[11] Their awareness towards better living conditions, about their own and their children's health and their opinion regarding key decisions taken in their family and community have been analysed in this study. The survey among Santhal and Mahali women of 23 villages shows that they have positive awareness regarding water. Women of both these communities used tubewells for drinking water and only 5 per cent Santhal women used tap water for drinking purposes. All tribal families surveyed used open fields for excretion and had no exposure to modern sanitary facilities. Only 5 per cent Santhals used sanitary toilets.

Majority of the tribal women (Santhal 71.08 per cent, Mahali 58.24 per cent) took doctor's advice during pregnancy. Negligence and ill behaviour of the staff of government hospitals are important causes deterring these women from availing pre-natal and post-natal facilities. Mothers were generally aware of the immunization programme for children administered by rural sub-centres or primary health centres. This study did not report a single case of mothers taking their children to local private doctors for vaccination. About 60 per cent tribal women of both communities completed the immunization course for their children. About 69 per cent Santhal and 78 per cent Mahali women preferred small families, 9 per cent Santhals and 14 per cent Mahalis preferred middle-sized families, and 22 per cent Santhals and 8 per cent Mahalis preferred large families. More Mahali women (about 54 per cent) tended to accept family planning practices and preferred small-sized families slightly more than the Santhals.

From such studies focussing on different tribes, one may conclude that healthcare for tribal women in West Bengal needs to be planned and reorganized differently keeping in mind area-specific and age-specific needs and constraints and the role of traditional tribal medicine in remedying illnesses.

Employment and Work

Looking at tribal communities in India, one cannot ignore the fact that barring some acculturated sections, tribal societies are generally economically undifferentiated and tribals practice little specialization. Those families which undertake farming—settled or slash-and-burn—are involved also in other subsidiary occupations like animal husbandry, wage-labour handicrafts, gathering of food and forest produce, etc. A study by Buddhadeb Chaudhuri[12] on the distribution pattern of occupation shows that settled cultivation is practiced by 139 communities, shifting cultivation by 84 communities, handicrafts by 49 communities, wage labour by 40 communities, food gathering by 39 communities, hunting by 19 communities, animal husbandry by 15 communities, terrace cultivation by 11 communities, fishing by 7 communities and trade and commerce by 7 communities. Indeed, it has been correctly pointed out by Chaudhuri that the pattern does not reflect the percentage of population dependent on each of these occupations. The most significant fact is that about 90 per cent of the tribal population depends on cultivation, whether settled or shifting, either directly as peasant-cultivators or indirectly as farm-labourers.

Women play bigger social and economic roles in tribal societies than in non-tribal societies. They work in fields,

[10] Chowdhuri, M.K., S. De and A. Debnath, 'Impact of Prevalent Diseases among the Tribals of Tribal Concentrated Areas of West Bengal', in Buddhadev Chaudhuri (ed.), *Tribal Health: Socio-Cultural Dimensions*. Inter India, New Delhi, 1986.

[11] Manna, Samita, 'Awareness of Tribal Women for Better Living—A Comparative Study of Two Groups in Similar Ecology', *Bulletin of Cultural Research Institute*, 20, 1998.

[12] Chaudhuri, Buddhadeb, 'Tribal Women and the Economy', in J.P. Singh, N.N. Vyas and R.S. Mann (eds), *Tribal Women and Development*. MLV Tribal Research and Training Institute, Udaipur, 1998.

forests, homes and markets. In 1987, Fernandes and Menon showed that a tribal housewife puts in, on an average, 14 hours of active work every day. On account of deforestation, she also has to walk three to four hours to fetch fuel for the family. On the other hand, men work for 10–11 hours every day.[13] With increasing pressures and degradation of natural resources, life has been growing tougher, demanding more and more physical exertion from tribal women mostly. However, tribal women have largely remained in the Plan-shadow relative to their specificities. The National Commission for Women, in its report in 1998 on tribal women and employment, had focussed on three central issues.[14]

1. While considering the employment of tribal women there is the need to address the diversification of their occupational pattern and their induction into secondary and tertiary sectors constituting modern sectors. But we cannot afford to lift our focus from the primary sectors of agriculture and forestry and related self-employment activities which absorb a vast majority at present.

2. Tribal women have been engaging themselves in two main economic pursuits, i.e., agriculture and forestry. But tribal society is generally economically undifferentiated

and they also engage in other subsidiary occupations like animal husbandry, wage-labour, handicrafts, collection of food and forest produce, etc.

3. The planning process in our country has been androcentric, i.e., male-oriented, specifically for tribal society and generally for all social groups. This has created a distinct handicap, a drawback and a hiatus.

In West Bengal we find that women as active workers constitute a large section of the tribal force in particular and women's labour force in general. Table 8.7 gives the district-wise percentage of ST female in the total ST population of West Bengal according to different workgroups in 1981 and 1991.

Either as agricultural labourers, tea garden labourers and at times industrial and construction labourers, tribal women work as bread winners or as active producers at home. Besides being engaged in various agricultural activities like sowing, weeding, transplanting and harvesting, tribal women collect minor forest produce such as leaves, gum, fruits, seeds, herbal plants, broom grass and forest grass, which are useful for domestic as well as commercial purposes. The role of tribal women in minor forest produce component (which can be as high as

Table 8.7
District-wise Percentage of ST Females in Total ST Population according to Different Workgroups (1981–91)

District	Percentage of females in total ST population		Total main Workers		Marginal workers		Non-workers	
	1981*	1991**	1981	1991	1981	1991	1981	1999
Koch Bihar	47.45	47.59	17.69	22.99	76.25	87.56	64.84	61.39
Jalpaiguri	48.58	48.81	33.88	34.78	63.44	72.61	56.87	55.37
Darjeeling	48.44	48.77	34.88	37.65	65.37	69.19	56.81	55.88
W. Dinajpur	48.91	49.16	26.71	35.87	80.14	91.22	62.26	59.16
Maldah	51.10	49.82	22.35	35.53	81.21	90.87	65.65	58.90
Murshidabad	49.49	49.27	36.18	37.77	81.55	92.45	58.65	56.10
Nadia	49.56	48.82	32.58	31.49	64.10	83.79	60.95	60.23
24-Parganas	49.62	48.80	24.52	26.27	66.88	87.87	64.74	60.82
Calcutta	32.55	40.84	9.13	12.01	20.00	37.17	57.49	58.65
Haora	43.46	46.50	30.07	31.82	55.72	37.64	59.65	59.51
Hoogli	49.32	49.44	45.49	46.27	67.53	77.38	53.01	52.22
Medinipur	49.45	49.20	38.80	41.06	75.76	83.15	56.00	52.95
Bankura	49.71	49.28	38.29	40.87	71.37	85.53	55.80	52.97
Purulia	49.29	49.03	30.37	36.79	78.71	87.30	57.87	52.54
Bardhaman	48.86	49.21	59.73	41.60	64.96	71.24	55.91	54.93
Birbhum	49.57	49.38	65.30	39.26	84.88	86.39	58.70	54.79

Source: Chowdhuri, M.K. and A.De. 'Imprints of Four Decades: Scheduled Tribes of West Bengal', Cultural Research Institute, 19 (3): 5, 1997.
Notes: * *Census of India 1981*, Series-23, West Bengal, SC and ST State Primary Census Abstract for Scheduled Tribes.
        ** *Census of India 1991*, Series-26, West Bengal, SC and ST State Primary Census Abstract for Scheduled Tribes.

[13] Fernandes, Walter and Menon, Githa, *Tribal Women and Forest Economy—Deforestation, Exploitation and Status Change*. Indian Social Institute, New Delhi, 1987, p. 99.
[14] *Report on Tribal Women and Employment*. National Commission for Women, New Delhi, 1998.

60 per cent of the total tribal household income budget) has not been precisely evaluated, but observers see it as preponderant.[15]

Tribal women contribute no less than their male counterparts in mining, mineral collection and other industrial operations. The major contribution of tribal women labourers is in the construction industry. Women are employed in large numbers at various levels of construction work like soil-lifting, sand-cement mixing and lifting of bricks. Table 8.8 gives decadal statistics on the sex-wise distribution of scheduled tribe workers in different industrial categories in the state.

From Table 8.8 it is clear that the percentage of female workers as cultivators and agricultural labourers has increased in every decade. It is interesting that among male workers the percentage of cultivators shows a decrease, though an increase is evident in the percentage of male agricultural labourers. It is significant that the percentage of females engaged as cultivators increased from 8.41 in 1971 to 20.95 in 1991, though the percentage was much higher in 1961. The percentage of female agricultural workers has decreased from 67.29 in 1971 to 61.27 in 1991, though in the same category there has been a phenomenal increase from 32.64 per cent in 1961 to 61.27 per cent in 1991. In livestock, forestry and fishing, percentage of female workers is much higher than the males. But the percentage of women working in this sector registers a steady decline from 17.20 in 1971 to 11.05 in 1991.

Projects for Tribal Women

The West Bengal Tribal Development Cooperative Corporation Limited (WBTDCCL) looks after the economic interest of the tribals. At present, 121 Large-sized Multipurpose Cooperative Societies (LAMPS), 2 mahila samitis, a Labour Contract Cooperative Society are affiliated to WBTDCCL. Since the seventies, several projects have been initiated in some of the tribal districts of West Bengal. For instance, in Bankura, in order to empower rural women, the first women's collective called the Grameen Mahila Shramik Unnayan Samiti was formed in Jhilimili in 1981. The Centre for Women's Development Studies (CWDS), New Delhi, played a leading role in organizing the women here. The women had taken a brave decision to withstand the pressure of going in for seasonal migration. Alternative employment was found for them in the form of collection of tendu and sal leaves from the adjoining forest. These were sold by the samiti to the local unit of LAMPS. The women of the samiti got a monopoly in this work and were guaranteed a minimum price for their collection. The guarantee of a minimum price acted as a tremendous spur for the women. The success attained by this samiti and a desire for extension led to the formation of two more mahila samitis in Chendapathar and Bhurkura. In Bhurkura, about 7–8 acres of land were donated to the samiti, which was a much needed support for the women as it enabled them to embark on the path of finding employment which could be sustained for a prolonged period. They began to organize work on wasteland on which they could plant arjun and asan trees and breed tassar silkworms. Thus, the success of one project spawned off others. Finally, it was in 1986 that the Nari Bikash Sangha (NBS) was formed to function as an apex body to coordinate the activities of the mahila samitis in the villages. The CWDS report says, 'The Bankura project has reached a plateau. After 16 years of great hardship the women are still

Table 8.8
Sex-wise Percentage Distribution of Scheduled Tribe Workers

Industrial Categories	1961		1971		1981		1991	
	M	F	M	F	M	F	M	F
Total workers	58.48	41.55	54.43	19.90	53.51	29.08	52.57	33.30
Cultivators	50.95	45.54	39.13	8.41	37.67	18.44	35.11	20.95
Agricultural labourers	25.46	32.64	42.54	67.29	42.58	60.42	44.24	61.27
Livestock, forestry, fishing, etc.	–	–	8.67	17.20	9.70	14.35	8.51	11.05
Mining and quarrying	13.69	13.32	1.23	0.79	1.28	0.65	1.23	0.46
Household industry	1.03	1.79	0.99	1.09	0.85	1.43	0.99	1.71
Other than household industry	1.70	2.00	1.55	1.70	2.84	2.93	3.31	2.62
Construction	0.39	0.24	0.36	0.50	0.49	0.29	0.64	0.23
Transport and storage	0.53	0.07	0.96	0.13	1.12	0.11	0.51	0.10
Other services	5.79	4.15	3.72	2.63	2.93	1.13	3.51	1.32
Non-workers	41.52	58.45	45.57	80.10	46.49	70.92	47.43	66.70

Source: *Bulletin of Cultural Research Institute*, 9(3): 5, 1997.

[15] Gupta, Ratna (ed.), *Profiles of Tribal Women in West Bengal*. Scheduled Castes and Tribes Welfare Department, Government of West Bengal, 1990, p. 93.

happy with the little prosperity that they have won and with their new found social status.'[16] The 24 samitis cover a little more than 60 villages and 2,500 members. It involves a handful of the women. 'It has not turned out to be a "movement" sweeping through the region.'[17] Since the late nineties, the government has taken the policy of forming self-help groups to organize women. A women's cooperative society was established in Koch Bihar in 1999–2000 for improved housing and dairy schemes. The women beneficiaries are being given improved breeds of cows. A 10,000-litre capacity dairy plant has been set up in Koch Bihar for processing and marketing milk and milk products.

Forest Management and Women

Tribal women's dependence on forest is well-known. In 1988, Government of India adopted the policy of participatory management of forests. In West Bengal, the Joint Forest Management policy was implemented by a government order in 1989 and the first Forest Protection Committees (FPCs) were formed in 1991 under the initiative of the forest department. FPCs are village-based committees with representation from each household, which protect and manage the forests. For this they hold regular meetings in the presence of forest department staff or by themselves. The FPCs have executive committees which discuss various issues related to the forest as well as the community. In West Bengal, women were not roped in adequately in the beginning. Later, in November 1991, an amendment to the State Government Order of 1989 was passed which bestowed joint FPC membership on the husband and wife. In spite of this there has been little active participation of women in the decision making or functioning of the FPCs. The 1991 Amendment does not deal with situations where a man has more than one wife or where either the husband or the wife is simply not there (due to death, divorce, abandonment, etc.). There is no provision for the representation of women in the executive committees. Yet the necessity of soliciting women's active participation in the FPCs is acknowledged and perceived to be important as women are the major collectors, processors and users of forest produce.[18] There are 11 all-women FPCs in the state, of which 3 are formed solely of tribal women. But the inability of women to read and write make them over-dependant on the male members. However, the JFM policy has helped tribal women on the whole because they have got free access to non-timber forest produce (NTFP) and to fuel. Much more can be achieved if women's representation in the FPCs is made compulsory and women are represented adequately in the decision making process.

Socio-cultural Aspects

Although the status of tribal women varies between regions and tribes, it is widely recognized that they enjoy a better status within their own communities than women in mainstream Indian society. It must, however, be mentioned that tribal women enjoy equal participation only in relation to economic activities. In the traditional forest-based adivasi economies, women's important role as gatherers of forest food and subsistence goods made them economically valued members of the community. This is reflected in the tradition of bride-price among most adivasi communities, whereby the groom's father has to pay a price to the bride's father. Bride-price is common to all the tribes. While negotiating a match, information is sought about the working capacity of the mother and aunts of a girl. They are looked upon as an addition to the family workforce. Among the Birhor tribe, if the groom's side is too poor to pay the bride-price, the groom works in the would-be bride's family even before marriage. This works as a payment of the bride-price in kind. In the communities which follow the custom of bride-price, the daughter is not regarded as a burden as she might bring in material wealth and parents do not have to dread the time when she will have to be married. A change from bride-price to dowry has undermined the status of women in tribal society in recent times. For example, among the Bhumij tribe, bride-price is being replaced by dowry to be paid to the groom's family by the bride's father. This practice is being adopted by the relatively well-to-do in the Bhumij community, who are taking more and more to the caste-Hindu norms and practices.

Marriage among tribal females is said to be generally universal. All physically and mentally sound females are married. The practice of child marriage is rare among the tribals in West Bengal, the only exception being the Shabar tribe who reside in Purulia and Dinajpur. Tribal marriage rituals are simple but are long-drawn and require the involvement and participation of the entire village community. In the 'Sanga' system of marriage, the bride-price is low and there is hardly any community festival. There is another kind of wedding which

[16] Sarkar, Chanchal, 'Tilting against Odds: Bankura's Rural Women Organized for Empowerment'. CWDS, New Delhi, 1998, p. 48.

[17] Ibid.

[18] Sarin, Madhu. 'Who is Gaining? Who is Losing: Gender and Equity Concerns in Joint Forest Management'. Society for Promotion of Wasteland Development, New Delhi, 1998.

is very rare. In case an unmarried woman gets pregnant and the name of the father is not revealed, then it becomes necessary to find someone to marry the girl. This is necessary to provide the unborn child a legal status as well as a clan name. Often, to get a boy one has to spend a lot of money as dowry. Once someone agrees to marry, he accepts the girl as wife in front of the village elders and the marriage is declared legal. In case noone agrees to marry the pregnant girl, the child is allowed to be born and he gets the clan and family name of the community manager, called 'Jaga-majhi', who has the responsibility of managing and guiding the young boys and girls of the community. Polygamy is generally not practised, though in cases where no children are born to the first wife, a second wife is allowed by the community.

Remarriage of widows or divorcees is an accepted norm in all tribal societies of West Bengal. In the case of widows, one cannot by rule marry the elder brother of the dead husband, though nuptial bond may be tied to the younger brother. In case the younger brother refuses to marry the widow, she can marry anyone else. The community ratifies such alliances. In the case of a widower, he is allowed to marry the younger sister of the dead wife and not the elder sister.

Divorce is a commonly accepted practice in tribal societies. Divorce proceedings are conducted by the village/tribal panchayats with the pradhan or the chief playing a decisive role. Divorce can be initiated by either the husband or the wife. A man can seek divorce on three grounds—wife being lazy, adulterous or barren. Women can ask for divorce on grounds of the husband being cruel. Divorce is granted by the tribal panchayats and involves a simple act of ritualistic tearing of a sal leaf in front of the community leaders. In case of divorce, the bride-price given before marriage is returned. A divorced woman can remarry. However, after divorce or widowhood, all rights are not bestowed on a woman who has remarried. For example, a remarried woman is not allowed to enter the sacred place of the household where the family deities or ancestors are worshipped. Even the rituals of a second marriage are different.

Property Rights

As such, tribal women have no right to property. This is the same for all tribal societies of West Bengal with small variations. For example, among the Ho tribe, who inhabit the forest fringes bordering Bihar, a daughter can enjoy some land of residence if she is the only child in the family. But this can happen only if the panchayat of the community agrees to it. Even then the land is not transferred in her name or in the name of her husband, and if she has no male child, the land reverts back to her paternal family at her death. The responsibility of unmarried sisters rests with the brothers, particularly the eldest. As per the social norms enforced by the village elders, both unmarried daughters and widows are looked after by their families.

However, according to Santhal customary laws, only males can inherit land. Sons jointly succeed the father. Except in a few circumstances, females have no right to inheritance. If brothers are co-sharers in a holding and one brother dies, the surviving brothers and the sons of the deceased inherit his share. While an unmarried Santhal daughter has no rights to the immovable property of her family, any property that a Santhal woman acquires out of her own wages is her own. Succession of property of an unmarried daughter devolves first to her father, after that to her brothers or their sons, then to her mother followed by her paternal uncles and, finally, in the absence of all male agnates to her sisters or their heirs. In the event of a man having no son and only daughters, the Santhal custom permits him to take a son-in-law into his house and give him all rights of a son. Thus, a daughter is marginalized. Even a widow has no claim over her deceased husband's property if there are agnates. She can keep the landed property of her husband only with the consent of the agnates. However, the Santhal Parganas Tenancy Act, 1949, contains in Section 20 a special provision by which a Santhal male can, with the previous written permission of the deputy commissioner, gift land to a sister or a daughter. It also provides that with the previous written permission of the deputy commissioner, a man may make a grant with respect to his land, not exceeding one half of the area of the holding, to his widowed mother or to his wife for her maintenance after his death.[19]

Even in the Santhal society, customary rules against female succession have been changing under pressure of public opinion. As Jayanti Alam has argued, in certain other respects, a Santhal woman is as free as a man.[20] In household matters, she has an equal say as her husband. In matters of arranging marriages of her children, her role is often decisive. She can open and independently manage a shop in a public area. Even in village meetings, women are virtually at par with men. Moreover, she is now not debarred from owning land and can also own certain types of movable property. But the pace of change is very slow on account of illiteracy and a lack of awareness. Furthermore, with the gradual creation of a middle class within

---

[19] Quoted in *Report on Tribal Women and Employment*, 1998.
[20] Alam, Jayanti, *Tribal Women Workers: A Study of Young Migrants*. Raj Publications, New Delhi, 2000, p. 51.

the tribal society, certain middle class values have also been imbibed by the Santhals. The socio-economic identity of the schedule tribes are getting more varied and complex. The previous identity of Santhal girls labouring in the fields have subtly been replaced by that of office-going Santhal girls. New ventures like eateries are being set up by tribal women as a source of income.

Witch-hunt

The other kind of oppression that women face in a tribal society is witch-hunt. Once identified as a witch, a woman is usually hounded and often killed. Among tribals, a part of the public sphere that is reserved for men is the ritual, magico-religious sphere. This ritual knowledge, which is used to increase the productivity of the forest and to protect the group from danger, is something from which women are excluded. This reflects the male control over knowledge within tribal society.[21] The male access to ritual knowledge is used to institute control over women's labour and has been used consistently to impose oppression on women. It has taken the form of a superstition which thrives in poverty and in socially restive situations. Moreover, as Mahasweta Devi writes, the tribals today are pressed from all sides. They have lost their lands and are forced to work as migrant workers. Their culture is threatened by the vulgar onslaught of *jatra*, films and video parlours. Political forces have created an exploitative elite class within them who exercise undue power. The dowry system has made its way into the tribal society. Faced with such absolute erosion of traditional norms and culture, the tribals have held on to the witch cult with a vengeance in order to assert their identity.[22] It is thriving with the active support of the police, and the women are the victims. Between 1951 and 1979, 96 witch killings took place in Maldah alone.[23] The July–December issue of *Bortika*, 1991,[24] lists the number of witches killed or hounded out of their villages between 1996 and 1999. Witch-hunt killed a total of 21 in 6 districts of the state in these four years. In 1996, 3 witches were killed, 1 each in Bardhaman, Darjeeling and Jalpaiguri. In the following year, 11 witches were killed in the districts of Jalpaiguri, Purulia and Bardhaman. In 1998, a witch was killed in Bankura and in 1999, 6 were killed in Purulia, Maldah and Jalpaiguri. For attempting to murder and hounding women out of their villages on the

charge of being witches, 25 cases were reported from 7 districts of the state between 1996 and 1999. These are from Medinipur, Bardhaman, Bankura, Maldah, Koch Bihar, Uttar Dinajpur and Jalpaiguri. The 1996 figures are 9, the 1997 figures are 7, the 1998 figures are 4 (Bardhaman only) and the 1999 figures are 5 (Uttar Dinajpur only). Witch-hunt is now used for settling all kinds of scores—land disputes, political disputes among parties and personal animosities.

Conclusion

The last three decades of the twentieth century have seen some policy changes with the objective of bringing the tribals at par with the general population. This effort has had a somewhat mixed impact on women. Indeed, a policy of development based on technology and with an emphasis on the private sector paves the way for a higher degree of concentration of capital and extremely exploitative situations with very serious implications for women. The tribal women generally have been at the receiving end. The forces of caste, class and gender have produced devastating results for these women. The exploitation of tribal women working in the stone quarries in the town of Mallarpur in Birbhum district is a case in point. Mallarpur is situated around 50 km north of Santiniketan in the economically backward Rampurhart-1 block of Birbhum district. The only industry in the area adjoining Mallarpur in Rampuhart-1, Mayureshwar-1 and Muhammad Bazar blocks is stone quarrying. Large numbers of quarry workers are Santhal women who are drawn from this desperately impoverished area. Many of them are teenaged girls. They are made to work 10 to 12 hours a day, are paid a pittance and are not provided with mandatory safeguards such as masks. They receive no medical treatment and no compensation if they are injured in the course of their work. The tribal women working here suffer from serious health problems, such as asthma, as a result of inhaling stone dust. All existing environmental laws and statutes of West Bengal are violated by the quarry owners. Many of these quarries have been dug on land which belonged to the Santhals.[25] As the Deputy Superintendent of Police (DSP), Birbhum, reports: 'The quarry owners occupied the lands either through deceitful means or through political influence from the tribals at a minimum cost violating the Indian

---

[21] Nathan, Dev, *From Tribe to Caste*. Indian Institute of Advanced Studies, Shimla, 1997, p. 248.

[22] Ghatak, Maitreya (ed.), *Dust on the Road: The Activist Writings of Mahasweta Devi*. Seagull Books, Calcutta, 1997, p. 168.

[23] Ibid.

[24] Devi, Mahasweta (ed.), *Bortika*, July–December 1991.

[25] Report submitted by the Deputy Superintendent of Police, Birbhum, to the Women's Commission, Government of West Bengal, July 2002.

Constitution',[26] which prohibits any transfer of tribal land in the form of sale or mortgage. This is a clear indication of the collusion of vested interests and political and administrative corruption, all of which by nature are caste-dominated. Besides, the women workers as well as their teenaged girls are sexually exploited by the rich owners. Generally, the police collude with the quarry owners. One such case that was widely reported in the media revealed the extraordinary clout of the owners, administrative and political.[27] The whole incident came to light because of an FIR lodged by Hupni Kishku, a Santhal woman of the area. The case was taken up by a local NGO which had been working towards organizing the workers. It finally led to the arrest of Kunal Deb who headed the NGO. The gender angle was clear when Hupni Kishku was punished by the tribal council and paraded naked around the village on the allegation that in spite of her being married she had a relationship with a non-tribal man.[28] This is a glaring example of double-edged gender oppression. Finally, the women who have struggled to get themselves educated and employed feel a tremendous pressure. While they get alienated from their own kind, they are not easily accepted at par by other communities. This was the tragedy of Chuni Kotal, the first woman Lodha graduate, who found it difficult to cope with these pressures and committed suicide.

Chuni Kotal was the first woman from a primitive tribe to have passed the higher-secondary examination. In 1983, she was appointed a social worker at the Jhargram ITDP office. From childhood, despite starvation, working in the fields and having no money to purchase books, she doggedly continued to study. In 1985, she graduated and in 1987, she was appointed superintendent of Rani Shiromoni SC and ST Girls'

Hostel in Medinipur. That she was a Lodha, a hated name in the district, clung to her like a stigma. Some of the hostel staff were against her because of her origins. Chuni felt suffocated in the job. Matters became worse when she enrolled herself at the local Vidyasagar University as an M.Sc. student in anthropology. From the very first day, a certain male professor started abusing her calling her a member of a criminal tribe who had no right to study M.Sc. The same professor failed her twice, as a result of which she lost two years. Then she became a victim of the inner politics between the members of the faculty. Chuni kept complaining to the university and the government but the enquiry commission set up to probe her complaints did nothing. Cornered from all sides she realized that being a Lodha she should never have dreamt of higher studies. She committed suicide on 16th August 1992.

Tribal women are oppressed from both sides—they are oppressed by their communities, where superstition thrives and traditional authority is exercised by Jana-gurus and other leaders. On the other hand, development processes have also led to the loss of their home and hearth. Lack of adequate number of schools, particularly upper-primary and high schools, have kept them away from education. Schools with hostel facilities are too few and far between for girls. A complete lack of minimum healthcare renders the tribal society helpless and fosters a breeding ground for superstitions. This in turn leads to witch-hunt. Inadequate village-based support system for women and their non-involvement in the planning process keeps them away from economic empowerment. This chapter has tried to highlight some of these gaps which need to be bridged in order to improve the status of tribal women in West Bengal.

[26] Ibid.
[27] *The Times of India*, Kolkata, 27 April 2002.
[28] *The Times of India*, Kolkata, 29 April 2002.

Micro Studies and Statistics

PART B
APPENDICES

Tables on Demography

Table A1
Select District-wise Demographic Profile of West Bengal, 1971–2001

District	Population 2001 (fig. in '000s)			Average annual population growth (%)			Density per sq. km				Urban population as % of total population		
	Male	Female	Total	1971–81	1981–91	1991–2001	1971	1981	1991	2001	1971	1981	1991
Koch Bihar	1,272	1,207	2,479	2.5	2.2	1.4	418	523	641	732	6.8	6.9	7.8
Jalpaiguri	1,753	1,650	3,403	2.7	2.6	2.2	280	356	450	547	9.6	14.1	16.4
Darjeeling	826	780	1,606	3.1	2.7	2.4	254	325	413	510	23.1	27.6	30.5
West Dinajpur				2.9	3.9	–	357	449	585	–	9.3	11.2	13.3
Uttar Dinajpur	1,261	1,181	2,442	–	3.4	2.9	–	–	604	778	–	–	–
Dakshin Dinajpur	770	732	1,502	–	2.4	2.2	–	–	555	677	–	–	–
Maldah	1,689	1,601	3,290	2.6	3.0	2.5	434	544	706	881	4.2	4.8	7.1
Murshidabad	3,004	2,859	5,863	2.5	2.8	2.4	550	695	890	1,101	8.5	9.4	10.4
Nadia	2,365	2,239	4,604	3.3	3.0	2.0	568	755	981	1,172	18.7	21.6	22.6
24 Parganas (S)	3,564	3,345	6,909	1.9	3.0	2.1	612 (N+S)	441	574	694	35.2	51.0	13.3(S)
24 Parganas (N)	4,635	4,295	8,930	2.7	3.2	2.3	–	–	1,179	2,181	–	–	51.2(N)
Kolkata	2,506	2,075	4,581	1.9	0.7	0.4	30,276	22,260	23,784	24,760	100.0	100.0	100.0
Haora	2,242	2,031	4,273	2.3	2.6	1.5	1,640	2,022	2,543	2,913	41.9	45.1	49.6
Hoogli	2,588	2,452	5,040	2.4	2.2	1.6	913	1,130	1,383	1,601	26.5	29.5	31.2
Medinipur	4,929	4,709	9,638	2.2	2.4	1.6	401	479	592	685	7.6	8.5	9.9
Bankura	1,635	1,557	3,192	1.7	1.8	1.4	295	345	408	464	7.5	7.6	8.3
Purulia	1,298	1,237	2,535	1.6	2.0	1.4	256	296	355	405	8.3	9.0	9.4
Bardhaman	3,603	3,317	6,920	2.3	2.5	1.4	557	688	861	985	22.8	29.4	35.1
Birbhum	1,546	1,467	3,013	1.8	2.2	1.8	390	461	562	663	7.0	8.3	9.0
West Bengal	41,488	38,733	80,221	2.3	2.5	1.8	504	615	767	904	24.8	26.5	27.5
India	531,277	495,738	1,027,015	2.5	2.4	2.1	177	216	267	324	19.9	23.3	25.7

Sources: Government of West Bengal, *Statistical Abstract: West Bengal, 1994–95*, Tables 1.3, 1.5, 1.6.
Census of India 2001, Provisional Population Totals, Paper 1 of 2001, pp. 44, 84.

Table A2
District-wise Female Literacy in West Bengal, 1991–2001

District	Female literacy		Total literacy		SC/ST literacy		Female literacy SC/ST	
	1991	2001	1991	2001	T.SC 1991	T.ST 1991	SC 1991	ST 1991
Koch Bihar	33.3	57.0	45.8	67.2	33.3	23.1	21.7	16.7
Jalpaiguri	33.2	52.9	45.1	63.6	33.4	18.0	21.3	9.7
Darjeeling	47.8	63.9	58.0	72.9	38.6	33.7	27.7	26.4
West Dinajpur								
Uttar Dinajpur	22.9	37.2	39.3	48.6	26.4	15.3	15.1	7.3
Dakshin Dinajpur	35.3	55.1		64.5				
Maldah	24.9	41.7	35.6	50.7	24.0	12.2	16.1	4.7
Murshidabad	29.6	48.3	38.3	55.1	26.1	12.9	19.5	6.5

(Contd.)

(Table A2 Contd.)

District	Female literacy		Total literacy		SC/ST literacy		Female literacy SC/ST	
	1991	2001	1991	2001	T.SC 1991	T.ST 1991	SC 1991	ST 1991
Nadia	44.4	60.1	52.5	66.6	37.4	17.8	28.6	9.1
24 Parganas (N)	58.0	72.1	66.8	78.5	44.6	20.0	34.3	9.8
24 Parganas (S)	40.6	59.7	55.1	70.2	40.4	20.0	27.1	8.6
Kolkata	72.1	78.0	77.6	81.3	49.6	44.4	41.1	25.0
Haora	57.8	70.9	67.6	77.6	26.8	30.0	27.0	20.0
Hoogli	56.9	67.7	66.8	75.6	33.1	22.7	22.5	11.5
Medinipur	56.6	64.6	69.3	75.2	43.8	32.4	31.9	19.8
Bankura	36.6	49.8	52.0	63.8	21.8	26.9	10.4	11.2
Purulia	23.2	37.2	43.3	56.1	25.1	22.2	10.5	8.6
Bardhaman	51.5	61.9	61.9	71.0	29.6	20.2	19.9	11.4
Birbhum	37.2	52.2	48.6	62.2	22.3	11.2	13.4	4.5
West Bengal	46.6	60.2	57.7	69.2	34.3	22.4	23.4	12.0
India	18.2	54.2	52.2	65.4	37.4	29.6	23.8	18.2

Sources: *Census of India 1991*, Series-26, Preliminary Census Abstract, West Bengal, Part II-B(ii), *Scheduled Caste and Scheduled Tribes.*
Census of India 2001, Series-20, Provisional Population Totals, West Bengal, Paper 1 of 2001, p. 52.

Table A3
Proportion of Married, Widowed and Divorced/Separated People in West Bengal (60 Years and above), 1991

District		Married (%)			Widowed (%)			Divorced/Separated (%)		
		(60–69)	(70–79)	(80+)	(60–69)	(70–79)	(80+)	(60–69)	(70–79)	(80+)
Koch Bihar	Male	86.8	80.6	61.8	10.6	16.8	18.5	0.6	0.7	0.4
	Female	31.0	19.6	18.7	67.7	78.6	69.0	0.6	0.5	0.5
Jalpaiguri	Male	82.9	75.6	64.8	14.3	19.8	25.0	0.5	0.8	1.5
	Female	40.2	24.7	22.7	58.8	74.0	69.0	0.4	0.3	0.9
Darjeeling	Male	82.4	71.4	55.7	13.6	23.7	24.4	0.7	0.3	0.3
	Female	52.7	32.2	21.0	44.0	65.1	69.7	1.0	0.4	0.3
West Dinajpur	Male	87.0	80.5	60.5	10.1	16.4	20.2	0.4	0.5	0.9
	Female	36.9	23.7	17.3	61.2	74.3	72.2	0.8	0.6	0.7
Maldah	Male	86.0	79.8	50.1	10.6	16.2	13.8	0.4	0.2	0.5
	Female	39.2	21.6	18.0	58.5	74.7	56.1	0.7	0.4	1.0
Murshidabad	Male	91.0	85.2	73.2	6.7	11.9	17.9	0.4	0.4	0.9
	Female	38.9	22.2	20.2	50.6	76.6	75.4	0.7	0.5	1.0
Nadia	Male	89.8	84.0	62.4	7.2	12.5	13.3	0.2	0.1	0.4
	Female	37.8	18.0	14.2	61.0	80.4	75.8	0.5	0.2	0.2
24 Parganas (N)	Male	89.9	83.8	62.6	6.6	12.0	11.5	0.3	0.4	0.3
	Female	43.3	23.7	18.8	55.2	74.8	71.1	0.5	0.6	0.4
24 Parganas (S)	Male	88.8	82.9	59.8	7.6	12.9	11.2	0.4	0.3	0.2
	Female	42.3	24.2	18.9	56.3	73.9	66.4	0.5	0.3	0.2
Calcutta	Male	87.7	83.7	74.2	5.4	10.1	14.4	0.1	0.2	0.1
	Female	49.9	26.2	24.2	47.8	69.6	70.2	0.2	0.3	0.1
Haora	Male	90.3	85.2	61.4	6.0	10.7	13.7	0.1	0.2	0.1
	Female	42.7	23.2	20.1	56.3	75.8	69.0	0.2	0.1	0.1
Hoogli	Male	89.4	84.4	71.2	7.2	12.6	18.3	0.2	0.3	1.0
	Female	40.2	21.2	18.6	58.7	77.1	76.1	0.3	0.5	0.2
Medinipur	Male	89.2	81.6	66.5	8.5	16.1	20.5	0.5	0.3	0.6
	Female	38.0	18.6	12.7	61.1	80.2	82.9	0.5	0.5	0.6
Bankura	Male	85.5	76.0	58.3	11.8	20.3	18.4	0.2	0.2	0.2
	Female	31.2	15.2	13.7	67.9	83.8	73.5	0.2	0.2	–
Purulia	Male	83.5	74.5	58.5	14.9	24.0	32.2	0.5	0.3	2.9
	Female	35.1	18.5	13.5	64.3	81.1	85.8	0.4	0.3	0.2
Bardhaman	Male	88.2	81.3	57.7	8.9	15.3	14.4	0.4	0.2	2.1
	Female	38.2	21.0	19.6	60.6	77.7	68.5	0.4	0.2	0.5
Birbhum	Male	82.8	72.4	49.4	14.3	23.4	12.4	0.5	0.2	0.7
	Female	32.3	15.5	18.7	66.3	81.8	61.8	0.5	0.3	0.6
West Bengal	Male	88.1	81.1	62.7	8.6	14.5	15.8	0.3	0.3	0.7
	Female	39.7	21.7	18.2	59.0	76.7	72.1	0.5	0.4	0.4
India	Male	85.4	77.6	61.7	12.0	19.6	25.4	0.3	0.3	0.5
	Female	52.5	32.7	23.4	46.3	66.1	69.8	0.4	0.4	0.3

Source: *Census of India 1991, West Bengal District Profiles and District Profiles of India.*

Table A4
Percentage Distribution of Population by Age Groups in West Bengal (1981–91)

Age group (Year)	Sex-ratio		Total population		Male population		Female population	
	1981	1991	1981	1991	1981	1991	1981	1991
0–14	966	963	38.9	36.9	37.8	35.8	40.0	37.5
15–19	923	901	10.4	9.3	10.3	9.3	10.5	9.2
20–24	908	978	9.4	9.3	9.5	9.1	9.4	9.5
25–29	876	1,027	8.3	9.0	8.5	8.7	8.2	9.4
30–39	858	873	12.3	14.0	12.6	14.6	11.9	13.3
40–49	811	861	9.3	9.2	9.8	9.7	8.7	8.6
50–59	802	950	5.8	6.1	6.2	6.3	5.5	5.8
60+	992	1,081	5.6	6.5	5.3	6.5	5.8	6.7

Sources: *Census of India 1981*, Series-23, Social and Cultural Tables, West Bengal, Part IVA.
Census of India 1991, Series-26, Social and Cultural Tables, West Bengal, Part IVA.

Table A5
Selected Indicators of Nuptiality in West Bengal (Rural Areas), 1971–91

District	Percentage of never married women aged 20–24 years			Percentage of ever-married women aged 15–19 years			Percentage of currently married women with age at marriage below 18 years who married during	
	1971	1981	1991	1971	1981	1991	1981–86	1986–91
Koch Bihar	5.3	6.9	9.0	59.6	57.5	44.0	64.2	56.5
Jalpaiguri	14.5	16.9	18.3	55.7	38.4	31.3	46.9	41.9
Darjeeling	33.3	NA	34.2	30.2	26.7	24.4	22.2	38.6
West Dinajpur	–	10.5	10.8	61.0	46.3	39.4	58.1	51.2
Maldah	6.1	12.2	11.5	62.7	45.4	47.6	63.4	59.5
Murshidabad	3.3	8.7	8.5	70.8	57.6	51.5	68.6	61.2
Nadia	6.5	12.1	11.8	63.5	44.4	42.3	63.1	57.9
24 Parganas	9.2	10.4	–	58.2	46.7	–	–	–
24 Parganas (N)	–	–	12.4	–	–	43.5	68.7	59.7
24 Parganas (S)	–	–	11.7	–	–	37.4	65.5	56.8
Calcutta (Urban)	3.5	45.6	46.1	22.0	15.3	13.4	29.5	21.6
Haora	8.3	17.9	19.0	42.4	31.3	23.4	57.4	43.1
Hoogli	7.8	18.4	16.6	48.9	32.8	29.5	54.3	43.4
Medinipur	4.8	9.9	12.1	69.9	47.5	39.4	65.2	55.7
Bankura	4.5	10.1	14.4	68.8	45.0	36.7	62.7	53.0
Purulia	3.7	6.0	8.5	68.3	55.6	51.2	67.2	65.6
Bardhaman	5.6	11.4	11.8	64.8	41.5	38.3	61.5	50.9
Birbhum	1.7	10.0	10.1	70.0	49.5	45.2	62.8	55.1
West Bengal (Rural)	7.5	11.7	12.7	62.0	44.9	39.6	62.6	54.3
West Bengal (Urban)	25.6	37.0	36.9	30.5	22.9	19.3	38.9	30.3
West Bengal (U + R)	12.3	19.0	19.5	NA	37.5	33.0	56.5	48.3

Source: *Census of India 1991, Social and Cultural Tables, West Bengal District Profile.*

Tables on Health and Nutrition

APPENDIX B

Table B1
Low Birth Weight Among Children in India

	Not weighed			Weighed			Below 2.5 kg			2.5+ kg			Don't know/missing		
	Urban	Rural	Total	Urban	Rural	Total	Urban	Rural	Total	Urban	Rural	Total	Urban	Rural	Total
NFHS-1															
W. Bengal	38.2	83.2	73.0	61.8	16.8	27.0	10.6	4.0	5.5	42.6	9.3	16.9	8.6	3.5	4.7
India	49.7	87.8	79.1	50.3	12.2	20.9	10.0	1.9	3.8	28.0	5.8	10.8	12.3	4.5	6.3
NFHS-2															
W. Bengal	21.1	69.3	60.6	78.9	30.7	39.4	14.9	7.1	8.5	57.3	17.8	24.9	6.7	5.8	6.0
India	40.2	78.6	70.1	59.8	21.4	29.9	10.8	4.2	5.7	40.3	13.4	19.4	8.7	3.7	4.8

Source: Findings from National Family Health Survey-1 (NFHS-1) (1992–93), International Institute of Population Sciences, Mumbai; National Family Health Survey-2 (NFHS-2) (1998–99), International Institute of Population Sciences, Mumbai.

Table B2
Birth Weight Percentage of Babies Weighed and Birth Weight, in India and 15 States, 1998–99

	Percent distribution of babies weighed and found							
	Babies weighed within two days of birth		Below 2,500 gm		2,500 gm and above		Weight not known	
	%	Rank	%	Rank	%	Rank	%	Rank
Andhra Pradesh	46.0	4	18.2	10	66.5	8	15.2	9
Assam	22.7	8	11.8	2	77.9	3	10.2	6
Bihar	7.4	14	14.0	3	75.5	4	10.6	7
Gujarat	42.5	5	17.0	8	75.5	4	7.6	3
Haryana	21.4	9	20.2	13	58.7	10	21.1	11
Karnataka	42.5	5	19.5	12	70.6	6	10.0	5
Kerala	95.1	1	14.8	4	79.7	2	5.3	1
Madhya Pradesh	16.4	10	16.5	7	48.9	12	34.7	14
Maharashtra	55.4	3	18.9	11	72.5	5	8.6	4
Orissa	16.0	11	15.2	5	69.4	7	15.4	10
Punjab	28.9	7	15.3	6	56.8	11	27.9	12
Rajasthan	12.4	12	21.9	14	47.4	13	30.8	13
Tamil Nadu	76.5	2	10.8	1	82.6	1	6.7	2
Uttar Pradesh	7.9	13	17.3	9	37.0	14	45.7	15
West Bengal	35.1	6	22.1	15	64.9	9	13.0	8
India	28.0		16.9		68.2		14.9	

Source: Reproductive and Child Health Programme, Rapid Household Survey (RCH-RHS) (Phase I and II) (1998–99), International Institute of Population Sciences, Mumbai, 2001, Table 4.1 p. 54.

Table B3
Nutritional Status of Children in India and in 15 Major States

| State | Weight for age | | | | | | | | Height for age | | | | Weight for height | | | |
| | % below –3SD | | % below –2SD | | | | | | % < –3SD | | % < –2SD | | % < –3SD | | % < –2SD | |
	1992–93	Rank	1998–99	Rank	1992–93	Rank	1998–99	Rank	1998–99	Rank	1998–99	Rank	1998–99	Rank	1998–99	Rank
Andhra Pradesh	15.6	5	10.3	4	49.1	6	37.7	6	14.2	4	38.6	4	1.6	3	9.1	3
Assam	18.7	8	13.3	6	50.4	8	36.0	4	33.7	15	50.2	11	3.3	8	13.3	6
Bihar	31.1	15	25.5	15	62.6	15	54.4	13	33.6	14	53.7	14	5.5	13	21.0	12
Gujarat	17.6	6	16.2	7	50.1	7	45.1	8	23.3	9	43.6	8	2.4	6	16.2	8
Haryana	9.0	2	10.1	3	37.9	2	34.6	3	24.3	10	50.0	10	0.8	2	5.3	1
Karnataka	19.4	10	16.5	9	54.3	11	43.9	7	15.9	5	36.6	3	3.9	11	20.0	11
Kerala	6.1	1	4.7	1	28.5	1	26.9	1	7.3	1	21.9	1	0.7	1	11.1	4
Madhya Pradesh	22.3	12	24.3	14	57.4	13	55.1	14	28.3	11	51.0	12	4.3	12	19.8	9
Maharashtra	21.3	11	17.6	10	54.2	10	49.6	10	14.1	3	39.9	6	2.5	7	21.2	13
Orissa	22.7	13	20.7	11	53.3	9	54.4	13	17.6	7	44.0	9	3.9	10	24.3	14
Punjab	14.2	4	8.8	2	45.9	4	28.7	2	17.2	6	39.2	5	0.8	2	7.1	2
Rajasthan	19.2	9	20.8	12	41.6	3	50.6	11	29.0	12	52.0	13	1.9	4	11.7	5
Tamil Nadu	13.3	3	10.6	5	48.2	5	36.7	5	12.0	2	29.4	2	3.8	9	19.9	10
Uttar Pradesh	24.6	14	21.9	13	59.0	14	51.7	12	31.0	13	55.5	15	2.1	5	11.1	4
West Bengal	18.4	7	16.3	8	56.8	12	48.7	9	19.2	8	41.5	7	1.6	3	13.6	7
India	20.6		18.0		53.4		47.0		23.0		45.5		2.8		15.5	

Source: NFHS-1, Table 10.10, NFHS-2, Table 7.17. Height for age and weight for height not available for W. Bengal in 1992, hence not shown for others.

Notes: Figures are for children under four years for NFHS-1 and under three years for NFHS-2. Each of the indices is expressed in standard deviation units (SD) from the median of the International Reference Population. The per cent of children who are more than 3 and more than 2SD units below the median of the International Reference Population (–3SD and –2SD) are shown according to selected characteristics.

Each index is expressed in standard deviation units (SD) from the median of the International Reference Population. '% below –2SD' includes children who are below –3SD from the International Reference Population median, International Institution of Population Sciences, Mumbai. '% below –2SD' would mean undernourished and '% below –3SD' would mean severely undernourished.

Table B4
Anaemia among Children in India and in 15 Major States, 1998–99

| | % Children age 6–35 months classified as having iron-deficiency anaemia | | | | |
| State | Any anaemia | | | | |
	%	Rank	Mild anaemia (%)	Moderate anaemia (%)	Severe anaemia (%)
Andhra Pradesh	72.3	5	23.0	44.9	4.4
Assam	63.2	2	31.0	32.2	0.0
Bihar	81.3	12	26.9	50.3	4.1
Gujarat	74.5	7	24.2	43.7	6.7
Haryana	83.9	14	18.0	58.8	7.1
Karnataka	70.6	4	19.6	43.3	7.6
Kerala	43.9	1	24.4	18.9	0.5
Madhya Pradesh	75.0	8	22.0	48.1	4.9
Maharashtra	76.0	9	24.1	47.4	4.4
Orissa	72.3	5	26.2	43.2	2.9
Punjab	80.0	11	17.4	56.7	5.9
Rajasthan	82.3	13	20.1	52.7	9.5
Tamil Nadu	69.0	3	21.9	40.2	6.9
Uttar Pradesh	73.9	6	19.4	47.8	6.7
West Bengal	78.3	10	26.9	46.3	5.2
India	74.3		22.9	45.9	5.4

Source: NFHS-2, Table 7.19.

Note: The haemoglobin levels are adjusted for altitude of the enumeration area.

Table B5
Iron-deficiency Anaemia among Children (6–35 Months) by Sex in West Bengal and India, 1998–99

| | % Children with any anaemia | | % of children with | | | | | | Number of children | |
| | | | Mild anaemia | | Moderate anaemia | | Severe anaemia | | | |
Sex	India	W. Bengal	India	W. Bengal	India	W. Bengal	India	W. Bengal	India	W. Bengal
Male	75.1	78.1	22.2	26.5	47.0	46.3	5.9	5.3	10,477	485
Female	73.3	78.5	23.7	27.2	44.8	46.3	4.8	5.1	9,539	444
All	74.3	78.3	22.9	26.9	45.9	46.3	5.4	5.2	20,016	929

Sources: NFHS-2 India, Table 7.11.
NFHS-2, W. Bengal.

Table B6
Anaemia among Women by State, Percentage of Ever-married Women Classified as having Iron-deficiency Anaemia, by Degree of Anaemia, in India and in 15 Major States, 1998–99

| | No anaemia | | Any anaemia | | Mild anaemia | | Moderate anaemia | | Severe anaemia | |
	%	Rank	%	Rank	%	Rank	%	Rank	%	Rank
Andhra Pradesh	50.2	8	49.8	9	32.5	8	14.9	8	2.4	9
Assam	30.3	14	69.7	15	43.2	13	25.6	13	0.9	3
Bihar	36.6	13	63.4	14	42.9	12	19.0	12	1.5	5
Gujarat	53.7	4	46.3	4	29.5	4	14.4	6	2.5	10
Haryana	53.0	5	47.0	5	30.9	5	14.5	7	1.6	6
Karnataka	57.6	3	42.4	3	26.7	2	13.4	3	2.3	8
Kerala	77.3	1	22.7	1	19.5	1	2.7	1	0.5	1
Madhya Pradesh	45.7	9	54.3	10	37.6	11	15.6	9	1.0	4
Maharashtra	51.5	6	48.5	7	31.5	6	14.1	5	2.9	11
Orissa	37.0	12	63.0	13	45.1	14	16.4	11	1.6	6
Punjab	58.6	2	41.4	2	28.4	3	12.3	2	0.7	2
Rajasthan	51.5	6	48.5	6	32.3	7	14.1	5	2.1	7
Tamil Nadu	43.5	10	56.5	11	36.7	10	15.9	10	3.9	12
Uttar Pradesh	51.3	7	48.7	8	33.5	9	13.7	4	1.5	5
West Bengal	37.3	11	62.7	12	45.3	15	15.9	10	1.5	5
India	48.2		51.8		35.0		14.8		1.9	

Source: NFHS-2, Table 7.7.
Note: The haemoglobin levels are adjusted for altitude of the enumeration area and for smoking when calculating the degree of anaemia.

Table B7
Nutritional Status of Women by State, among Ever-married Women, Mean Height, Percentage with Height below 145 cm, Mean Body Mass Index (BMI), and Percentage Below Specified Levels of BMI, in India, and in 15 Major States, 1998–99

| | Height | | | | Weight-for-height* | | | |
	Mean height (cm)	Rank	% below 145 cm	Rank	Mean body mass index (BMI)	Rank	% with BMI below 18.5 kg/m²	Rank
Andhra Pradesh	151.2	10	12.7	10	20.3	7	37.4	9
Assam	149.9	14	17.3	13	20.1	9	27.1	4
Bihar	149.5	15	19.5	15	19.4	14	39.3	12
Gujarat	151.8	6	10.2	6	20.7	5	37.0	8
Haryana	154.3	2	4.6	2	21.3	3	25.9	3
Karnataka	152.0	5	9.6	5	20.4	6	38.8	11
Kerala	152.6	4	8.8	4	22.0	2	18.7	2
Madhya Pradesh	151.7	7	10.8	7	19.8	12	38.2	10
Maharashtra	151.4	9	11.9	8	20.2	8	39.7	13
Orissa	150.5	11	14.9	11	19.2	15	48.0	15
Punjab	154.5	1	4.1	1	23.0	1	16.9	1
Rajasthan	153.7	3	5.6	3	19.9	11	36.1	7
Tamil Nadu	151.5	8	12.0	9	21.0	4	29.0	5
Uttar Pradesh	150.3	12	16.4	12	20.0	10	35.8	6
West Bengal	150.0	13	19.2	14	19.7	13	43.7	14
India	151.2		13.2		20.3		35.8	

Source: NFHS-2, Table 7.5.
Note: * Excludes women who are pregnant and women with a birth in two preceding months. The body mass index (BMI) is the ratio of the weight in kilograms to the square of the height in metres.

Table B8
Singulate Mean Age at Marriage, by Sex from 1961 to 1998–99 and Percentage of Women Marrying before 18 Years

| | 1961 Census | | 1971 Census | | 1981 Census | | 1991 Cencus | | NFHS-1 | | NFHS-2 | | % women marrying <18* | |
	Male	Female	Male	Female	Male	Female	Male	Female	Male	Female	Male	Female	%	Rank
Andhra Pradesh	22.3	15.2	22.8	16.3	23.1	17.3	23.5	18.3	23.6	18.1	23.9	18.3	37.3	10
Assam	25.9	18.6	25.8	18.7	U	U	U	U	27.9	21.6	27.8	21.7	28.7	5
Bihar	18.9	14.3	20.0	15.3	21.6	16.6	22.1	17.5	23.2	18.0	23.8	18.8	58.2	15
Gujarat	21.7	17.1	22.4	18.5	23.3	19.6	23.4	19.9	23.9	20.2	24.4	20.2	25.3	4
Haryana	U	U	20.9	17.7	25.2	17.9	22.8	18.8	23.1	18.4	24.6	19.8	31.6	7
Karnataka	24.7	16.4	25.2	17.9	26.0	19.3	26.2	20.1	26.1	19.6	26.7	20.1	35.3	9
Kerala	26.6	20.2	27.0	21.3	27.5	22.1	27.7	22.2	28.1	22.1	27.9	21.5	9.1	1
Madhya Pradesh	18.7	13.9	19.5	15.0	20.8	16.6	21.7	17.8	22.0	17.4	23.5	18.9	51.4	13
Maharashtra	22.6	15.8	23.8	17.6	24.4	18.8	24.8	19.7	24.9	19.3	25.3	19.8	30.9	6
Orissa	21.9	16.4	22.7	17.3	24.3	19.1	25.0	20.2	25.6	20.7	26.6	21.2	32.2	8
Punjab	22.6	17.5	24.1	20.1	25.0	21.1	24.3	21.0	24.8	21.1	25.7	22.1	11.2	2
Rajasthan	19.6	14.2	19.9	15.1	20.6	16.1	21.3	17.5	22.7	18.4	22.3	18.3	57.1	14
Tamil Nadu	25.3	18.4	26.1	19.6	26.1	20.3	26.4	20.9	26.4	20.5	26.6	20.9	19.1	3
Uttar Pradesh	19.4	14.5	19.8	15.5	21.3	16.7	21.9	18.0	23.0	18.6	23.3	19.0	49.8	11
West Bengal	24.3	15.9	24.6	18.0	26.0	19.3	25.9	19.7	25.9	19.2	26.2	19.6	51.1	12
India	21.9	15.9	22.6	17.2	23.3	18.4	24.0	19.3	25.0	20.0	24.9	19.7	36.9	

Source: NFHS-1, Table 4.3 and NFHS-2, Table 2.4; RCH-RHS, Appendix I, pp. 121–36.
Notes: * RCH = % of girls marrying below age 18.
U: Not available.

Table B9
Current Use of Family Planning Method by Women in India and 15 States. NFHS 1 and 2 (per cent)

| | Not using any method | | Using any method | | | | Using traditional method | | | | Using any modern method | | | |
	1992–93	1998–99	1992–93	Rank	1998–99	Rank	1992–93	Rank	1998–99	Rank	1992–93	Rank	1998–99	Rank
Andhra Pradesh	53.0	40.4	47.0	9	59.6	5	0.5	15	0.5	14	46.5	6	58.9	2
Assam	57.2	56.7	42.8	10	43.3	11	22.9	1	15.8	2	19.8	14	26.6	13
Bihar	76.9	75.5	23.1	14	24.5	15	1.5	10	1.6	11	21.6	13	22.4	14
Gujarat	50.7	41.0	49.3	7	59.0	6	2.4	7	5.6	7	46.9	5	53.3	6
Haryana	50.3	37.6	49.7	6	62.4	4	5.3	5	8.9	4	44.3	8	53.2	7
Karnataka	50.9	41.7	49.1	8	58.3	7	1.8	8	1.7	10	47.3	4	56.5	3
Kerala	36.7	36.3	63.3	1	63.7	3	8.9	3	7.8	5	54.4	1	56.1	4
Madhya Pradesh	83.5	55.7	36.5	11	44.3	10	1.0	13	1.4	12	35.5	10	42.6	10
Maharashtra	46.3	39.1	53.7	4	30.9	13	1.2	12	1.0	13	52.5	2	59.9	1
Orissa	63.7	53.2	36.3	12	46.8	9	1.6	9	5.6	7	34.8	11	40.3	11
Punjab	41.3	33.3	58.7	2	66.7	1	7.4	4	12.4	3	51.3	3	53.8	5
Rajasthan	38.2	59.7	31.8	13	40.3	12	0.9	14	1.9	8	30.9	12	38.1	12
Tamil Nadu	50.2	47.9	49.8	5	52.1	8	4.6	6	1.8	9	45.2	7	50.3	8
Uttar Pradesh	80.2	71.9	19.8	15	28.1	14	1.3	11	5.7	6	18.5	15	22.0	15
West Bengal	42.6	33.4	57.4	3	66.6	2	20.1	2	18.5	1	37.3	9	47.3	9
India	59.4	51.8	40.6		48.2		4.3		5.0		36.3		42.8	

Source: Compiled from NHFS-1, Table 6.7 and NFHS-2, Table 5.7.

Table B10

Ante-natal Care Indicators in India and in 15 Major States

Percentage of births in three years preceding survey for which mothers received

	At least one ante-natal check up				Three or more ante-natal check ups			Two or more TT injections				Iron/Folic acid tablets				% Received all types of recommended ante-natal care (3)		
	1992–93		1998–99		1992–93	1998–99		1992–93		1998–99		1992–93		1998–99		1992–93	1998–99	
	%	Rank	%	Rank	%	%	Rank	%	Rank	%	Rank	%	Rank	%	Rank	%	%	Rank
Andhra Pradesh	86.3	4	92.7	3	NA	80.1	3	74.8	4	81.5	5	76.4	3	81.2	4	NA	35.6	4
Assam	49.3	12	60.1	11	NA	30.8	10	34.9	13	51.7	13	39.4	12	55.0	10	NA	15.8	11
Bihar	36.8	14	36.3	14	NA	17.8	13	30.7	14	57.8	10	21.4	15	24.1	14	NA	6.4	14
Gujarat	75.7	7	86.4	6	NA	60.2	6	62.7	9	64.2	9	69.3	7	78.0	6	NA	25.0	7
Haryana	72.7	9	58.1	12	NA	37.4	9	63.3	8	79.7	6	59.9	8	67.0	9	NA	20.8	9
Karnataka	83.5	5	86.3	7	NA	71.4	4	69.8	7	74.9	7	74.9	4	78.0	6	NA	41.5	3
Kerala	97.3	1	98.8	1	NA	98.3	1	89.8	2	86.4	3	91.2	1	95.2	1	NA	64.9	1
Madhya Pradesh	52.1	11	61.0	10	NA	28.1	11	42.8	11	55.0	11	44.3	11	48.9	11	NA	10.9	12
Maharashtra	82.7	6	90.4	4	NA	65.4	5	71.0	5	74.9	7	70.6	6	84.8	3	NA	31.0	6
Orissa	61.6	10	79.5	8	NA	47.3	8	53.8	10	74.3	8	49.9	10	67.6	8	NA	21.4	8
Punjab	87.9	3	74.0	9	NA	57.0	7	82.7	3	89.9	2	73.6	5	79.6	5	NA	31.7	5
Rajasthan	31.2	15	47.5	13	NA	22.9	12	28.3	15	52.1	12	29.2	14	39.3	12	NA	8.3	13
Tamil Nadu	94.2	2	98.5	2	NA	91.4	2	90.1	1	95.4	1	84.1	2	93.2	2	NA	50.8	2
Uttar Pradesh	44.7	13	34.6	15	NA	14.9	14	37.4	12	16.9	14	29.5	13	32.4	13	NA	4.4	15
West Bengal	75.3	8	90.0	5	NA	57.0	7	70.4	6	82.4	4	56.3	9	71.6	7	NA	19.7	10
India	62.3		65.4		NA	43.8		53.8		66.8		50.5		57.6		NA	20.0	

Source: Compiled from NFHS-1, Table 9.7 and NFHS-2, Tables 8.7 and 8.13.

Notes:
1. The cut off date in 1992–93 was four years whereas in 1998–99 it was three years.
2. Data for NFHS-1are based on births in the period 1–47 months prior to the survey. Data for NFHS-2 include only the two most recent births during the three years preceding the survey.
3. Three or more ante-natal check ups (with the first check up within the first trimester of pregnancy), two or more tetanus toxoid injections, and iron and folic acid tablets or syrup for three or more months.

Table B11

Type of Ante-natal Care (ANC) for Women in India and 15 States (per cent)

	ANC provided						Check up						Treatment given					
	Any		In first trimester		3+ visits		Weight taken		BP measured		Abdominal check up		IFA tablets		At least 1 TT injection		Full ANC	
	%	Rank	%	Rank	%	Rank	%	Rank	%	Rank	%	Rank	%	Rank	%	Rank	%	Rank
Andhra Pradesh	94.2	3	56.1	4	87.5	3	81.9	3	84.2	3	85.9	3	72.9	4	89.9	3	63.4	3
Assam	56.0	12	28.2	10	29.2	11	28.4	9	38.9	9	52.5	8	57.7	8	68.3	12	24.8	10
Bihar	29.7	15	14.4	15	17.1	15	11.8	14	16.2	13	25.4	15	16.9	15	64.6	13	10.1	15
Gujarat	79.1	8	36.5	6	55.0	8	40.7	7	43.4	8	53.0	7	68.1	6	77.9	10	42.7	6
Haryana	77.7	9	31.8	8	41.3	10	27.5	10	30.6	10	50.1	9	48.7	10	81.0	8	23.9	11
Karnataka	88.9	4	59.5	2	78.0	4	54.3	5	67.1	4	82.4	4	72.6	5	83.0	7	60.1	4
Kerala	99.3	1	83.2	1	98.3	1	83.0	2	96.0	1	87.8	2	90.0	1	95.7	2	86.1	1
Madhya Pradesh	52.4	13	18.5	13	28.0	13	17.8	12	19.9	12	40.1	12	45.3	11	69.8	11	20.2	12
Maharashtra	87.6	5	41.0	5	65.8	5	66.0	4	65.5	5	79.7	5	76.8	3	89.5	4	54.8	5
Orissa	72.9	10	28.8	9	43.7	9	27.3	11	28.6	11	43.8	11	60.8	7	79.7	9	32.5	8
Punjab	87.2	6	32.4	7	56.4	6	33.9	8	47.4	7	64.9	6	42.7	12	88.5	5	25.4	9
Rajasthan	62.3	11	19.9	12	28.3	12	13.2	13	19.9	12	33.5	13	34.5	13	62.0	14	16.6	13
Tamil Nadu	98.4	2	56.2	3	94.2	2	89.2	1	87.5	2	89.3	1	79.1	2	98.0	1	75.3	2
Uttar Pradesh	46.8	14	14.6	14	19.6	14	8.0	15	10.0	14	25.7	14	27.7	14	60.5	15	11.2	14
West Bengal	84.1	7	27.5	11	55.4	7	46.8	6	47.9	6	48.9	10	54.7	9	86.4	6	33.4	7
India	65.3		29.7		44.2		34.5		38.2		49.4		48.7		74.7	10	31.8	

Source: RCH-RHS, 2001, Table 3.4, p. 32.

Table B12
Percentage of Women Who Received any Ante-natal Care (ANC) by Source in India and 15 States

	Percentage of women who had any ANC		At home from health worker		In govt. health facility		In private health facility	
	%	Rank	%	Rank	%	Rank	%	Rank
Andhra Pradesh	94.20	3	48.00	2	34.70	11	55.80	3
Assam	56.00	12	10.30	12	40.80	7	12.90	10
Bihar	29.70	15	4.60	15	7.10	15	19.30	9
Gujarat	79.10	8	34.10	5	23.90	13	37.90	5
Haryana	77.70	9	5.70	14	39.50	9	22.90	8
Karnataka	88.90	4	40.00	3	41.90	5	41.10	4
Kerala	99.30	1	39.30	4	35.80	10	65.60	1
Madhya Pradesh	52.40	13	22.00	9	25.30	12	12.90	10
Maharashtra	87.60	5	31.90	7	41.20	6	37.90	5
Orissa	72.90	10	33.40	6	43.30	4	12.10	12
Punjab	87.20	6	6.70	13	47.80	2	37.20	6
Rajasthan	62.30	11	23.50	8	39.90	8	8.80	13
Tamil Nadu	98.40	2	48.40	1	43.80	3	59.70	2
Uttar Pradesh	46.80	14	13.60	11	23.60	14	12.80	11
West Bengal	84.10	7	18.20	10	49.30	1	34.90	7
India	65.30		22.00		31.60		26.20	

Source: RCH-RHS, Table 3.2, p. 29.

Table B13
Maternal Care Indicators in India and 15 Major States in 1992–93 and 1998–99

	Birth delivered at home						Birth delivered in medical institution						Safe delivery					
	NFHS (1992–93)		NFHS (1998–99)		RCH (1998–99)		NFHS (1992–93)		NFHS (1998–99)		RCH (1998–99)		NFHS (1992–93)		NFHS (1998–99)		RCH (1998–99)	
	%	Rank	%	Rank	%	Rank	%	Rank	%	Rank	%	Rank	%	Rank	%	Rank	%	Rank
Andhra Pradesh	67.2	6	50.2	5	49.1	4	32.8	6	49.8	5	50.6	4	49.3	5	65.2	3	59.8	5
Assam	88.9	15	82.4	14	75.5	10	11.1	15	17.6	13	23.6	10	17.9	14	21.4	15	31.9	12
Bihar	87.9	12	85.4	15	84.9	15	12.1	12	14.6	15	14.9	15	19.0	13	23.4	13	19.0	15
Gujarat	64.4	5	53.7	6	53.3	6	35.6	5	46.3	6	46.1	6	42.5	7	53.5	7	55.9	6
Haryana	83.3	9	77.6	11	74.1	9	16.7	9	22.4	10	25.7	9	30.3	9	42.0	9	32.7	10
Karnataka	62.5	4	44.9	3	49.6	5	37.5	4	51.1	4	50.0	5	50.9	4	59.1	6	59.9	4
Kerala	12.2	1	7.0	1	2.9	1	87.8	1	93.0	1	97.0	1	89.7	1	94.0	1	97.4	1
Madhya Pradesh	84.1	10	79.9	13	78.1	13	15.9	10	20.1	12	21.5	13	30.0	10	29.7	12	27.5	13
Maharashtra	56.1	3	47.4	4	42.6	3	43.9	3	52.6	3	57.1	3	53.2	3	59.4	5	61.2	3
Orissa	85.9	11	77.4	10	76.2	11	14.1	11	22.6	9	23.4	11	20.5	12	33.4	11	32.7	11
Punjab	75.2	8	62.5	8	58.9	7	24.8	8	37.5	8	40.5	7	48.3	6	62.6	4	54.7	7
Rajasthan	88.4	13	78.5	12	77.2	12	11.6	13	21.5	11	22.5	12	21.8	11	35.8	10	33.4	9
Tamil Nadu	36.6	2	20.7	2	20.9	2	63.4	2	79.3	2	78.8	2	71.2	2	83.8	2	82.4	2
Uttar Pradesh	88.8	14	64.5	9	83.4	14	11.2	14	15.5	14	16.2	14	17.2	15	22.4	14	20.8	14
West Bengal	68.5	7	59.9	7	61.0	8	31.5	7	40.1	7	38.9	8	33.0	8	44.2	8	45.6	8
India	74.5		66.4		65.9		25.5		33.6		34.0		34.2		42.3		40.2	

Source: Compiled from NFHS-1, Table 9.7; NFHS-2, Table 3.8; RCH-RHS.
Notes: 1. Tables for NFHS-1 are based on births in the period 1–47 months prior to the survey. Tables for NFHS-2 include only the two most recent births during the three years preceding the survey.
2. Health Professionals: In NFHS-1 only allopathic doctor or nurse/midwife; in NFHS-2 doctors, auxillary nurse midwife, nurse, midwife, lady health visitor, or other health professional; in RCH-RHS safe deliveries includes institutional deliveries and home deliveries assisted by doctor/nurse/ANM.

Table B14
Pregnancy, Delivery, and Post Delivery Complications in India and 15 States (per cent)

	Percentage of Women									
	Who had pregnancy complication during pregnancy		Who had delivery complication		Who had post delivery complication		Who sought* treatment for pregnancy complication		Who sought* treatment for post delivery complication	
	%	Rank	%	Rank	%	Rank	%	Rank	%	Rank
Andhra Pradesh	41.3	15	31.4	7	24.5	14	70.2	6	69.1	6
Assam	60.5	10	66.2	3	39.9	8	38.6	13	38.9	13
Bihar	76.4	2	73.4	2	64.2	1	31.5	15	29.0	15
Gujarat	66.5	7	76.0	1	49.7	5	59.8	7	51.2	7
Haryana	49.1	13	14.4	15	22.5	15	53.7	9	58.0	9
Karnataka	43.4	14	21.6	11	28.4	12	72.9	4	71.3	4
Kerala	80.4	1	28.8	8	28.2	13	86.3	1	80.8	1
Madhya Pradesh	62.9	8	45.5	5	46.7	6	39.2	12	33.5	12
Maharashtra	69.1	6	56.0	4	54.6	4	71.1	5	64.9	5
Orissa	72.8	4	35.1	6	62.9	2	41.5	11	25.7	11
Punjab	59.3	11	20.0	12	29.5	11	75.7	2	48.9	2
Rajasthan	57.1	12	19.0	13	30.9	10	42.0	10	56.4	10
Tamil Nadu	69.5	5	27.6	9	36.9	9	73.8	3	41.4	3
Uttar Pradesh	62.0	9	17.8	14	41.3	7	37.1	14	48.4	14
West Bengal	74.3	3	25.3	10	59.2	3	56.3	8	46.2	8
India	63.6		37.0		44.4		46.7		46.6	

Source: RCH-RHS, Table 3.12, p. 52.
Note: * % refers to those who had complications.

Table B15
Per 1,000 Distribution of Mothers by Type of Delivery

	Type of Delivery											
	Normal						Operation					
	Rural	Rank	Urban	Rank	Total	Rank	Rural	Rank	Urban	Rank	Total	Rank
Andhra Pradesh	917	11	848	12	900	12	52	5	118	3	88	2
Assam	962	1	847	13	956	2	11	10	133	2	17	9
Bihar	918	10	935	3	920	9	10	11	31	11	12	11
Gujarat	954	4	918	5	944	4	21	8	67	7	34	8
Haryana	913	13	939	2	918	11	61	2	37	10	56	5
Karnataka	942	6	868	10	926	7	24	7	83	6	37	7
Kerala	779	15	753	15	773	15	171	1	197	1	177	1
Madhya Pradesh	929	8	903	7	925	8	9	12	46	8	16	10
Maharashtra	940	7	903	6	928	6	29	6	86	5	47	6
Orissa	920	9	902	8	919	10	5	13	24	12	7	13
Punjab	903	14	876	9	896	14	57	4	83	6	64	4
Rajasthan	949	5	922	4	945	3	9	12	19	13	11	12
Tamil Nadu	916	12	860	11	898	13	58	3	108	4	74	3
Uttar Pradesh	957	3	944	1	956	1	13	9	44	9	17	9
West Bengal	960	2	833	14	937	5	13	9	133	2	34	8
India	935		891		927		23		76		32	

Source: National Sample Survey Organization, 1995–96. NSS 52nd Round. Department of Statistics, Government of India, Table 4.7, pp. 107–9.

Table B16
Symptoms of Reproductive Tract Infections in India and 15 Major States, 1998–99

	Percentage of currently married women reporting various symptoms of reproductive tract infections												
	% with any abnormal vaginal discharge		% with symptoms of a urinary tract infection (1)		% with any abnormal vaginal discharge or symptoms of a urinary tract infection (1)		% with painful intercourse (often)		% with bleeding after intercourse (ever) (2)		% with any reproductive health problem	
	%	Rank	%	Rank	%	Rank	%	Rank	%	Rank	%	Rank
Andhra Pradesh	38.2	14	18.8	9	44.0	13	16.9	15	2.9	9	48.5	14
Assam	41.2	15	20.6	13	47.3	14	14.7	11	4.1	11	50.6	15
Bihar	33.7	10	25.7	15	42.2	12	11.4	9	2.4	8	44.2	11
Gujarat	23.0	4	10.3	3	26.3	4	6.9	3	1.6	4	28.6	5
Haryana	32.2	9	12.6	6	35.9	7	8.3	4	1.0	3	38.2	7
Karnataka	13.5	1	7.2	1	17.7	1	2.7	1	0.3	1	18.8	1
Kerala	26.3	6	19.8	11	35.7	6	16.8	14	3.7	10	42.4	9
Madhya Pradesh	34.8	11	22.5	14	41.2	9	16.7	13	4.2	12	44.9	12
Maharashtra	30.7	8	20.1	12	37.1	8	10.4	6	1.8	5	40.0	8
Orissa	18.2	2	11.0	4	22.9	2	11.0	7	1.9	6	27.5	2
Punjab	23.9	5	8.5	2	26.3	4	5.6	2	0.9	2	28.3	4
Rajasthan	36.8	13	19.1	10	41.3	10	11.1	8	1.8	5	43.2	10
Tamil Nadu	18.6	3	12.3	5	24.2	3	8.5	5	2.2	7	27.8	3
Uttar Pradesh	28.0	7	17.9	7	33.9	5	16.4	12	2.4	8	38.1	6
West Bengal	35.8	12	18.4	8	41.8	11	14.6	10	1.9	6	45.3	13
India	30.0		17.8		35.9		12.5		2.3		39.2	

Source: NFHS-2, Table 8.16.
Notes: (1) includes pain or burning while urinating or more frequent or difficult urination.
(2) Not related to menstruation.

Table B17
Prevalence of RTI, STI among Men Aged 20 to 54 Years and Women Aged 15 to 44 Years in India and 15 States

	Having at least one symptom of RTI/STI*				Sought treatment for RTI/STI*			
	Men		Women		Men		Women	
	%	Rank	%	Rank	%	Rank	%	Rank
Andhra Pradesh	7.6	12	18.8	13	65.0	2	46.5	4
Assam	15.1	6	28.5	9	40.9	13	38.3	7
Bihar	17.7	3	37.7	2	59.1	4	37.0	9
Gujarat	15.3	5	32.0	6	51.3	11	36.1	10
Haryana	9.8	10	32.3	5	54.0	8	38.2	8
Karnataka	4.4	15	16.3	14	58.6	5	53.8	1
Kerala	4.9	14	27.7	10	58.6	5	50.8	2
Madhya Pradesh	10.2	9	26.1	11	54.6	7	43.7	5
Maharashtra	8.9	11	25.4	12	69.2	1	47.9	3
Orissa	17.3	4	15.6	15	52.4	10	36.1	10
Punjab	5.4	13	30.0	8	61.0	3	42.4	6
Rajasthan	12.5	7	45.0	1	51.0	12	22.6	14
Tamil Nadu	10.7	8	36.5	3	25.9	14	31.5	12
Uttar Pradesh	18.0	2	36.4	4	55.0	6	35.8	11
West Bengal	18.1	1	30.4	7	53.4	9	30.2	13
India	12.3		29.7		55.1		37.6	

Source: RCH-RHS, Table 7.2, p. 117.
Note: * Refers to three months prior to survey.

Table B18
Communicable Diseases, West Bengal (January–July 2002)

Diseases	Patients treated (OPD + IPD)				Deaths (IPD)			
	Male	Female	Total	% Female	Male	Female	Total	% Female
Acute Diarrhoeal Diseases	581,673	522,910	1,104,583	47.3	457	381	838	45.5
Diphtheria	126	107	233	45.9	2	6	8	75.0
Acute Poliomyelitis	4	3	7	42.9	0	0	0	0.0
Tetanus Neo-natal	130	98	228	43.0	57	36	93	38.7
Tetanus other than Neo-natal	459	358	817	43.8	83	89	172	51.7
Whooping Cough	630	591	1,221	48.4	3	2	5	40.0
Measles	4,760	3,876	8,636	44.9	11	7	18	38.9
Pneumonia	21,110	20,124	41,234	48.8	388	307	695	44.2
Enteric Fever	13,250	11,049	24,299	45.5	37	15	52	28.8
Viral Hepatitis	2,794	1,494	4,288	34.8	88	64	152	42.1
Japanese Encephalitis	184	93	277	33.6	52	25	77	32.5
Meningococcal Meningitis	1,012	608	1,620	37.5	158	97	255	38.0
Rabies	126	27	153	17.6	126	27	153	17.6
STD	14,232	40,753	54,985	74.1	1	0	1	0.0
Tuberculosis	45,425	23,058	68,483	33.7	542	247	789	31.3
Malaria	16,926	12,776	29,702	43.0	78	43	121	35.5
Kala Azar	608	427	1,035	41.3	4	2	6	33.3
ARI (including Influenza & Excluding Pneumonia)	368,218	363,604	731,822	49.7	333	171	504	33.9
Dengue	96	83	179	46.4	1	0	1	0.0

Source: Report on Communicable Diseases in West Bengal, State Bureau of Health Intelligence, West Bengal, 2002.

Table B19
Abortions Rates in 15 Major States, India

	Abortion per 1,000 live births	Abortions per 1,000 women in 15–44 age group
Andhra Pradesh	512	60.21
Assam	431	54.58
Bihar	434	62.55
Gujarat	485	58.01
Haryana	403	63.34
Karnataka	495	58.38
Kerala	728	52.02
Madhya Pradesh	372	63.99
Maharashtra	508	60.77
Orissa	467	60.24
Punjab	481	60.39
Rajasthan	380	64.62
Tamil Nadu	641	56.20
Uttar Pradesh	373	67.92
West Bengal	493	60.23
India	452	–

Source: Rami Chhabra and Sheel C. Nuna, *Abortion in India: An Overview*. Virendra Printers, New Delhi, 1993, Table 3.

Table B20
Estimated Number of Abortions in 15 Major States, India in 1991

	Total abortions ('000)	Induced abortions ('000)	Abortions per 1,000 couples	Induced abortions per 1,000 couples
Andhra Pradesh	887	532.2	74	44.4
Assam	299	179.4	91	54.6
Bihar	1,152	691.2	73	43.8
Gujarat	551	330.6	80	48.0
Haryana	220	132.0	82	49.2
Karnataka	600	360.0	82	49.2
Kerala	388	232.8	91	54.6
Madhya Pradesh	883	529.8	76	45.6
Maharashtra	1,052	631.2	79	47.4
Orissa	422	253.2	81	48.6
Punjab	270	162.0	91	54.6
Rajasthan	587	352.2	77	46.2
Tamil Nadu	745	447.0	79	47.4
Uttar Pradesh	1,855	1,113.0	78	46.8
West Bengal	908	544.8	83	49.8
India	11,185	6,711.0	78	46.8

Source: Same as Table B19, Table 2.

Table B21
Proportion of Ill-timed and Unwanted Births in 15 Major States, India, NFHS, 1992–93

	Ill-Timed	Unwanted
Andhra Pradesh	8.9	5.2
Assam	19.2	9.7
Bihar	14.2	9.3
Gujarat	5.7	2.5
Haryana	10.8	9.6
Karnataka	26.9	7.8
Kerala	16.8	2.4
Madhya Pradesh	8.7	7.4
Maharashtra	15.0	7.1
Orissa	17.3	9.4
Punjab	9.7	6.1
Rajasthan	6.0	7.6
Tamil Nadu	16.9	8.7
Uttar Pradesh	13.1	10.8
West Bengal	19.9	15.3
India	13.8	8.8

Source: U.S. Mishra, Mala Ramanathan and S. Irudaya Rajan, 'Induced Abortion Potential among Indian Women', Trivandrum Working Paper, Centre for Development Studies, Trivandrum, 1997, Table 3.

Table B22
Differential Assessment of Induced Abortion Potential

	Possible induced abortion	Potential no. of induced abortion projected, 1991	No. of abortions as per NFHS	No. of MTPS, govt. records
Andhra Pradesh	79,435	240,712	13,598	13,357
Assam	NA	NA	NA	NA
Bihar	164,998	499,995	8,794	10,383
Gujarat	31,411	95,186	9,541	15,846
Haryana	41,958	127,140	9,543	20,073
Karnataka	142,658	432,296	12,521	12,889
Kerala	39,026	118,262	10,123	36,727
Madhya Pradesh	116,146	351,957	13,281	32,262
Maharashtra	168,908	511,841	23,209	126,983
Orissa	75,094	227,558	7,725	21,583
Punjab	29,470	89,302	9,504	15,436
Rajasthan	60,834	184,344	15,285	26,778
Tamil Nadu	126,613	383,676	64,497	49,859
Uttar Pradesh	405,004	1,227,285	48,826	120,995
West Bengal	226,153	685,312	17,076	55,673
India	2,071,524	6,277,346	333,413	631,141

Source: Same as Table B21, Table 7.

Table B23
Gender Difference Child Immunization: Findings of NFHS-1 and NFHS-2

	Fully vaccinated				Not vaccinated			
	1992–93		1998–99		1992–93		1998–99	
	Male	Female	Male	Female	Male	Female	Male	Female
Andhra Pradesh	46.6	43.5	47.8	55.9	14.6	20.4	5.0	4.0
Assam	18.4	20.4	22.3	9.2	41.6	45.6	30.2	37.7
Bihar	12.5	8.8	12.1	9.0	47.7	59.6	15.1	18.9
Gujarat	51.3	48.3	49.5	47.0	20.3	17.4	6.7	6.5
Haryana	56.6	49.9	62.4	63.2	15.9	19.3	9.2	10.8
Karnataka	50.7	54.0	62.8	57.1	15.1	15.3	8.3	7.0
Kerala	55.8	52.9	76.3	82.6	8.7	14.3	2.5	1.9
Madhya Pradesh	32.6	25.4	27.3	17.9	30.9	38.2	11.5	16.1
Maharashtra	61.2	67.1	80.3	76.3	7.1	7.8	2.1	1.8
Orissa	37.8	34.1	44.1	43.3	25.0	31.5	8.3	11.0
Punjab	68.9	54.2	74.5	69.2	8.2	27.7	5.2	12.9
Rajasthan	23.5	18.5	15.6	16.6	45.8	51.3	21.8	23.3
Tamil Nadu	68.3	61.9	81.3	74.6	3.5	3.1	X	0.6
Uttar Pradesh	22.5	17.0	23.6	18.8	40.2	46.6	27.5	31.5
West Bengal	31.8	36.5	43.7	43.5	23.6	21.3	12.9	14.3
India	36.7	34.1	X	X	27.8	32.3	X	X

Source: *National Human Development Report 2001*, Planning Commission, Delhi, 2002, Table 5.36.

C1
Micro Study on Participation of SC/ST Girls in Professional (Teachers' Training) Education

Kamal Kumar Chattopadhyay and Dipali Nag

Introduction

The premier women teachers' training college of the state, Institute of Education for Women, Hastings House, Alipore, Calcutta has been identified for the micro study. This college offers a 10-month course leading to a B.Ed. Degree of the University of Calcutta. The course is meant for secondary and higher secondary schoolteachers teaching various subjects of the secondary school curriculum.

The in-take capacity of the institution is 250 including both deputed and non-deputed (fresher) students. The principle of reservation for SC/ST women as per government rules is being strictly followed. Therefore, a good number of SC/ST girls are enrolled every year for professional training as secondary and higher secondary schoolteachers.

As the institute is regarded as one of the efficient teachers' training institutes for women in the state, the applicants belong to all major districts of West Bengal and they possess very high academic qualification, viz., postgraduate/honours degree, in different subjects. Hence the selection of the institution is justified and it fulfils all the requirements of the micro study. It may be noted that practically all SC/ST students for the session 2000–2001 belong to non-deputed (fresher) category.

Approach

For an in-depth study, it has been decided that the group of selected SC/ST students will be interviewed based on well-structured questionnaire and opinionnaire at different levels so as to elicit their opinion, perception and personality indicators (viz., interest, aspiration, awareness, attitude and leisure time activities) in respect of the *issues* that may be classified as follows:

i. Background: environment in the family and in the neighbourhood—early successes in academic career and the factors leading to those circumstances.
ii. Professional goals and related issues.
iii. Opinion and perceptions on individual and social issues.
iv. Personality characteristics and professional competencies (IAAAL and CROLI).

Collection of Data

The study has been conducted at two-levels:

A. A general survey of selected SC/ST trainees (N = 50)
B. An in-depth study of a small group (N = 25) through face-to-face interaction on the basis of structured tools.

Tools of Study

Questionnaire and opinionnaire on the following areas:

Sections	Contents	Items
i.	Identification/academic background/communication skills	6
ii.	Family and social background/economic status/social environment/sources of motivation	10
iii.	Participation in social/developmental activities/community welfare	5
iv.	Opinion and perceptions on reservation policy. Sectors: educational, occupational and high professional	8
v.	Opinion and perceptions on government policy on reservation—factors of illiteracy, ill-health,	10

Sections	Contents	Items
	underdevelopment, backwardness of women— suggestions for community upliftment	
vi.	Personality indicators and professional competencies	30
	IAAAL—interest/aspiration/awareness/attitude/ leisure time activities	
	CROLI—communication/report/organization/ leadership/innovation	

First Stage of the Study

The present academic session (2000–2001) begins in the month of July 2000 and will continue up to April 2001. A general investigation will be undertaken in respect of 50 SC/ST women trainees of the current session. The areas of investigation are the following:

i. Age of the selected women trainees
ii. Special academic qualifications (honours degree in different subjects)
iii. Guardians' occupations
iv. Total family income
v. Professional aspiration

The sources of information are admission records which include trainees' admission forms, office records and questionnaire.

Second Stage of the Study

An in-depth face-to-face dialogue is planned for every trainee and it may continue up to several hours. They will be requested to submit written statements on their perceptions as member of scheduled caste/ scheduled tribe in the society generally dominated by upper caste men and women. The number of this phase of study is limited to 25 women trainees.

The entire records of the dialogue will be noted in the structured response sheets for analysis and interpretation. The personalities of these trainees will be further scrutinized at practice teaching sessions in different experimental schools of the training college. The areas of observation are:

i. Communication skills (C)
ii. Rapport with children (R)
iii. Competency in class management (O)
iv. Leadership (L)
v. Power of innovation (I)

Survey Data and its Implications

Age of Women SC/ST Trainees

The maximum number of subjects belong to the range 24–25 years (vide Table C1.1) and as such it may be observed that most of the SC/ST women trainees are eager to take up a professional course (here B.Ed Course) after completing their degree and masters degree in specific areas of school curriculum. It will be apparent after face-to-face dialogue that like the girls of the upper caste, the SC/ST girls are equally keen to prepare themselves for economic self-sufficiency as soon as possible.

Table C1.1

Age	Number
22–23 years	8
24–25 years	34
26–27 years	7
28–29 years	0
30–31 years	1
Total	50

Academic Qualifications

It is noteworthy that practically all SC/ST women trainees possess honours and some of them have postgraduate degrees. Their subject specialization has been achieved more in social science areas (viz., history and geography) rather than in basic science subjects (vide Table C1.2).

Table C1.2

Subject area	Number
History	16
Geography	12
Bengali	8
Zoology	8
Physics	1
Chemistry	1
Anthropology	1
Pass (B.A./B.Sc.)	3
Total	50

Guardians' Occupation

The socio-economic status of a family can be best understood from two data—one, occupation of the guardian and, two, total income of the family. The classified occupational information may be seen in Table C1.3.

Table C1.3

Occupational area	Number
Service	27
Agriculture	12
Business	4
Miscellaneous	6
N.A.	1
Total	50

The data in Table C1.3 clearly show the half of the subjects belong to families whose heads are office employees. As such, they presently reside in urban areas and some of them maintain telephones in their homes or staff quarters for central/state government employees. The socio-economic status of SC/ST women trainees will be further confirmed by data on family income (vide Table C1.4).

Monthly Family Income

For convenience of analysis, Rs 8,000 has been accepted as the cut-off income level between lower and middle-income groups. On the basis of this criterion, 8 out of 25 families may be designated as lower income group. Some of the families belong to the category earning more than Rs 10,000. The nature of the guardian's occupation and facts on monthly income confirm the socio-economic status of the new generation of educated SC/ST families. This aspect of the changing character of the deprived classes will be further confirmed from the data on the case-histories of six SC/ST women trainees.

Table C1.4

Income	Number
Below Rs 2,000	2
Rs 2,001–4,999	4
Rs 5,000–7,999	2
Rs 8,000–Rs 9,999	15
Over Rs 10,000	2
Total	25

Professional Aspiration

This aspect of the study is based on the data regarding method subjects preferred by the trainees during the current training period. The college has specific guidelines in this regard. The subjects offered at honours/postgraduate courses are generally taken up by the trainees as their method subjects. In the case of science subjects or geography, this principle is strictly followed. As a rule, the trained teachers are known as subject teachers of the same method subjects.

Table C1.5 shows that nearly 50 per cent of SC/ST trainees have their combinations of method subjects in the areas of Science and Geography. Needless to say, the aspiration level of SC/ST women trainees is quite high as the areas concerned are in great demand in priority list of subject teachers in employment market.

Table C1.5

Subject combinations	Number
Pure science	10
Pure arts	12
Mixed with science subjects	2
Mixed with arts subjects	11
Mixed with geography	15
Total	50

Experiment on Teaching Skills (CROLI)

A novel experiment have been undertaken to assess teaching skills of SC/ST women trainees in five areas of classroom interaction. They are:

C = > Skills in communicating the learning materials effectively and with definite purpose.
R = > Skills in establishing rapport with the learners.
O = > Skills in ensuring effective classroom management and organization.
L = > Skills in effective handling of classroom situations as denoted by the term 'leadership'.
I = > Skills in manipulating classroom situation with newer and innovative steps.

The results of the experiment are remarkable. As a group, the ST women trainees (among them two deputed teachers) have performed well. Five out of six ST women secured 80 per cent and above in numerical scores based on 5-point qualitative grading. Similarly, nine out of twelve SC women trainees equally performed to that level of teaching excellence (vide Table C1.6).

Table C1.6

Name of the women SC/ST trainees	Status: deputed (D)/ fresher (F)	Caste SC/ST	Teaching skills 5-point scale in five skill areas C R O L I					Score 5 × 10 = 50
Swarnalata Toppo	F	ST	A	A	B	A	B	46
Subhadra Hembram	D	ST	A	A	A	B	A	48
Dipa Mondal	D	SC	A	A	A	A	A	50
Ruma Barua	D	ST	A	A	A	B	A	48
Parbati Das	F	SC	A	A	B	B	B	44
Debjani Hansda	F	ST	A	A	A	A	B	48
Manasa Soren	F	ST	D	C	B	D	B	30
Bijali Barman	F	SC	A	A	B	B	A	46
Santana Kanji	F	SC	A	A	B	B	B	44
Rajasree Naskar	F	SC	A	B	B	C	C	38
Madhabi Sanpui	F	SC	A	A	B	B	C	42
Jhuma Das	F	SC	B	B	B	B	A	43
Baisakhi Saha	F	SC	C	B	B	B	A	40

(Table C1.6 Contd)

(Table C1.6 Contd)

Name of the women SC/ST trainees	Status: deputed (D)/ fresher (F)	Caste SC/ST	Teaching skills 5-point scale in five skill areas					Score 5 × 10 = 50
			C	R	O	L	I	
Tapati Halder	F	SC	A	A	B	B	A	46
Indrani Halder	D	SC	B	B	C	C	A	38
Sikha Bapari	F	SC	C	D	C	D	C	26
Paramita Mondal	F	SC	B	B	B	C	A	40
Jharna Murmu	F	ST	A	B	B	C	A	42

Results

1. 5 out of 6 ST trainees secured 80 per cent and above
2. 9 out of 12 SC trainee secured 80 per cent and above
3. 1 ST trainee secured 60 per cent
4. 2 ST trainee secured 75 per cent
5. 1 SC trainee secured 52 per cent

A creditable performance. Except one, all ST trainees have secured more than 80 per cent. Except one, all deputed teachers also have performed well.

Selected Case Studies

Manasa Soren

She belongs to the Santhali tribe. As a student activist she has participated in different programmes of the All Bengal Santhali Students Association for three years. She has regularly taken part in different programmes organized by the Santhali section of AIR. Presently she is a member of ASEKA, a social organization for the upliftment of the Santhali community.

The main earning member of her family is her father who earns more than Rs 8,000 per month as an employee in the office of the accountant general of West Bengal. He also holds a degree though her mother is illiterate. Previously, the family resided at Hirabandh in Bankura district. She usually stayed at students' hostels in Calcutta.

As a social activist, she is eager to campaign for the spread of education in her community. Majority of the members of her community still do not know much about social opportunities provided by the government in the form of scholarships, hostel accommodation, Ashram school, reservation quota in educational institutions, training institutes and employment sectors. She tries to propagate those information among her own community.

As the new state of Jharkhand is full of natural resources, she wants to see Santhali people in the role of entrepreneurs. At the same time, she does not like to take up the role of a politician in the new state. Her role model is Mahashweta Devi as she plays the role of a spokesperson for the tribal people and their aspirations.

It is true that she is a product of the new generation of enlightened Santhali women. She attributes her success to her parental help and co-operation. She has an M.Sc. and a B.Sc. (Hons) in geography. She has been educated in Sarisha Ramkrishna Mission and in Bethune College and School, Calcutta.

The entire family has come to stay in Calcutta thanks to reservation policy. Though she supports the policy she thinks that higher professional jobs and promotional procedure should not come under the reservation quota system. In these cases the selection should be done on the principle of merit.

In practical demonstration of her skills in classroom teaching, she is good in class management and innovativeness in teaching. But, as a teacher, she lacks power of communication and leadership. Her score in teaching practice experiment is 60 out of 100.

Subhadra Hembram

[Tribe: Santhal. Status: Deputed. Life Science/Physical Science Teacher. Passed Madhyamik in first division. Working in Girls' High School, Garden Reach. Originally resided in the town Subhaspally, Jhargram. Afterwards stayed at Kharagpur. Highly qualified family—brothers are doctor and engineer. Parents also qualified. She is also a mother.]

She has one of the most qualified families. Father is a graduate, mother has passed School Final, and out of her two brothers, one has passed IIT (engineer) and the other MBBS (doctor). She undoubtedly belongs to the 'second generation educated tribal family'. She can communicate in four languages: Santhali, Bengali, Hindi and English.

Just like a well-to-do general caste upper middle class family staying in Calcutta Port area, she is inclined to educate her child in an English-medium school. At the same time, she is quite conscious about the miserable condition and plight of her own community living in the villages.

She is socially aware and participates in community songs and dances at the time of community marriage ceremonies. She teaches her family maid (ayah) to read and write. Though she aspires to be a teacher, she is ambitious about being an independent businesswoman.

She supports the reservation policy but only till all backward men and women become literate, are educated up to elementary levels and secure jobs for a modest living. At the same time, she appreciates the selection of researchers and higher professionals on the basis of merit for maintaining quality. She attributes underdevelopment to poverty, adverse social environment, parental illiteracy and lack of initiative on the part of government officials belonging to upper castes.

She prescribes some measures for upliftment of her community:

1. To create awareness about the facilities provided by the government and extend support to ignorant tribals.
2. To propagate the benefits of the reservation policy.
3. To make her community literate and educated.
4. To adopt poverty-elimination programmes for men and women living below the poverty line.

As a mother, she spends her leisure time playing with her girl-child, loves cooking for her child and her husband, decorates living rooms and reads story-books. She wants to do something specially for children of her community and make their environment joyous and pleasant. She identifies child labour as a major obstacle to universal primary education.

Subhadra represents the 'second-generation enlightened tribal woman' and she is committed to the mission of women's liberation, specially Santhali women. Judging critically, she is a part of the 'creamy layer' of tribal communities—a typical phenomenon among the tribal families living in urban areas.

In the field experiment, she excels in skill area of CROI scoring 10 out of 10 but in the area of leadership (L) she scores 8 out of 10. In all, her performance is quite satisfactory compared to assessment standards for all women trainees of the institute.

Ruma Barua

[Belongs to the Magh tribe. Staying at present in Patuli Natunpara, P.O. Jadavpur. Deputed teacher from Muralidhar Girls' School, South Calcutta. Father was an office employee. Mother tongue: Bengali. Excels in teaching skills and possesses co-curricular experience in sports, Bratachari and drama. Belongs to moderate income group earning more than Rs 10,000 (two earning members).]

She is distinctly conscious of a separate identity of the ST as against SC communities. Tribal society and culture are much more developed and their women occupy respected and distinctive place in the community.

She is part of the 'first generation educated family' with three brothers and sisters, all graduates. Her father was a primary level literate but her mother is literate at the secondary level. Family income is more than Rs 10,000. She has had to struggle hard for her education and social development.

Though she is academically mediocre, she acquires competence in sports, arts, drama and dance. Moreover, she is a Montessori trained teacher. All these qualifications help her to become a good teacher as demonstrated in the Teaching Practical Field Experiment.

She is socially aware of the plight of the Magh tribe living in hilly tracts of remote places in the north-eastern region of our country. Abject poverty of her community has made her more conscious about the need for an effective reservation policy for the upliftment of the backward tribal people, both socially and economically. At the same time, she is frank enough to admit that for the development of the country as a whole, promotional policy and appointment in high professional jobs should be done on merit.

Her professional aim is to educate herself more so that she can excel in teaching. She possesses finer qualities in art and handwork.

Apart from her candid interview, she voluntarily submits a long note elaborating upon her logical views on long-term development of scheduled tribes, particularly those residing in remote corners of her land.

She scores 10 out of 10 in 4 skills areas of CROI except leadership (L) where her score is 8 out of 10. This is truly a creditable achievement. Her Montessori training has helped her in her present B.Ed. course.

Debjani Hansda

[Belongs to the Santhali tribe. Qualified science teacher. Belongs to the village Bapmara. P.O. Panchmura, Bankura. Her specialization is in life science/physical science. Honours in zoology and scored first division in Madhyamik. Underwent secondary education at Sarisha Ramkrishna Mission. At the degree level, good performance in zoology and mathematics in Bethune College, Calcutta. Resided in hostels. Belongs to high income group, two earning members, both brothers. Father is retired AG Bengal employee. 'Second generation' educated Santhali family.]

She comes from an educated Santhali family. Her father is a graduate and her mother is educated up to the primary level. Her elder sister is M.Sc. in Zoology, B.Ed. and at present teaches at Nadia Palashpara High School. Her two brothers are also graduates. She is educated at Jagacha Primary School, RKM Sarada Vidyamandir, Sarisha, Howrah Girls' College for her higher-secondary and degree courses. Her role model is her elder sister. One of the brothers is employed at Calcutta Corporation and the other at a local secondary school.

From 7+ onwards, she has been residing in urban areas. She belongs to the higher income group. Her ambition is to be a college teacher and she also wants to work as an activist of the All India Adibashi Parishad. She is a strong supporter of the reservation policy, but feels that promotions and appointments in higher occupations like teacher, technologist, medical practitioner and researcher should be made on merit. She appreciates the activities of NGOs, particularly in areas of education, women's liberation and self-awareness.

She is keen to help the women folk of her community. According to her, Santhali women are not only ignorant but also become mothers of four to five children at an early age. She personally loves to lead a life of comfort her hobbies being listening to music, watching TV, watching plays and travelling. All these are indicative of the culture loaded society of higher caste people. Her favourite historical personalities are Buddha and Subhash Chandra Bose. It may be mentioned here that the influence of Buddhism is a characteristic feature among educated Santhali families. Her favourite film artist is Soumitra Chattopadyay and writer is Samaresh Majumdar.

By nature, she is an 'introvert' though she belongs to the 'creamy layer' of the Santhali community, she retains a feeling of commitment towards the upliftment of the Santhali community as a whole.

In the practical training experiment, she secured 10 out of 10 in CROL areas and 8 out of 10 in innovativeness (I). Her total score is 48 out of 50, which is a remarkable achievement.

Debjani Hansda belongs to the new generation of emancipated Santhali women, precursor of the social reform among the backward community.

Swarnalata Toppo

[Belongs to the Oraon tribe. Resident of Aliporeduar, Jalpaiguri. Father is a farmer. Her mother-tongue is Hindi. Presently, she resides at Salt Lake RBI quarters. Her religion is Christianity. Educated in good institutions. All three sisters are graduates and one of them is employed as Inspector of Customs. She has done History (Hons).]

Swarnalata is educated at The Nirmala Government Primary School, Jalpaiguri, Nirmala Girl's High School, Lady Brabourne (higher-secondary) and Scottish Church College (degree level).

She comes from an educated family. Her father and three sisters are all graduates but her mother read up to the primary level. Up to 12+ she stayed in Jalpaiguri and then shifted to Calcutta. One of her teachers inspired her to pursue academic studies.

Her career options are teaching and administration. Her role model is her sister who has also taken up a career in administration. She attributes her success to her family and school environment. She does not mention the Christian culture as one of the contributing factors in her life.

A novel formula is suggested by her regarding the reservation quota. Those who are economically well off among the ST community should compete with the general category, and the poor and backward candidates should enjoy the benefits of the reservation quota.

She is of the opinion that women of her community should not be termed as socially underdeveloped. She says that in her society, women are not only conscious but more self-sufficient than women of the upper caste.

She is proficient in Hindi. Her favourite writer is Manu Bhandari. Her favourite film actor is Salman Khan. She likes the questionnaire and interview schedule and appreciates the role of the interviewer. Though a member of the upper caste, the interviewer is still so sympathetic towards SC/ST problems. She is happy to communicate the problems of her community to the interviewer.

Her performance in practical teaching is remarkable. In skill areas CRL, her scores are 10 out of 10, while in O and I areas, she secures 8 out of 10. Her total score is 46 out of 50.

Dipa Mondal (SC)

She belongs to a family which is educationally and economically self sufficient. She is married and represents enlightened womanhood among the backward schedule caste. She resided at a village in Sundarban region at Gosaba in 24 Parganas (S). Her academic career is bright. She is a B.Sc. (Hons) and M.Sc. in geography. At present, she is a deputed teacher.

In her parental family, the earning members are her father and her elder brother. Her other three brothers and sisters are all graduates of Calcutta University.

Regarding the reservation policy her opinion is somewhat different. Though she supports the policy, she still points out its negative impact in creating an artificial division among the society at large. She is sorry about the attitude of her upper caste friends who suspect their potential and merit in the fields of education and employment. She thinks SC students are very much capable and in some cases they excel in academic performance. She supports reservation because her community residing in rural areas are so backward and poverty-stricken that without state support they will never come out of the present deplorable situation.

She is very much critical of those in her community who are urban based and employed in government and private offices. They have monopolized and cornered all the facilities of the SC quota awarded by the government and they do not share them with hapless brothers and sisters of their own community.

She wants to serve the community as a 'mother' providing nutritious food to sick and undernourished children. Her comments on the questionnaire are constructive. She praises the attitude of the interviewer for her depth of understanding of the SC/ST problems. She readily writes a special note on the problems of SC/ST communities in society. She is also keen in eradicating social and educational hindrances. Not only as a student but also as a teacher she possesses various good qualities, namely, communication rapport, organization, leadership and innovativeness (CROLI). Her assertion that the women of backward communities may surpass their counterparts in the general caste communities is not an idle dream but a glaring reality. Her own example proves the point.

Analysis of the Structured Responses of SC/ST Women Trainees on Questionnaire and Opinionnaire

This is not a quantitative study in the sense of 'how many' on different social issues and problems but a study to understand the depth of feeling and perception of those who will be engaged in a sensitive sector like 'teaching' in the near future. These women teachers occupy a pivotal position in their own community. They are the *creators* of public opinion. From the point of view of national integration, these SC/ST women teachers will play either a positive or a negative role on different social and national issues.

The first point which has come out from this time-consuming face interaction is the fact that there exists deep-rooted distrust, lack of faith and trust in the mind of the backward class intelligentsia towards the society in general and the general caste in particular.

The perception of these selected women trainees is generally in favour of the reservation policy but with a significant qualification. In matters of promotion to higher positions of selection and in some specialized professions like medicine, law, research, engineering, etc., the principle should be, according to them, on the basis of merit. This is a significant advance towards a democratic standpoint on the basis of which a national consensus may be built up.

On the vital question of progress of women's education among SC/ST communities, it is evident that many of the women trainees belong to 'first or second generation' learners. The pace of the progress of education among them has accelerated during the seventies, eighties and nineties. There are families where the father is a graduate and employed in a government office while the mother is illiterate, but their sons and daughters have degrees. Undoubtedly these educated young SC/ST people are the products of the reservation policy.

The evidences of affluence in day to day living and lifestyle among backward caste families have also been identified. Their social perceptions towards problems of SC/ST communities in turn, have undergone a critical change similar to the intelligentsia belonging to the upper caste. It is also noted that some ST families who have been influenced by the Christian Church are definitely more advanced. They may be characterized as the 'creamy layer' of the SC/ST communities.

It is true that these affluent families are few in number. The majority of SC/ST people are still submerged in the ocean of illiteracy, ill-health and are without any minimum means of subsistence. The first decade of the twenty-first century should be devoted to the problems of primary and secondary education for all SC/ST children.

All the selected trainees for the study have stressed that lack of information on social opportunities provided by the state is a major problem particularly in the rural areas. The department of the state government concerned with backward and tribal welfare should undertake a massive awareness programme in this regard.

The benefits of the reservation policy are limited but all the facilities are still not availed by SC/ST children in the field of primary, secondary and vocational education. The women trainees have appreciated the activities of the NGOs in the areas of elementary education, women's awareness, childcare and nutrition, development of vocational skill and handwork and cooperative efforts among SC/ST women. Invariably the NGOs are very much interested in dissemination of information in these regards.

There is also lack of information on important educational schemes meant for the scheduled communities. Book grant, fee for Madhyamik examination, maintenance grant, hostel grant, ashram hostel, special merit scholarships in secondary and higher-secondary stages, residential school for girls, stipend for students engaged in unclean occupation, etc., are some of the examples in this regard.

Non-implementation of the reservation quota in the government and government sponsored primary, secondary, higher-secondary, degree college, university, medical, engineering and other technical institution are delaying the progress of education of SC/ST communities.

The educational statistics show that the SC/ST communities have made substantial progress since 1980 and the rate of progress is quite high. The number of first or second generation educated families among the 'experimental group' (N = 25) confirms this contention.

Educated ST women seem to be more committed to community welfare than their counterparts in the SC community and some of them are eager to play their role as activists of different NGO tribal organizations.

One discerning fact has been revealed in the study, that is, the lifestyles of the well-to-do SC/ST families do not represent the cultural ethos of their own tribes. Not a single trainee has referred to Dr Ambedkar as her 'favourite' personality and very few of them participate in community cultural functions, characteristics of a tribal society. But these families have practically monopolized all the socio-economic benefits of the reservation policy.

As suggested by many women trainees of the study, the tools of the investigation, the questionnaire and the opinionnaire may be refined and used for further studies involving bigger samples. The refined tools may answer some of the unanswered questions in this study. The questions are:

(*i*) Is there any significant difference between the SC/ST trainees in respect of social awareness, perception and personality indicators?

(*ii*) Is the difference between the SC/ST and general category students in respect of academic and professional achievement quantitative or qualitative in nature?

The selection of the topic of this micro study for understanding the changing status of women from the seventies to the nineties, has proved to be correct in respect of SC/ST educated women. The methodology adopted in this study is also justified on the basis of the results achieved.

List of SC/ST Women Trainees under Study, Institute of Education for Women Hastings House, Alipore, Calcutta, Session 2000–2001

Serial no.	Name
ST Women Trainees	
1.	Swarnalata Toppo
2.	Subhadra Hembram
3.	Manasa Soren
4.	Jharna Murmu
5.	Debjani Hansda
6.	Ruma Barua
SC Women Trainees	
7.	Parbati Das
8.	Kaberi Das
9.	Santana Kanji
10.	Bijoli Barman
11.	Shila Roy
12.	Sarmistha Mondol
13.	Rina Makal
14.	Sikha Bapari
15.	Paramita Mondal
16.	Indrani Halder
17.	Jhuma Das
18.	Tapati Halder
19.	Baisakhi Saha
20.	Jayati Teli
21.	Rajashree Naskar
22.	Srabanti Naskar
23.	Madhabi Sanpai
24.	Dipa Mondal
25.	Sima Mondal
26.	Sumana Giri (Sikdar)
27.	Mousumi Saha
28.	Shilarani Gupta
29.	Madhumati Saha
30.	Kana Mondal
31.	Dipshikha Hazra
32.	Sampa Saha
33.	Maumita Pramanik
34.	Sucheta Mallick
35.	Mili Hira
36.	Susmita Pramanik
37.	Mahuya Purkait
38.	Aparna Biswas
39.	Bipasa Sarkar
40.	Srilekha Mondal
41.	Paramita Saha
42.	Mausumi Biswas
43.	Sipra Gayen
44.	Sumita Howladar
45.	Anupama Mondal
46.	Karabi Mondal
47.	Sudipta Das
48.	Lila Das
49.	Rupali Malakar
50.	Swati Mondal

C2
Education of Muslim Women in West Bengal

Ratnabali Chattopadhyay

The work was undertaken as a micro study of the educational status of Muslim women in the context of women's education in West Bengal. In all past studies, it was assumed that Muslim women were generally in a backward position compared to the dominant group of Hindu women. Yet the Fourth Quinquennial Review of Education (1897–1902) revealed that Muslim girls were in a better position compared to Hindu girls in Madras, Bombay, the United Provinces and Central Provinces, but behind them in Bengal. In the face of this information we needed to look at the special condition prevailing in Bengal both historically and in the contemporary situation.

History

Historically Bengal stood apart in the context of Islamization of the entire country, a region where the Muslims were the majority but distinctly aloof. There were clear indications of a mixed culture as 'Popular Islam' was considered as an apt term to describe the religious rituals followed by Muslims in rural Bengal. Dominated by an agrarian economy, they responded very little to the questions of upper Indian's Muslim identity. The Faraizi and Wahabi movements, in which local Muslim women were equally involved, were intrinsically related to the Muslim peasant identity.

Some of the most important factors which caused migration and popular dislocation due to communal tensions in both pre- and post-independence era underplayed women's role in the community. It also affected the general well-being of the Muslim women who faced onslaughts from the Hindus as well as the fundamentalist Muslims. Though education according to the Quaranic authorities was compulsory and universal, since it is prescribed in Islam that 'every Muslim man and woman' must go to the furthest corner of the globe to acquire knowledge, the actual situation was far from this set ideal. There were primarily two institutions catering to education, the *makhtab* and the *madrasah*. The *makhtab* was the primary school, which was co-educational, and the usual age to begin in it was seven after the initiation ceremony. The syllabus included teaching of Persian and Arabic calligraphy, Bustan and Gulistan of Sadi and a little arithmetic. Though the Muslim society was divided into Ashraf (aristocratic) and Altaf (common people), no special mention of how education was imported to women of these classes are made. It is generally assumed that women received their education in the aristocrats' exclusive space of the *zenana*. Medieval Bengali folk-lores, like Laila Majnu and Dewane Medina, bear evidence of girls and boys studying together in the *makhtab*.

Women's inability to step into the public space is symbolized by the *purdah* (veil). As both Hindu and Muslim women carried their *purdah* to protect them from the public gaze, their education was hampered in a big way. For the Muslim girls who were barred from going out in public after the age of 12, the progress from *makhtab* to *madrasah* could not take place.

In the first half of the nineteenth century, English and American missionaries started schools for girls in Calcutta. The Female Juvenile Society of the Baptist Mission set up a free school at Gouribari in the Ultadanga area of Calcutta, and quite a few Muslim girls attended this school. This is known from contemporary records and newspapers. Between 1823 and 1830, schools numbering around 30 were set up by Miss Cooke and her associates. Reports of the Female Juvenile Society mentioned that a number of Muslim girls were attending the schools at Janbazaar and Entally. It is also known that a few Muslim girls went to the school set up by Raja Baidyanath Roy. Most of these girls came from poor families and were generally married off at an early age. Women of the Ashraf community continued with their traditional learning of Arabic and the religious texts in the privacy of the *zenana*.

After 1857, the government began to move out of its apathy and make special efforts towards the promotion of the education of Muslim girls. The Fourth Review of Education cited indifference, even resistance, on the part of the Muslim community as the cause for slow progress of female education.

In 1901–2, the percentage of schoolgoing Muslim girls was 0.8 in Bengal, which was considerably lower than in Bombay or Madras. In 1907, the DPIA made proposals to W.S. Milne, Under Secretary of the Government of Bengal, Calcutta for the promotion of education among Mohammedan girls. A special syllabus to be used for the special schools for Muslims in connection with *zenana* education was proposed. The syllabus was restricted in nature, in strict adherence to orthodox tradition. Distinction was made not just between Hindu and Muslim girls but between Muslims of the Shia and Sunni communities as well. The syllabus was also limited to the teaching of Arabic and Urdu. In 1909, on the basis of Curzon's recommendation, the Female Education Committee for Eastern Bengal and Assam made some special arrangements for the education of Muslim girls, but even now stress was on Urdu and Hindi, and teaching of Bengali was avoided. Right through the colonial period, both for Hindus and Muslims, Western education became the basis for availing of jobs.

Since upper class Muslim identity continued to revolve around Urdu, the elites of Bengal responded to it and the knowledge of English and Urdu became a sign of class. Thus, from its inception, education in the vernacular for Muslim women was pushed to a second position.

The initiative of setting up secular schools for Muslim girls came from the Muslim women themselves. They were supported by private institutions interested in imparting instructions to both men and women in Bengali. The fusion of these common interests helped to create an environment in which education of Muslim women came to the forefront in Bengal.

In 1873, Fairunnissa Chowdhury set up a school at Comilla in Bangladesh, which exists to date. In 1895, Khairunnissa Khatun started a school in the village of Hussainpur in Siraiganj in Bangladesh. The first Muslim girls' school in Calcutta was set up at Khidirpur in 1897 by Nawab Begum Firdaus Mahal of Murshidabad. In 1909, Khujista Begum established the Suharwardy Pardanashin School. The same year witnessed Begum Roquiya establishing the Sakhawat Hussain Memorial School. Between 1910–20, several girls' schools were set up in the districts. In the same decade, the number of schoolgoing Muslim girls rose to 3.5 per cent.

The year 1920 marks a turning point in the life of Bengali Muslim women. Not only were there significant contributions from the elite women, but also two major government schools were established— the Suharwardy Memorial School, which received Rs 200 per month and Sakhawat Memorial School, which initially received Rs 71 per month that was raised to Rs 448 as government grants. The *makhtabs* received between Rs 2 and Rs 4 per month only. Most of these were co-educational. The sudden increase in the number of Muslim girls' schools (about 3,031) in the remote regions of Bengal indicated not only a governmental concern but an awareness within the community that education was a process of empowerment for women.

The Ninth Quinquennial Reviews of Education (1922–27) noted that the Muslim population of British India was 59.5 million (i.e., 24 per cent of the total population). The numerical data shows that although Muslim participation was lower than the average for all communities and all regions other than the Central Provinces, there was a steady rise in the number of Muslim schools in proportion to the Muslim population over the five year period. The most remarkable was the rise in numbers of Muslim women scholars in Bihar, Orissa and the Central Provinces. The Punjab had also shown

a dramatic increase in girl students. In Bengal, between 1921–26, the average of Muslim scholars was around 3.4 in 1921 and 4.4 in 1926. The girls had risen from 1.4 per cent to 1.8 per cent of the total number of Muslim scholars, which showed slow development.

In 1937, the proportion of Muslim scholars to the Muslim population increased steadily for both men and women. They increased their share in proportion to the total population except in Bengal and Delhi (Tables C2.1 and C2.2).[1]

Table C2.1
Hindu and Muslim Girls Attending Public Schools as a Percentage of the Total Girls of Schoolgoing Age in Their Respective Communities

Province	Hindus	Muslims
Bombay	3.7	4.0
Madras	3.1	5.9
Bengal	2.0	0.8
Punjab	1.6	0.5
Central provinces	1.0	2.3
United provinces	3.0	0.7

Sources: Fourth Quinquennial Review of Education, India, 1897–1902, Supdt. of Govt. Printing, Calcutta, 1904, p. 308; Shahida Lateef, 1990, *Muslim Women in India*. Kali for Women, Delhi, p. 49.

Table C2.2
Comparison of Education of Muslim and Non-Muslims

Province	Year	Per cent of Muslim male pupils to population	Per cent of other males	Per cent of Muslim female pupils to population	Per cent of other females
Madras	1916	4.9	3.6	1.8	1.4
	1926	7.9	4.1	3.1	2.3
Bombay	1916	3.1	3.8	–	–
	1926	4.5	5.4	1.4	2.1
Bengal	1916	3.2	3.9	1.3	1.3
	1926	3.8	4.6	1.4	1.6
U.P.	1916	1.7	1.6	–	–
	1926	3.1	2.5	–	–

Source: Memorandum on progress of education in British India, 1916–26. Same as Table C7.1.

In Bengal the progress of Muslims showed a slight decline in education as compared to the all-India figures between 1932–37. The number shows a slight dip from 55.5 per cent in 1932 to 55.2 per cent in 1937. Interestingly, this does not agree with the general observations of British writers. Kingsley Davis had related that educational differential between Muslims and other communities to urbanization and the socio-economic status was quite marked. He noted that since the turn of the nineteenth century, Muslims had improved their relative position, and that between 1891–1931, their percentage among the various religions communities was the highest in terms of gains in literacy.

The issue of women's education at the end of the nineteenth century was related more to regional norms and responses and less to the needs of the specific communities unlinked as it was to the widening of economic opportunities. Muslim women's attempts at

---

[1] Lateef, Sahida, *Muslim Women in India*. Kali for Women, New Delhi, 1990.

education tended to follow this pattern while reflecting the tensions of both internal and external communal strife.

After 1947, Muslim women as citizens of a democracy had certain legal, economic and social rights. Different regions had to deal with questions of how to maintain these rights. Bengal was one of the two Muslim majority states that was partitioned in 1947. Muslims in Calcutta were only a small percentage of the city's population. Bengali Muslims mingled with the migrants from other neighbouring states who flocked to the city to seek employment.

In 1977, a survey was conducted by the women running the Calcutta Muslim orphanage, which was limited to Muslim areas and aimed mainly towards assessing the needs of the Muslim women. They found that Muslim women, despite poverty and illiteracy, were conscious of the need to educate their children and to limit the size of the family. The orphanage provided girls with education and vocational training and it also arranged their marriages using a standard *Nikahnama* which rules out the possibility of unilateral divorce or polygamy. Such contracts, according to those in-charge, were in use even before 1947 (M. Tahir, Secretary, Calcutta Muslim Orphanage, 30 September 1977).

Due to the partition of the province at the turn of the century and in 1947, communal skirmishes continued to plague the Muslims. Also, in spite of the need for greater contact between the Muslim elite and the masses to address the social problems facing the community, there was no notable Muslim leadership in Calcutta. Several Muslim organizations, however, began to operate in the city. The Khilafat Committee was established in the twenties which was attached to the main mosque, and was active in promoting women's education and mediating in marital disputes. The Anjuman Mufidul Islam was similarly involved and had both men and women members. Like women of other communities, Muslim women in Calcutta had to face hardships due to lack of opportunities in both employment and education. In this study we have tried to take samples both from institutions which have been in continuous existence and those that were set up after 1947 to cater to the needs of Muslim women.

Educational Institutions in Calcutta

Since Bengali Muslim women in the rural areas shared many customs and practices which were followed by Hindus, a separate study has been conducted in three villages where a stable Muslim population has continued to live long before 1947. A comparison has been attempted between the rural and urban set up.

The two schools which have been surveyed in Calcutta are Anjuman Girls' High School and the Sakhawat Memorial Government Girls' High School. While the latter shows a degree of continuity both in its curriculum and its methods of teaching, the Anjuman Girls' High School aims to meet the demands of the post-independence situation. Sakhawat Memorial Government Girls' High School was established as early as 1911. It is one of the oldest schools for Muslim girls situated at 17 Lord Sinha Road, Calcutta 700 071. The school is at present directly under the control of the Director of School Education, Government of West Bengal. The working hours are divided into two shifts—morning (6.30 AM to 10.30 AM) and afternoon (10.40 AM to 3.50 PM). The building is owned by the government. The school has modern facilities for teaching science and offers certain extracurricular activities to the students. Apart from the Roquiya Trust Fund, it has no other private bodies to offer grants to students.

The school at present caters to girls of all communities and the media of instruction are English Bengali and Urdu. Since no record is kept of teachers or students who have graduated from the school, it was difficult to form any impressions about how the curriculum of the school had changed or how from an institution which was meant to house mainly Muslim girl students it has turned into a multicultural institution where no Muslim religious festivals are specially observed.

Anjuman Girls' High School derives its name from the organization who tried to help the under-privileged Muslim youth. They collected money from the charity, i.e., *zakat* offered by the whole community. In 1947, the school was recognized by the new government. The institution houses about 24 permanent teachers and quite a few part-time teachers. The medium of instruction is still Urdu. Total number of students amounts to 1,500, which includes students who opted for science and arts. Unfortunately, after higher-secondary examinations, students rarely go in for B.A. This is mainly because they find it difficult to follow either Bengali or English. Without Urdu textbooks, they cannot proceed further than the school level. Since there is a strict observation of Muslim customs, most girls wear either a *burkha* or a *chadar*. Even the headmistress is never seen in public without a *chadar*. Both the students and the teachers complained bitterly about their exclusion from mainstream education, where both the medium of instruction and the curriculum did not leave them any space.

College

In some ways, Lady Brabourne College in its early years represented the cultural needs of the community revealed by the students of Anjuman School. The college was founded in July 1939 in a rented house in the Park Circus area of Calcutta. It was named after Lady Brabourne, wife of the then governor of Bengal. The faculty consisted of only nine members and the students numbered 35 Muslim girls. The curriculum included Urdu and Persian, along with other arts' subjects. Though primarily meant for the education of Muslim girls, the college, which celebrated its diamond jubilee in 1999 and is now considered a premiere institution in West Bengal, houses students from all communities.

Postgraduate

The need to create a separate department for Islamic history and culture was expressed by Sri Ashutosh Mukherjee in his presidential address to the Bihar and Orissa Research Society as early as 1923. Unfortunately, his death in 1924 pushed back the founding of the department to 1939. The then Vice Chancellor Sri Azizul Haque moved the government for the necessary funds.

Table C2.3
Progress of Education for Muslim and Non-Muslim
Males and Females, 1932–37

Province	Year	Male			Female		
		Per cent of Muslim population total population	Per cent of Muslim pupils to Muslim population	Per cent of Muslim pupils to total pupils	Per cent of Muslim population to total population	Per cent of Muslim pupils to Muslim population	Per cent of Muslim pupils to total pupils
Madras	1932	7.5	9.7	10.9	7.5	5.1	11.5
	1937	–	10.8	11.2	–	6.3	11.4
Bombay	1932	8.8	5.8	19.4	8.4	2.9	19.8
	1937	–	11.6	13.7	–	6.9	12.4
Bengal	1932	54.9	5.4	51.7	55.2	2.3	55.5
	1937	–	6.0	51.7	–	3.0	55.4
UP	1932	14.8	3.9	18.6	14.9	0.8	15.7
	1937	–	4.2	18.3	–	1.0	15.5
Delhi	1932	32.5	6.4	30.0	32.2	2.6	23.3
	1937	–	7.7	31.0	–	3.8	25.5
British India	1932	24.7	5.2	26.7	24.1	2.0	26.0
	1937	–	5.5	26.1	–	2.5	25.6

Source: Derived from Tables CXXIII of the 1932–37. Review of Education vol. 1, pp. 242, 243, Calcutta 1939.
   Same as Table C2.1.

While undergraduate courses were started at the Islamia College (now Maulana Azad College) from the academic session of 1940–41, the postgraduate studies began in the university colleges of arts and commerce. At first the classes were held in the history, Persian and Arabic departments. A full-fledged department came to function from 1942. Interestingly, the establishment of this department came to be regarded as a part of the liberalizing process in which the university is engaged.

Though Islamic culture formed the major thrust of the curriculum, the teaching faculty included well-known scholars in medieval Indian history like Dr Makhanlal Roychoudhury. Knowledge of Arabic and Persian was considered essential for research, but as time progressed the department drew in more and more students who took up these subjects as a branch of history. Though from its inception the curriculum included the history of Islam, students began to be interested more in the development of Islamic culture in India. The number of Muslim students, particularly girls, was reduced. At present, except for those who study Islamic history and culture at the B.A. Honours level in Maulana Azad College, few communicate in Urdu. Since the department does not maintain a proper register of old students, a correct assessment of the girl students and the number of Muslim girls who had graduated could not be made. The only data made available to us was of 1995, which noted a total of 126 students of which only 10 per cent were Muslim girls. The department also has no special holidays for celebration of Islamic festivals (Table C2.4).

Survey of Three Villages

The three villages under survey belong to Diamond Harbour Block 1 in 24 Parganas (S). The villages Panchagram, Bardrone and Chauda are situated at a distance of 5 to 7 miles from each other. These were chosen mainly because of the stable Hindu and Muslim population that has existed and continues to exist even now. The three villages have no *madrasahs*. They only have one high school, one junior high school and five primary schools. There is only one health centre which caters to the needs of the residents of these villages.

Panchagram houses the high school, which was set up by Pramath Nath Deb, the successor of Nabakrishna Deb of the Sovabajar Rajbari. It was due to the personal efforts of Pramath Nath Deb, and the then MLA Charu Chandra Bhandari that all the developmental work of the villages was undertaken. The residents of Panchagram consist of an equal number of Hindu and Muslim families.

Bardrone is an older settlement with a predominantly Hindu population. It has an old library and a Bardrone Social Welfare Organization which has looked after the welfare of the people for many years.

Chauda, has a larger Muslim population than the others and they form the dominant group in the village. There is no high school and only one primary school. Most of the women are illiterate and, apart

Table C2.4
Urban Study on Muslim Institution in Calcutta

Name of the institution	Establishment year	Affiliated to	Free studentship	Working hours		Current enrolment
Sakhawat Memorial Govt. G.H. School	1911	W.B.B.S.E. 1936	Yes Roquiyya Trust Fund	6.30 AM–10.40 AM	10.30 AM–3.50 PM	390
Anjuman Girls' High School	1947	W.B.B.S.E. 1947	Yes	11.00 AM	4.30 PM	1,600
Lady Brabourne College	1939	C.U.	No	10.15 AM	4.30 PM	1,500
Islamic History Deptt., C.U.	1944	C.U.	No	10.30 AM	5.30 PM	

Source: Survey findings.

from tending to their households, work in the fields as wage labourers. With a few exception all three villages reveal that the families live in acute poverty. The men, if they work at all, take time off for their own recreation and leave the entire managing of the household to the women. Yet, women have no options for education or skill training. Their voices regarding the education of their children are rarely heard though most want their children and specially their daughters to get some education.

An interesting factor which cropped up during our survey was the way 'literacy' could be measured. For us it opened up new avenues of communication with the women in the villages. Quite a few claimed to be literate, though they could only read the Koran and knew the Arabic script. Yet, they neither understood Arabic, which could reveal to them the religious knowledge for which they

hankered, nor did they read or write Bengali, which was their only language of communication.

The accompanying tables show the large number of drop-outs from school. Since there is no *madrasah* in the vicinity (Tables C2.5, C2.5a, C2.5b, C2.5c), it was not possible to compare either the curriculum or the way respondents related to the syllabus that they followed. At the same time, we were stuck by the strong motivation expressed by both young and old women to acquire knowledge. Education was considered a marker of empowerment for them and they expressed their resentment at being excluded quite strongly. Dowry (which has been mentioned in our study on violence) acted as one of the main deterrents to the education of young girls. It also revealed how the minority community was being influenced by the dominant groups.

Table C2.5
Level of Age and Education of Respondents (Muslims)

Distribution of age (years)	Level of Education					
	Illiterate	Literate	Primary	Secondary	Higher-secondary	B.A. and above
18–24	9	6	10	8	5	1
24–30	11	13	17	6	2	2
30–36	14	9	8	3	1NF	–
36–42	12	8	11NF	NF	NF	–
42 and above	7	5	3NF	NF	NF	–
Total	53	41	48	17	8	3
Percentage	31.1	24.1	28.2	10	4	1

Note: Tables C2.5, C2.5a, C2.5b, C2.5c reveal surveys of the three villages belonging to 24 Parganas (S), Diamond Harbour Block. They are Bardrone, Chauda and Panchagram. This table shows the level of age and education of Muslim from all three villages.

Chart C2.1
Age and Education of Respondents (Muslims)

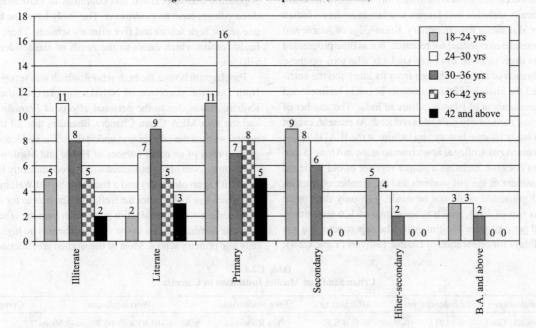

Source: Table C2.5.

Table C2.5a
Level of Age and Education of Respondents (Hindus)

Distribution of age	Level of Education					
	Illiterate	Literate	Primary	Secondary	Higher-secondary	B.A. and above
18–24	5	2	11	9	5	3
24–30	11	7	16	8	4	3
30–36	8	9	7	6	2	2
36–42	5	5	8	3NF	NF	–
42 and above	2	3	5	2NF	NF	–
Total	31	26	47	28	11	7
Percentage	20.6	17.3	31.3	18.6	7.3	4.6

Note: The table shows the level and age of the Hindus who form respondents from the control group.

Chart C2.2
Age and Education of Respondents (Hindu)

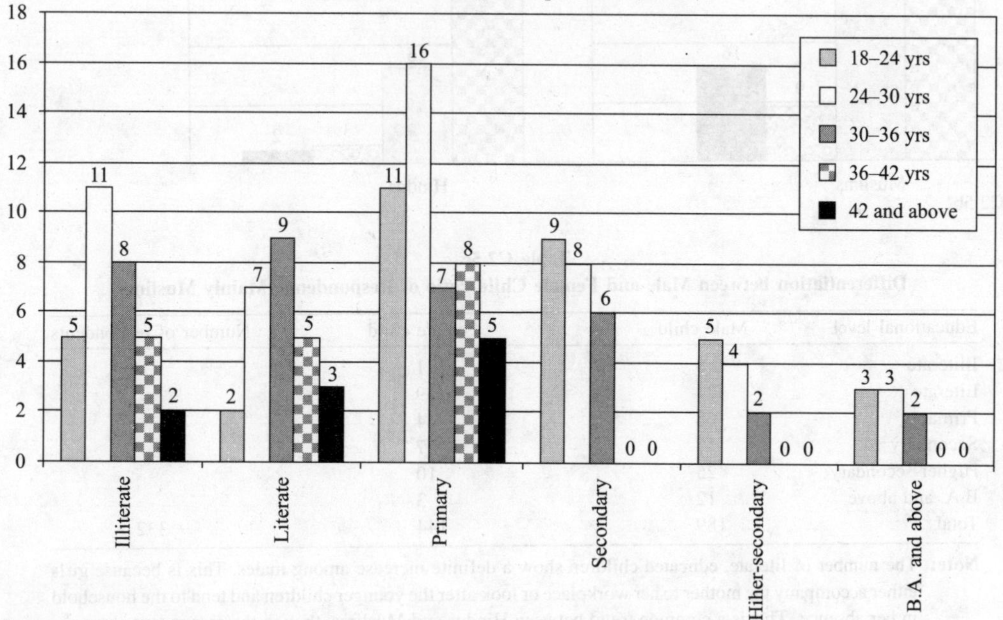

Source: Table C2.5a.

Table C2.5b
The Table Shows the Reasons for Drop-outs among both Hindus and Muslims

Religion-wise	Economic	Employment	Dowry	Lack of interest of student	Lack of interest of guardians	Grand total
Muslim	85 (26.56)	33 (10.31)	27 (8.43)	9 (2.81)	16 (5)	170
Hindu	77 (24.06)	52 (16.25)	16 (5)	3 (0.93)	2 (0.62)	150
Total	162 (50.62)	85 (26.56)	43 (13.43)	12 (3.75)	18 (5.62)	320

Note: The reasons for drop-outs are mainly due to poverty. According to the survey, 48 girls have acquired primary education and the number of illiterates is 5. But in spite of this there is a strong motivation for education and even illiterate mothers want their daughters to go to school.

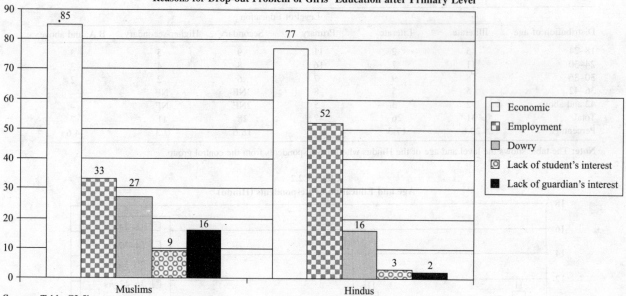

Chart C2.3
Reasons for Drop-out Problem of Girls' Education after Primary Level

Source: Table C2.5b.

Table C2.5c
Differentiation between Male and Female Child-ratio of Respondents, Mainly Muslims

Educational level	Male child	Female child	Number of respondents
Illiterate	5	21	
Literate	24	39	
Primary	68	44	
Secondary	52	27	
Higher-secondary	25	10	
B.A. and above	12	3	
Total	189	144	332

Note: The number of literate, educated children show a definite increase among males. This is because girls either accompany the mother to her workplace or look after the younger children and tend to the household in her absence. This is a common trend between Hindus and Muslims, though the respondents here are mainly Muslims.

Status of Women with Respect to Work: Report of Primary Surveys in Bankura and Hoogli

Ishita Mukhopadhyay

It has been mentioned earlier that all the features of participation of women in work cannot be assessed from the available secondary data. To answer some of these queries, a primary survey was undertaken in two districts of the state—Bankura and Purulia. In the sample chosen from both the districts were those women who worked either in agricultural fields or in home-based work or in informal industrial sectors as subcontracted workers. The sample was thus a purposive one. The sample size was 209 in Bankura and 270 in Hoogli. The pattern of women's work was analysed with respect to the land-size holdings of their families, their educational attainment, their job availability and job opportunity, hours of work and their economic empowerment through work. The sample presentation is: Among the 209 women respondents in Bankura, 106 were from landless agricultural labour families, 35 from families of marginal farmers, 55 from farmers with land-size holdings between 1 and 5 bighas, and 13 were from families of farmers with land-size greater than 5 bighas; none came from sharecropper families. Among 270 women respondents in Hoogli, 221 were from families of landless agricultural labour, 22 from families of marginal farmers, 8 from families with land-size holdings between 1 and 5 bighas, 2 from families with land-size greater than 5 bighas and 17 from sharecropper families. The following sections analyse the pattern of women's participation in work with respect to the factors stated earlier.

Land-size and Women's Work

Women's participation in the job market is more intensive when they come from poor and very poor households. Women's income in particular becomes a means of survival of the poor people. This was felt from the response of the respondents in both the districts. In poor families, women enter the job market at a very tender age, in fact, as girl children. This was revealed from the primary survey. Since the survey was conducted in the year 2000, the respondents who entered the job market as girl children did so one or two decades

before that. Hence, it is not to be inferred that girl children enter the job market even at present.

Charts D1.1 to D1.6 describe the entry age in the job market. It was revealed that 53.77 per cent of the landless respondents in Bankura and 41.63 per cent of landless respondents in Hoogli entered the job market between the ages of 6 and 15 years. This was higher than women coming to work from small, marginal or large holdings. But here we find a difference between the two districts. In Hoogli, 64.70 per cent of women coming from sharecropper families joined work at this tender age, but this was not so in Bankura. Poor women enter the job market either at a very tender age or immediately after marriage in both the districts. This is an indication of the level of poverty in the family. Charts D2.1 to D2.5 give an account of the number of hours of work of these working women. Women coming from families with land-size greater than 5 bighas work for lesser hours during the day, but the result is reverse for women coming from families of landless agricultural labourers and small and marginal farmers. They generally tend to work from 6 to 8 hours during the day and when they need more money, they work more. The proportion of females who wish to work more is lesser in Bankura district and more in Hoogli district. The reason is probably that Bankura is more an agricultural district than Hoogli and families are mostly agricultural households. So when we see women working, we find them working in various non-agricultural occupations, whose urge is greater in Hoogli than in Bankura. Charts D3.1 to D3.5 describe the kind of domestic work done by women during the whole day. Women divide their time between household work and tending towards animal husbandry, which they term as caring for pets and poultry. This forms the range of their domestic household duties. We find that as land-size increases, women allocate more and more time to animal husbandry. This is true in both the districts, though household work still tends to take the lion's share of their time during the day. For the respondents, household work includes home-based work and other expenditure saving activities of the household, and this is clearly unpaid work. The entry into this world of unpaid work is also at a very tender age for poor landless and small, marginal farmers' families. With higher land-size holdings, women become more and more oriented towards only household work and they retreat from income-earning job types.

Education-wise Job Opportunity to Women

In the process of analysing the socio-economic changes of working women in the two districts, we tried to look at the relationship between educational attainments and the type of jobs which women are doing. This analysis is important from the view of understanding the role of education in the economic empowerment of women. We found that most of the women who work here are just literate in the sense that they can only sign their names. In Hoogli, many women who are working could not even sign their names. Most of the women who work are just literates or attained only primary educational levels. Most of them who studied up to Class VIII are engaged either in *bidi* making or sewing and tailoring. These two occupations appeared to be the occupations of educated women, if education means middle school level. Illiterates and neo-literates are mostly working in agro-based occupations and the middle school educated women are working in off-farm home-based occupations. The role played by education has only been to make women aware of the variations in working opportunities possible. They have added to the pool of unskilled and semi-skilled work.

There is practically no relationship between attainment of training for small and cottage-based production and the kind of jobs which the women are doing at present. In most of the cases, the training has not translated into jobs that utilize the training. Training was not imparted in most of the cases, and when it was, hardly any provision was made for conditions augmenting the utilization of training. This was true in both the districts. Training needs to be followed by institutional assistance and other conditions congenial to utilization of the training potentiality by the women among whom training is imparted.

Job Availability and Job Opportunity

This section looks into the variations in job availability among the working women. This was also an attempt to understand the ways in which poor women earn their livelihoods in the two districts. The identified livelihoods were the following:

1. making mats,
2. making plates out of leaves,
3. making bricks,
4. making garlands,
5. husking rice,
6. *muri* making,
7. umbrella making,
8. making woolen garments,
9. making bamboo products,
10. pottery,
11. *bidi* making,
12. making cotton threads,
13. stone crushing,
14. making products out of *mohua*,
15. making paper bags,
16. embroidery,
17. spectacle making,
18. elastic making,
19. wagon unloading,
20. handgloves making,
21. *bodi* making,
22. potato sorting,
23. spice packaging, and many other items which are either directly produced or assembled.

Some of the these occupations are found only in Bankura, some in Hoogli and others are found in both the districts. Most of these job types are those which are home-based, and cottage and small-scale industries. Women are engaged in these jobs clearly as a means to earn for the family. Sometimes teenage girl children are also employed so that they earn enough for their siblings. The diversity of these jobs is worth mentioning.

We tried to look at the extent of job shifting and switching among the working women, which is shown in Charts D4.1 to D4.5. The seasonal shifting was found to be perceptible among landless and marginal farmer families in Bankura, but this is not perceptible among them in Hoogli. Hoogli is relatively an industrial area and there is a trend of seasonal migration from Bankura to the Bardhaman rice bowl, which is not so in Hoogli. However, permanent job shifting and switching over to new jobs are significant among women from landless and marginal families in Hoogli. The new jobs indicate the corresponding of jobs to training programmes, and the assembling and subcontracting job opportunities opened up due to the globalization process. Permanent job shifting is significant in the Hoogli district for women coming from families of small, medium and large farmers also.

As far as availability of working women is concerned, these jobs are more or less available to the women when they want or look for them. Very few complained of non-availability of jobs. They can work if they are willing to do work; however the wages are not rewarding. The women are compelled to do these ill-paid jobs in order to provide some earnings for the family.

Working Hours of Women

A criterion indicating status of women's work is hours of work. Duration of work is a point of severe concern for women throughout the world after the policies of globalization have been implemented. There have been complaints of longer working hours in subcontracted jobs. We took eight hours a day as benchmark and tried to see who worked less or who more than eight hours. We found that the standard working hours were six. Some do not get even six hours of work a day. The earnings of this type of work depend on the intensity of work or number of hours of work. Those who do not get even six hours of work get less pay. Again, there are many women who make plates out of *sal* leaves in Bankura and who are engaged in embroidery work for more than eight hours. But these are piece-rated jobs, that is, their pay depends on the number of pieces that they actually make and not how long they work. This reflects the informalization aspect of jobs, which has quickly set in after globalization in the country.

The extent of exploitation due to longer working hours is pronounced in the work in rice mills, as agricultural labourer and as *bidi* worker, where working hours are sometimes as long as 11 to 12 hours. In all these cases, a subsistence wage rate is paid to the female workers, though we found that half of the women workers in the two districts were working between six and eight hours a day and earning due wage rates. But the exploitation exists with respect to the other half of the women workers.

Question of Economic Empowerment

This section deals with the question of whether working of women can lead to economic empowerment? This question cannot be simply answered, thus we tried to look at various manifestations of empowerment of working women. It is always true that a woman may be empowered vis-à-vis one kind of manifestation, but not be empowered with respect to another kind of manifestation. These manifestations and the results obtained are narrated here.

1. The reason for dropping out of studies and taking to work: Most of the women in both the districts stated that they were not direct drop-outs. They could have carried on with their studies if they wanted to, but they found work to be profitable. However, they also knew that dropping out of middle school and going to work was the only alternative for the poor families. The poor women were hence not in a position to exercise their choices, and social and economic compulsions forced them to leave their studies. Although the women felt that they could exercise their choice in this respect, they were hardly in a position to do so and this freedom of choice cannot be taken to be empowerment.

2. The age of entry into work: With respect to this question, we find a difference in responses in Bankura and Hoogli. In Bankura, most of the women enter work at a very tender age. This is not so in Hoogli, where most of them enter work after marriage or birth of the first child. As can be inferred, Bankura is an agricultural district where women work in the fields from a very early age. Hoogli is an industrial district, where women enter into small-scale production when required by the family to supplement their income. It is not empowerment when women enter work at an early age, but if they enter work at an adult age, they have the freedom to choose from among the jobs available. In small-scale production, they have

this opportunity, but when it is compulsory work in agricultural fields they do not have this opportunity.

3. Decision to enter into job market: Most of the women in the two districts reported that entry into the job market was their own decision. They objected to the view that there was coercion in the family which forced them to work and earn. The problem is that women can hardly distinguish between what is coercion and what is their own free will. When they feel the compulsion of situations—the poverty of the families, young siblings or children to feed and bring up—they voluntarily join work. Here we must again distinguish between an adult's decision and a child's decision to join work. Hence, though they reported that they were free to decide and coming to work was their own decision, this cannot be taken to be empowerment.

4. Hours of work: Women in both the districts reported more or less six to eight hours of work. The longer working hours of women in the post-globalization era in developing countries cannot be found in the state. However, many women reported that they do not work more as more work is not available. Again, the linking of wages to hours of work also exists here. The more they work, the more they earn. If they do not work more hours, they earn less. If they fall sick, they again earn less. This means that women are becoming economically empowered but the conditions of work are not satisfactory.

5. Domestic duties: Questions were asked to understand how domestic duties are performed when women come out to work or women are engaged in home-based production. Women perform domestic duties even when they work and they need the same kind of input from the family members. But we found that women hardly receive any help from other family members and even if they are devoting time to supplement the family income, they have to perform all domestic duties. They are not empowered to share domestic chores with other family members, especially the male members. Only sometimes we find the elder daughter taking up the domestic duties of her working mother, but then she is doing so by dropping out from school.

6. Women's share in the earnings from the family occupation: Women participate in the family occupation, which is almost mandatory for the family members. Most of them know what their earnings and share are and have control over them, but as far as the spending of the family earnings is concerned, they have little control. They are empowered as far as earnings are concerned, but not with respect to spending the earnings.

7. Savings and possession of personal assets: Women in Bankura show significant empowerment as most of them save and possess personal assets. But this is not so for most women in Hoogli. They earn but they do not have savings or personal assets. This is because of the fact that Bankura is a rich agricultural region, and women in Hoogli are dependent on small-scale industries. They do not earn enough to save or to possess personal assets.

The empowerment position of women in both the districts is ambiguous as one can see empowerment with respect to some indicators, but not with respect to others. However, the environment of women's work in both the districts and the limited empowerment that we have seen have been nurtured within the socio-political empowerment process of people, including women, through the panchayat system. The socio-political empowerment is thus interlocked here with economic empowerment and is reinforcing each other in the process.

The primary surveys in the two districts have exposed the scope for possible action regarding the question of women's economic empowerment in the state. They have marked out some problems in the social conditions which prohibit full economic empowerment to be achieved by women even if they have an independent income and contribute to the family income. The very attitude of considering women's income supplementary and something not preferred if the family has no financial problems raises problems for women's empowerment. This has been clearly revealed from the primary surveys in the two districts. The two districts are fairly representative of the state as Bankura is an agricultural region and Hoogli is an industrial region.

Chart D1.1
Entry Age of Work

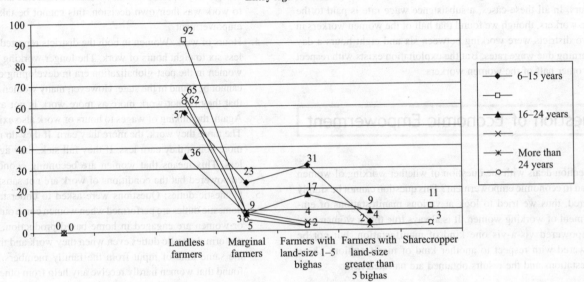

Chart D1.2
Time of Entry for Landless Farmers

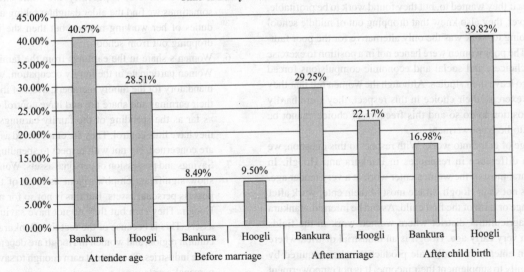

Chart D1.3
Time of Entry for Marginal Farmers

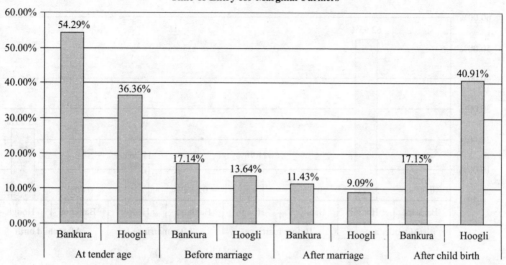

Chart D1.4
Time of Entry for Farmers with Land-size 1–5 Bighas

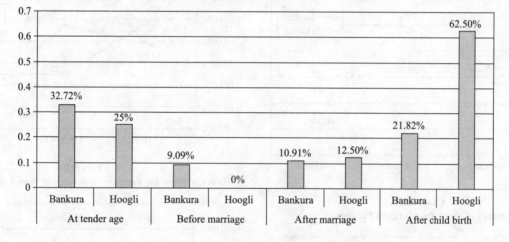

Chart D1.5
Time of Entry for Farmers with Land-size Greater than 5 Bighas

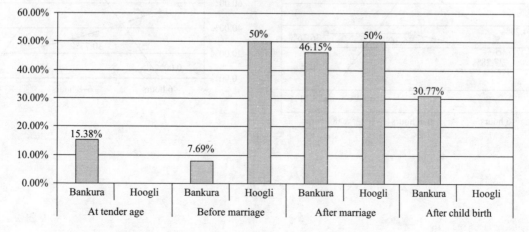

Chart D1.6
Time of Entry for Sharecroppers

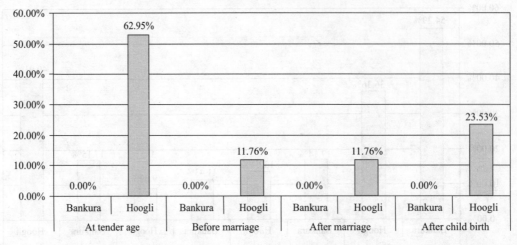

Chart D2.1
Hours of Work for Landless Farmers

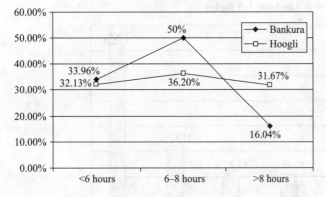

Chart D2.3
Hours of Work for Farmers with 1–5 Bighas of Land

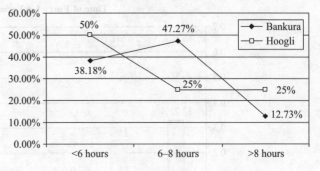

Chart D2.2
Hours of Work for Marginal Farmers

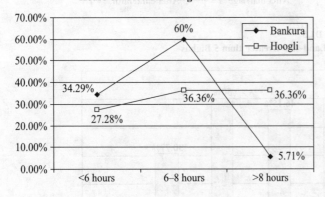

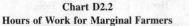

Chart D2.4
Hours of Work for Farmers with Greater than 5 Bighas of Land

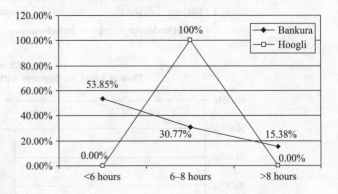

Chart D2.5
Hours of Work for Sharecroppers

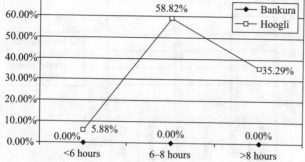

Chart D3.3
Kind of Work done by Women during the Whole Day

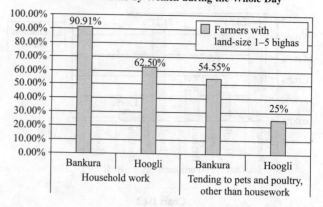
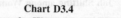

Chart D3.1
Kind of Work done by the Women during the Whole Day

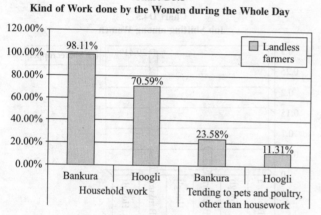

Chart D3.4
Kind of Work done by Women during the Whole Day

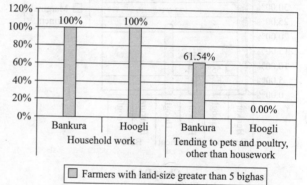

Chart D3.2
Kind of Work done by the Women during the Whole Day

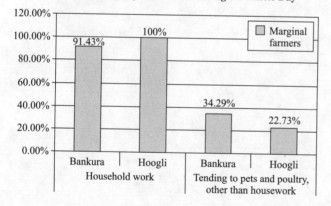

Chart D3.5
Kind of Work done by Women during the Whole Day

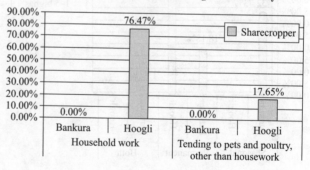

Chart D4.1
Job Shifting among Women

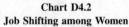
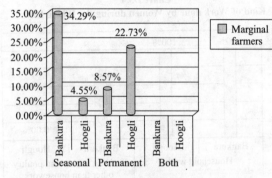

Chart D4.4
Job Shifting among Women

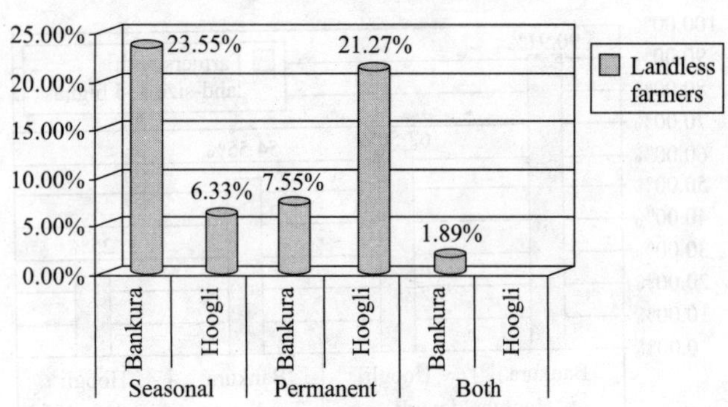

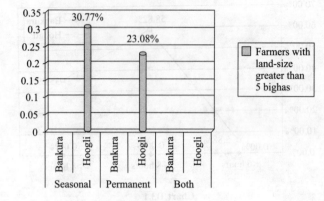

Chart D4.2
Job Shifting among Women

Chart D4.5
Job Shifting among Women

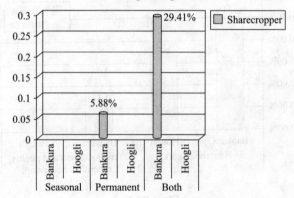

Chart D4.3
Job Shifting among Women

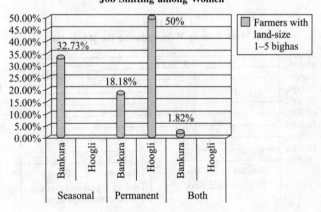

List of Women Lok Sabha MPs from West Bengal (1952–2000)

Name of the MP	Party	Constituency	Lok Sabha terms
Mamata Banerjee	AITC	Calcutta South	8, 10, 11, 12, 13
Sandhya Bauri	CPI (M)	Vishnupur (SC)	11, 12, 13
Malini Bhattacharya		Jadavpur	9, 10
Indumati Bhattacharya	INC	Hoogli	8
Krishna Bose	AITC	Jadavpur	11, 12, 13
Maitreyee Bose	Independent	Darjeeling	4
Renu Chakravarty	CPI	Barrackpore	1, 2, 3
Bibha Ghosh Goswami	CPI (M)	Nabadwip (SC)	5, 6, 7, 8
Phulrenu Guha	INC	Contai	8
Abha Maiti	Janata Party	Panskura	6
Geeta Mukherjee	CPI	Panskura	7, 8, 9, 10, 11, 12, 13
Maya Ray	INC	Raiganj	5
Renuka Ray	INC	Malda	2, 3
Uma Roy	INC	Malda	4
Minati Sen	CPI (M)	Jalpaiguri	12, 13

List of Women Rajya Sabha MPs from West Bengal

Period		Name of the MP	Party
10/07/1975	09/07/1981	Pratima Bose	INC
03/04/1952	02/04/1958	Maya Devi Chettry	INC
03/04/1958	02/04/1964	Maya Devi Chettry	INC
03/04/1964	02/04/1970	Phulrenu Guha	O
03/04/1990	02/04/1996	Sarla Maheshwari	CPI (M)
19/08/1999	18/08/2005	Sarla Maheshwari	CPI (M)
03/04/1960	04/03/1962	Abha Maity	O
03/04/1978	02/04/1984	Kanak Mukherjee	CPI (M)
03/04/1984	02/04/1990	Kanak Mukherjee	CPI (M)
03/04/1970	02/04/1976	Purabi Mukhopadhyay	INC
03/04/1976	02/04/1982	Purabi Mukhopadhyay	INC
19/08/1993	18/08/1999	Chandra Kala Pandey	CPI (M)
19/08/1999	18/08/2005	Chandra Kala Pandey	CPI (M)
03/04/1996	02/04/2002	Bharati Ray	CPI (M)

E3
List of Women MLAs in West Bengal (1952–2000)

List of Women MLAs in West Bengal (1952–2000)

Year	Name of the MLA	Name of the constituency	Year	Name of the MLA	Name of the constituency
1952	Bina Bhowmick	Calcutta General	1967	Nanda Rani Dal	Ghatal (SC)—Medinipur
	Bivabati Bose	Calcutta South		Sudharani Dutta	Onda—Bankura
	Janab Husan Ara Begam	Murshidabad		Abha Maiti	Bhaganpur—Medinipur
	E.M. Ricketts	Anglo-Indian		Biva Mitra	Kalighat—Calcutta
1954	Mira Dutta Gupta	Bhowanipur		Ila Mitra	Manicktala—Calcutta
	Mani Kuntala Sen	Kalighat		Purabi Mukhopadhyay	Taldangra—Bankura
	Abha Maiti	Khejri—Medinipur		Geeta Mukhopadhyay	Panskura—East-Medinipur
	Purabi Mukhopadhyay	Taldangra—Bankura		Nurunnesa Sattar	Mangalkot—Bardhaman
	Renuka Ray	Ratua—Maldah		Shakila Khatun	Basanti—24 Parganas
1956	Santi Das	Nominated	1969	Nirupama Chatterjee	Bagnan—Haora
	Anila Debi	Presidency Division North		Nanda Rani Dal	Ghatal (SC)—Medinipur
	Labonyaprova Dutta	Nominated		Abha Maiti	Bhagabanpur—Medinipur
1957	Maya Banerjee	Kakdwip—24 Parganas		Ila Mitra	Manicktala—Calcutta
	Sudharani Dutta	Raipur—Bankura		Protiva Mukhopadhyay	Suri—Birbhum
	Labanya Prova Ghosh	Purulia—Purulia		Geeta Mukhopadhyay	Panskura—East-Medinipur
	Anjali Khan	Medinipur—Medinipur		Parul Saha	Gaighata—24 Parganas
1960	Maya Banerjee	Kakdwip—24 Parganas	1971	Nirupama Chatterjee	Bagnan—Haora
	Maitreyee Bose	E. Calcutta		Nanda Rani Dal	Ghatal (SC)—Medinipur
	Sudharani Dutta	Raipur—Bankura		Anila Debi	Manicktala—Kolkata
	Labanya Prova Ghosh	Purulia—Purulia		Protiva Mukhopadhyay	Suri—Birbhum
	Parbati Hazra	Tarakeswar—Hoogli		Geeta Mukhopadhyay	Panskura—East-Medinipur
	Anima Hare	Kalchini—Jalpaiguri		Ila Roy	Jorabagan—Kolkata
	Anjali Khan	Medinipur—Medinipur	1973	Ila Mitra	Manicktala—Kolkata
	Abhalata Kunda	Bhahar—Bardhaman		Geeta Mukhopadhyay	Panskura—East-Medinipur
	Olive Pemantle	Nominated		Nurunnesa Sattar	Purbasthati—Bardhaman
	Manikuntala Sen	Kalighat—Kolkata		Ila Roy	Jorabagan—Kolkata
	Shakila Khatun	Canning—24 Parganas		Amala Saren	Ranibandh (ST)—Bankura
	Tusar Tudu	Garbatta—Medinipur	1975	Ila Mitra	Manicktala—Kolkata
	Purabi Mukhopadhyay	Vishnupur—Bankura		Mira Rani Mitra	Gaighata—24 Parganas
1963	Maya Banerjee	Kakdwip—24 Parganas		Geeta Mukhopadhyay	Panskura—East-Medinipur
	Santi Das	Chakdah—Nadia		Nurunnesa Sattar	Purbasthati—Bardhaman
	Sudharani Dutta	Raipur—Bankura		Ila Roy	Jorabagan—Kolkata
	Radhrani Mahatab	Bardhaman—Bardhaman		Amala Saren	Ranibandh (ST)—Bankura
	Niharika Majumdar	Rampurhat—Birbhum	1977	Nirupama Chatterjee	Bagnan—Haora
	Biva Mitra	Kalighat—Kolkata		Chhaya Ghosh	Murshidabad—Murshidabad
	Ila Mitra	Manicklata—Kolkata		Aparajita Goppi	Koch Bihar North—Koch Bihar
	Santilata Mondal	Bishnapur—24 Parganas		Renu Leena Subba	Kalimpong—Darjeeling
	Purabi Mukhopadhyay	Taldangra—Bankura	1978	Nirupama Chatterjee	Bagnan—Haora
	Olive Permantle	Nominated		Chhaya Ghosh	Murshidabad—Murshidabad
	Shakila Khatun	Basanti—24 Parganas		Aparajita Goppi	Koch Bihar North—Koch Bihar
	Tusar Tudu	Garbetta—Medinipur		Renu Leena Subba	Kalimpong—Darjeeling

(*Contd.*)

(*Contd.*)

Year	Name of the MLA	Name of the constituency	Year	Name of the MLA	Name of the constituency
1980	Nirupama Chatterjee	Bagnan—Haora		Santi Chatterjee	Tarakeswar—Hoogli
	Chhaya Ghosh	Murshidabad—Murshidabad		Nirupama Chatterjee	Bagnan—Haora
	Aparajita Goppi	Koch Bihar North—Koch Bihar		Arati Dasgupta	Falta—24 Parganas (S)
	Renu Leena Subba	Kalimpong—Darjeeling		Minati Ghosh	Gangarampur—Medinipur
1981	Nirupama Chatterjee	Bagnan—Haora		Aparajita Goppi	Koch Bihar North—Koch Bihar
	Chhaya Ghosh	Murshidabad—Murshidabad		Anju Kar	Kalna—Bardhaman
	Aparajita Goppi	Koch Bihar North—Koch Bihar		Maharani Konar	Memari—Bardhaman
	Renu Leena Subba	Kalimpong—Darjeeling		Mamtaz Begum	Ratua—Maldah
1982	Aparajita Goppi	Koch Bihar North—Koch Bihar		Jayasree Mitra	Barjora—Bankura
	Renu Leena Subba	Kalimpong—Darjeeling		Mamata Mukherjee	Purulia—Purulia
	Nirupama Chatterjee	Bagnan—Haora		Kamal Sengupta (Bose)	Habra—24 Parganas (N)
	Chhaya Bera	Medinipur—Medinipur	1990	Chhaya Bera	Nandanpur—Medinipur
1983	Chhaya Bera	Medinipur—Medinipur		Sandhya Chatterjee	Chandannagore—Hoogli
	Nirupama Chatterjee	Bagnan—Haora		Santi Chatterjee	Tarakeswar—Hoogli
	Chhaya Ghosh	Murshidabad—Murshidabad		Nirupama Chatterjee	Bagnan—Haora
	Aparajita Goppi	Koch Bihar North—Koch Bihar		Arati Dasgupta	Falta—24 Parganas (S)
	Anju Kar	Kalna—Bardhaman		Minati Ghosh	Gangarampur—Medinipur
	Maharani Konar	Memari—Bardhaman		Aparajita Goppi	Koch Bihar North—Koch Bihar
	Renu Leena Subba	Kalimpong—Darjeeling		Anju Kar	Kalna—Bardhaman
1984	Chhaya Bera	Medinipur—Medinipur		Maharani Konar	Memari—Bardhaman
	Nirupama Chatterjee	Bagnan—Haora		Mamtaz Begum	Ratua—Maldah
	Chhaya Ghosh	Murshidabad—Murshidabad		Jayasree Mitra	Barjora—Bankura
	Aparajita Goppi	Koch Bihar North—Koch Bihar		Mamata Mukherjee	Purulia—Purulia
	Anju Kar	Kalna—Bardhaman		Kamal Sengupta (Bose)	Habra—24 Parganas (N)
	Maharani Konar	Memari—Bardhaman	1993	Chhaya Bera	Nandanpur—Medinipur
	Renu Leena Subba	Kalimpong—Darjeeling		Kumkum Chakraborti	Behala East—24 Parganas
1985	Chhaya Bera	Medinipur—Medinipur		Tania Chakraborty	Panihati— 24 Parganas (N)
	Nirupama Chatterjee	Bagnan—Haora		Sandhya Chatterjee	Chandannagore—Hoogli
	Chhaya Ghosh	Murshidabad—Murshidabad		Santi Chatterjee	Tarakeswar—Hoogli
	Aparajita Goppi	Koch Bihar North—Koch Bihar		Nirupama Chatterjee	Bagnan—Haora
	Anju Kar	Kalna—Bardhaman		Nanda Rani Dal	Keshpur (SC)—Medinipur
	Maharani Konar	Memari—Bardhaman		Arati Dasgupta	Falta—24 Parganas (S)
1987	Chhaya Bera	Medinipur—Medinipur		Chhaya Ghosh	Murshidabad—Murshidabad
	Nirupama Chatterjee	Bagnan—Haora		Minati Ghosh	Gangarampur—Medinipur
	Santi Chatterjee	Tarakeswar—Hoogli		Gillian Rosemary Harti	Nominated
	Sandhya Chatterjee	Chandannagore—Hoogli		Arati Hembram	Ranibandh (ST)—Bankura
	Arati Dasgupta	Falta—24 Parganas (S)		Anju Kar	Kalna—Bardhaman
	Minati Ghosh	Gangarampur—Medinipur		Maharani Konar	Memari—Bardhaman
	Aparajita Goppi	Koch Bihar North—Koch Bihar		Mamtaz Begum	Ratua—Maldah
	Anju Kar	Kalna—Bardhaman		Jayasree Mitra	Barjora—Bankura
	Mamtaz Begum	Ratua—Maldah		Sabitri Mitra	Araidanga—Maldah
	Jayasree Mitra	Barjora—Bankura		Mamata Mukherjee	Purulia—Purulia
	Mamata Mukherjee	Purulia—Purulia		Maya Rani Paul	Berhampore—Murshidabad
	Kamal Sengupta (Bose)	Habra—24 Parganas (N)		Anuradha Putatunda (Dev)	Magrahat West—24 Parganas (S)
1988	Chhaya Bera	Nandanpur—Medinipur		Rubi Noor	Sujapur—Maldah
	Sandhya Chatterjee	Chandannagore—Hoogli		Bilasi Bala Sahis	Para (SC)—Purulia
	Santi Chatterjee	Tarakeswar—Hoogli		Kamal Sen Gupta (Bose)	Habra—24 Parganas (N)
	Nirupama Chatterjee	Bagnan—Haora	1996	Chhaya Bera	Nandanpur—Medinipur
	Arati Dasgupta	Falta—24 Parganas (S)		Susmita Biswas	Barjora—Bankura
	Minati Ghosh	Gangarampur—Medinipur		Kumkum Chakraborti	Behala-East—24 Parganas (S)
	Aparajita Goppi	Koch Bihar North—Koch Bihar		Shanta Chhetri	Kurseong—Darjeeling
	Anju Kar	Kalna—Bardhaman		Nanda Rani Dal	Keshpur—Medinipur
	Maharani Konar	Memari—Bardhaman		Gillian Rosemary Harti	Nominated
	Mamtaz Begum	Ratua—Maldah		Ibha Dey	Jangipara—Hoogli
	Jayasree Mitra	Barjora—Bankura		Kanika Ganguly	Bally—Haora
	Mamata Mukherjee	Purulia—Purulia		Minati Ghosh	Gangarampur—South Dinajpur
	Kamal Sengupta (Bose)	Habra—24 Parganas (N)		Deblina Hembram	Ranibandh—Bankura
1989	Chhaya Bera	Nandanpur—Medinipur		Mili Hira	Haringhata—Nadia
	Sandhya Chatterjee	Chandannagore—Hoogli		Anju Kar	Kalna—Bardhaman

(*Contd.*)

(*Contd.*)

Year	Name of the MLA	Name of the constituency	Year	Name of the MLA	Name of the constituency
	Sadhana Mallik	Mangalkot—Bardhaman		Kanika Ganguly	Bally—Haora
	Sabitri Mitra	Araidanga—Maldah		Minati Ghosh	Gangarampur—South Dinajpur
	Mamata Mukherjee	Purulia		Deblina Hembram	Ranibandh—Bankura
	Sakuntala Paik	Kulpi—24 Parganas (S)		Mili Hira	Haringhata—Nadia
	Maya Rani Paul	Berhampore—Murshidabad		Anju Kar	Kalna—Bardhaman
	Sakti Rana	Gopiballavpur—Medinipur		Sadhana Mallik	Mangalkot—Bardhaman
	Rubi Noor	Sujapur—Maldah		Sabitri Mitra	Araidanga—Maldah
	Tapati Saha	Taltola—Kolkata		Mamata Mukherjee	Purulia
	Bilashi Bala Sahis	Para—Purulia		Sakuntala Paik	Kulpi—24 Parganas (S)
	Kamal Sen Gupta	Bijpur—24 Parganas (N)		Maya Rani Paul	Berhampore—Murshidabad
1999	Sushmita Biswas	Barjora—Bankura		Sakti Rana	Gopiballavpur—Medinipur
	Kumkum Chakraborti	Behala-East—24 Parganas (S)		Rubi Noor	Sujapur—Maldah
	Shanta Chetri	Kurseong—Darjeeling		Tapati Saha	Taltola—Kolkata
	Nanda Rani Dal	Keshpur—Medinipur		Bilashi Bala Sahis	Para—Purulia
	Gillian Rosemary Harti	Nominated		Kamal Sen Gupta	Bijpur—24 Parganas (N)
	Ibha Dey	Jangipara—Hoogli			

A Micro Survey of the Status of Women Rural Artists of West Bengal

APPENDIX F

Malini Bhattacharya

This survey was undertaken with the help of the West Bengal Folk and Tribal Cultural Centre between February–April 2000 and is based on facts collected from 134 women rural artists coming from the districts of Jalpaiguri, Uttar Dinajpur, Dakshin Dinajpur, Maldah, Murshidabad, Birbhum, Bankura, Purulia, Medinipur, Bardhaman, Nadia, Hoogli, 24 Parganas (N) and 24 Parganas (S). They represent a number of cultural forms spread out over these 14 districts; some of these forms are exclusive to women artists, while others are performed jointly by men and women. The objective of the survey was to study the economic, educational, familial and social status of these women not just as women but also as artists, to examine the circumstances in which they carry out their artistic practice and to find out how they perceive their own practice as artists. We received some infrastructural support for this study from the School of Women's Studies, Jadavpur University and the first workshop at which the survey was conducted was partly funded by the Eastern Zonal Cultural Centre.

Some Basic Premises of the Survey

First, 'rural artists' in our sense are those whose daily life and livelihood are inextricably linked with production in the rural sector, particularly agricultural production, and those who practise their art-forms principally to educate and entertain millions of poor people living in rural areas. There are some cultural forms prevalent among them, in the performance of which the entire community participates. Many of these are parts of seasonal folk festivals and the audience itself takes active part in the performance. The artistic expertise is shared by the villagers or the community as a whole. *Bhadu*, *Tushu*, tribal singing and dancing are examples of this. Again, there are other forms of performance where more of professional expertise is required. The artists are vocationally engaged in these and they have to go through a special training which is handed down through master-artists or 'gurus'. *Alkaap*, *Leto*, *Baul*, puppetry, *Pat* narration or narration from scroll-paintings are examples of these. Both among community-performers and professional performers, women are to

be found. Of handicraft-makers, we have only a few samples. This, no doubt, requires a separate survey.

Second, there are performances associated with seasonal rituals which are enacted within the family or the immediate neighbourhood. Very often these are exclusively female occasions: Bhanjo, Sanjha, Ashtak, Jalmanga, marriage-songs among certain communities exemplify such all-female forms. Again, sometimes we find that a particular form is dominantly female when it is performed within the familial space. The same form may be taken over by men when it moves outside the neighbourhood. Thus, *Bhadu* singers who travel seasonally from village to village are all men, though a small girl (or boy) dressed up as 'Bhadu-rani' or Princess Bhadu accompanies them. In dramatic forms, women artists are fewer. Sometimes men perform in women's roles. The presence of women in mixed teams has always been a subject of controversy, but so far as we can see, although their number has been smaller, remarkable women artists have been associated with these forms. There are some exclusively male forms, too, like *Chhau* and *Gambhira*; here any exceptions only prove the rule. Again, the *Jhumur* form of singing and dancing has given rise to a whole class of talented women performers—the *nachnis*, who are now on the way to being extinct because of the sexually vulnerable lives they have been forced to lead. Kabigan has also produced some remarkable women artists, but they are small in number because of the pressure on most of them to become full-time professionals. We have not been able to include any *nachnis* in our survey, but we have interviewed a number of women artists who perform professionally in mixed dramatic teams. We have also included performers from all female teams.

Third, it may be observed that in the so-called folk forms that we have been talking of, generally both the performers and the audience come from among the rural poor. The large majority of them are landless labourers, sharecroppers, small and poor peasants, small artisans, fishermen, small traders, etc. The capitalist transformation of agriculture in Europe, which reduced pre-capitalist rural cultural forms to museum-pieces a century-and-a half-earlier, remained incomplete in India. The continuing preeminence of the agricultural sector in our country, where the penetration of industry has not completely transformed pre-capitalistic social formations, has allowed traditional cultural forms to retain their vitality. However, the penetration of audiovisual electronic media even in rural areas during the last 10 or 15 years and the changes in agrarian economy ushered in by the structural adjustment programme have also had a very profound impact on such traditional cultural forms. The work-pattern of women in the rural sector has changed; it may be expected that the pattern of their cultural participation would also change.

Fourth, the situation in West Bengal is somewhat special. The limited but effective land reforms during the Left Front regime have ensured some marginal benefits for landless labourers, poor peasants and sharecroppers. The rural artists, most of whom belong to these classes, have also benefited from the general effects of these. Apart from this, the Left Front has for quite a long time had a small but separate budgetary allocation for rural artists, which has been used to assist them to develop their artistic skills by providing more opportunities to perform in the panchayat areas and at the block and district levels, by organizing workshops and training camps for rural artists and by providing special assistance to old and sick artists. Rural artists are being involved in government programmes of literacy, sanitation and health, which are not only providing them with supplementary income but giving them recognition. As a result, many cultural forms in the rural areas have retained their vitality and their popularity even without the sponsorship of the forces that dominate the national and international cultural market. The status of women rural artists in West Bengal has to be understood in this context too.

Fifth, there is no doubt that poverty is one of the problems that tend to stifle the creativity of the artist. On the other hand, the entry of the forces dominating the national and the international market for culture is a lure that individual artists can hardly resist. But by succumbing to these forces, the rural artist tends to get alienated from his/her proper milieu, from the demands of the audience supplied by the rural poor. All these problems also affect the woman artist. But apart from these, she also has to confront other difficulties that are gender-based. For instance, to what extent is a woman prevented from developing her creativity in a society where she has been given a stereotyped role? What kind of leisure and opportunity does she get to practise her skill regularly? Does her family and her community allow her the space that is required by her if she wishes to practise her art as a professional or a semi-professional? To what extent does society tolerate her mobility which as an artist, takes her, outside the domestic sphere? All these tensions constitute the woman rural artist's life and determine her status.

Finally, the question of the articulation of the woman's voice in these creative practices. There are some forms which describe an exclusively female space but can we invariably say that all the anonymous songs and verses which pertain to the daily lives of women and to the rituals observed by them were therefore composed by women? Very often such orally transmitted compositions are imbued with patriarchal values. Can we then say that they were composed by men to be recited by women? We think it would be very simplistic to imagine that those compositions which represent patriarchal values indicate a male composer, whereas voices of resistance against patriarchy are invariably women's. Patriarchy as a dominant system of values may find articulation through women as well as through men. On the other hand, a male composer may very well resist this hegemony. Orally transmitted rural culture, as

it is passed on with conscious or unconscious modifications by men and women who use them, is often quite conservative, but again, strands of resistance against gender as well as class hegemony are often found to be embedded in such 'traditional' texts. But we cannot say that such notes of resistance are any certain indication of their having been composed by women. It is only in more recent times when the note of resistance to patriarchal values coincides with the emergence of the individual identity of the woman artist from the collective creative effort of which she was a part that we can talk of the presence of a distinctive 'woman's voice'. Thus, in wedding songs sung by women in the Muslim community, there have always been elements of social criticism. This does not mean that all the songs were women's compositions. It is only in present times, when the woman singer of these songs deliberately fights against social conservatism to transfer these songs from the familial ritual space to the public space, that she consciously begins to introduce the theme of protest into them and that we may hear a distinctive 'woman's voice'.

Aims and Objectives

In this micro-study, our objective has been to focus on the cultural lives of the majority of women in West Bengal, that is, those who belong to the rural sector. We are not taking a segregationist approach here. In other words, we do not think that the status of the woman rural artist can be studied completely in isolation from the general status of such artists, male or female, in West Bengal. However, we do think that it is necessary to study the gender dimension of cultural practice specifically. When rural artists engage in their cultural practice, they generally do so as a group. But even within the group, there are stratifications. Very often, it is the male leader of the group who acts as its spokesman. Even when we have a group of women, the male who is in the position of the escort speaks on behalf of the entire group. Unless we can find a strategy whereby the woman artist may be made to speak, we cannot be sure how she perceives her own role as an artist and a performer. We considered it important to record her own version of her artistic practice. The main parameters of her status and her own perception of it that we sought to explore are as follows:

1. Her age, educational standard, religion, caste and ethnic identity: religion, caste and ethnic identity are important because these often determine the cultural genre that she is associated with;
2. The role/roles she plays as an artist, such as singer/dancer/ actor/instrumentalist/dramatist/composer/trainer, etc.
3. Her economic position: while we have sought to understand this from an assessment of the amount of land (including agricultural and) possessed by the family, we have also sought to find out other sources of family income; the personal possessions/earnings of the artist have also been the subject of our enquiry; whether she has any say in the spending of her family income/her own income was also asked.

4. Marriage and children: apart from more general queries regarding age of marriage and marital status, we have wanted to know whether she married within the same caste/community/ethnic group, the number of children she has had, whether they have been to school, whether she/her husband/both practise family planning.

5. About the specific characteristics of her cultural practice: such as details regarding her training, whether her 'guru' was a woman, how she manages to find time to practise her skill, whether she faces any social stigma or any opposition from the family or from her community, whether she has introduced any new themes in her art, etc.

6. Apart from this, the influence on their lives of the general cultural ambience that they share with others was another object of our inquiry. For instance, they were questioned about their exposure to mass-media like cinema, radio and television, about books and journals they may read, about their contact with people from other communities, possible incidences of inter-caste/community marriage in their locality, their opinion on dowry. We also asked them questions about their mobility as artists, performances outside the village/the district/the state in which they participated; and also about government programmes they performed in, and/or government assistance of various kinds that they might have received.

Method

We have tried to make our survey representative of different cultural forms in different districts. We are not entirely sure whether the 134 artists we have chosen can fully represent these varieties. We have not been able to include Koch Bihar, Darjeeling and Haora in our survey. Again, some important forms where women are known to participate (e.g., Banbibir Pala) have remained unrepresented. While admitting these limitations, however, we can say that we have been able to bring in a number of crucial variants which may help us to form a general idea about the status of such women artists in West Bengal.

The survey was done through a questionnaire which had 40 different questions in it, both quantitative and qualitative. A one-day intensive training camp was held for 10 field workers who collected the facts subsequently by interviewing the women. The interviews were taken through five workshops held in (*i*) Banipur, (*ii*) Maldah, (*iii*) Balurghat, (*iv*) Bolpur and (*v*) Bangaon where the interviewers met the artists and collected their responses. Apart from Banipur, where participants were present from 10 districts, those from the districts of Maldah, Uttar and Dakshin Dinajpur, and Birbhum were present at the workshops held in Maldah, Balurghat and Bolpur respectively. In the Banipur workshop, 78 correspondents were present; 17, 13 and 8 participants respectively were present at the workshops held in Maldah, Balurghat and Bolpur. At the Maldah workshop, a woman Alkaap artist came from Murshidabad and was included. In Bangaon, a mixed group of women performers came. Moreover, three handicraft makers, two from Uttar Dinajpur and one from Bankura, have been included in the survey as stray samples.

The data collected through the surveys were put together and a quantitative analysis was made of the whole. Also, certain qualitative information emerged from the conversations of the interviewers with the artists. These have also been included in our report. As far as we know, no other work of this kind with female folk artists has been done before. We are also aware that our sample size is quite small, but we have tried to introduce different variables in a manner that might enable us to hypothesize on some general trends.

Samples of Data

1. Total number of women folk artists: 134.
2. Representation from different districts: Jalpaiguri—14, Uttar Dinajpur—9, Dakshin Dinajpur—17, Maldah—12, Murshidabad—17, Birbhum—8, Bankura—5, Purulia—11, Medinipur—6, Bardhaman—6, Nadia—9, Hoogli—4, 24 Parganas (N)—14, 24 Parganas (S)—2.
3. Representation of different forms:
   Baul—23 (Jalpaiguri—2, Uttar Dinajpur—2, Dakshin Dinajpur—13, Birbhum—3, Nadia—3)
   Tribal dance and song—24 (Dakshin Dinajpur—2, Maldah—4, Birbhum—4, Bankura—4, Purulia—4, Medinipur—4, 24 Parganas (N)—2)
   Muslim wedding song—23 (Maldah—2, Murshidabad—9, Bardhaman—6, Nadia—6)
   Khan—2 (Uttar Dinajpur—1, Maldah—1)
   Jalmanga—2 (Uttar Dinajpur—2)
   Bhawaiya—6 (Jalpaiguri—2, Uttar Dinajpur—2, Dakshin Dinajpur—2)
   Chor-Churni—2 (Jalpaiguri—2)
   Bishahara—2 (Jalpaiguri—2)
   Rabha dance—6 (Jalpaiguri—6)
   Sanjha—1 (Maldah—1)
   Rajbangshi wedding song—2 (Maldah—2)
   Bhanjo—4 (Maldah—2, Murshidabad—2)
   Chaain wedding song—3 (Murshidabad—3)
   Kabigan—2 (Murshidabad—1, 24 Parganas (N)—1)
   Meleni Mashir Gan—1 (Murshidabad—1)
   Tushu—8 (Purulia—5, Birbhum—1, 24 Parganas (N)—2)
   Puppet—2 (24 Parganas—2)
   Leto—4 (Hoogli—4)
   Pater Gan—2 (Medinipur—2)
   Jhumur—2 (Purulia—2)
   Alkaap—1 (Murshidabad—1)
   Dokra—1 (Bankura—1)
   Bamboo and cane work—2 (Uttar Dinajpur—2)
4. The artist's role: singer—114, instrumentalist—15, actress—25, dancer—55, writer of plays—4, writer of songs—8, composer—17, instructor—1, others—3 (There are many artists who perform more than one function in their own forms.)
5. Age: up to 16 years—21; 17 to 30 years—45; 31 to 55 years—9 (The youngest artist is Mariam Khatun of Murshidabad aged six and the seniormost artist Sarala Das of Jalpaiguri aged over 80.)

6. Education: illiterate—14, can sign own name—26, primary level—41, secondary level—46, higher secondary —2, above higher secondary—5. (Among the 14 illiterate artists, 3 are aged between 17 and 30, 7 are aged between 31 and 55 and 4 are over 55.)

7. Religion: Hindu—79, Muslim—24, Christian—4, others—26. (Quite a few among the Bauls and a few among the tribals did not describe themselves as Hindu. Their statements have been recorded exactly and we have put them under the category 'others'. A singer of Rajbangshi wedding songs has said 'I do not know what religion is'. One artist who sings Baul songs as well as Muslim wedding songs has said that although she is Muslim by birth, she follows the religion of the Bauls. One Baul artist from Birbhum has said that earlier her title was Ankur [Dom], now her title is Baul.)

8. Caste or ethnic group: Caste Hindu—6, scheduled caste—58, tribal—32, others—12. (This classification has not included 24 Muslim artists. One Bhawaiya artist has described herself as *vaishnab* without mentioning any separate caste. One Patua has said she has no caste.)

9. Economic condition: landless—45, only homestead land—27, the others have some agricultural land, 7 artists have homestead/agricultural land in their own names, 6 hold land jointly with husband or other relatives. An artist of Muslim wedding songs has informed us that her husband has divorced her because she had no children, but he has given her 1 bigha land in her name as compensation. The sole earning of 26 artists is from performances. There are 62 artists who have incomes from land or some other source apart from performances. There was 1 artist who said that she has no income of her own. There are 11 artists who are the sole earners in their families. There are 106 artists who help partially to run the family, and there are 16 artists who are dependent on the income of others.

10. Marital status: married—77, unmarried—39, widows—12, deserted—5, divorced—1. (Among the unmarried artists, 21 are below 16 years, 15 are between 17 and 30, 3 are between 31 and 55.) There are 22 artists who have married husbands of their own choice, 11 who have married outside their own caste, 69 who were married before they were 18, 22 who were over 18 when they got married, and 4 who could not tell us at what age they got married. In 59 cases, the husbands are also artists.

11. Children: 16 artists have no children, 35 have 3 or more children. Of these, 4 are below 31, 25 are below 36 and 6 are above 55. Again, of these 35 artists Hindus are 14, and Muslims are 7. There are no Christians and 14 others are none of these. In 2 cases the child died at an early age. The children of 65 artists go to school, in 5 cases the child is too small to go to school and in 10 cases the children never went to school. In 2 cases the son goes to school but the daughter does not. In 1 case we have not been able to find anything.

In 65 cases, either the children themselves practise the artistic form of the mother or the mother wishes to train her children in it. There is 1 Baul who wants to teach her form only to her son, another only to her daughter. There are 27 artists who do not want their children to learn their form. A Jalmanga artist said it would be useless to do so because her form is not in demand. There is 1 deserted tribal artist who has told us that if she has a child after remarriage she will train him/her in her form and 1 unmarried artist said if she has a child after marriage she will train him/her. There is 1 Baul and 1 Khan artist who said that their children do not like their forms, so they cannot force them.

There are 20 artists who gave birth in hospitals and 54 at home. In the case of 10 artists some of the children were born at home, others at the hospital. In 2 cases we have no information.

There are 27 who have recourse to family planning. Of these, 16 are Hindus, 7 Muslims, 1 Christian, and 3 belong to other categories. Again, 11 are aged 17 to 30 years and 16 are aged 31 to 55. There are 30 who have not taken recourse to family planning. We were unable to get any information in 26 cases. There are 4 artists who have said that they will take recourse to family planning later. Of them, 1 is between 16 and 30 years and 3 are between 31 and 55 years and all 4 are Hindus. There are 3 artists who follow Baul methods of family planning. Of them, 2 are between 17 and 30 years and 1 is between 31–55; 1 is a Hindu, 1 is a Muslim and the third belongs to the 'others' category. Ligation is the most popular method of family planning. There is a single case of taking pills and in another case the husband has undergone vasectomy.

12. Support from family: in 13 cases, there is support from family. In 3 cases we have no information. There is 1 interviewee who has said that the family does not support her going out for performances because this hampers her education. There is 1 unmarried artist who has said that the family does not support her because they think no-one will marry an artist. In 1 case we were told that the father is unwilling but there is support from the mother. Another artist said that her bedridden husband supports her but her son does not like her going out.

13. Training: from the family—74, through gurus—29, personal initiative—9, through some organization—11, both from family and guru—2, from guru through personal initiative—1, family and personal initiative—2, family and some organization—4, personal initiative and some organization—1.

14. Learned the form from a woman—44, man and woman—3, not known—11.

15. There are 13 artists who spend their money themselves. There are 22 who spend for themselves and for the family. In 3 cases artists spend some money for themselves and the family and give the rest to the husbands. In 1 case the artist spends for herself and gives her husband the rest. In 12 cases we have no information. (One artist of Muslim wedding songs said that she has no income at present. However, if she earns anything, she will keep the major part for herself and give her husband a few rupees, if he needs it.)

16. There are 29 artists who have said that whether they go for a performance or not is their own decision. There are 6 who

have said that it is a joint decision. In 2 cases we have no information.

17. There are 9 artists who have said that women did not have a function in that particular form previously. (Of these, 2 are Patuas, 1 is a Baul, 1 is a puppeteer, 1 is a Bishahara performer, 1 a Sokra artist.) In 1 case, there is no information.

18. There are 4 artists who perform only within family circles, 29 both within the family circle and the village, and 27 have performed at the district level. In 82 cases, we find women performing outside their own districts. In 2 cases, there is no information.

19. There are 82 artists who have informed us that they do not face any social strictures for their performances. There are 46 who have said that there are no such strictures now, although earlier these had been there. In 2 cases, there is no information. (Among those who have said that social strictures are there, we have 5 Bauls, 2 Bhawaiya singers, 2 Chor performers, 2 Bishahara performers, 5 Rabha dancers, 12 Muslim wedding songs singers, 1 tribal artist, 3 Chaain artist, 1 Kabigan singer, 5 Manasha-bhasan singers, 3 Tushu singers, 1 puppeteer and 4 Leto performers. 1 in Khan, 1 in Bhanjo and 1 in Alkaap said that there had been social strictures previously.)

There are many forms which are performed within family circles. When family performances are sought to be transferred to a public space one faces social impediments. A singer of Muslim wedding songs has informed us that at one stage their family had been ostracized by their community for about 7 years. Another artist in the same form has said that her group consists of young unmarried girls who drop out from the group as soon as they get married. The actresses in the Leto and puppeteering troupes have told us that in the village they have a lower social status because they perform outside their homes. An artist of Kabigan has mentioned the unfriendliness of other male kabiyals.

20. The extent of acquaintance with modern audiovisual medium: In answer to this question, 22 artists have said that they listen only to the radio, 6 have only seen films, 4 have only seen video shows and 14 have watched television. There are 73 artists who are acquainted with more than one kind of audiovisual medium. There are 12 artists who are not acquainted with any. In 2 cases we have no information. A singer of Muslim wedding songs from Bardhaman, when asked about the names of films that she had seen, mentioned *Nayak, Shakha-Prashakha, Paromitar Ekdin* and *Hajar Churashir Ma*. There are 74 artists who read either books or newspapers or journals. In 5 cases there is no information and there are 55 artists who do not read books, journals or newspapers.

21. Most artists observe some religious rites. There are 25 artists who do not observe any religious rites, and in 5 cases there is no information.

22. Majority of the artists do not participate in the religious rituals of other communities in the village. There are 58 such artists. In 4 cases we have no information.

23. This survey shows few instances of inter-community or inter-caste marriages. There are only 23 cases where such marriages have taken place. There are 9 artists who have said that they would not mind if such marriages were to take place. In 9 cases there is no information.

24. There were two questions asked regarding dowry. Those artists who had children were targeted and asked whether they would give or take any dowry at the marriage of their daughter or son. There are 25 who have said that they would take dowry for their son's marriage. But 45 have said they would not do so. In fact, some have said that when their sons got married they did not take dowry. Among the tribals 5 have said that they would give bride-price for their son's marriage. In 4 cases there is no information. The question was generally posed to women with children, but there are 2 young, unmarried artists who have said that if they get married and have sons they would not take any dowry. There is 1 artist who has said that if the bride is beautiful she will not take dowry. Another has said that she won't take any dowry if she does not have to give dowry for her daughter's marriage.

There are 34 artists who have said they would give dowry when their daughters get married. Another 34 have said that they would not do so. There is 1 tribal artist who has said that she will not take bride-price for her daughter' marriage but 1 tribal and 2 non-tribals said they would do so. In 16 cases there is no information. An unmarried Muslim girl said that large amount of dowry had to be given when her elder sister got married. Dowry would have to paid for her own wedding also. But if she ever has children she will neither give nor take dowry. One artist has said that in their community a bride-price of Rs 12.50 is compulsory and will have to be given.

25. There are 18 artists who have received some government assistance. There is 1 who has received a government award. In 1 case there is no information.

26. Before this, 86 artists have participated in some government organized programme or workshop. In 2 cases there is no information.

27. There are 76 artists who have told us that apart from traditional themes they are also introducing new themes in the form that they practice. In 3 cases there is no information.

General Conclusions

We have already spoken about the limitations of the survey that must be kept in mind when drawing general conclusions. All data were collected from the artists themselves which one has tried to accurately record. It may very well be that in some cases we have talked at cross-purposes, the real implication of some of their answers may have been misunderstood by us, or they may not have understood our questions accurately. Occasionally, they may have provided us unintentionally or even intentionally with data that are not wholly accurate. Those who are saying that they do not approve of dowry and will not take dowry may in fact have already done so under social pressure. When someone has described her family as supportive she may have done so tactically or because she is not willing to air her grievances publicly. The method we have followed includes these minor hazards. On the other hand, most of the artists have been very articulate and quite happy to be able to talk about themselves. When we compare the evidence given by one artist with that given by others, some patterns emerge. From these, more or less accurate conclusions may be arrived at:

1. There is evidence of greater mobility from one district to another and greater interaction between one form and the other. The traditional boundaries of a particular form within which an artist has developed herself have become more blurred. An artist singing 'Lalangeeti' may also learn to sing Bhawaiya; a woman Baul singer may also be adept at singing Muslim wedding songs. In all such cases, we have classified the artist in accordance with the form first mentioned by her. This mobility of the artists may be an indication of greater rapport among the forms and greater interaction among the artists themselves. This is a very positive sign particularly for women artists because it shows that the opportunity for picking up new forms has increased. That 82 artists included in this survey have performed either at different places within the district or outside the district or the state is a sign of this increased mobility.

2. According to the data of the Mass Education Directorate, literacy rate of women in West Bengal has risen from 45.56 per cent to 60.31 per cent between 1991 and 1995. In our survey we have found 14 women who are completely illiterate and 26 women can only sign their own names. Even if we exclude them, about 70 per cent of our interviewees are found to have had some modicum of education. Even if we assume that some of the most backward sections among the folk artists have not been included in our survey, the percentage of literacy may be taken to represent the general progress in elementary education. On the other hand, it may be noticed that one young artist has said that her family is unwilling to allow her to go for performances because this would hamper her education. It should also be observed that no artist under 16 years is illiterate. The number of illiterate artists between 17 and 30 years is only three. This indicates growing commitment to literacy and education. Majority of the children of married artists are going to school or have been to school. There are some examples, too, of such children looking down upon and being alienated from the cultural forms practised by their parents, as a result of education.

3. The number of caste-Hindus is very small. Members from the scheduled caste categories constitute the largest chunk. Apart from this, there are tribals, whose percentage in our survey is fairly high. So far as Muslims and Christians are concerned, their percentage in the survey closely reflects their percentage in the total population of West Bengal. Possession of land is one indication of the economic status of the participants. In our survey, we have found that 72 persons,

that is, a little above 50 per cent are either landless or have homestead land only. Most of the participants who have some agricultural land were unable to estimate the exact amount. But through indirect questions it came out that very few have land more than 15–20 bighas. Only one or two are fairly prosperous. The proportion of land possessed by tribal families seems to be higher. In very few cases do women own land in their own names or even jointly with their husbands. This indicates that while women are engaged in agricultural work, their right to land does not yet have wide recognition. Generally, we hear that in rural areas women-headed families are on the increase. In our survey, however, only 11 such families have been found. There are few women engaged in non-agricultural work. There is one ICDS worker, one bank employee and two or three panchayat members. Generally speaking, almost all artists come from the poorer sections; the number of completely destitute artists is three to four.

4. About 69 women, that is, majority of the married women were married when they were under 18 years. This statement applies even to women married in the recent past. The number of deserted/divorced women is quite low. About 22 artists married out of their own choice; the number is considerable. In quite a large number of cases, the men whom they married are also artists. The number of inter-caste marriages is small. From the data collected, we have come to the conclusion that the dowry system is very widespread in rural areas. The respondents have said that sometimes girls remain unmarried because they cannot pay dowry. Even Muslim women have said that dowry worth Rs 30,000 to Rs 40,000 is sometimes demanded. Among scheduled castes and tribals, the system of bride-price still exists; one respondent has said that the groom has to pay Rs 12.50 at the time of marriage as a ritual gesture. Adivasi boys in service are now demanding dowry in a roundabout way, according to the evidence. Many respondents have said that one has to abide by existing conventions if one lives in society, but generally, younger women have severely criticized the dowry system. Though noone has really supported it. Some artists have said that they are speaking up against dowry through their performances.

5. Of 95 women who are married, widowed, divorced or deserted, 35 have three or more children. Among them, only a few are below 30; the majority are between 31 and 55. There is no discernible religious divide between women who have a larger number of children and those who do not. Probably, economic stratifications are of more significance here, that is, whether Hindu or non-Hindu, younger women with a better economic status tend to have fewer children. There are exceptions to this—between two women in the same community, of the same age group and with a similar economic status, one may have more children than the other. Most women artists still give birth at home. A few, however, went to the hospital to have the second child. About sending children to school or training them in their own art, little discrimination is found to be made between girls and boys. There are 65 artists who want to train their children in their own art.

6. The question on family planning was asked more cautiously. Only women fieldworkers were instructed to ask this question, even then one was unable to do so with women above 55 years. However, of those that we have been able to question, 27 have said they have adopted some family planning methods. Another 4 have said that they will do so, but not right now. Respondents under 55 seem to be aware of the issue. Differences along religious lines are not perceivable on this issue; economic status, on the other hand, may have a more significant role to play. However, almost in all cases, a terminal method, namely, ligation, seems to have been adopted. The husband has undergone vasectomy only in one case. It becomes very clear from this that in government programmes, the main target is still the woman. Another interesting thing is that some Baul artists have informed us that they use their own indigenous methods of family planning.

7. Only a few artists have said that they face restrictions from their family. In fact, in the rural community, women would not have even been able to come outside the family sphere in most cases if they did not have some support from the family. Where the husband or father is also an artist, often the woman collaborates with him and moves together with him. Quite a few of the artists on the other hand—46 in all—have spoken of social impediments. It seems that the impediments become more pronounced for those artists who take their performances outside the family or the village into the public sphere. Particularly forms that require a professional commitment, like Leto, Alkaap and puppetry, expose women to the disspproval of rural society. However, many of our respondents felt that in spite of this, the number of women engaged in these performances has not decreased. Also, a significant few have said that when they are invited to perform, they take their own decisions regarding agreeing or not, without waiting for their male guardian's consent. On the other hand, very few artists spend their own earnings only on themselves. When asked how they find time for rehearsals in the midst of their work, most of them did not consider it a problem. Some have said that they rehearse in the evenings and others have said that they do it at night; some have commented that if one has the motivation, one can always find time.

8. A few questions were asked to assess their awareness about the social changes going on around them. It emerged that rural women are not unaware of these changes. We have already said that above 82 artists have performed in different places in and outside the district. Also, we find that about 74 artists, that is more than 50 per cent, read books, pamphlets, newspapers and journals. Similarly, about 90 per cent are familier with the audiovisual media. Few artists have received financial assistance from the government, but most have participated in government programmes at some level or the other. This is also a route by which one may get acquainted with the world outside. This awareness has encouraged more than 50 per cent the artists to introduce new themes in their performances. Apart from themes related to government schemes, like literacy, other themes are also becoming popular. A few have said that they wish to introduce new themes, but feel constrained because of being less educated.

9. Religious rituals and practices have a significant presence in rural life. Most artists observe some religious practices, though 25 artists have specifically said that they do not observe any such practices. However, these religious practices seem to have fairly flexible boundaries and members of one community widely participate in the religious festivals of another community. We have found very few instances of cross-community marriages. Some people have voiced their reservations about such marriages. But a good number have also said that they would not object if such marriages took place.

A Report on Findings from a Study of Women's Status in Birbhum District of West Bengal

APPENDIX G

Atis Dasgupta and Suraj Bandyopadhyay

Contents

Study assisted by Rabindranath Jana, Sonali Chakraborty, Susmita Bharati, Dipankar Sen and Anil Chaudhuri (Sociological Research Unit, Indian Statistical Institute, Kolkata).

Advice and suggestions of Professors T.J. Rao and Debapriya Sengupta (Statistics-Mathematics Unit, ISI, Kolkata) and Anjali Ghosh (Psychological Research Unit, ISI, Kolkata) at different stages of study are gratefully acknowledged.

Introduction

Preamble

During the last few decades increasing concern with policies of egalitarian development, welfare of the backward sections of the society and making social justice and equity accessible to the weaker classes has spurred great interest in women's studies in our country. Various research activities including doctoral dissertations have been initiated by scientists, scholars and policy makers (Anju Vyas and Sunita Singh, *Information Sources, Services and Programmes*, Sage Publications, Newbury Park 1993).

The studies have been, on the whole, guided by major streams of thought such as: structural functional views based on socio-cultural background of tradition, values and norms; welfare focussed liberal orientation; unequal economic exchange; patriarchal pattern of relationships of domination-subordination; and so on. Some were inspired by socio-cultural norms traditionally attributing status of high respect to the role and position of Indian women while some others have studied exploitation of women in India as a consequence of unequal economic exchanges. Again, oppression through relationship of domination-subordination formed the central thrust of many scholars drawing research materials from the field of social anthropology. Discrimination and relative deprivation could be located at the centre of many of the enquiries. They would also argue the case in the context of lack of assimilation or integration with the mainstream. Thus, most of the women's studies bear some type of ideological connotation as indicated earlier.

As distinct from the above thrusts, the present study is primarily empirical. It is based on observations of quite a large number of women in the settings of their daily life and living. Furthermore, for this purpose, the women were not selected purposively but probabilistically in order to obtain an unbiased representation of the universe. The purpose is not to study women as if on a priority defined distinct class for itself. It rather aims at drawing valid inferences about women's status from interpretations of their interactions and experiences of daily life. While gender inequalities are not assumed to have become extinct with women's participation as equal partners in various processes of modernization and development, the central query around which the study veers is that, in spite of persisting gender inequalities and strains, how the society and, for that matter, its key units at the grassroots, such as households or families, still tend to survive.

Logistics of Field Selection, Sampling and Survey Design

Field Selction

The district of Birbhum was selected as the field of the study. It is a major rice producing district of the state in central West Bengal. The western part bordering Bihar is mostly the tail end of the East Indian plateau. Stretches of plain land criss-cross the eastern side of the district. Agriculture, which provides the principal source of livelihood for the majority of the population, has remained traditionally both rain-fed and irrigated. Community composition of population is quite heterogeneous. Large number of villages are reachable throughout the year, while there is still a considerable number of village areas inaccessible during the rainy season. All these features make it a typical district of West Bengal.

Besides, the official sources indicate that recently various measures of development in economic, socio-cultural and administrative spheres have been implemented in the district. These are, to give a few examples, small and minor irrigation projects, distribution of land among the landless and registration of sharecroppers, functioning of three-tier elected panchayats. Total Literacy Campaign (TLC), specially among the women, construction of all weather roads, and so on. It is quite natural to expect that these development measures would change the socio-economic and cultural environment of the district. Consequently, its impact will be felt in the women's life and living as well. In fact, a few indications in this regard have already been stated in some recent reports based on survey undertaken by Indian Statistical Institute such as: *A Study on the Impact of Total Literacy Campaign (TLC) in the District of Birbhum (West Bengal)* (December 1993); *Survey of Possibilities and Problems of Small-scale Industries in Birbhum* (August 1996); *In-depth Studies on the Levels of Development of Scheduled Castes and Scheduled Tribes* (December 1998); and *Social Network Analysis of Survival Strategy of the Rural Poor: A Case Study in the Context of Decentralized Planning* (November 1998).

The background of the district makes it more pertinent for the study. The focus of the study becomes wider and enables us to explore whether exposure to the exogenous forces of modernization intervening through developmental measures are likely to alter women's status, their attitudes and normative values, at the grassroots level.

Sampling Scheme

A district in West Bengal is officially divided into a number of subdivisions (SD), each of which has its boundary unambiguously demarcated. Natural and physical, or, broadly speaking, ecological variations within a district are confounded with SDs. So also are some village characteristics such as proximity or remoteness to rivers, roads and urban or commercial/industrial centres. Again, each SD is further administratively divided into a number of police stations (PS) which are later turned into community development blocks (CDB) or, simply, blocks. Often a PS as such becomes a CDB; but sometimes considering the size of a PS, more than one CDB is created out of one PS. A CDB consists of a number of *mouzas* (or revenue villages), which may be inhabited or not. The former are commonly identified as villages bearing social significance. In the district of Birbhum, there are 3 SDs, 14 PSs, 19 CDBs and 2,479 *mouzas* out of which 2,245 are inhabited villages.

Logistics of sampling was broadly similar in rural and urban areas. Exact designs, however, were different. We would, first, describe the design for the rural areas. There are three SDs in the district, namely, Sadar, Bolpur and Rampurhat with seven, four and eight CDBs respectively. In order to grasp the effects of ecological variations in the study, each SD was treated as a stratum. Keeping in view the socio-economic composition of the CDBs in each SD, two, three and three CDBs (altogether eight CDBs) were drawn to form the first stage units for sampling in rural areas by simple random sampling without replacement (SRSWOR). Inhabited villages in a CDB formed the second stage sampling units. A fixed number of moderate six inhabited villages was drawn for the study by SRSWOR from each CDB.

A list of all the households inhabiting a sampled village was obtained from the records maintained by the respective gram panchayat. The list was scrutinized by on-the-spot visits, as and where required, and an updated list of households was prepared. Household was considered to be the last stage unit for sampling. Twenty households from each village were selected. Thus, a total of 960 (= $20 \times 6 \times 8$) rural households was drawn as sample for the purpose of field interviews for the study.

At the stage of sampling of households, however, an intervening stratification by categories of communities was introduced. This was the division of households in a village among four strata formed by caste and community affiliation: scheduled caste Hindus (SC), scheduled tribes (ST), Muslims (Mu) and others (G). This was done due to the fact that several social scientists have pointed out the adverse consequences of uneven economic development, persistent socio-cultural backwardness and religious orthodoxy among some of them. Hence, the present study of women's status was visualized both as an aggregative study of the entire sample as well as disaggregated by categories of communities in order to construct, as and where necessary, a valid profile of probable variation among the categories stated here.

Accordingly, the total number of 20 households to be selected in each village was distributed among the four categories proportional to the total numbers of households in each of them in every village. The households were then selected separately from each of the earlier mentioned four intra-village strata by the method of circular systematic sampling without replacement. This was done to eliminate the risk of any unanticipated bias, if it exists due to the ordering of households in the list. Obviously, the number of households of each category surveyed differed from village to village according to their sizes in the villages.

For the purpose of sampling in urban areas, one town was selected from each subdivision, i.e., a stratum. Out of three towns in Sadar subdivision, one was drawn by SRSWOR and one out of two was drawn in Rampurhat subdivision. Since there was only one town in Bolpur subdivision, it was automatically selected. Thus, Dubrajpur, Bolpur and Rampurhat were the three selected towns.

There were 16, 18 and 18 wards respectively in the three towns. As for drawing sample in rural areas, we decided to draw a sample of 6 wards by SRSWOR in each town and then a sample of 20 households in each ward, i.e., altogether 120 (= 20×6) households in each town. However, since 1 ward in the town of Rampurhat consisted of mostly shops, market and quarters of railway staff, the households of this ward were largely characterized by a sort of 'floating population' of single males. Hence, excluding this ward, there remained 17 wards, out of which 5 instead of 6 wards (for operational reasons) were drawn by SRSWOR for the purpose of

the study. In this town, therefore, 24 households were drawn from each of the 5 sample wards in order that the sample size by households remains the same, i.e., 120 (= 24×5), like the other 2. Thus, the size of the urban sample became 360 (= 120×3) households altogether.

An updated list of all households in each sample ward of a town was prepared from the records stored in respective municipal office, which were scrutinized by spot visits. The listed households were stratified into four caste-community categories. Subsequent steps of sample design were similar to what was done in case of drawing the rural sample of households.

Survey Design

Besides the overall rationale of methodology of the selection of field and the design of sampling, there are few specificities of survey design which need to be explicated here.

Unlike the usual survey researches, where relevant household data are gathered from the *karta* (the male 'head' of the household), data for the present study were collected from a household by interviewing its *kartri*, i.e., the 'female head' of the household. This change was introduced in order to reduce the risk of non-sampling error due to gender bias of the male respondent affecting the quality of data. A male head (*karta*) might unconsciously contaminate or skip the intricacies of female attitudes and motivations. He may not be aware of the significance of the tasks performed by the females considering them to be 'too obvious to be noteworthy' or 'just day-to-day routine work required to be done anyway'. He may, therefore, fail to report them while answering the queries asked in the survey.

Another aspect of survey design was to select local female workers for the survey and train them as field investigators. They have interviewed the *kartris*. This step was required to be added to ensure the validity of the data for two reasons. It helps the dialogue between the investigator and the respondent to be frank and uninhibited. At the same time, rapport building with the respondent can be achieved quite easily by a local investigator. Without a good rapport, credibility of the study in the field suffers, having an adverse impact particularly on sensitive issues like those concerning intra-familial or marital tensions and conflicts.

The third feature of the survey design was the selection of a special sample of male respondents. After the questionnaire based survey of sample households in the village (or in a sample ward, in case of a town) was completed, two male heads of households in the village (or, the ward), other than those sampled for the survey of the *kartris*, were identified by discussions with the *kartris*. The intention was to find out 'typical' male heads whose response to gender based attitudinal and value oriented questions may be considered to represent the common male response. The purpose was to compare the pattern of female response to male response. Thus, altogether 130 male respondents were purposively selected; 96 (= $6 \times 8 \times 2$) among them were from the villages and the remaining 34 (= 17×2) were from urban areas.

On the whole, the logistics of the sampling design was the selection of small numbers of ultimate last stage units of study, i.e., households in the present case, by means of deep stratification of the universe for the purpose of an intensive exploratory study.

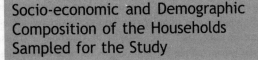

Socio-economic and Demographic Composition of the Households Sampled for the Study

- By mother tongue, the *kartris* were mostly Bengali speaking. Some spoke Santhali. Only a few have reported three other languages as their mother tongues—Hindi, Kora (a tribal language) and Urdu. Rural–urban dichotomy does not make any noteworthy change in the pattern. Distributions remain similar.

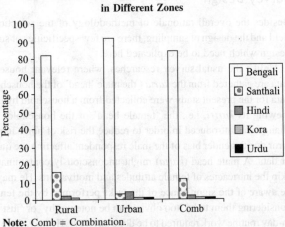

Kartris with Different Mother Tounges in Different Zones

Note: Comb = Combination.

- By caste and community categories, however, the *kartris* are more or less equally distributed among the scheduled caste (SC) Hindus, the general castes and communities (G) who are mostly the non-SC Hindus and the others. Again, the latter are almost equally divided between the two categories, the Muslims (Mu) and the scheduled tribe (ST). The pattern, however, differs in the urban areas from the rural areas. Incidence of SC and ST communities, particularly that of ST, are low in the towns. Major chunk of *kartris* belong to the general non-SC Hindu castes.

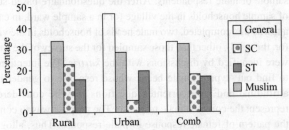

Kartris of Different Castes/Communities in Various Zones

Locally gathered information in the course of fieldwork indicates that this is not likely to be a matter of sampling fluctuation. Rather, this feature is intrinsic to the social contour of distribution of caste and community categories. The tribal and, to some extent, the SC communities have not yet settled down in the towns and they are yet to be integrated as parts of urban life and living. Their neighbourhoods, unlike those of

the other communities, often remain separate or outside the ambit of the towns. They interact and contribute to the urban economy, but remain somewhat isolated from the social life. In this regard, the next observation on the distribution of households of *kartris* by occupational class, along with its cross-classification by caste and community categories, becomes indicative.

- As mentioned earlier, instead of classifying the *kartris* by exact sources of livelihood of respective households, they are classified into three occupational classes formed out of the sources of livelihood. These are broadly identified as lower, middle and upper.

The lower occupational class consists of occupations such as labourers (whether agricultural or non-agricultural, *mahindars*, factory labourers, marginal or small farmers, owning less than 5 acre of agricultural land, sharecroppers, hawkers and ped-dlers, domestic workers, *mistris* and so on. The middle class consists of middle farmers owning 5–10 acre of agricultural land, retail shop owners, craftsmen and artisans, priests, clerical service holders, masons, electricians, mechanics and others. Last, the upper class consists of large farmers owning 10 acre or more of agricultural land, large scale or wholesale traders or businessman, and profes-sionals such as doctors, teachers, engineers, etc.

Although a considerable section of the *kartris* belong to the households whose principal source of livelihood is occupations of upper or middle class, the majority of their households depend upon lower class occupations. While this feature is sharply focussed and more explicit in the rural areas, it becomes reversed in the urban areas. There, unlike the rural areas, the majority of households depend upon principally the middle class occupations. Besides, those who are primarily engaged in upper class occu-pations are also considerable in number in the towns. Obviously, urban economic milieu has provided more possibilities of upwardly mobile sources of livelihood by creating diverse opportunities.

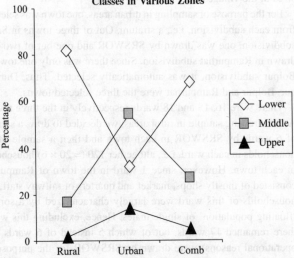

Kartris belonging to Different Occupational Classes in Various Zones

But, as one can see from the figure pertaining to *kartris* belonging to different occupational classes, the urban occupational opportunities have not sufficiently ameliorated the occupational class scenario of the *kartris* of SC and ST communities and make it considerably egalitarian as in case of general (G) or Muslim communities. The pattern of occupational class structure of the SC and ST *kartris* has remained similar in rural and urban areas. The gaps have not reduced much.

● Education and, for that matter, the extent of formal education and the level attained are considered pertinent measures of potential for advancement in the society. However, the majority among the *kartris* have not received any formal education in a school. A similar scenario is observed among the *kartris* in rural areas. In urban areas, however, it changes, though not upside down, sharply reducing the number of those who have not attended any school at all. The majority among the 'once school-goer' *kartris* in urban areas have attended Class VI or more.

Kartris belonging to Different Occupational Classes

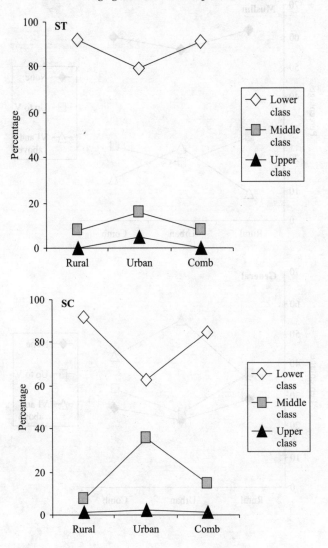

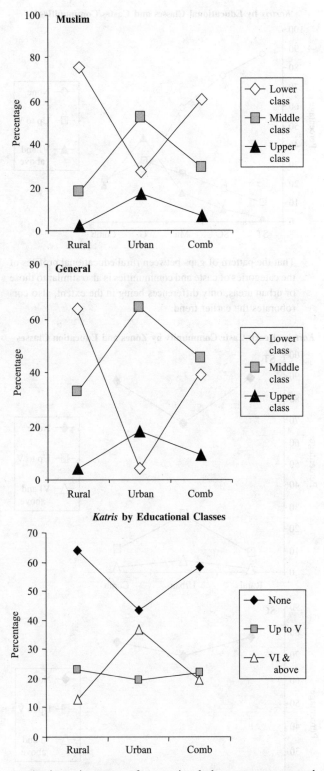

Katris by Educational Classes

Again, as in respect of occupational class structure, upward educational mobility has been comparatively achieved more by the *kartris* of Muslim and general castes or communities other than the SC and the ST. Since orthodox religious rituals are likely to be more prevalent among them, their positive response to education does not suggest any intrinsic orthodoxy inhibiting the spread of education.

***Kartris* by Educational Classes and Castes/Communities**

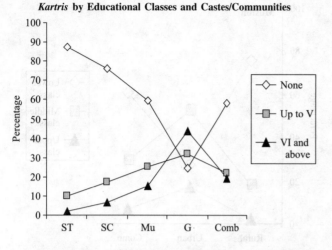

That the pattern of gaps between rural educational profiles of the categories of caste and communities is also similar to those of urban areas, only differences being in the extent, also corroborates the earlier trend.

Besides the level of formal school education of a *kartri*, period of how long her household has been exposed to that, or since when it has first been initiated in the household, is another comprehensive indicator of cultural milieu. Her propensity to receive school education has set in most of the families, whether in rural or urban areas, more than 10 years back in the present generation or earlier. Urban areas have advanced earlier, but rural areas have taken up recently under the impact of TLC.

- Age is, no doubt, quite a pertinent demographic characteristic for the study of variation of status structures. Its sociological connotation is that, being chronologically organized, it reflects temporal trends. However, the majority among the *kartris* belong to the age group 31–45 years. The next are distributed somewhat asymmetrically to the lower side of the scale. Since the pattern of age group-wise distribution is similar in both the rural and urban areas, it has not been taken up as an explanatory variable in addition to the rural–urban dichotomy. It is likely to have affected both sides of the dichotomy in the same way and, thus, has become confounded with it.

***Kartris* of each Caste/Community by Zones and Education Classes**

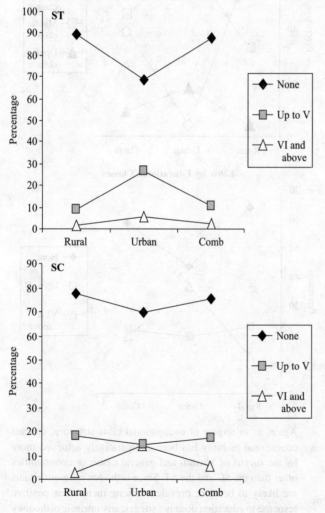

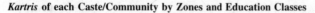

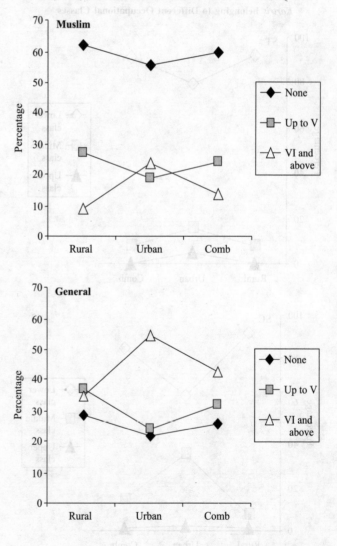

Beginning of School Education in *Kartris'* Households

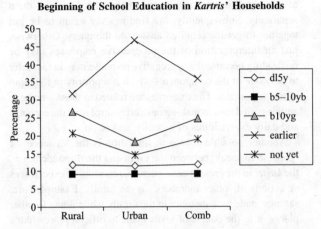

Notes: dl5y = during last 5 years, b5–10yb = between 5–10 years back, b10yg = before 10 years in this generation.

***Kartris* by Age**

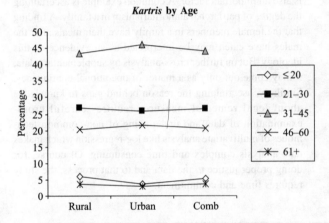

- For the same reason as in the case of age, family structure (of a *kartri*) identified by the kinship composition of her household remains excluded from the scheme of analysis. On the whole, the substantive part of the matter is that there are few instances (n = 27) where a *kartri*, whether unmarried or married, widowed,

***Kartris* by Family Type**

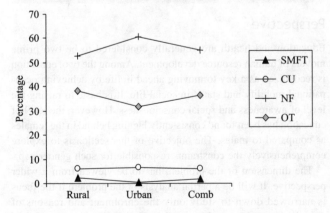

Notes: SMFT = Single member female (whether unmarried, married, divorced or separated); CU = Conjugal unit; NF = nuclear family; OT = others considered together.

divorced or separated, is not living with husband and/or unmarried children, i.e., broadly speaking, within the ambit of the family of procreation. This holds for both the rural and urban areas. Most of the few female single member households (about 85 per cent) occurred in rural areas among whom a large number are widowed living by themselves.

Parameters Selected for the Study

- In the course of discussions in the previous section, it comes out empirically from the data that rural–urban dichotomy and caste community affiliation would be the most pertinent global parameters for the study. These are not only *a priori* given in contextual conditions of stable societal action and interaction, but they also provide models of meaningful contrasts for the purpose of understanding variation in women's status.
- 'Rural' as such can be conceptualized as social entity which provides a field of agglomeration of impacts of various administrative and collective measures of planned development. These are implemented with an egalitarian ideological goal to redress various gaps and inequities of society, including those of gender. The 'urban' entity, on the other hand, connotes a ground of play of individualistic goals and competitive efforts as in a market. Thus, substantively it becomes a sub-system in contrast with the former. It is true that the rural entity may be further classified by access differential in respect of infrastructural facilities and opportunities. Yet, due to the overall scenario of developmental measures the system continues to maintain its district character.
- Caste and community affiliation refers to a different dimension. It triangulates a system of power in the society, status discrimination based on orthodox religious scriptures and customary usages enforcing deprivations. On the other hand, there are, no doubt, attributes which are socio-economically or demographically important. These are treated as local parameters, so to speak, for the study because they are individualistic characteristics and their variations are either confounded or they are invariant with respect to the global parameters selected for the study. Occupational class or level of education are examples of the former type. Age and family structure belong to the latter category. Obviously, there are many such characteristics. Such attributes have been considered as variables for analysis of variation.

Possibilities of Limitations of the Study

- There are possibilities of three types of limitations of the study. One of these arises from the sampling design. Research design is another source of limitation. The last one comes out of the mode of analysis of variables and interpretation of the results.
- One of the critical issues in sampling design is how to find out an appropriate balance among the number of units to be selected at different stages. In the present study, the blocks are the

first stage units. The second stage units consist of the villages within a selected block. Last, the third stage units are the households in a sampled village. The question is how to decide about the number of units to be selected at each stage. Usually, the textbook type guideline for making decisions in this regard focusses upon minimizing the sampling error of estimates and reducing the costs to be incurred per unit of investigation at different stages. An optimum balance is obtained among them against the given funds available for fieldwork.

This approach is appropriate for a study primarily aiming at a generalization for a universe, i.e., estimation of various characteristics for a given population. The objective of the present study differs from that. It is exploratory and aims at an analysis of patterns of variation of the characteristics. The number of units at different stages need to be decided accordingly. Hence, decomposition of variability of a characteristic by different stages is required to be done and the balance among the number of units to be selected at different stages needs to be decided with that information as the backdrop. But no specific information was available at the time of preparing the present sampling frame. As it has been stated earlier, the decisions regarding allocation of numbers of units to be selected at successive stages were made on the basis of some broad *a priori* general assumptions. However, using the findings from analysis of data collected for the present study, the relative weights of different stages can be ascertained later for the future studies. The remaining two sources of limitations are discussed next. As it can be seen, these are as such important by themselves and only tangential to what is usually meant as 'non-sampling errors'.

- An appropriate research design for the purpose of a study, as the present one has to encapsulate both quantitative and qualitative survey methods. Though this strategy was envisaged at the beginning of the study, it could not be pursued always for various unanticipated operational reasons. A few examples are as follows.

  It was planned to organize group discussions with females of different age groups including local experts or knowledgeable persons in various neighbourhoods in the villages as well as undertake case studies specially selected as being typical of those aspects about which in-depth information is required. But only a few of them were arranged since a comprehensive plan for effective implementation of these strategies could be made only after the queries were identified in the course of analysis of field data. As it is not merely a matter of collecting some additional supplementary data, but of exploring deeper meanings, proper planning is a key to its successful completion.

- Analysis and interpretation of the results may also add to the limitations of a study. There are different reasons responsible for this. Most difficult one is often confounded with the nature of query. Few examples are briefly discussed here.

  A query as such may appear intuitively to be quite 'simple', and its response in the field may also come quite 'immediately' or without any hesitation on the part of the respondent. But, on scrutiny, the query may be found to be a composite one which, for a valid analysis, needs to be desegregated into a set

of meaningful components and analysed by each of them separately. Subsequently, the findings are again to be put together to get the required answer to the query. Otherwise, just an interpretation of the progressive responses may be misleading because the aggregative response may in fact refer to only one of the components which is a priority in the mind of the respondent. The examples are related to those who have authority in decision making or exert control over the earnings and daily expenditures of a family, and so on.

Another possible source of limitation is the 'distance' or 'gap', so to speak, between the event and the respondent, i.e., the *kartri* in the present case, such as, reporting of experiences or actions of 'other members' in the family. Examples are: savings made by a member in the family while going to other places or in the course of visits made to official places like a health centre.

Last, the selection of variables for interpretation of findings is also an important factor. A common example is ascertaining the degree of patriarchal authoritarianism in a family. A finding that the female members in a family have their meals after the males have eaten may be interpreted as an evidence of this ideology. But on further cross-analysis by supplementary data, it may come out only as a matter of operational contingency. Similarly, ascertaining the reason behind gaps in knowledge about legal remedial measures requires careful cross-examination of data and undertaking of non-common techniques of multivariate analysis like log-regression which makes data analysis complex and time consuming. Of course, for doing proper justice to the data and to that process, the study requires time and commitment.

Intra–household Gender-wise Situation

Discontinuity of Education

Perspective

Education and health are generally considered to be two prime movers of human resource development. Among the two, education is recognized as a key to moving ahead in life by achieving occupational mobility and status in social life. It is basic to raising the level of awareness and social consciousness. However, the level of education has been found consistently lagging behind in the females as compared to males. The objective of this section is to explore comprehensively the constraints responsible for such gender gap.

The dimension of the problem has to be viewed from a wider perspective. It will be a partial analysis of the problem if the focus is narrowed down to study only the enrolment and reasons of dropping out, after enrolment, of the females in the age group of 6–11 years. Instead, for a generalized understanding of the problem of why females lag behind males, the upper age limit is required to be largely extended. To be comprehensive, a study should cover the domain of potential adult literates as well. It is to be extended to include the persons up to the middle age group of, say, 35 to 45 years of age. Naturally, this population should be considered as the effective sample (n_e) for the purpose of this part of the study.

The study should examine why breaks or discontinuities occur in the process of education in totality rather than at the point of dropping out only at the beginning of the process. The principal query is directed to explore gender specific constraints to impart education among the females. In addition, it tangentially aims to find out whether gender gaps are rooted culturally in the perception of desired levels of differential educational attainments for males and females as well as the expected future goals of role performance set for the female and the male children in the family when they grow up. It is worthwhile to mention in this context that there are serious thinkers still inclined to subscribe mainly to culturological explanation of persisting gender gap such as 'more conservative nature of Indian village society', 'cultural norms', 'cultural perception of women' and so on (see, for example, Mira Seth, *Women and Development: The Indian Experience*, Sage Publications, New Delhi, 2001). These are argued to be responsible for the prevalence of a sort of lackadaisical attitude to female education.

Why do Discontinuities Occur: Constraints in Real Life Situation

Investigation of why breaks or discontinuities of education occur, however, point out otherwise. The findings point out various specific structural reasons embedded in the social system. Instead of considering them as such, they have been divided into six different types in the following manner:

Economic:	(i)	Earning livelihood for the family or providing partial financial assistance (E);
	(ii)	Assisting family profession or trade (P);
Familial:	(iii)	Undertaking domestic responsibilities (D);
	(iv)	Lack of familial care and encouragement or support in the family for continuing education for various reasons, such as, lack of interest of other family members after parents' death, or, of in-laws after marriage of girls, and so on (F);
Health condition:	(v)	Suffering from chronic disease, or, ill health (I); and,
School related:	(vi)	Different factors concerning schooling, such as distance of schools, 'unattractive' and 'poor quality' of teaching, lack of clothes for girls to attend schools, there being no one to help while studying at home, etc. (S)

Of the six types of factors mentioned above, E and P reflect economic compulsions, D and F arise out of familial environment, I is personal health status and, S refers to quality of infrastructural situation concerning schools. Even though data analysed are gross and aggregative, indications of certain trends emerge unambiguously.

Socio-economic Categories and How the Constraints are Distributed

On the whole, the economic burden (E and P) of maintaining the family is the constraint causing breaks in the educational process of the majority (52.68 per cent) among the females. Intra-familial educational milieu (D and F together) comes next (35.45 per cent), each being responsible in the same proportion. Incidence of ill health or chronic illness is negligible (0.51 per cent). But factors associated with formal schooling can not be ignored (11.36 per cent). The data, thus, show that there is no single factor responsible for discontinuity of education. Rather, multiple types of constraints need to be taken into account for a comprehensive understanding of the problem. The high value of standardized entropy confirms that there is high uncertainty arising out of multiple reasons.

Gender and Constraints

Gender-wise disaggregation, however, brings out a sharp contrast. The single major constraint among a substantial majority of males remains the economic one, the incidence increasing to 66.42 per cent. It comes out, no doubt, also as a major reason among females, but its incidence decreases to 38.33 per cent, closely followed by the incidence of the burden of domestic duties (D). Increase in the pressure of domestic duties (D) upon females restrain a large number of them (28.63 per cent) from moving ahead in education. Comparatively, its incidence is quite low in case of the males (7.13 per cent).

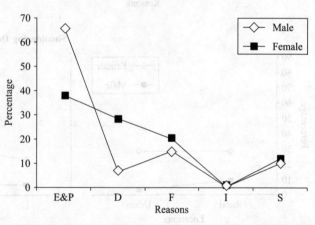

Distribution of Women (Rural + Urban)

Again, structurally whether rural or urban, or, by community-wise affiliation, such as SC, ST, Muslim (Mu), other Hindu castes and communities (G), or, being socio-economically stratified as lower (L), middle (M) and upper (U) occupational classes, the problem of earning livelihood remains the single major constraint.

A further gender-wise disaggregation of the structural categories mentioned earlier brings into focus that irrespective of location, caste and community affiliation, and occupational class stratification, the viability of female education has to overcome the pressure on the women to provide, fully or partially, economic support to the family in addition to shouldering the burden of domestic chores, while males share only the economic constraint in most cases. Furthermore,

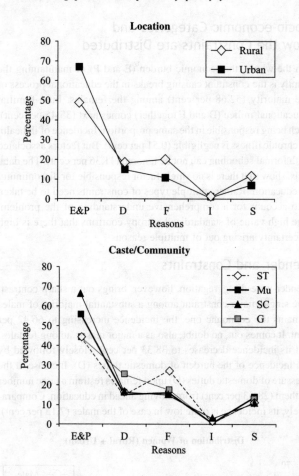

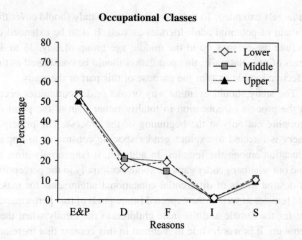

while females of different social and economic categories face economic pressure in a varying order, its intensity is relatively much low among females of particularly the general castes and communities, while that of domestic chores affects them much more than the rest. Its impact upon males is only marginal.

Since the sharing of domestic responsibilities can start at quite an early age, breaks in education of females appear perhaps earlier than among males. Cumulatively, this may contribute significantly to widen the gender gap in educational attainments. But this cannot be explained away as a matter of general cultural attitude to female education prevailing among all sections of the society. Because, if at all, at the most, domestic duties are found to be imposed at the cost of education upon females of the general castes and communities

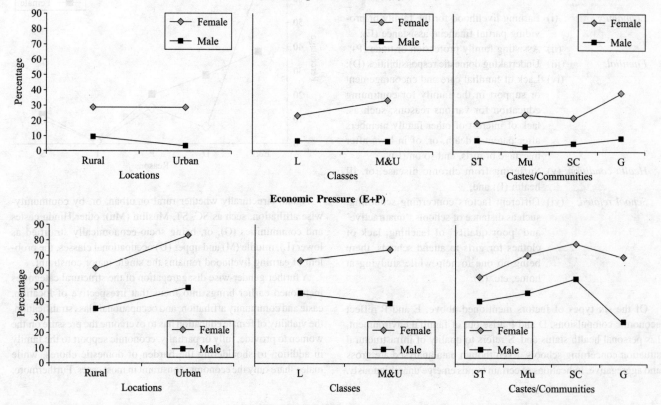

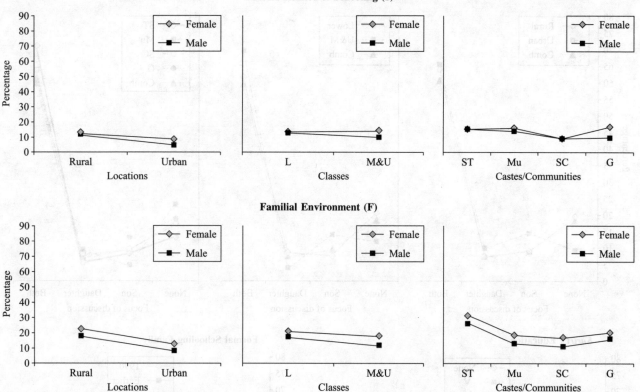

Factors Related to Schooling (S)

Familial Environment (F)

while they are too young. It may be argued to indicate a sort of myopic view of the latter about the role performance of their female children when they grow up. The pressure of domestic chores also affects, no doubt, the females of upper and middle class families more than those of the lower class. However, it is caste more than class which matters more in the given context.

Families of General Castes and Communities

Occupational class	% females discontinuing education for 'domestic' reasons
Upper and middle (n_e)	42.25 (284)
Lower (n_e)	41.54 (272)

Some Aspects of 'Gender Bias' and Socio-economic Categories

(i) In family decisions about children's future

What comes out of the analysis of some auxiliary data in this context suggests that it will not be valid to consider the earlier finding as a random phenomenon. Rather, it may be a part of various indications of gender-oriented slant regarding the choice of 'future' of female children when they grow up. It is manifested in discussions in a family concerning children's education and future career. Such discussions take place more in urban families of upper and middle occupational classes belonging to the general caste and communities other than the SC, ST and Muslim communities. Education and future career of both son and daughter receive, no doubt, attention

of the majority of the families irrespective of socio-economic categories. But the families of these categories particularly prioritize son's education and future career in their discussions in relatively high proportion. Daughter's education and future career receive emphasis in a small proportion of families in these categories.

Furthermore, the above pattern of gender bias is not suppressed in the families where *kartris* have received formal education. On the other hand, gender gap appears to widen a little with formal education of the *kartris*.

Contrarily, Total Literacy Campaign (TLC) has possibly produced a somewhat egalitarian impact in this regard since the nineties. Families, which have begun formal schooling during this period, are observed to have put emphasis on sons and daughters in equal proportions.

(ii) Expected levels of education for children

Yet, one cannot be claim that TLC has gone deep below the surface from behavioural to ideational depth because the *kartris* themselves expect that levels of formal institutional education imparted to a female and a male should be different. In other words, paradoxically, gender gaps have been internalized by even the *kartris* themselves in their subconscious minds. According to their expectation, the desired level of education that should be normally attained by a male is higher in most of the cases than that of a female. It is corroborated by the result of testing the value of T^+ obtained from Wilcoxon matched-pairs signed rank test computed from differences in expected levels of education to be imparted to a male and a female according to each *kartri* considered individually (S. Siegel:

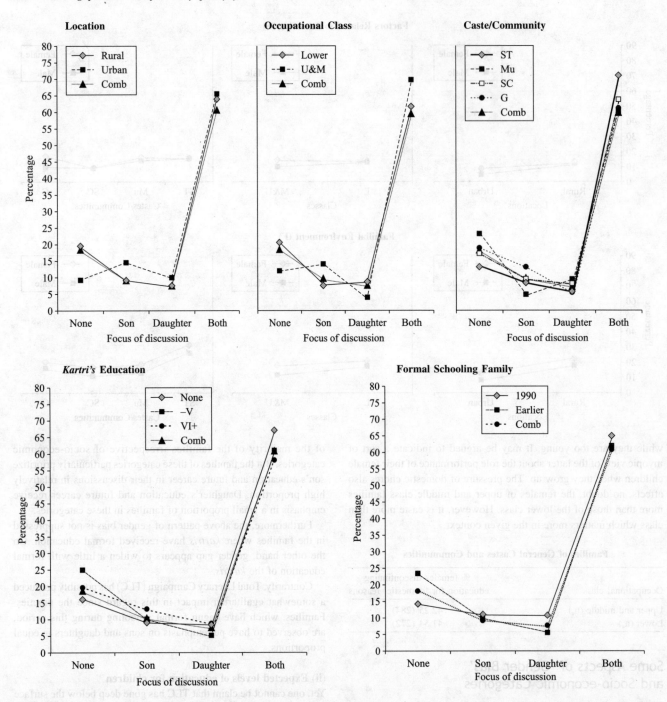

Location

Occupational Class

Caste/Community

***Kartri's* Education**

Formal Schooling Family

Non-Parametric Statistics for Behavioural Sciences, McGraw-Hill Book Co., New York, 1956, pp. 75–83). Note that obtained $[\{T^+ - E(T^+)\} / \sigma_{T}^+] = 18.4$.

Data on expected levels of education for female children, arranged in a tripartite summary format, veer around the higher secondary or equivalent level (HS), as the cut-off point brings out a simple pattern explicitly. The other two parts of the format are 'lower than HS level' and 'higher than HS level' which move from college level upwards. Incidentally, there are few strong reasons for selection of HS level as the cut-off point. It marks the 'transition zone' in one's role model and building career orientation for future. Furthermore,

until recently, secondary education was mostly an elitist, urban phenomenon (Usha Nayer, 'Cultural Roots of Oppression: Patterns of Women's Education in India', in Susheela Kaushik (ed.), *Women's Oppression Patterns and Perspectives*, Shakti Books, Delhi, 1985, pp. 50–51, 71). It is quite pertinent, therefore, to treat HS level as a critical dividing line in the field of education in general and that of female education in particular.

Again, primary level may be the feasible attainable limit for large sections of female population such as those in rural areas, or those who belong to a lower occupational class as well as in SC, ST and Muslim communities, or those who have become newly literates, or are yet without any formal school education. Large sections of female population in these categories may have been exposed to TLC, but have so far not been able to go for any level of formal education at all. Hence, the fact that the *kartris* in these categories in large numbers report primary level to be the desired maximum level of education to be attained by a female may possibly be an indicator of mass impact of TLC as well.

On the other hand, for considerable numbers of the *kartris* belonging to contrasting population categories such as urban, upper and middle occupational classes, general castes and communities or, with formal school education of Class VI or above, a female should have at least some college level formal education or even higher. On the whole, while the modal value of expectation of *kartris* of educational level for males is college or above, it is primary or HS for females.

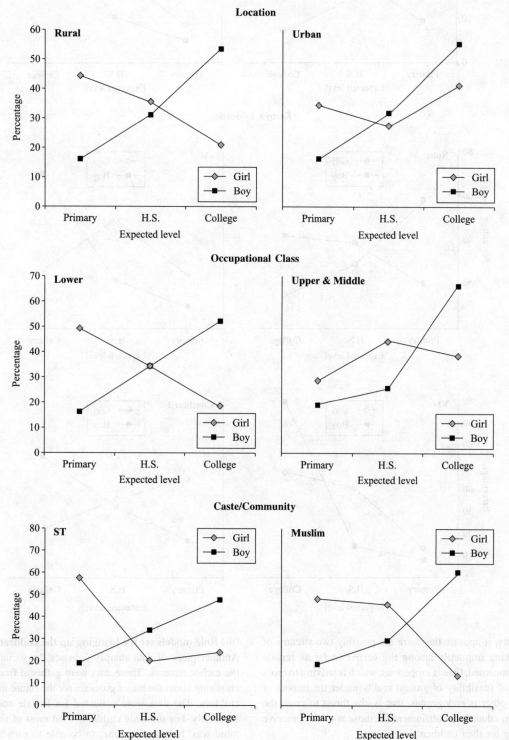

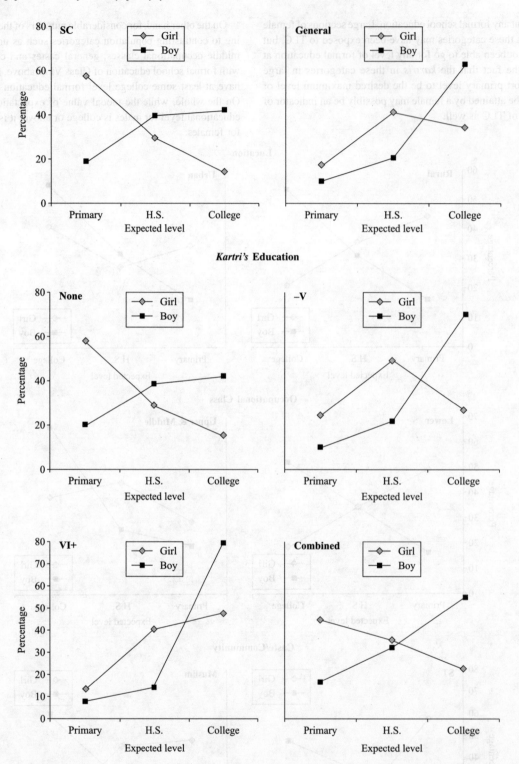

Kartri's **Education**

Consequently, it appears that there are possibly two streams of thoughts working implicitly among the *kartris* so far as female education is concerned. One is exogenous, which is striving to cross the threshold of feasibility of ground reality under the impact of TLC, and the other is endogenous, that is, the thrust to cross the dividing line in educational attainment for those who can perceive career building for their children.

(iii) Role models set for bringing up the children

Another piece of data sharply focusses the social significance of the earlier features. These data were gathered from the *kartris* by enquiring about the major goals set for the future in bringing up the children. The data were collected for female and male children separately. For the male children, what most of the *kartris* had in mind was, broadly speaking, to be able to earn a livelihood and

Formal Schooling Started in the Family

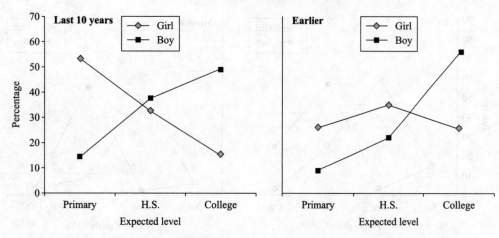

provide for the family. But, so far as the female children were concerned, two different types of responses were obtained. Some would like the female children to be able to earn a livelihood and thus provide for the family by themselves, if necessary, when they would grow up. On the other hand, some *kartris* would like the female children mainly to look after their family.

Location

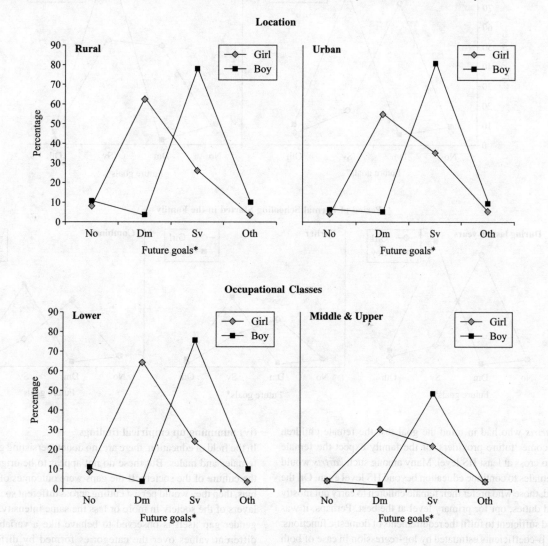

Occupational Classes

Notes: *No = No idea; Dm = Domestic work in the family; Sv = Becoming engaged in a service or profession; Oth = Others

Caste/Community

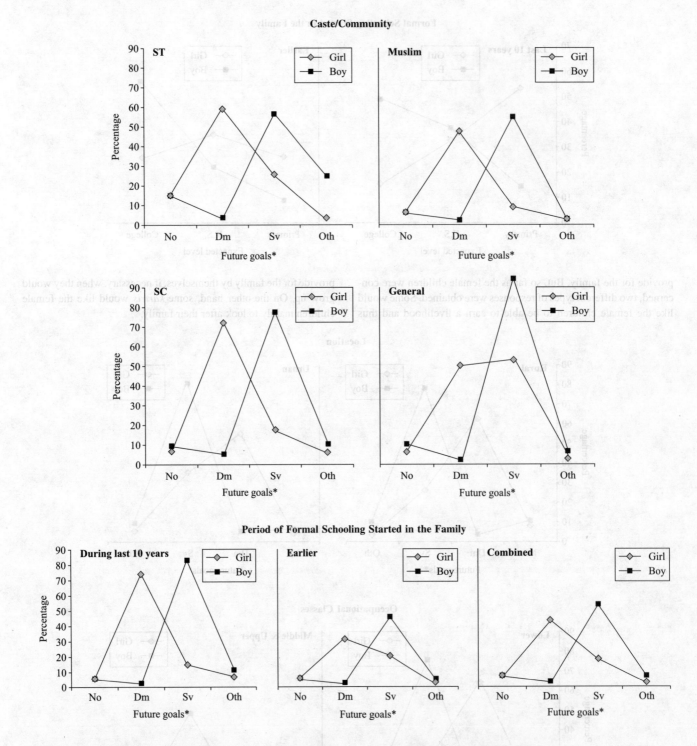

Period of Formal Schooling Started in the Family

The *kartris* who had in mind the goal that the female children would become 'future providers' of the family expect the female children to cross at least HS level. Many among such *kartris* would like the females to continue education beyond HS level even. On the other hand, those who prefer their female children to carry out mostly household duties, opt for primary level at the best. Perhaps, it was considered sufficient to fulfil the requirements of domestic functions. Values of β-coefficients estimated by log-regression in case of both the former and latter relationships are statistically significant.

(iv) Summing up empirical findings

In the field of education, there are, no doubt, persisting gaps between females and males. But these do not appear to be originating from the culture of the society. If the gaps were outcomes of that kind of bias, then they would persist cutting across different socio-economic layers of the society in more or less the same intensity. Instead, the gender gap itself is observed to behave like a variable assuming different values over the categories formed by different socio-economic attributes, which are rooted in the multi-factorial structure

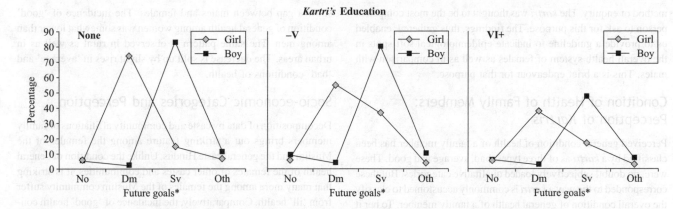

Notes: * No = No idea; Dm = Domestic work in the family; Sv = Becoming engaged in a service or profession; Oth = Others.

of the social situation. The pattern of variations in gender gaps is not exactly lineal. But the results of analysis bring out that dichotomies formed out of three attributes of a family can substantially capture its broad outline. These are: background attributes of the educational level of the *kartri* of a family and its caste and community affiliation in combination with its occupational class position. The variation in gaps corresponds to an ordered arrangement of the categories formed by them.

Kartri's education	Caste/Community	Occupational classes	Code
Class VI or higher (VI+)	General (G)	upper or middle (UM)	1
		lower (L)	2
	SC, ST, Muslim	UM	3
	(O)	L	4
Class V or lower upto literate (–V)	G	UM	5
		L	6
	O	UM	7
		L	8
Non-literate (NL)	G	UM	9
		L	10
	O	UM	11
		L	12

Finally, what has been observed earlier is not a matter of mere surface level association among some population attributes. Its complexity can be gauged by the fact that the *kartris* themselves have internalized the rationale which sustains the process. Hence, the meaning attributed by the actors is also worth pondering, that is, whether the *kartris* consider it as a 'gender gap' or a matter of pragmatic division of functions within a family as the unit of social action.

Health

Preliminaries

Unlike education, assessment of health status, in the true sense of the term, requires a health survey which may be undertaken by professionally trained medical practitioners. Besides, such an

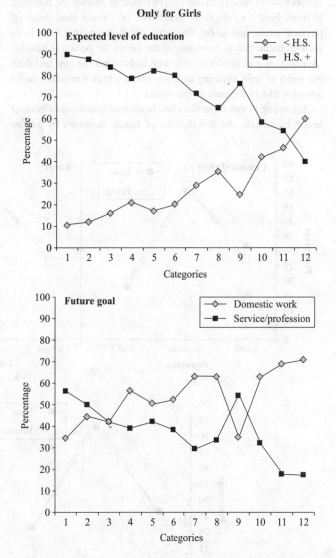

investigation necessitates a study design of its own, while that of the present one is geared to enquire about women's status in its totality. For the purpose of a survey like the present one, perception of condition of one's health was considered to be the appropriate method of enquiry. The *kartri* was thought to be the most competent person to ask for this purpose. The findings, thus gathered, enabled us to provide a guideline to indicate epidemiological soft spots in the overall health system of females as well as in comparison with males. This is a brief endeavour for that purpose.

Condition of Health of Family Members: Perception of *Kartris*

Perceived general condition of health of a family member has been classified by a *kartri* as of three types: bad, average and good. These were, no doubt, subjectively loaded qualitative categories. But these corresponded to the way a *kartri* is commonly accustomed to classify the overall condition of general health of a family member. To her it is 'bad' (i.e., ill health) if, in case, a member lacks 'immunity' and suffers time-to-time from one kind of illness or another, or, is unable to work hard for 'physical weakness', or, cannot bear much of physical strain, and so on. The term 'good' means that there is no such problem; that is, according to the *kartri*, the person is healthy. 'Average' is a kind of tolerable state in-between the two and does not mean at least anything to worry about which demands careful attention like in the case of the former.

According to this three tier classification of condition of general health by *kartris*, the distributions of family members by gender show a gap between males and females. The incidence of 'good' condition of general health among women was somewhat lower than among men. The same pattern is observed in rural as well as in urban areas. The decrease is split up by slight rises in 'average' and 'bad' conditions of health.

Socio-economic Categories and Perception

Decomposition of data by caste and community affiliations of family members brings out a striking feature among the females of the Muslim and the general caste Hindus. Unlike the condition of general health of the females of other castes and communities, it is striking that many more among the females of the Muslim community suffer from 'ill' health. Comparatively, the incidence of 'good' health condition is more and that of 'bad' is less among Muslim males. In fact, the incidence of 'bad' condition of health among Muslim females is highest among all categories of females. On the other hand, both males and females of Hindu general castes enjoy highest incidences of 'good' health condition among all categories. But the gap between the genders with respect to 'good' health condition is noteworthy, that of females being less than of males. However, the condition of health of general caste Hindu females is more of 'average' type, while 'bad' condition is the lowest among all categories.

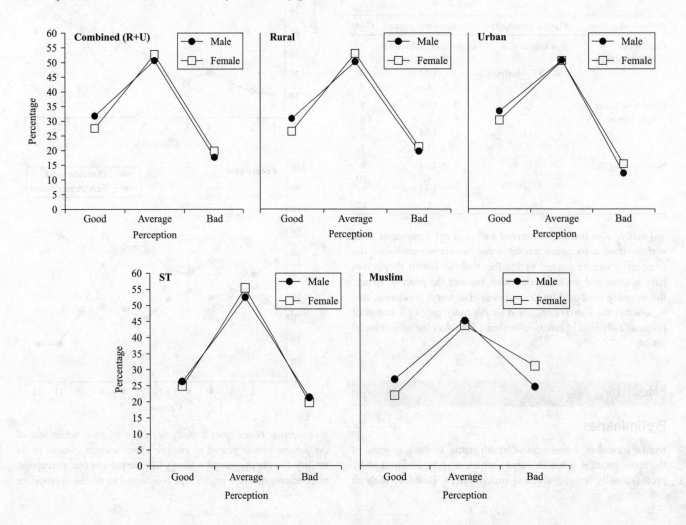

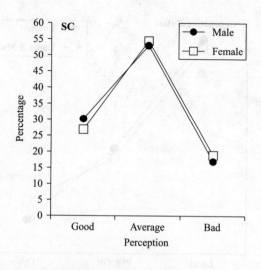

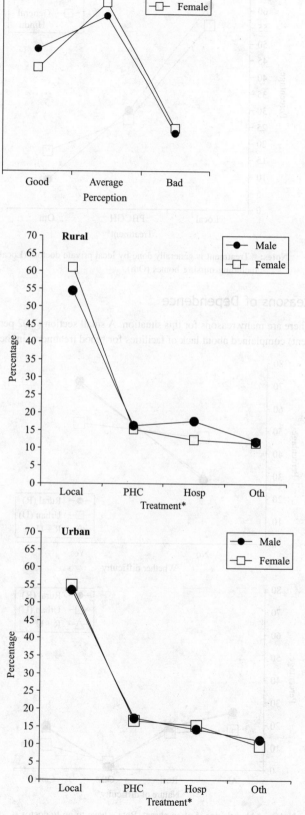

Dependence upon Private Doctors

For treatment of male or female members, more in case of the latter, local private doctors were consulted in majority of the cases. Primary health centre (PHC) or government hospital was contacted by a smaller proportion of *kartris* for treatment.

This pattern is observed in rural as well as in urban areas among both the genders.

The majority of females, particularly those belonging to SC, ST and Muslim communities, normally go to local private doctors for treatment. In the case of females of lower occupational class, it occurs a little more than among the upper and middle class females. Treatment at nursing homes, etc., is noteworthy among upper and middle class as well as among Hindu general caste females.

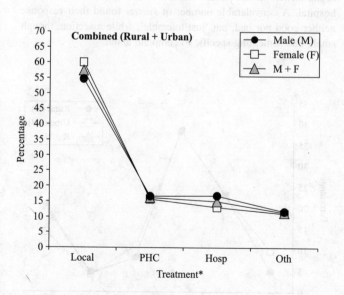

Notes: * Treatment is generally done by local private doctors (Local), primary health centre (PHC), government hospital (Hosp), Others (Oth).

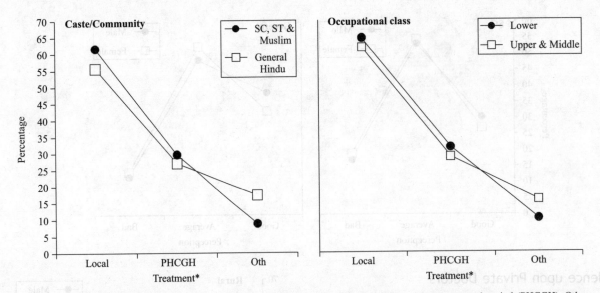

Notes: * Treatment is generally done by local private doctors (Local), primary health centre and government hospital (PHCGH), Others including nursing homes (Oth).

Reasons of Dependence

There are many reasons for this situation. A small section (7.02 per cent) complained about lack of facilities for 'good treatment' in the

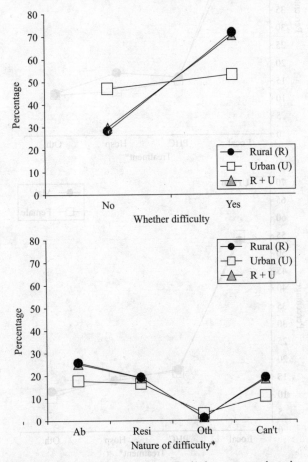

PHC or government hospital or in nearby areas whether for females (6.85 per cent) or males (7.19 per cent). Due to this factor, 'proper medical treatment' could not be taken up.

The major reason for the reluctance of the *kartris* to go to a PHC or a government hospital is the difficulty in getting a doctor. Either they have to wait for a long time to meet the doctor since the doctor is not present in his chamber or go to his residence. Either way, this often becomes inconvenient for a female. Even in urban areas, though somewhat less than in rural areas, these problems vex the majority of the *kartris*.

Moreover, one other factor which contributed to the reluctance of the *kartris* was the pattern of interaction with the staff at PHC or hospital. A considerable number of *kartris* found their response neither good nor bad, but 'just tolerable', while a section, though small, had something specific to complain about.

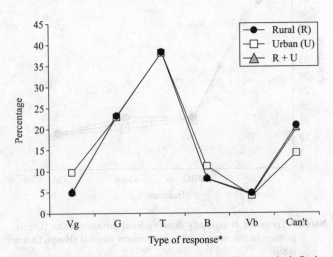

Notes: *Ab = doctor is often absent, Resi = have to go to doctor's residence; Oth = Others; Can't = Cannot specify.

Notes: *Vg = very good; G = good; T = tolerable; Vb = very bad; Can't = cannot specify.

In this regard, however, a *Bhadralok* (gentleman) oriented, i.e., somewhat elitist, bias may be implicitly acting behind the pattern of response of the staff to patients or their relatives and friends. Less educated *kartris* or *kartris* of lower occupational class or those who belonged to SC, ST and Muslim communities recalled unfavourable experiences at PHCs or hospitals relatively more often than the others. A simple three part classification of interaction with the staff makes this explicit.

Implications

Indications are not, therefore, that lack of proper attitude and motivation or awareness and knowledge make females depend upon local private medical practitioners. It is the inefficiency of the medical service system provided by the official structure that has to bear the responsibility of the failure. Therefore, only a thorough health survey

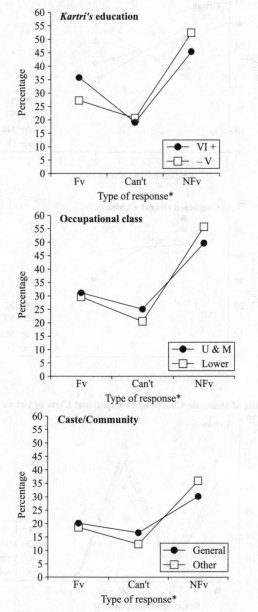

Notes: *Fv = favourable (very good + good); Can't = cannot specify; NFv = not favourable (others).

can find out whether and why the health condition of females has become more vulnerable. An overwhelming majority of the *kartris* (67.72 per cent) reported that even though there were instances when a treatment or at least some consultation with a medical practitioner was necessary, that could not be done for financial reasons (due to 'lack of money' to meet the costs of private treatment). This happened to occur in the case of both female (66.44 per cent) and male (69.06 per cent) family members. However, it affects much more the access to treatment of females belonging to SC, ST and Muslim communities and also of lower occupational class, that is, the lower socio-economic rung of the society. It was observed that no medical treatment was undertaken in case of 71.05 per cent females of the former category and 70.48 per cent females of the latter due to lack of funds. Among the general caste Hindu females and upper and middle class females, the proportions of lack of medical treatment for the same reasons were 50.00 per cent and 56.10 per cent respectively. The reasons for lack of treatment of females among the socio-economic categories were of somewhat different type such as, 'lack of time for females to go for medical treatment', 'females either ignoring or not taking note of seriousness of the need for their own treatment', 'family's inconveniences', and so on. Altogether, this situation may indicate, on the one hand, a kind of gender bias. Again, on the other hand, it may possibly be also a matter of how a person perceives his/her own illness, that is, a matter of cultural definition of health.

At present, one can only conjecture about the future consequences of this.

Performance of Household Chores

So far the findings regarding women's educational and health status have been discussed. We now shift the focus of discussion to various dimensions of their role performance in shouldering the responsibilities of routine intra-household domestic chores undertaken in order to run the daily life of the household. A set of intra-household domestic chores were listed and from each *kartri* (who was, incidentally, the respondent), it was ascertained for which set she took the sole responsibility and for which set she provided assistance to others or participated casually or did not participate at all. The following 12 domestic chores were selected for the purpose of the present enquiry:

1. preparing bed and cleaning the house;
2. cleaning utensils and washing dishes;
3. cooking food for lunch and dinner;
4. gathering fuel and collecting potable water for drinking and cooking;
5. washing clothes;
6. looking after the aged and the children;
7. helping children in their studies;
8. looking after domestic animals, specially in the case of rearing goats, poultry and cattle;
9. helping cultivation of family farm;
10. providing help to non-agricultural pursuits of the family;
11. doing daily marketing, going to collect ration, etc.; and
12. manufacturing rice and rice products such as Muri, Chira for home consumption and/or sale.

The domestic chores will be analysed aggregatively instead of being considered in terms of individual details of each attribute because only by looking at the totality of performance of these chores as a single parameter, one can capture an inner view of how a household continues to function as a micro-system of social organization as well as the role of the female head and, for that matter, of women in that system. Incidentally, although the total number of domestic chores remains *a priori* fixed as 12, their relative values in percentage scales instead of their exact counts have been used as simple measures suitable to highlight the findings of the analysis.

Our concern in this regard is the following: How much prevalent is gender-sharing in the performance of the above intra-familial responsibilities? If not, how is the structure of distribution organized among the females? Our finding is that neither gender-sharing nor sharing within the gender is the dominant norm. Rather, it is mostly the 'duty' of the female head (*kartri*) to shoulder them single-landedly.

On the whole, the female head is found to be responsible for regular performance of most of the domestic chores (in 63.75 per cent cases). In about half of the chores (49.75 pe cent), she has to perform solely by herself (W_1), and the remaining ones (14.00 per cent) with the assistance of female members in the household (W_2). Rarely the male members provide any regular help in these matters except in the case of 'going to shops or markets' or for matters related to family crafts or trade and business or occasionally 'helping children in their studies'.

The incidence of gender-sharing of domestic chores (W_2) as such remains more or less low whether in rural or urban areas. But a significant feature in urban areas is the increased involvement of females other than the *kartri* in reducing her domestic burden (W_0).

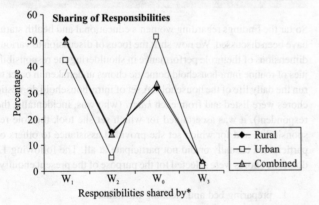

Sharing of Responsibilities

Notes: * W_1 = *Kartri* herself; W_2 = *Kartri* and other females; W_0 = other females excluding *Kartri*; W_3 = Rest.

A community-wise comparison, however, brings out a sort of contrast among SC, ST and Muslim families on the one hand, and the general caste Hindu families on the other. The *kartris* in the families of the latter category undertake relatively less responsibilities by themselves, whether in rural or urban areas (W_1). 'Other females' undertake as substitute actors (W_0).

The urban pattern of intra-familial distribution of performance of domestic chores may, no doubt, be explained by occupational class character of the families because the pattern comes out in the figure 'Sharing of Domestic Chores by Occupational Class in Urban Areas'.

Sharing of Domestic Chores by Caste/Community Categories

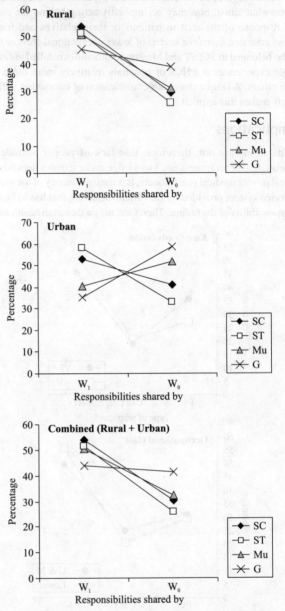

Sharing of Domestic Chores by Occupational Class in Urban Areas

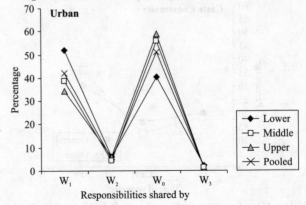

Sharing of Domestic Chores by Occupational Class in Rural Areas

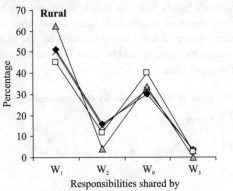

Combined (Rural+Urban)

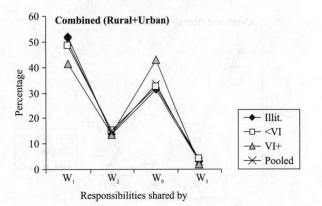

In the rural areas, on the contrary, categorization by occupational classes indicates only a unique feature of the middle class *kartris* with respect to W_1 and W_0, instead of bringing out any systematic trend by class as such.

Hence, occupational class does not provide any consistent explanation of ecological variation. Rather, educational level of the *kartri* comes out as an effective indicator of how the performance of domestic chores is organized within the family irrespective of its location in rural or urban area. Hence, instead of a social stratification-based structural approach to explain the distribution of pressure of intra-familial domestic chores, one may need a sort of alternative hypo-

thesis as more appropriate for a consistent explanation of variation such as cultural attribute like educational level of *kartri*.

Moreover, inadequacy of structural explanation is further corroborated by another finding. The socio-economic status of the *kartri* being gainfully employed to earn livelihood for the family, i.e., being a 'working *kartri*' does not ameliorate the condition of being overwhelmed with additional responsibilities by undertaking a substantial share of regular domestic duties. A 'working *kartri*', whether in rural or urban area, has to bear the double pressure of both earning for the family as well as for sharing domestic responsibilities.

Sharing of Domestic Chores by *Kartri's* Level of Education

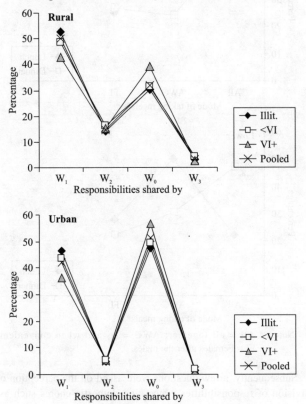

Sharing of Domestic Chores by *Kartri's* Working Status

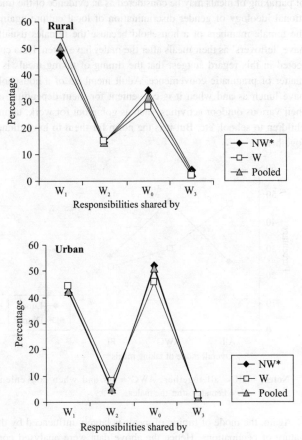

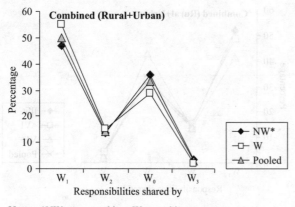

Notes: *NW = not working; W = working.

So far empirically observed behavioural pattern of performance of intra-familial domestic responsibilities have been analysed. In this context, it is pertinent to probe whether they reflect traditional ideological orientation persisting deep beneath the surface of behaviour in the way of functioning of the families, or, whether the observed patterns of behaviour have been shaped, on the whole, by the pragmatic contingencies of micro socio-economic milieu within the household.

That the latter hypothesis can be a strong contender as an alternative is amply clear from the following illustration. Prevalent mode of partaking of meals may be considered as an evidence of the traditional ideology of gender discrimination of local culture against the female members of a household because the females usually have 'leftovers' as their meals after the males have eaten. Data collected in this regard suggest that the timing of taking meals is a matter of pragmatic convenience. Adult members of a household have lunch as and when it is convenient for them depending on their various outdoor activities, such as going out for work, taking children to school, etc. But it is the norm for them to have dinner together.

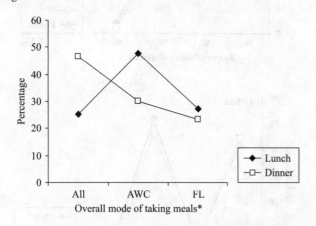

Notes: * All = all together; AWC = As and when convenient; FL = Females after the males.

Again, the mode of timing of meals is largely influenced by the nature of occupations. Hence the above data were analysed controlling for occupational class. The members of households belonging to lower occupational class have to often pursue odd irregular jobs to supplement their earnings from the main occupation in order to maintain their family. Male and female members of the households in this class, therefore, largely have lunch as and when convenient. This pattern changes sharply during dinner time. The change is less pronounced in the case of middle class households and the least among the upper class.

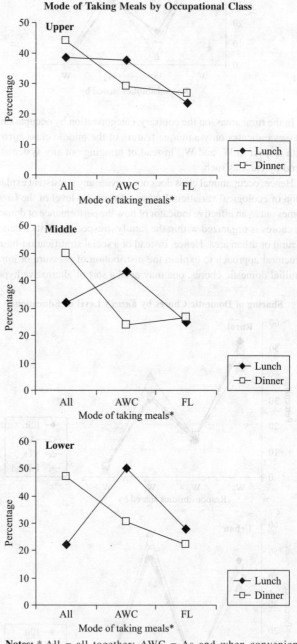

Notes: * All = all together; AWC = As and when convenient; FL= Females after the males.

Subsequently, a few questions were asked on the perception of division of responsibilities concerning domestic chores such as: whose duty should it normally be to prepare meals in a family and serve it as well as wash the dishes and cooking utensils? Whose duty should it be to wash clothes and clean the house? It was also asked as to who should look after the studies of children in a family. But the latter is a conditional question since its response depends upon the presence of children in a family, and is excluded from the present analysis. Data, thus gathered, were not merely a kind of 'instant opinion' expressed by the *kartris*. Rather, these indicated normative values embedded in their minds. The responses explained, in the Weberian sense, the meaning imputed to—value orientation—own action by actors themselves. For the remaining four domestic chores, i.e., preparing meals, dish-washing, washing clothes and clearing the house, most of the *kartris* almost unequivocally responded asserting that normally females should perform those domestic chores. Relevant data are given in the table.

Domestic chores	Domain of only the females according to the perception of the *kartri* (in %)
Cooking and serving meals	88.61
Dish washing	92.90
Home cleaning	81.60
Cloth washing	75.78

The pattern remains similar for different categories of caste/communities, occupational class and educational level of *kartris*. Broadly speaking, therefore, the findings do not show any noteworthy contradiction between empirical behaviour and value perception.

As the data show, traditional orientation prevails over the overall scenario of perception of *kartris*. However, log-regression test brings out a subtle statistically significant trend which suggests that a process of deviation from mainstream thinking is possibly brewing among women as well. The test shows that a 'working *kartri*' is more likely to expect males to share to some extent the burden of domestic chores compared to a 'non-working *kartri*' even though a comparison of their relative frequencies cannot ascertain this feature unambiguously. Relevant data are given in the table.

Domestic chore	$\hat{\beta}$ (on *Kartri* working –1/ not – 0) ± s.e.	$\hat{\beta}$ /s.e.	Per cent *kartris* expecting male members in a household to share a domestic chore	
			Working	Not working
Preparation of meals (cooking)	0.48 ± 0.218	2.20	13.77	10.05
Washing dishes/ cooking utensils	–0.15 ± 0.255	–0.59	06.54	07.44
Cleaning the house	0.60 ± 0.172	3.49	23.25	17.67
Washing clothes	0.38 ± 0.163	2.33	37.71	22.19

To conclude, one may compare these findings with those of a macro-level cross-country survey on gender inequality sponsored by the International Sociological Association (ISA) covering four countries that have different political systems, namely, Canada, Italy, Poland and Romania (Mino Vianello, and Renata Siemienska, *Gender Inequality: A Comparative Study of Discrimination and Participation, Sage Studies in International Sociology*, London, 1990). This study considers three orientations to the gender issue: traditional, egalitarian and radical (p. 21). It is hypothesized whether orientation and attitudes towards performance of domestic chores

are shaped by systemic ideology or by a combination of socio-economic and cultural factors (p. 30). The findings of the survey show that all the above domestic chores fall under women's domain in all those countries (p. 86). The only difference with the present study is that whether women work or not does not influence whether they shoulder the responsibilities of performing domestic chores or not in those four countries. The authors of the international study ask whether women are more traditional, as they are more conservative than men (p. 92). In that sense, are the working women in Birbhum more egalitarian than the aforesaid ones?

Shouldering Economic Responsibilities

The discussion in this chapter has been arranged to focus on the issue from two different angles with two different queries: (*i*) to describe role performance of the *kartris* in the sphere of income generation for their respective families, whether directly or tangentially; and (*ii*) to what extent the role performance enables a *kartri* to attain a position of authority and power vis-à-vis the *karta* of the economic chores of family life.

Economic Role Performance: Brief Description

Domestic chores, performed by the *kartris*, which have been discussed in the last chapter, carry no economic connotation. But that does not mean that they do not work to make any contribution to provide for the family. In fact, quite a considerable number among them (35.74 per cent) are earning, being engaged in some gainful occupation whether fully or partly. A notable number among them (8.53 per cent) even occupy the rank of principal earner in the family, though among all the *kartris*, whether working or not, only a smaller proportion (3.06 per cent) has attained the position as the *kartri* (female head) of the family by virtue of being its principal earner. Thus, in the domain of income generation also, *kartris* directly contribute in a large number of families in addition to their routine performance of household 'duties'.

Furthermore, there are three other dimensions of household activities through which the *kartris* add to its economic stability. Usually these remain unaccounted at the time of ascertaining a *kartris* contribution to provide support for a family's livelihood. One of these areas is growing various vegetables in the homestead labelled as 'kitchen garden'. The products of a kitchen garden are used as substitute of vegetables purchased from the market and that way it helps to save income for other purposes. A moderate proportion of the *kartris* are engaged in maintaining kitchen gardens (13.08 per cent). Besides, they sell a part of the products in the market as well. Obviously, the income earned thereby forms another channel contributing to the earnings of a family.

The rearing of domestic animals, such as keeping goats or poultry or ducks, taking care of milk cows, and so on, constitutes another domain of almost exclusively the female members of a family. The incidence of such activities among the *kartris* is quite noteworthy (22.38 per cent).

Besides this, the *kartri* tacitly plays an important role in order to supplement a family's requirements for livelihood at the time of an emergency. Thus a *kartri* undertakes to meet an urgent need by borrowing in kind or cash when a family is running short of food or, say, for treatment of a sick family member, for a social or religious event in the family and so on. Nowadays children's education has also become a significant issue in this regard. This is a sort of exchange relationship in the form of 'help in need' which flows in the village or a town along various types of relationship among the families different from what a moneylender or pawnbroker formally lends.

An overwhelming majority of the *kartris* (74.69 per cent) have reported the prevalence of informal borrowing, whether in kind or cash or both, by their respective families from others in the village or town. In this regard, the managerial role a *kartri* plays with respect to the 'little economy', so to speak, of her family comes out as more significant than that of the *karta* (i.e., the male head of a family). While the 'cash' mobilized by *kartris* through informally borrowing from others on different occasions to provide support for their respective families is only somewhat less than that of the male head (*karta*), their informal borrowing in kind occurs at quite a higher rate than that of the *karta*.

Informal Borrowing

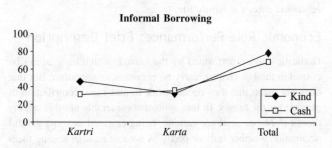

Before analysing data in order to answer the second query, let us explore if there is any pattern of variation in the economic participation of the *kartris*.

Ecologically, the pattern is interesting. The *kartris* in urban areas are engaged in gainful employment much less (13.14 per cent) than those in the rural areas (37.71 per cent). But among the former, quite a large number of them (45.81 per cent) occupy the position of principal earner in the family, which is much less in rural areas (7.48 per cent). Instead, if all the *kartris* of urban areas are considered, the percentage of a *kartri* being the principal earner of the family falls steeply (6.02 per cent), but still remains somewhat greater than the corresponding percentage in rural area (2.82 per cent). The reason behind these two opposite trends indicate that a *kartri* in an urban area has taken up a job to maintain her family mainly by her own earnings. In the rural areas, a *kartri* has possibly either taken up any type of occupation readily available outside the family to supplement the earnings of her family or has become engaged in the network of division of labour of 'family occupation', so to speak.

So far as earning from 'kitchen garden' and rearing of domestic animals by the *kartris* is concerned, there is no significant difference in their incidence between rural and urban areas.

In the case of informal borrowing, the rural—urban dichotomy brings out more sharply the association between gender and type of borrowing. The pattern of informal borrowing in kind does not change much in rural areas (i.e., the *kartris* borrow much more in kind than the male head). In urban areas, they also borrow in kind

more, but the incidence as well as the difference are quite low, whereas the male heads (*kartas*) informally borrow cash much more than the *kartris* in urban areas.

Kartri's Supplementary Earning

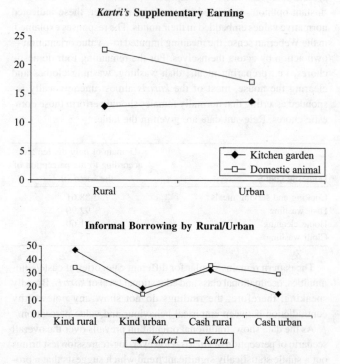

Thus, ecological situation as a macro-contextual variable does not introduce anything new in the overall pattern of variation in economic participation of the *kartris*. On the other hand, it can be studied whether micro-level egocentric attributes depicting the demographic and socio-economic position of a *kartri* exerts any influence instead of introducing any new element in variation. Age, caste and community affiliation, level of formal education and occupational class of a *kartri* have been considered as relevant variables in that respect.

Age of a *kartri*, a demographic variable, is related to physical strength of a person. Again, ageing is a decaying process. Hence, obviously, rate of work participation to earn is expected to be negatively correlated with the age of the *kartri*. This is what is observed and remains so both in rural as well as urban areas. The only point that may be noted is that the rate of participation of a *kartri* in gainful economic activities reaches its peak in the age group of 30–45 years. Incidentally, 4.51 per cent of the *kartris* whose age could not be ascertained reliably were not included for the purpose of the present analysis (4.65 per cent in rural and 3.66 per cent in urban areas). This phenomenon of a plateau-like relationship, however, becomes manifest as a function of a natural biological process.

Work participation of the *kartris*, on the other hand, bears a definite socio-economic connotation. Its incidence is quite high among the SC, ST and Muslim families, and among those whose level of formal education is low and who belong to lower occupational class. There is an interaction with the rural–urban dichotomy without, however, altering the overall pattern.

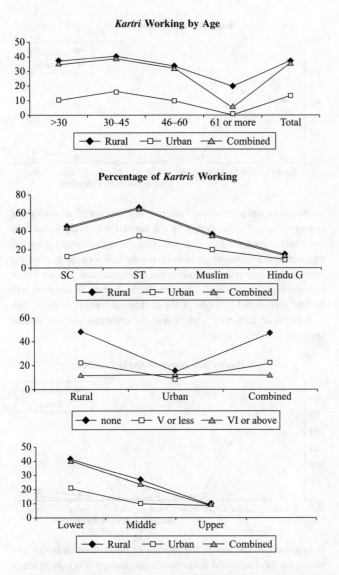

Kartri Working by Age

Rural — Urban — Combined

Percentage of *Kartris* Working

Rural — Urban — Combined

none — V or less — VI or above

Rural — Urban — Combined

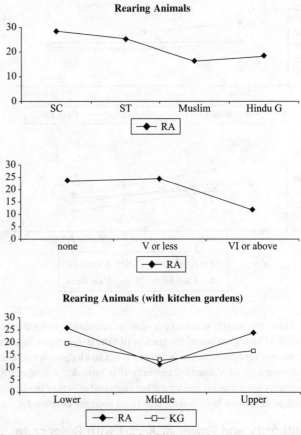

Rearing Animals

RA

RA

Rearing Animals (with kitchen gardens)

RA — KG

Notes: RA = Rearing animals; KG = Kitchen garden.

Informal borrowing in case of an emergency, whether in kind or cash, occurs, no doubt, relatively more among the families in the lower rung of the society. In general, however, when it is a matter of shouldering the responsibility, the *kartris* undertake the burden more than the male heads (i.e., the *kartas*) in case of borrowing in kind such as items of food, materials for repairing the house, and so on. This is particularly visible in the families in the lower socio-economic strata, but when it is a matter of informal borrowing, whether in cash or kind, the *kartri* plays a less prominent role compared to the *karta* in the urban families of the upper strata considered by caste and community affiliation or with respect to formal education or occupation. In the matter of informal borrowing of cash, however, the *karta* plays a consistently more important role in urban areas.

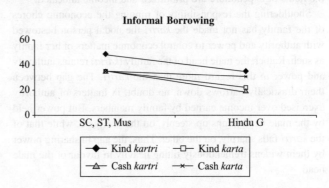

Informal Borrowing

Kind *kartri* — Kind *karta* — Cash *kartri* — Cash *karta*

Of the two supplementary sources of livelihood, incidence of kitchen garden is more or less the same across all the caste and community categories and also over different levels of formal education. It is rather a function of possession of homestead land ($\hat{\beta} \pm$ s.e. $= 0.33 \pm 0.18$).

Incidence of rearing animals as a supplementary source of livelihood is relatively higher among SC, ST and Muslim *kartris*, belonging to the lower occupational class category, where the level of formal education is somewhat low. Again, monetary affluence provides a better access to resources to invest in the industry. Hence, the trend of rearing animals becomes U-shaped, rising considerably among the upper class *kartris* similar to the case of 'kitchen gardens'. A large chunk of lower and upper class families are related to agricultural activities while these of the middle class to non-agricultural. Hence, the shape of the curve becomes an interesting pointer to possibly the middle class 'choosiness' by 'prestige of jobs'. Since the patterns in rural and urban areas are similar, only the combined overall trend as per each attribute is presented in the figure.

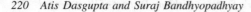

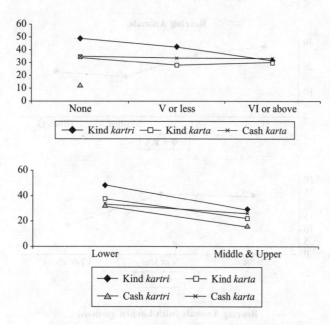

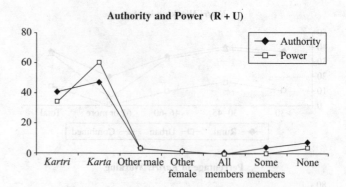

Authority and Power (R + U)

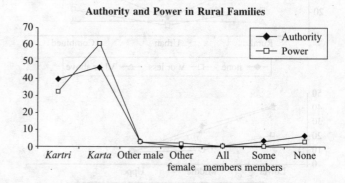

Thus, the *kartris* undertake a vital responsibility to enable her family to firmly withstand the gusts of life and living. Since in terms of the market economy, one's activity is acknowledged as real contribution against vulnerabilities only if it provides a noteworthy monetary contribution, piecemeal but sustained efforts of the *kartris* such as described here remain unnoticed and unaccounted for.

Authority and Power of *Kartri* with Respect to Economic Chores of the Family

For the present purpose, the concepts of authority and power are used in the following sense. Namely, the base of authority under consideration refers to voluntary obedience while power is identified in terms of situated roles of the incumbents (Dennis H. Wrong, *Power Its Forms, Bases and Uses*, The University of Chicago Press, Chicago, USA, 1988, pp. 14, 23). A quite simple but direct measure of authority is to ascertain who keeps the income (in cash) earned by family members. Is it the *kartri* or someone else? That is, more specifically, whether they voluntarily accept her authority in matters of centralizing the income of the family. Similarly, a direct indicator of intra-family location of power is to investigate who is endowed with the responsibility of running family expenditures, that is, how the items of expenditure are prioritized and income allocated.

Shouldering the responsibility of running the economic chores of the family has not made the *kartri* the nodal person bestowed with authority and power to control economic matters of her family as such. Rather, the male head of the family (*karta*) retains authority and power in this regard more than the *kartri*. The gap between them drastically narrows down, no doubt, in matters of authority exercised over income earned by family members. But power held by the male head jumps up steeply, on the one hand, while that of the *kartri* falls sharply, on the other. Thus, the gap in sharing power by them widens tremendously tilting heavily in favour of the male head.

However, only the overall relative distribution of authority and power exercised in the family by the *kartri* vis-à-vis the *karta* have been discussed so far. But for a deep understanding of the phenomenon one has to go beneath the surface looking beyond the analysis by marginals controlling the ecological and various socio-economic characteristics. Accordingly, the pattern of variation will be first considered in terms of the ecological context of the actors.

Pattern of authority and power differentials remain almost unchanged in rural areas.

Authority and Power in Rural Families

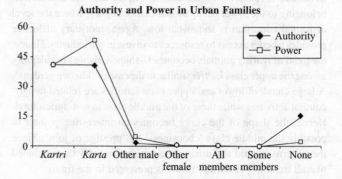

Authority and Power in Urban Families

In urban areas, the gap in the sharing of position of authority and power by the *kartri* and *karta* decreases, though it occurs through different processes. In the case of authority, proportionally less number of male heads in urban areas share responsibility as compared to rural areas. However, this responsibility does not come specifically on anyone else in the family. The share of the *kartri* changes slightly. The position of authority taken up by the *kartri* and *karta* thus becomes almost equal in urban areas.

On the other hand, the gap in the intra-family distribution of economic power persists. In the case of exercising control over expenditures, the share of the *karta* decreases by a considerable proportion compared to the rural areas, which is gained by the *kartri*.

But why does the widening gap between *kartri* and *karta* in respect of intra-family power of control over family's income tend to decrease in urban areas? Is it embedded in the intrinsic nature of urban areas? Or, does it arise out of its cosmopolitan culture and economic heterogeneity? In order to get a comprehensive answer to this query, the urban impact is investigated combined with the socio-economic and cultural attributes of the *kartri* such as her caste and community affiliation, level of formal education and occupational class position of her family. These are introduced as intervening variables between ecology and sharing of power between the *kartri* and *karta*.

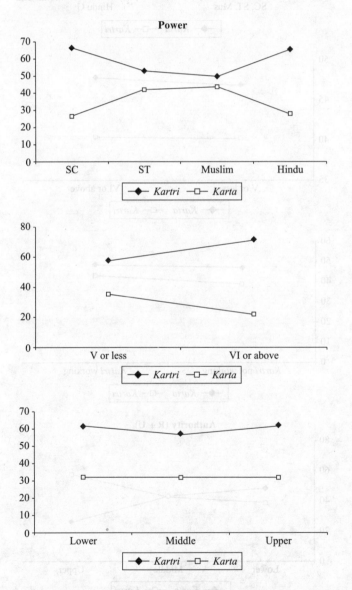

indicates interaction of the rural–urban dichotomy with the intervening attributes. Incidence of power is lowest among the *kartris* belonging to Hindu general castes, attaining a relatively higher level of formal education and upper occupational class in rural areas. On the other hand, it reaches a peak among the urban lower strata. These strata consist of SC, ST and Muslim communities as well as the families whose *kartris* do not have a relatively high formal education, or, those who belong to the lower occupational class in urban areas.

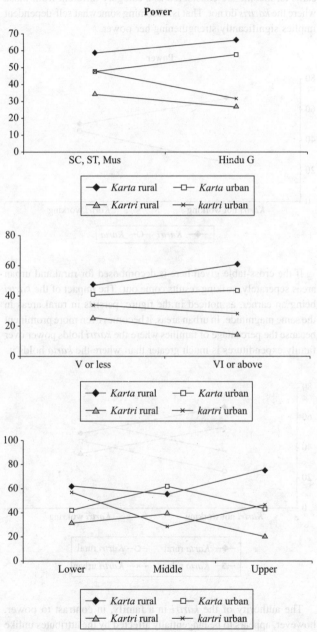

The overall marginal effects of the earlier mentioned variables are not very convincing, but desegregation of their effects by eco-logical contexts brings out the urban impact sharply. Desegregation

The characteristic occupational class refers to the family of a *kartri* as a social unit. But there is another economic characteristic which refers to just the *kartri* herself, namely, whether a *kartri* is working or not. Furthermore, this attribute provides a direct link between being an income earner of the family and having an access to economic power through control of expenditures incurred by the family. In other words, it leads to indicate to what extent economic self-dependence, even if partly, of a *kartri* helps her to assert her power in the family.

First, even when one looks at the overall impact of whether a *kartri* is working or not, one can immediately notice the significance of the impact of this dimension in balancing power proportion. The *kartri* is almost at par with the *karta* if the families where the *kartri* earns an income are considered as a category different from those where the *kartris* do not. That is, becoming somewhat self-dependent implies significantly strengthening her power.

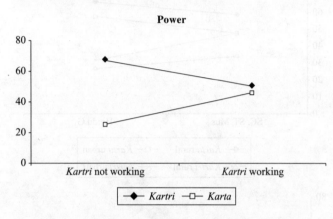

If the cross-table given here is decomposed for rural and urban areas seperately, striking results come out. The impact of the *kartri* being an earner, as noticed in the figure, persists in rural areas in the same magnitude. In urban areas, it becomes even more prominent because the percentage of families where the *kartri* holds power over family expenditures is much greater than where the *karta* holds it.

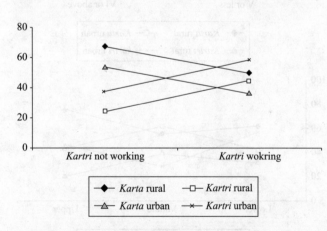

The authority of the *kartri* in a family, in contrast to power, however, appears to be tangentially affected by the attributes unlike what is observed in the case of power.

Only one of the attributes considered earlier, namely, occupational class of the family of the *kartri*, indicates that the authority exerted by the *kartri* becomes more and more prevalent as one moves from

lower to upper class. But this feature, on the other hand, is found to be characteristic of rural areas. It shows no consistent lineal pattern in urban areas although there, the authority of the *kartri* is more prevalent in upper class families than in other classes.

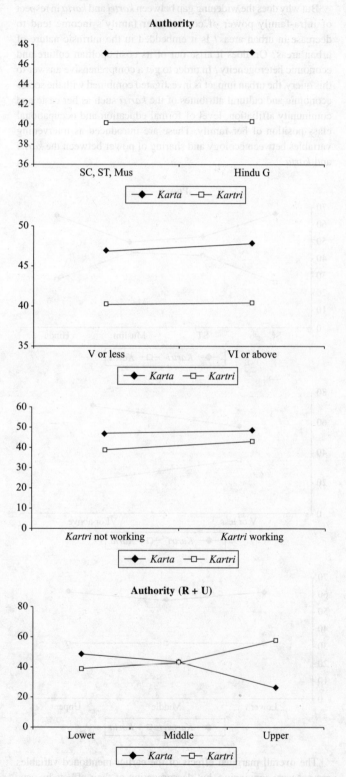

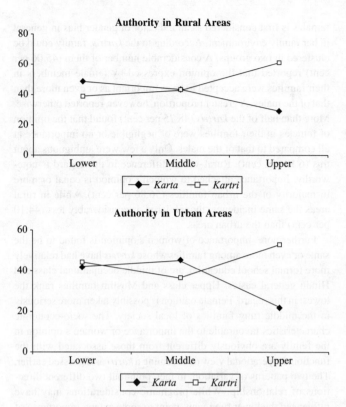

Authority in Rural Areas

Lower　Middle　Upper

◆ *Karta* □ *Kartri*

Authority in Urban Areas

Lower　Middle　Upper

◆ *Karta* □ *Kartri*

In contrast, in rural areas, it does not make any noteworthy difference whether a *kartri* works to earn an income or not. The authority of the *kartri* is less prevalent than that of the *karta*. Only in urban areas, the authority of a working *kartri* is more prevalent than that of a male head, but this relationship does not hold in rural areas.

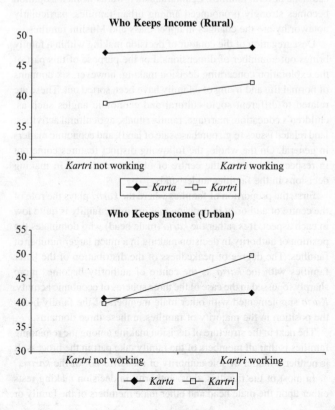

Who Keeps Income (Rural)

Kartri not working　*Kartri* working

◆ *Karta* □ *Kartri*

Who Keeps Income (Urban)

Kartri not working　*Kartri* working

◆ *Karta* □ *Kartri*

Is the high incidence of *kartris* endowed with economic authority, seen in upper class families in particular, just a matter of a chance empirical occurrence? Or, does it indicate any underlying social mechanism confounded with the process of income earning by upper class families? One plausible explanation which was suggested in group discussions is that income earners of an upper class family usually consisted of an earner supported by one or more earning dependents engaged in different occupations. Hence, the need for 'someone to look after the pooled income' is felt more in such families. This responsibility was assigned to the female head of the family. The authority of the *kartri* was, therefore, more prevalent among upper class families. That is why neither the level of formal education nor caste and community affiliation of a *kartri* show any significant pattern. But so far as power or control over expenditures was concerned, these characteristics of a family mattered little. The male head retained the power unless the female head herself participated in the 'production process', so to speak, and contributed to the family income only when upward mobility in the power scale was observed. Achieved economic status of a *kartri* helps her to gain intra-family power more than the normatively derived position in the status hierarchy of the social unit of which she is the head.

To sum up, the underlying message of the findings in this section is that the *kartris*, in large numbers, are inclined to utilize time and resources at their disposal as efficiently as possible, in addition to performing domestic chores, in order to supplement family demands in kind or cash to maintain proper functioning of the family. But their sustained efforts to support the family neither provide them with authority nor power over the routine day-to-day financial matters. That becomes amply evident from the fact that while 40.2 per cent of them keep the earnings of the family members, only in 32.9 per cent cases do they control the expenditures. The male head retains the key to power in almost half the families (47.1 per cent to be precise) and keeps the earnings of the family members. On the other hand, a large majority among them (60.6 per cent) assert power.

Decision Making

The *kartri's* domain of decision making will be viewed from two angles. One is the position of authority over the domain in an aggregative sense and the other is her role in decision making in a disaggregated sense. In the latter case, decision making will be decomposed into some selected constitutive dimensions and her position will be studied with respect to each of them seperately.

First, what comes out from the aggregative analysis? The reason a female member of the family is accepted as the *kartri* of the family gives a reasonable indication of her position in the family's decision making process. A *kartri* may perceive her own position to arise from being the wife of the male head. If this is the self-perception, a *kartri* can mainly play a titular role in the family. On the other hand, there are other distinct categories of ego's role perception which indicate the possibility that the incumbent is much more involved in the family's decision making matters. One of these categories is undertaking the responsibilities of running the family. She acts as a sort of central point in the network of intra-family functional relations. The *kartri's* distance from others is minimal.

She becomes endowed with easy access to influence the family. Another one ascribes a pivotal role to provide the economic mainstay of the family. Last, being the 'eldest' (i.e., the seniormost in the family), a *kartri* holds a traditionally ascribed high status position which she can utilize as an instrument of assertion of her own views. In a way, this is a normatively ordained attribute of status ranking.

In most of the cases, the self-perception of the *kartri* is that she is a *kartri* because she is the 'wife of *karta*'. However, reasons of status or functional importance cannot be ignored either, though these are less prevalent. The pattern remains almost unaltered in rural or urban areas. However, one may note that economic and other reasons are somewhat more visible, which substitute 'wife of *karta*' in urban families. Incidentally, a few *kartris* had no idea why they were held as '*kartri*' and that happened a little more in the case of rural families.

Personal socio-economic characteristics of *kartris* bring out a few additional features concerning the self-perception of a *kartri* regarding her position. These are as follows.

Among the rural ST and Muslim families, one observes a considerable incidence (28.37 per cent) of shouldering the responsibility of running the family, which makes the incumbent its *kartri*. There is a decrease in the perception of a *kartri* being the wife of the *karta*. On the contrary, among the SC and Hindu general caste families in rural areas, the traditional basis of status, normatively derived from being either wife of the male head or being the eldest or seniormost in the family, predominate (82.59 per cent). The same incidence among the ST and Muslim families, though large, is less than the former (66.10 per cent). Inter-caste and community variation is not sharply delineated among urban families.

Again, those who have received comparatively low level of formal education in schools, have been considered to be *kartris* less frequently simply by virtue of being the wife of the male head of the family whether in rural or urban areas. Instead, performance of daily operational and functional responsibilities in a family exert more influence in this regard.

Analysis by occupational class tangentially indicates that becoming a *kartri* of a family by undertaking its day-to-day operational and functional responsibilities happens comparatively more within the lower class, while within the middle and upper class the *kartri* of a family is more likely to be the 'eldest' or 'senior most' female member. It possibly indicates that lower class families are more pragmatically structured while whatever remnants of normative tradition exist are found within the middle and upper class families. This pattern does not change by rural–urban division and is a feature of the overall class situation as such.

Thus, in the aggregative sense, the authority of a *kartri* in the family is derived from her status as being the wife of the male head in majority of the cases whether in rural or urban areas. However, it is also to be noted that functional and operational factors also play a considerable role, though it is conspicuous by its presence comparatively more among the so-called 'marginalized sections' of the society such as the families of ST and Muslim communities, lower occupational class, those who are exposed to the initial phase of formal educational profile, that is, say, primary education or below including neo-literates and even the so-called formally 'illiterates'.

As a prelude to the *kartri's* role in decision making in the family in a desegregated sense, importance attached to the opinion of the females is first considered as an indicator of gender bias in general in her family environment. According to the *kartris,* family could be clustered in two groups. A considerable number of them (45.06 per cent) reported that the opinion expressed by female members in their families were accepted to be as important as or even more than that of the males. A greater proportion, however, reported otherwise. More than half of the *kartris* (48.75 per cent) found that the opinion of females in their families were of negligible or no importance at all compared to that of the males. Only a few were ambiguous about this (6.19 per cent). Rural–urban difference in this regard is noteworthy. Importance attached to women's opinion is equal or more in majority of the urban families (56.86 per cent), while in rural areas the same incidence, though large, is considerably less (44.10 per cent) than the urban areas.

Furthermore, importance of women's opinion is found to be the same or even more among families whose *kartris* have had relatively more formal school education, are of middle occupational class and Hindu general castes. Upper class and Muslim families rank the lowest in this regard. Female opinion is possibly taken more seriously in the middle rung families of local society. The socio-economic characteristics favourable to the importance of women's opinion in the family are obviously different from those associated with the functional-operational view of becoming a *kartri* as discussed earlier. The two patterns of variation, in fact, point out two different directions of relationship. While pragmatic considerations may have influenced the lower rung view-point to some extent, importance of female's voice in the family remains, perhaps, a matter of ideology of the middle stratum of society. On the other hand, gender biased male authoritarianism throttles the upper class and Muslim families much more in particular, though the bias comes out more as a characteristic of rural families. Egalitarianism towards women's opinion becomes strongly pronounced among urban families, particularly noteworthy are the changes in upper class and Muslim families.

Desegregation of the contour of decision making within a family brings out a number of dimensions. For the purpose of this part of the exploration concerning decision making, however, six domains of normal life and living of a family have been sorted out. These are related to different socio-cultural and economic angles such as, children's education, marriage, family rituals, agricultural activities, land related issues (e.g., purchase/sale of land), and economic matters in general. On the whole, the following distinct features come out in respect of locating the centre of ultimate authority in making decisions in the families under study.

First, the proportion of families where the *kartri* plays the role of the centre of authority in decision making in the family is quite low in each aspect. It is rather the *karta* (male head) who dominates the position of authority in decision making in a much larger number of families. The degree of peakedness of the distribution of the latter families with the *karta* as the centre of authority becomes more sharply focussed in the case of the three spheres of economic activity. *Karta* supplemented with other male members of the family holds the position in the majority of families in these three domains.

The next in the structure of decision making among the remaining families is that all members of the family take part in the process. It is neither a matter of sole authority of the *karta* nor of the *kartri*.

In most of the families, thus, authority in decision making rests either upon the male head and other male members of the family or involves everyone in the family. The *kartri* plays her role of authority only in a small proportion of the families whether in rural or urban areas. The data are presented in two parts, A and B, concerning non-economic and economic matters respectively.

In fact, in order to make the comparison of decision making across the six areas more precise, patterns need to be standardized excluding the event that did not occur recently. That, however, instead of bringing any change in the pattern, sharpens the contrast between the position of women's authority in the family, i.e., of the *kartri* and other females, compared with men's, i.e., of *karta* and other males, polarized in economic matters marked by male authoritarian peakedness.

Furthermore, male authoritarianism is found to dominate decision making that particularly concerns the economic activities of majority of rural families. It persists irrespective of caste and community or occupational class affiliation or level of formal education of the *kartri*.

Interaction Outside the Household

In the Village

Experiences of 'teasing' are experiences of motivated humiliation of one's ego. These may not occur frequently, but may not be negligible either and quite traumatizing. Muslim women in particular complain more about being objects of teasing in villages as well as in towns. In towns, the cases of 'teasing' tend to increase slightly. The weakening of normative social control over public behaviour and attitude towards gender in the towns was argued to be at the root of this phenomenon by the female participants in group discussions held on this issue.

The complaint is particularly high among working women concerning the place of work (33.92 per cent). In rural areas, 35.04 per cent of working *kartris* have reported suffering from teasing at their respective places of work. Teasing at the place of work in urban areas is, however, somewhat more (37.15 per cent).

Interaction among persons of different genders is not normatively valued highly in local society. However, measures enforcing such restrictions become quite relaxed at the place of work. A distorted consequence of the change in scenario is the expression of the latent attitude of male superiority in the form of teasing the younger *kartris* relatively more than the older *kartris*, both in rural and urban areas, though the rate of complaints to this effect in urban areas is greater than that in rural areas.

In Health Centres and Hospitals

Investigation regarding another important area of social interaction concerns experience of interaction with the local bureaucracy. Normally most of the *kartris*, 79.20 per cent in rural and 85.81 per cent in urban areas (about 80 per cent altogether), visit local primary health centres (PHC) or hospital for one reason or another. This

happens for *kartris* of all castes, communities, occupational classes and educational categories.

In the process, they interact with both ranks of the official bureaucracy: staff workers (lower in rank) and doctors (upper in rank). The *kartris* evaluated their personal experiences of interaction with the staff in terms of a five point scale as follows.

Only a small proportion of *kartris* were not happy with their experiences when they visited a PHC or hospital for medical reasons and requested the co-operation of staff workers. Among them, however, grievances came more from those urban *kartris* whose level of formal education is low (24.54 per cent) and who belonged to SC and ST communities. Incidentally, residing in urban areas, their experiences are those that they have faced in hospitals.

On the other hand, the experience of interaction of majority of the *kartris* with doctors in urban areas was quite favourable. The complaints largely came from among the ST *kartris* (30.07 per cent). The misgivings in the minds of the *kartris* were not related to gender discrimination. These were rather concerned with systemic inefficiencies predominately affecting rural areas as there were no complaints about experiencing any gender discrimination.

In Public Organizations

For the purpose of the present study, public organization includes elected local public bodies such as gram panchayat, panchayat samiti, zila parishad, on the one hand, as well as mass organizations based on class and gender like krishak sabha (farmers' association) and mahila samiti (women's organization) on the other hand. In this section it refers to the interaction of *kartris* or any female member of their families with these organizations in the form of contacts through visits to their offices or becoming a member or an office-bearer and so on. Whichever way it may be, interaction has been categorized as whether it exists at all or not. In a way, broadly speaking, it explores involvement outside the family with any civic institution.

Furthermore, the process of decision making, where the *kartris* discuss with someone about choosing a candidate to vote for in an election, has been considered a form of interaction with the public-political arena. It may be undoubtedly taken to be a very common experience of them. Unlike the previous situation here the focus lies upon how the process becomes structured.

Most of the *kartris* maintain contact with public institutions in one form or another, which is a manifestation of their high level of socio-political awareness.

Gram panchayat is the most widespread area of interaction for the rural *kartris*. Then is the gender-based association followed by the class-based organization. In this regard, the pattern of interaction is marked by two important features. First, its rate is relatively higher among the ST and Muslim communities, that is, the communities which are both socially and economically marginal in society are socio-politically most interactive. On the other hand, the interaction is consistently the lowest among the SC castes.

Occupational class does not bear any relationship to interaction with public organizations. However, the level of formal education indicates an inverted ∧ type of relationship because the rate of interaction becomes the highest at the middle level, i.e., literate or above, but up to Class V. It includes *kartris* educated up to the primary level as well as that stratum of *kartris* who have become neo-literates or are continuing primary education under the impact of the Total Literacy Campaign (TLC).

The process by which the *kartris* decide who to vote for in elections has been categorized into three types: self decision; discussion with husband and/or son; and consultation with 'others' in the village. The categories indicate self-perception of maturity to take decisions independently. The *kartris* believe that they somewhat less self-reliant and, hence, dependent upon others' opinion. Influence of males (*karta*, son and so on) percolate through the latter.

The overall incidence of self-reliance is of a moderate order. But in urban areas, the majority of *kartris* take decisions on their own while dependence on others, whether in the family or in the village, decreases significantly.

Formal school education accelerates the self-reliance of a *kartri*. It becomes quite suppressed among lower class, ST and Muslim *kartris* without any formal school education.

Social Values and Expectations

The present study, which is based on an empirical investigation, has indicated that it has been rewarding to undertake the study on gender issues structured as an exploration of a system of variations in terms of contextual, socio-cultural and economic parameters rather than as a study rooted in terms of traditional social norms and values. The present section is an illustration of enquiry into variations in a few selected indicators of social values and expectations based on survey research data. Some of these are related to pragmatic social expectations, such as expected age at marriage of one's daughter and son, and attitude to dowry. Some are concerned with traditional performance of rites by a household for the welfare of the family, e.g., performance of a *brata* or *parban*, lighting a lamp in front of the *Tulsi* (a sacred plant) in the evening. Again, a few ask normative guidance of women in a family in their behaviour vis-à-vis other members of the family.

First, the overall pattern of expected age of daughter's marriage is given here. Model age of marriage of a daughter, according to the majority of *kartris*, lies between 18–22 years or above.

Whether dowry should be asked for when negotiating the son's marriage refers to another important attitudinal dimension of social conflict, which often damage post-marital relationships. Though the majority among the *kartris* has expressed their opinion against dowry, attitudes of a considerable section remained ambivalent.

Again, quite a considerable section among the *kartris*, whether in rural or urban areas, perform *brata* or light a lamp in front of the *Tulsi* plant in the evening in order to pray for the well-being and increased affluence of the *karta* (as a symbol of the family) or the 'family' as such also.

Last, there were queries related to values guiding intra-family motivation influencing behavioural orientation. Two issues concerning traditional attitudes were raised. One was whether women should be more tolerant and patient in family matters. The other was whether women should first think of others in the family than about her own self. Overwhelming majority of the *kartris* positively agreed with the proposed attitudinal orientations both in rural as well as in urban areas.

The social orientations given earlier are not invariants. Patterns of their variation are associated with various personal socio-economic characteristics of the *kartris*. What has been gathered about expected age of marriage of one's daughter is found to vary with caste and community affiliation as well as the level of formal education of the *kartris*. *Kartris* belonging to Hindu general castes and those who have had formal education preferred an even higher age for daughter's marriage. The trend becomes reversed in rural areas among the Muslims and among those who are without any formal school education. But in urban areas there is no noteworthy variation in this respect.

Furthermore, the level of formal education of the *kartris* is also associated, but inversely, with attitude to dowry in both rural and urban areas. Education, therefore, plays a socially positive role. Its role also accelerates mental inclination to perform traditional rites for the well-being of the family. Religious reasons suppressed the performance of these rites mostly among ST and Muslim families, whereas a considerable number of SCs, and the least among Hindu general caste (non-SC) families could not perform these for financial reason.

An overwhelming majority of the *kartris* irrespective of socio-cultural and economic categories feel that women should be more tolerant and patient in the family. But when it comes to whether women should first think about 'others' in the family than herself, the attitude is manifest more among the *kartris* of Hindu castes, whether SC or not (85.41 per cent), as against 74.21 per cent of STs and Muslims. It becomes 90.10 per cent among the families where level of formal education is Class VI or above. These are perhaps gender invariant parameters.

Redressal of Gender Related Offence

Personal Efforts

In 13.83 per cent of families, the *kartris* have suffered torture within the family. Comparatively, this occurs much more among the SC as well as non-SC Hindu caste (18.32 per cent), whereas it is quite low (6.49 per cent) among the *kartris* of ST and Muslim families.

Moreover, 21.65 per cent of *kartris* have reported torture of female members in 'other' families in the village. Again, reporting is much more frequent from among Hindu castes, SC or non-SC, as earlier (26.32 per cent). The incidence comes down to 18.16 per cent among Muslim *kartris*, and steeply falls to 9.28 per cent among *kartris* of ST families.

Altogether, about 16.90 per cent of *kartris* have protested at least once against misbehaviour with women in the neighbourhood or village or town. In most of these instances they have protested individually, but it was of no avail.

Level of formal education does not make any impact in this regard.

Though survey research may not be an appropriate methodology for the purpose, yet, it provides a glimpse of the tip of iceberg, which helps to assess the extensiveness of the situation.

Legal Measures of Redressal of Offences against Women: A Matter of Individual Awareness or a Domain of Movement for Conscientization

The concern of this section is the extent of awareness about existing legal measures for redressal of various types of grievances of women, such as women's economic rights (same wage for same work; inheritance of paternal property or succession), liberalization of marriage system (Hindu Marriage Act, Special Marriages Act), women's post-marital welfare (maternity benefits), women's rights (prohibition of dowry; physical and mental torture; divorce/separation; alimony; age at marriage; representation in election). The number of *kartris* aware of economic and other specific rights is considerable. The majority, however, is aware only of the law enforcing the egalitarian economic right (same wage rate for same work without any gender discrimination). Level of awareness about other legal measures is quite lower than this.

Again, an ecological comparison brings out that awareness is proportionally quite large in urban areas compared to rural areas. The only exception is equal wage for equal work for male and female workers because, more rural *kartris* are aware than the urban ones. In fact, this legal measure comes out as a single significant case in the sense that the majority of *kartris*, irrespective of almost all socio-economic categories, is aware about it. This possibly indicates the impact of organized peasants' and women's movement in women's minds in general. Otherwise, awareness is usually low among SC and Muslim *kartris* than other castes and communities, but in the system of stratification by occupational class, the higher the status the more the awareness about legal measures of redressal. The intervening factor is the level of formal education of a *kartri*, which is positively associated with awareness.

On the whole, therefore, the urban Hindu non-SC caste and ST *kartris* with at least some formal school education belonging to upper and middle occupational classes are more aware about legal measures of redressal. Thus, the legal message has probably reached only the visible section of the stratum, maybe elites, through media or any informal network. Awareness of rights to succession or inheritance cannot push a system away from the state of inert social equilibrium by individual efforts alone. Not only lack of necessary resources but socio-cultural norms and ties, specially within the family, often restrain the incumbents from claiming redressal even if it is most appropriate to claim (Mira Seth, *Women and Development: The Indian Experience*, Sage Publications, New Delhi, 2001, pp. 259–60). What is required is an organized mobilization not only for legality to succeed, but even to spread awareness. That is why variability across socio-economic categories is very low in case of the measure 'same wage for the same work', which is supported by an organized movement as opposed to other movements against torture, dowry, etc. The former refers to bargaining with respect to the terms of contract in the labour market while the latter to gender specific property and other socio-cultural rights. Incidentally, one can also refer to the ambiguity of the *kartris* on whether to accept dowry or not in the son's marriage, as stated earlier. The sharp difference between the responses lends support to the proposition that women, based on gender and gender related issues, have not yet made a transition from the stage of women as a class in itself to women as a class for itself.

In this regard, a significant indication of far-fetched socio-political relevance is brought into focus by the local pattern of intra-regional variation. The extent of awareness is much more prevalent in a few village clusters, namely, in Illambazar, Rampurhat, Labhpur and Bolpur-Sriniketan blocks. Besides their close interaction with urban and market centres as well as the recent history of a long drawn anti-feudal peasant movement in some of them, another common source of inspiration is the strong impact of the Total Literacy Campaign. The latter, commonly known as *Saksharata* movement, had aimed at raising the level of consciousness of local villagers. Women form an integral part of these processes and the highs and lows that are observed in their level of awareness reflect the persistence of un-evenness in their conscientization under the impact of processes and is not a matter of any individual lag.

Concluding Remarks

The present study has attempted to focus upon some constitutive characteristics of women's status. These have been selected in terms of intrinsic socio-economic and psychological characteristics which are usually considered the bases of status (e.g., caste and community affiliation, level of formal education and occupational class) as well as hierarchical ordering such as authority, power and prestige, respect manifested through, say, importance bestowed on women's views (*kartris*, for example) and so on (ref. D.L. Sills (ed.), *International Encyclopedia of the Social Sciences*, Vol. 15, Macmillan Company and Free Press, USA, 1968, pp. 250–57). Consequently, that status has been considered embedded in a system of multi-dimensional variations can be inferred from empirically studied variables associated with social action and interactions.

In this context, a pragmatic approach to methodological strategies has been adopted by combining survey research with group discussions and case studies of typical events. Obviously, this has reduced the range of non-sampling errors contaminating the quality of data. Since the single major source of non-sampling error for the present study was gender bias, operational logistics consisted of obtaining response from female heads (*kartri*) by female investigators. The latter were properly trained for field surveys. Besides, they built good rapports with local villagers in general and female population in particular. Besides structural characteristics of women, their self-perception as actors and of their own role and position in the family provide important source materials for the studies. The survey, thus undertaken, was expected to make the study quite colourful.

Various official measures of development of social, economic and cultural levels have been implemented in the rural area under study and they have begun to make perceptible impact as well. Simultaneously, the area has experienced acceleration of interaction with external market and urban growth centres, which act as local modernizing agents in a veiled form. But whatever may be the extent of their impact, women's attachment to the family as the elementary social unit as well as their feeling of well-being for family members at the cost of their personal happiness remain the keystones in the structure of their value system and normative activities. Within the boundary of their own domain, the quality of women's role performance often excels that of male members of a family, but the 'reward' is not fully compensatory. In many instances, it leads to relative deprivation retrogressive to women's status. But they take it to mean a sort of normative cost to be shared for the family's sake by the incumbents. There is variation among different socio-economic strata, no doubt, but the sentiment percolates in different degrees through different layers of women.

Again, viewing the system endogenously, as actors within have indicated, leads to the strong possibility of contrast with viewing the system from without. If this contrast is not properly appreciated, there is a risk of misinterpreting it as arising out of an archetype of Bengali caste Hindu ideas about women and their roles as 'repositories of tradition' (Ben Rogaly, Barbara Harriss-White and Sugata Bose (eds), 'Introduction: Agricultural Growth and Agrarian Change in West Bengal and Bangladesh', in *Sonar Bangla*, Sage Publications, New Delhi, 1999, p. 25). Perhaps, herein lies the 'missing-link' in the transition to women becoming 'class for itself'.

Tables (based on estimated data otherwise specified)

Table G1

| Mother tongue of *kartri* | % | | |
	Rural	Urban	Combined
Bengali	81.63	91.94	84.44
Santhali	15.45	2.78	11.99
Hindi	1.77	4.16	2.43
Kora	0.63	0.56	0.61
Urdu	0.52	0.56	0.053
Total	100.00	100.00	100.00
(n)	(958)	(360)	(1,318)

Table G2

| Caste and community categories of *kartri* | % | | |
	Rural	Urban	Combined
G (Hindu general castes)	28.08	46.94	33.23
SC	33.82	28.62	32.40
ST	22.65	5.28	17.91
Muslim (Mu)	15.45	19.17	16.46
Total	100.00	100.00	100.00
(n)	(958)	(360)	(1,318)

Table G3

| Occupational class | % | | |
	Rural	Urban	Combined
Lower	82.15	31.67	68.36
Middle	16.08	54.44	26.56
Upper	1.77	13.89	5.08
Total	100.00	100.00	100.00
(n)	(958)	(360)	(1,318)

Table G4

| Caste and community categories of *kartri* | Area | % of occupational class | | | |
		Lower	Middle	Upper	Total (n)
ST	Rural	92.63	7.37	0.00	00.00 (217)
	Urban	78.95	15.79	5.26	100.00 (19)
	Combined	91.53	8.05	0.42	100.00 (236)
SC	Rural	91.67	7.10	1.23	100.00 (324)
	Urban	63.11	34.95	1.94	100.00 (103)
	Combined	84.78	13.82	1.40	100.00 (427)
Muslim	Rural	80.41	18.24	1.35	100.00 (148)
	Urban	27.54	55.07	17.39	100.00 (69)
	Combined	63.60	29.95	6.45	100.00 (217)
General	Rural	63.20	32.71	4.09	100.00 (269)
	Urban	8.88	70.41	20.71	100.00 (169)
	Combined	42.24	47.26	10.50	100.00 (438)

Table G5

| Level of formal education of *kartri* | % | | |
	Rural	Urban	Combined
None	64.09	43.61	58.50
Up to Class V	22.97	19.45	22.00
Class VI or above	12.94	36.94	19.50
Total	100.00	100.00	100.00
(n)	(958)	(360)	(1,318)

Table G6

| Categories of castes and communities of *kartri* | % attaining level of formal school education | | | |
	None	Up to Class V	Class VI and above	Total (n)
ST	87.71	10.17	2.12	100.0 (236)
SC	76.035	17.09	6.56	100.0 (427)
Muslim	59.91	24.88	15.21	100.0 (217)
General	24.66	31.73	43.61	100.0 (438)
Combined	58.50	22.00	19.50	100.0 (1,318)

Table G7

| Categories of castes and communities of *kartri* | Area | % of attaining level of school education | | | |
		None	Up to Class V	Class VI or above	Total (n)
ST	Rural	89.40	8.76	1.84	100.00 (217)
	Urban	68.42	26.32	5.26	100.00 (19)
	Combined	87.71	10.17	2.12	100.00 (236)
SC	Rural	78.40	18.21	3.39	100.00 (324)
	Urban	69.90	13.60	16.50	100.00 (103)
	Combined	76.35	17.09	6.56	100.00 (427)
Muslim	Rural	62.16	27.70	10.14	100.00 (148)
	Urban	55.07	18.84	26.09	100.00 (69)
	Combined	59.91	24.88	15.21	100.00 (217)
General	Rural	27.51	37.55	34.94	100.00 (269)
	Urban	20.12	22.48	57.40	100.00 (169)
	Combined	24.66	31.73	43.61	100.00 (438)

Table G8

| Beginning of education in a school in the house of *kartri* | % | | |
	Rural	Urban	Combined
During last 5 years	11.79	11.39	11.68
5–10 years back	9.29	9.17	9.36
Before 10 years in this generation	26.83	18.33	24.51
Earlier	31.63	46.67	35.74
Not yet	20.46	14.44	18.81
Total	100.00	100.00	100.00
(n)	(958)	(360)	(1,318)

Table G9

| Age (in years) of *kartri* | % | | |
	Rural	Urban	Combined
≤20	5.94	3.61	5.31
21–30	26.82	25.83	26.56
31–45	43.22	46.11	44.01
46–60	20.26	21.39	20.55
61+	3.76	3.05	3.56
Total	100.00	100.00	100.00
(n)	(958)	(360)	(1,318)

Table G10

Family type of *kartri*		%		
		Rural	Urban	Combined
Female	Unmarried	0.21	0.28	0.23
	Married	0.31	0.28	0.30
	Widowed	1.57	0.00	1.14
	Divorced/separated	0.31	0.00	0.23
	Total	2.40	0.56	1.90
Conjugal unit		6.26	6.39	6.30
Nuclear family		52.92	60.83	55.08
Others		38.42	31.67	36.57
Total		100.00	100.00	100.00
(n)		(958)	(360)	(1,318)

Table G11

Reasons for discontinuity of education	%	
	Male (M)	Female (F)
E	55.67	35.50
P	10.75	2.83
Economic	66.42	38.33
D	7.13	28.63
F	15.31	20.40
Familial	22.44	49.03
I	0.55	0.47
S	10.59	12.17
Total (n)	100.00	100.00
	(1,992)	(1,907)
St. E	0.73	0.80

Table G12

Reasons for discontinuity of education	Location		Caste/community				Occupational class		
	Rural	Urban	ST	Mu	SC	G	Lower (L)	Middle (Md)	Upper (Up)
E	41.46	61.44	38.16	49.78	57.43	36.01	46.21	44.98	42.75
P	7.21	5.66	6.22	5.93	6.16	8.73	6.44	8.23	7.25
Economic	48.67	67.10	44.38	55.71	63.59	44.74	52.65	53.21	50.00
D	18.39	14.98	14.23	14.96	14.54	25.31	16.28	21.53	21.01
F	19.93	10.14	27.51	14.81	12.95	17.83	18.86	14.09	19.57
Familial	38.32	25.12	41.74	29.77	27.49	43.14	35.14	35.62	40.58
I	0.52	0.47	0.60	1.04	0.39	0.27	0.49	0.68	0.00
S	12.49	7.31	13.28	13.48	8.53	11.85	11.72	10.49	9.42
Total	100.00	100.00	100.00	100.00	100.00	100.00	100.00	100.00	100.00
(n)	(3,051)	(848)	(836)	(675)	(1,266)	(1,122)	(2,874)	(887)	(138)
St. E	0.82	0.67	0.82	0.78	0.71	0.84	0.79	0.80	0.88

Table G13

	% (n)							
	Location		Occupational class		Caste/Community categories			
Gender	Rural	Urban	Lower	Middle and upper	ST	Muslim	SC	G
(D) Shouldering domestic duties								
Female	28.73	28.25	25.89	36.24	20.10	26.06	23.75	41.83
	(1,507)	(400)	(1,402)	(505)	(418)	(330)	(602)	(557)
Male	8.29	3.12	7.13	7.12	8.37	4.35	6.17	9.03
	(1,544)	(448)	(1,472)	(520)	(418)	(345)	(664)	(565)
(E + P) Economic pressure								
Female	35.50	49.00	40.37	32.67	36.60	42.42	51.33	23.16
	(1,507)	(400)	(1,402)	(505)	(418)	(330)	(602)	(557)
Male	61.53	83.26	64.33	72.31	52.15	68.41	74.70	66.02
	(1,544)	(448)	(1,472)	(520)	(418)	(345)	(664)	(565)
(S) Factors related to schooling								
Female	12.87	9.50	12.20	12.08	12.92	12.73	8.80	14.90
	(1,507)	(400)	(1,402)	(505)	(418)	(330)	(602)	(557)
Male	12.11	5.36	11.28	8.65	13.64	14.20	8.28	8.85
	(1,544)	(448)	(1,472)	(520)	(418)	(345)	(664)	(565)
Familial environment								
Female	22.56	12.25	21.25	18.02	29.90	17.58	15.78	19.93
	(1,507)	(400)	(1,402)	(505)	(418)	(330)	(602)	(557)
Male	17.36	8.26	16.58	11.73	25.12	12.17	10.39	15.75
	(1,544)	(448)	(1,472)	(520)	(418)	(345)	(664)	(565)

Discussion in the Family about Education and Future of Children

Table G14

Focus of discussion, if any	Location		Occupational class		Caste/community categories				
	Rural	Urban	Lower	Upper and middle	ST	Muslim	SC	General	Combined
None	19.43	9.17	20.77	11.95	14.00	23.42	17.57	19.31	18.64
Mostly about									
Son	9.07	14.67	8.12	13.85	8.36	4.87	9.37	13.22	9.50
Daughter	7.02	9.84	8.37	3.63	5.57	9.35	8.42	5.41	7.23
Both	64.48	66.32	62.74	70.57	72.07	62.36	64.64	62.06	60.83
Total*	100.00	100.00	100.00	100.00	100.00	100.00	100.00	100.00	100.00
(n')	(829)	(326)	(782)	(373)	(197)	(186)	(379)	(393)	(1,155)

Note: *n' is the number of families excluding those without any child for whom the question is not applicable and hence distributions of estimated percentages are comparable.

Table G15

Focus of discussion, if any	% by *kartri's* level of formal schooling			% by the period when formal schooling started in the family	
	None	– V	VI +	Last 10 years (since 1990)	Earlier
None	16.08	24.70	19.61	14.11	23.19
Mostly about					
Son	8.58	10.01	12.71	10.72	9.69
Daughter	8.02	4.41	8.46	10.64	5.71
Both	67.32	60.88	59.22	64.53	61.41
Total*	100.00	100.00	100.00	100.00	100.00
(n')	(662)	(261)	(232)	(251)	(717)

Note: Same as Table G14.

Table G16.1

Expected level of education	% by location				% by occupational class			
	Rural		Urban		Lower		Upper + Middle	
	Girl	Boy	Girl	Boy	Girl	Boy	Girl	Boy
≤ Primary	44.13	15.98	33.73	16.29	49.06	15.61	25.46	17.22
Higher-secondary or equivalent	35.33	30.73	26.66	30.72	32.93	33.29	40.15	22.70
College ≤	20.54	53.29	39.61	52.99	18.01	51.10	34.39	60.08
Total	100.00	100.00	100.00	100.00	100.00	100.00	100.00	100.00
(n)	(958)	(958)	(360)	(360)	(901)	(901)	(417)	(417)

Caste and Community Affiliation of *Kartri*

Expected level of education	ST		Muslim		SC		General	
	Girl	Boy	Girl	Boy	Girl	Boy	Girl	Boy
≤ Primary	57.12	19.17	45.46	17.39	57.07	18.97	19.14	10.04
Higher-secondary or equivalent	19.56	33.78	42.30	27.30	29.24	39.58	44.05	21.54
College ≤	23.32	47.05	12.24	55.31	13.69	41.45	36.81	68.42
Total	100.00	100.00	100.00	100.00	100.00	100.00	100.00	100.00
(n)	(236)	(236)	(217)	(217)	(217)	(217)	(438)	(438)

Level of Formal Education of *Kartri*

Expected level of education	None		– V		VI +		Combined	
	Girl	Boy	Girl	Boy	Girl	Boy	Girl	Boy
≤ Primary	57.16	20.14	24.32	9.55	12.83	8.08	43.34	16.01
Higher-secondary or equivalent	28.05	38.14	49.51	21.06	40.01	13.55	34.68	30.73
College ≤	14.79	41.72	26.17	69.39	47.16	78.37	21.98	53.26
Total	100.00	100.00	100.00	100.00	100.00	100.00	100.00	100.00
(n)	(771)	(771)	(290)	(209)	(257)	(257)	(1,318)	(1,318)

Table G16.2

Expected level of education	During last 10 years (since 1990)		Earlier	
	Girl	Boy	Girl	Boy
≤ Primary	52.69	13.79	29.98	10.31
Higher-secondary or equivalent	32.34	37.42	40.41	25.32
College ≤	14.97	48.79	29.61	64.37
Total	100.00	100.00	100.00	100.00
(n)	(276)	(276)	(794)	(794)

Table G17.1

% *kartris* bringing up their children with goals for future

	Location				Occupational class			
	Rural		Urban		Lower		Upper + Middle	
Goals for future	Girl	Boy	Girl	Boy	Girl	Boy	Girl	Boy
No idea	7.72	10.36	3.64	6.12	7.98	10.96	5.60	7.15
Domestic work in the family	62.50	3.15	55.41	4.28	65.09	3.18	52.15	3.42
Becoming engaged in a service or profession	26.49	76.88	35.38	81.37	23.92	75.26	37.35	83.34
Others	3.29	9.61	5.57	8.23	3.01	10.60	4.90	6.09
Total	100.00	100.00	100.00	100.00	100.00	100.00	100.00	100.00
(n)	(958)	(958)	(360)	(360)	(901)	(901)	(417)	(417)

Caste and Community Affiliation of *Kartri*'s Family

	ST		Muslim		SC		General	
	Girl	Boy	Girl	Boy	Girl	Boy	Girl	Boy
No idea	13.86	15.54	8.94	9.41	5.58	8.82	4.81	8.74
Domestic work in the family	58.72	3.60	73.60	3.45	72.30	5.03	44.68	0.92
Becoming engaged in a service or profession	24.57	56.33	14.07	84.10	17.01	76.30	48.46	85.30
Others	2.85	24.53	3.39	3.04	5.11	9.85	2.05	5.04
Total	100.00	100.00	100.00	100.00	100.00	100.00	100.00	100.00
(n)	(236)	(236)	(217)	(217)	(217)	(217)	(438)	(438)

Table G17.2

% *kartris* bringing up their children with goals for future

	During last 10 years (since 1990)		Earlier	
Goals for future	Girl	Boy	Girl	Boy
No idea	4.43	5.28	6.17	8.49
Domestic work in the family	74.34	1.48	54.74	3.09
Becoming engaged in a service or profession	14.78	81.92	36.06	79.48
Others	6.45	11.32	3.03	8.94
Total	100.00	100.00	100.00	100.00
(n)	(276)	(276)	(794)	(794)

Table G17.3

% *kartris* bringing up their children with goals for future

	None		–V		VI+		Combined	
Goals for future	Girl	Boy	Girl	Boy	Girl	Boy	Girl	Boy
No idea	9.56	12.25	5.10	8.61	1.57	2.53	7.40	10.04
Domestic work in the family	68.90	3.80	55.36	3.31	41.85	0.61	61.96	3.24
Becoming engaged in a service or profession	18.07	73.61	36.68	82.60	52.13	84.49	27.17	77.22
Others	3.47	10.34	2.86	5.48	4.45	12.37	3.47	9.50
Total	100.00	100.00	100.00	100.00	100.00	100.00	100.00	100.00
(n)	(771)	(771)	(290)	(290)	(257)	(257)	(1,318)	(1,318)

Table G18

| | | VI+ | | | | −V | | | | NL | | | |
| | | G | | Others | | G | | Others | | G | | Others | |
		UM	L	UM	L	UM	L	UM	L	UM	L	UM	L
Expectation of *kartri* about maximum level of education to beprovided to female children*	<HS	10.53	12.07	15.79	21.43	17.39	20.00	29.27	35.45	23.53	42.11	45.88	60.21
	HS+	89.47	87.93	84.21	78.57	82.61	80.00	70.73	64.55	76.47	57.89	54.12	39.79
Future goals in bringing up the female children	Domestic responsibilities	34.59	44.83	42.11	57.14	50.72	52.86	63.41	63.64	35.29	63.16	69.41	71.28
	Service/ Profession	56.39	50.00	42.11	39.29	42.03	38.57	29.27	33.64	54.90	31.58	17.65	17.13

Notes: * <HS = primary or below; HS+ = At least higher-secondary or above.
1. VI + = *kartri's* level of formal education is Class VI or higher;
   − V = *kartri's* level of formal education is Class V or below;
   NL = *kartri's* level of formal education is none.
2. G = *kartri's* caste/community is Hindu general caste;
   Others = *kartri's* caste/community is other than G.
3. UM = Upper + middle; L = lower.

Table G19

| Perception of general condition of health | % | | | | | |
| | Combined | | Rural | | Urban | |
	Male	Female	Male	Female	Male	Female
Good	31.72	27.55	30.62	26.24	34.70	31.47
Average	50.60	52.63	49.83	52.66	52.67	52.54
Bad	17.68	19.82	19.55	21.10	12.63	15.99
Total	100.00	100.00	100.00	100.00	100.00	100.00
(n)	(3,257)	(3,082)	(2,378)	(2,313)	(879)	(769)

Table G20

| Perception of general condition of health | % | | | | | | | |
| | ST | | Muslim | | SC | | General | |
	Male	Female	Male	Female	Male	Female	Male	Female
Good	26.25	24.83	27.89	22.68	30.11	26.81	38.80	32.94
Average	52.51	55.38	46.77	45.18	52.99	54.40	49.22	53.48
Bad	21.24	19.79	25.34	32.14	16.90	18.79	11.98	13.58
Total	100.00	100.00	100.00	100.00	100.00	100.00	100.00	100.00
(n)	(598)	(576)	(588)	(560)	(1,053)	(1,011)	(1,018)	(935)
% (Rural)								
Good	24.64	23.59	26.38	20.78	31.31	27.63	37.54	30.22
Average	54.35	56.60	40.95	39.48	52.34	55.39	48.48	54.02
Bad	21.01	19.81	32.66	39.74	16.49	16.98	13.98	15.76
Total	100.00	100.00	100.00	100.00	100.00	100.00	100.00	100.00
(n)	(552)	(530)	(398)	(385)	(770)	(789)	(658)	(609)
% (Urban)								
Good	23.91	19.57	10.00	15.43	18.02	25.23	8.33	9.51
Average	30.44	41.30	58.95	57.71	54.77	50.90	50.56	52.45
Bad	45.65	39.13	31.05	26.86	27.21	23.87	41.11	38.04
Total	100.00	100.00	100.00	100.00	100.00	100.00	100.00	100.00
(n)	(46)	(46)	(283)	(222)	(190)	(175)	(360)	(326)

Table G21

Generally treatment is done by	%			% (Rural)		% (Urban)	
	Male	Female	Combined	Male	Female	Male	Female
Local/private doctors	54.67	60.03	57.37	54.34	61.02	55.56	56.95
PHC	16.69	15.73	16.21	16.26	15.25	17.90	17.22
Government hospital	16.86	13.16	14.99	17.59	12.29	14.81	15.90
Others	11.78	11.08	11.43	11.81	11.44	11.73	9.93
Total	100.00	100.00	100.00	100.00	100.00	100.00	100.00
(n)	(611)	(623)	(1,234)	(449)	(472)	(162)	(151)

Table G22

Whether a *kartri* finds it difficult to get a doctor at PHCs or govt. hospital as and when required	% of *kartri*s		
	Rural	Urban	Combined
No	28.33	46.93	29.73
Yes (Reasons)	71.67	53.07	70.27
Doctor is often absent	28.36	19.59	27.69
Have to go to doctor's residence	21.14	18.16	20.91
Others	1.30	3.52	1.48
Cannot specify	20.87	11.80	20.19
Total	100.00	100.00	100.00
(n)	(957)	(360)	(1,317)

Table G23

Type of response of staff at PHC or govt. hospital to *kartri*	%		
	Rural	Urban	Combined
Very good	4.90	9.70	5.26
Good	23.11	22.81	23.09
Tolerable	38.26	38.07	38.25
Bad	8.18	11.14	8.40
Very bad	4.75	4.09	4.70
Cannot specify	20.80	14.19	20.30
Total	100.00	100.00	100.00
(n)	(958)	(360)	(1,318)

Table G24

Type of response of staff at PHC or govt. hospital to *kartri*	%					
	Kartris education		Occupational class		Caste/community	
	VI +	Less than VI	Upper and middle	Lower	General	Others
Favourable (very good + good)	35.78	27.13	29.44	28.00	30.09	27.60
Cannot specify	18.96	20.52	23.56	19.26	24.68	18.41
Not favourable (Others)	45.26	52.35	47.00	52.74	45.23	53.99
Total	100.00	100.00	100.00	100.00	100.00	100.00
(n)	(257)	(1,061)	(417)	(901)	(438)	(830)

Table G25

Normally treatment is done by	% of families by castes and communities		% of females by occupational class	
	SC, ST and Muslim	General caste Hindu	Lower	Upper and Middle
Local private doctor	61.62	55.69	60.83	58.20
PHC and government hospital	29.61	26.95	29.72	26.98
Others (including nursing homes)	8.77	17.36	9.45	14.82
Total	100.00	100.00	100.00	100.00
(n)	(456)	(167)	(434)	(189)

Table G27

Caste/ community category	Percentage of intra-familial domestic chores					
	R		U		R + U	
	W_1	W_0	W_1	W_0	W_1	W_0
SC	53.83	29.67	52.67	90.75	53.75	30.41
ST	51.08	25.33	58.33	32.75	51.25	25.50
Mu	50.75	31.08	40.67	52.00	50.17	32.33
G	45.33	38.75	35.08	58.83	44.00	41.25

Table G28

Occupational class	Mode of performance of intra-familial domestic chores of urban families (in per cent)				
	W_1	W_2	W_0	W_3	Total
Lower	51.76	5.86	40.28	2.10	100.00
Middle	38.56	4.44	55.81	1.19	100.00
Upper	34.20	5.84	58.56	1.10	100.00
(Urban) pooled	42.25	5.08	51.17	1.50	100.00

Table G26

Percentage of intra-familial domestic chores performed by	Rural (R)	Urban (U)	Combined (R + U)
Kartri herself (W_1)	50.33	42.25	49.75
Kartri and other females (W_2)	14.75	5.08	14.00
Other females excluding *kartri* (W_0)	31.75	51.17	33.25
Rest (W_3)	3.17	1.50	3.00
Total	100.00	10.00	100.00

Table G29

Occupational class	Mode of performance of intra-familial domestic chores of rural families (in per cent)				
	W_1	W_2	W_0	W_3	Total
Lower	51.35	15.60	29.71	3.34	100.00
Middle	45.23	11.41	40.10	2.76	100.00
Upper	62.57	4.88	33.35	0.00	100.00
(Rural) pooled	50.33	14.75	31.75	3.17	100.00

Table G30

Level of formal education of *kartri*	Mode of performance of intra-familial domestic chores (in per cent)				
	W_1	W_2	W_0	W_3	Total
Panel A: Rural					
Illiterate	52.45	14.13	30.46	2.96	100.00
Class V or below	48.48	15.97	31.40	4.15	100.00
Class VI or higher	42.62	15.53	39.36	2.49	100.00
(Rural) pooled	50.33	14.75	31.75	3.17	100.00
Panel B: Urban					
Illiterate	46.50	4.75	47.21	1.50	100.00
Class V or below	43.65	5.09	49.47	1.79	100.00
Class VI or higher	36.53	5.49	56.70	1.28	100.00
(Urban) pooled	42.25	5.08	51.17	1.50	100.00
Panel C: Rural and Urban Combined					
Illiterate	52.12	13.63	31.36	2.89	100.00
Class V or below	48.20	15.34	32.45	4.01	100.00
Class VI or higher	41.40	13.52	42.84	2.24	100.00
(R + U) pooled	49.45	14.00	33.25	3.00	100.00

Table G31

Kartri working or not	Mode of performance of intra-familial domestic chores (in per cent)				
	W_1	W_2	W_0	W_3	Total
Panel A: Rural					
Not working	47.42	14.50	34.08	4.00	100.00
Working	55.00	15.17	28.00	1.83	100.00
(Rural) pooled	50.35	14.75	31.75	3.17	100.00
Panel B: Urban					
Not working	42.00	4.67	52.00	1.33	100.00
Working	44.08	7.75	45.83	2.34	100.00
(Urban) pooled	42.25	5.08	51.17	1.50	100.00
Panel C: Rural and Urban Combined					
Not working	46.83	13.50	35.92	3.75	100.00
Working	54.75	14.92	28.50	1.83	100.00
(R + U) pooled	49.45	14.00	33.25	3.00	100.00

Table G32

Domestic chore	β (on *kartri* working (1) or not (0)) $\pm$ s.e.	β/s.e.	Per cent of *kartris* expecting male members to share the work	
			Working	Not working
Preparation of meals (cooking)	0.48 ± 0.218	2.20	13.77	10.05
Washing dishes and cooking utensils	−0.15 ± 0.255	−0.59	6.54	7.44
Cleaning the house	0.60 ± 0.172	3.49	23.25	17.67
Washing clothes	0.38 ± 0.163	2.33	37.71	22.19

Table G33

Domestic chore	Fall under the domain of only female according to the *kartri* (in %)
Cooking and serving meal	88.61
Dish washing	92.90
Home cleaning	81.60
Washing clothes	75.78

Table G34

Mode of taking meals by adult male and female members of a household	Lunch	Dinner
All together	25.10	46.67
As and when it is convenient	47.83	30.08
Females after the males have had their meals	27.07	23.25
Total	100.00	100.00

Table G35

Mode of taking meals by adult male and female members of a household	Occupational class					
	Lower		Middle		Upper	
	Lunch	Dinner	Lunch	Dinner	Lunch	Dinner
All together	22.34	47.00	31.95	49.57	38.57	44.14
As and when it is convenient	49.98	30.58	43.38	23.82	37.94	28.88
Females after the males have had their meals	27.68	22.42	24.67	26.61	23.49	26.98
Total	100.00	100.00	100.00	100.00	100.00	100.00

Table G36

Discussion in the family about 'children's education' and their 'future'	%		
	Rural	Urban	Combined
No idea	12.78	9.79	12.56
No discussion	16.95	8.27	16.30
Specially about			
sons	7.91	13.23	8.31
daughters	6.12	8.88	6.32
both	52.98	55.79	53.19
Yes: in a general manner	3.26	4.04	3.32
Total	100.00	100.00	100.00
(n)	(958)	(360)	(1,318)

Table G37

Discussion in the family about 'children's education' and their 'future'	% of *kartris* by maximum level of formal schooling			% of the period when formal schooling has started in the family	
	None	–V	VI +	During last 10 years (since 1990)	Earlier
No idea	13.98	9.64	10.98	6.66	11.11
None	13.83	22.31	17.46	13.17	20.61
Specially about					
Sons	7.38	9.04	11.31	10.01	8.61
Daughters	6.90	4.01	7.53	9.93	5.08
Both	53.52	53.47	51.22	54.49	52.47
Yes: in general	4.39	1.53	1.50	5.74	2.12
Total	100.00	100.00	100.00	100.00	100.00
(n)	(771)	(290)	(257)	(276)	(794)

Table G38

Discussion in the family	% by caste/community affiliation				% by occupational class	
	ST	Muslim	SC	Others	Lower	Middle + Upper
No idea	15.75	15.87	9.09	12.42	12.57	12.54
None	11.80	19.70	15.97	16.91	18.16	10.45
Specially about						
Sons	7.04	4.10	8.52	11.58	7.10	12.11
Daughters	4.69	7.87	7.66	4.74	7.32	3.18
Both	57.17	51.00	53.22	52.37	51.15	59.57
Yes: in general	3.55	1.46	5.54	1.98	3.70	2.15
Total	100.00	100.00	100.00	100.00	100.00	100.00
(n)	(236)	(217)	(427)	(438)	(901)	(417)

Table G39

Informal borrowing by*	% of families reporting informal borrowing in	
	Kind	Cash
Kartri	44.89	31.26
Karta	31.72	34.56
Total (including informal borrowing by others)	79.00	68.98

Note: * As and when required to meet the requirements of daily life.

Table G40

Source of supplementary livelihood of *kartri*	% of *kartris*	
	Rural	Urban
Kitchen garden	13.01	13.85
Rearing of domestic animal	22.80	17.18

Table G41

Informal borrowing by	% of families reporting informal borrowing in			
	Kind		Cash	
	Rural	Urban	Rural	Urban
Kartri	47.05	18.38	32.53	15.65
Karta	33.13	14.40	34.95	29.85

Table G42

Age (in years) of a *kartri*	% of *kartris* working to earn livelihood (excluding 'not available cases')		
	Rural	Urban	Combined
Less than 30	37.08	9.99	35.02
30–45	40.80	16.36	38.94
46–60	34.09	9.96	32.25
61 or more	19.81	0.00	5.02
Total	37.71	13.14	35.74

Table G43

Socio-economic characteristics of *kartri*	% of *kartris* working to earn livelihood in each socio-economic category		
	Rural	Urban	Combined
Caste and community affiliation			
SC	44.55	12.04	42.43
ST	64.84	34.40	64.14
Muslim	35.85	19.19	34.82

(Table G43 Contd.)

(Table G43 Contd.)

Socio-economic characteristics of *kartri*	% of *kartris* working to earn livelihood in each socio-economic category		
	Rural	Urban	Combined
Sub-total	47.12	16.65	45.47
Hindu general castes	14.11	9.61	13.55
Level of formal education			
None	48.47	15.10	46.68
Class V or below	22.21	8.90	21.44
Sub-total	41.45	13.35	39.91
Class VI or above	10.77	12.78	11.18
Occupational class of the family			
Lower	40.87	20.38	40.21
Middle	26.74	9.95	23.61
Upper	8.85	8.50	8.69

Table G44.1

Socio-economic characteristics of *kartri*	% of families reporting informal borrowing in			
	Kind		Cash	
	Kartri	*Karta*	*Kartri*	*Karta*
Caste and community affiliation				
SC, ST, Muslim combined	49.03	35.62	36.27	35.85
Hindu general castes	35.28	22.65	19.64	31.59
Level of formal education				
None	48.81	33.71	36.30	35.01
Class V or below	42.13	27.41	26.76	33.96
Class VI or above	31.91	29.84	16.17	33.59
Occupational class of the family				
Lower	49.89	33.75	32.84	38.25
Middle and upper	29.21	25.33	16.30	23.00

Table G44.2

Socio-economic characteristics of *kartri*	% of families reporting informal borrowing in			
	Kind		Cash	
	Kartri	*Karta*	*Kartri*	*Karta*
(Rural areas with urban areas in brackets)				
Caste and community affiliation				
SC, ST and Muslim families	50.18	36.77	36.84	36.09
	(28.86)	(15.66)	(26.23)	(31.62)
Hindu general castes	39.20	24.01	21.72	32.10
	(7.85)	(13.14)	(5.02)	(28.07)
Level of formal education				
None	49.91	34.89	36.81	35.19
	(29.52)	(12.98)	(27.14)	(31.84)
Class V or below	43.58	28.50	27.99	34.44
	(18.38)	(9.61)	(6.65)	(26.07)
Class VI or above	38.66	32.75	18.69	34.68
	(5.15)	(18.32)	(6.19)	(29.25)
Occupational class of family				
Lower	50.34	34.35	32.85	38.41
	(36.35)	(15.83)	(32.58)	(33.52)
Upper and middle	34.41	28.44	31.32	21.65
	(9.75)	(13.72)	(7.51)	(28.05)

Table G45

Socio-economic characteristics of *kartri*	% of *kartris* rearing animals as a supplementary source of livelihood in each category (rural and urban combined)	
Caste and community affiliation		
SC	28.48	
ST	25.23	
Muslim	16.15	
Sub-total	24.19	
Hindu general castes	18.18	
Level of formal education		
None	23.80	
Class V or below	24.83	
Sub-total	24.08	
Class VI or above	12.04	
Occupational class of the family*		(Kitchen garden)
Lower	25.67	(19.36)
Middle	10.90	(12.52)
Upper	23.32	(16.12)

Note: * % *kartris* engaged in kitchen gardening in each occupational class category shown within brackets.

Table G46

Actor endowed with the responsibility	% of families	
	Keeping the income earned by family members	Prioritization of different requirements and spend accordingly
Kartri	40.20	32.89
Karta	47.14	60.62
Other male members	2.26	2.71
Other female members	0.40	1.50
All members (sharing among themselves)	0.24	0.00
Some members (sharing among themselves)	2.96	0.00
None specifically	6.80	2.28
Total	100.00	100.00

Table G47

Actor endowed with the responsibility	% of families in rural areas	
	Keeping the income earned by family members	Prioritization of requirements and spend accordingly
Kartri	40.11	32.28
Karta	47.62	61.24
Other male members	2.32	2.56
Other female members	0.43	1.62
All members	0.24	0.00
Some members	3.13	0.00
None specifically	6.15	2.30
Total	100.00	100.00

Table G48

Actor endowed with the responsibility	% of families in urban areas	
	Keeping the income earned by family members	Prioritization of requirements and spend accordingly
Kartri	41.31	40.32
Karta	41.19	52.97
Other male members	1.52	4.51
Other female members	0.00	0.00
All members	0.28	0.00
Some members	0.93	0.00
None specifically	14.77	2.10
Total	100.00	100.00

Table G49

Socio-economic characteristics of *kartri*	Who has the power to prioritize requirements and spend accordingly (% families)	
	Karta	*Kartri*
Caste and community affiliation of *kartri's* family		
SC	66.40	26.60
ST	53.18	42.46
Muslim	50.13	43.40
Sub-total	58.61	35.19
Hindu general castes	65.26	27.55
Level of formal education of *kartri*		
Class V or below	58.71	34.78
Class VI or above	72.24	21.39
Occupational class of *kartri's* family		
Lower	61.83	31.60
Middle	56.28	32.10
Upper	61.89	31.71

Table G50

Socio-economic characteristics of *kartri*	Who has the power to prioritize requirements and spend accordingly (% families)			
	Karta		*Kartri*	
	Rural	Urban	Rural	Urban
Caste and community affiliation *of kartri's* family				
SC, ST and Muslim combined	59.21	48.18	34.45	48.20
Hindu general castes	66.33	57.78	26.83	32.50
Level of formal education of *kartri*				
Class V or below	59.13	51.45	34.29	43.23
Class VI or above	76.47	55.50	17.76	35.76
Occupational class of *kartri's* family				
Lower	62.50	41.99	30.75	56.81
Middle	55.03	61.75	39.43	28.98
Upper	76.38	44.34	19.35	46.69

Table G51

	% of families showing who has the power to prioritize requirements and spend accordingly (rural and urban combined)	
Kartri working	*Karta*	*Kartri*
No	66.89	25.78
Yes	49.27	45.46

Table G52

	% of families showing who has the power to prioritize requirements and spend accordingly			
	Rural		Urban	
Kartri working	*Karta*	*Kartri*	*Karta*	*Kartri*
No	68.21	24.42	55.44	37.65
Yes	49.23	45.08	36.71	58.70

Table G53

Socio-economic characteristics of a *kartri*	Who keeps incomes earned by members of the family (% families combining rural and urban areas)	
	Karta	*Kartri*
Caste and community affiliation of *kartri's* family		
SC, ST and Muslim combined	47.11	40.19
Hindu general castes	47.20	40.28
Level of formal education of *kartri*		
Class V or below	47.02	40.19
Class VI or above	47.86	40.28
***Kartri* working or not**		
No	46.58	39.03
Yes	47.86	42.28

Table G54

Occupational class of *Kartri's* family	Who keeps income (% families)	
	Karta	*Kartri*
Rural and urban areas combined		
Lower	48.81	39.06
Middle	43.48	42.39
Upper	26.59	57.41
Rural areas		
Lower	49.01	38.87
Middle	43.15	43.74
Upper	30.03	61.17
Urban areas		
Lower	42.78	44.54
Middle	44.95	36.47
Upper	22.41	52.85

Table G55

Kartri working or not	Who keeps income (% families)	
	Karta	*Kartri*
Rural		
No	47.21	38.92
Yes	48.02	42.07
Urban		
No	41.04	40.05
Yes	42.12	49.63

Table G56

Characteristics	Who keeps income (% families)			
	Rural		Urban	
	Karta	*Kartri*	*Karta*	*Kartri*
Caste and community affiliation of *kartri's* family				
SC, ST and Muslim combined	47.51	41.27	40.11	46.02
Hindu general castes	47.91	37.20	42.27	36.58
Level of formal education of *kartri*				
Class V or below	47.36	40.02	41.16	43.04
Class VI or above	49.53	40.74	41.24	38.45

Table G57

Why *kartri*	% of *kartris*		
	Rural	Urban	Combined
No idea	2.80	1.58	2.71
Being the 'wife of *karta*'	68.29	63.67	67.94
Looks after running the family	17.87	17.08	17.81
Being 'eldest' or 'senior most' in the family	8.04	6.29	8.06
Principal earner of the family	2.82	6.02	3.06
	3.00	9.38	3.48
Other reasons	0.18	3.36	0.42
Total	100.00	100.00	100.00

Table G58

Why *kartri*	% of *kartri* *			
	Rural		Urban	
	ST + Mu	SC + G	ST + Mu	SC + G
No idea	4.90	1.51	4.60	0.76
Being the 'wife of *karta*'	60.35	73.15	62.00	64.12
Looks after running the family	28.37	11.46	17.14	17.06
Being 'eldest' or 'seniormost'	5.75	9.44	11.20	7.50
Principal earner and other reasons	0.63	4.44	5.06	10.56
Total	100.00	100.00	100.00	100.00

Note: * + = and; G = Other non-SC Hindu castes.

Table G59

Why *kartri*	% of *kartris*					
	Rural		Urban		Combined	
	Class V or less	Class VI or above	Class V or less	Class VI or above	Class V or less	Class VI or above
No idea	2.74	3.27	2.02	0.83	2.70	2.78
Being the 'wife of *karta*'	66.92	78.15	58.18	72.75	66.44	77.06
Looks after running the family	18.47	13.56	16.90	17.38	18.38	14.33
Being 'eldest' or 'senior-most'	8.48	4.86	8.83	7.41	8.50	5.37
Principal earner and other reasons	3.39	0.16	14.07	1.63	3.98	0.46
Total	100.00	100.00	100.00	100.00	100.00	100.00

Table G60

Why *kartri*	% of *kartris* in each occupational class	
	Lower	Middle and upper
No idea	2.05	4.77
Being the 'wife of *karta*'	70.12	61.14
Being 'eldest' or 'seniormost'	4.99	19.77
Principal earner and other reasons	22.84	14.32
Total	100.00	100.00

Table G61

	% of *kartris* by occupational class			
	Rural		Urban	
Why *kartri*	Lower	Middle and upper	Lower	Middle and upper
No idea	2.06	5.65	1.88	1.43
Being the 'wife of *karta*'	70.36	60.36	62.85	64.07
Being 'eldest' or 'seniormost'	5.01	19.68	4.40	20.15
Principal earner and other reasons	22.57	14.31	30.81	14.35
Total	100.00	100.00	100.00	100.00

Table G62

Importance of opinion of the females in the family compared to that of the males	% of *kartris*		
	Rural	Urban	Combined
More	3.62	7.87	3.94
Equal	40.48	48.99	41.12
Less	28.26	18.37	27.51
Negligible	15.87	11.44	15.54
None	5.71	5.60	5.70
No idea or ambiguous response	6.06	7.73	6.19
Total	100.00	100.00	100.00

Table G63

Socio-economic characteristics of *kartri*	% of *kartris* reporting importance of women's opinion as same or higher than men's		
	Rural	Urban	Combined
Caste and community			
Muslim	29.45	59.20	31.70
ST	40.82	35.11	40.39
SC	45.42	44.67	45.36
Hindu general castes	54.98	65.36	55.76
Level of formal school education			
None	39.97	46.76	40.48
Class V or below	47.79	70.50	49.50
Class VI or above	58.86	62.50	59.13
Occupational class			
Lower	41.34	45.44	41.65
Middle	56.19	61.52	56.59
Upper	33.50	65.62	35.93

Table G64.1

Who takes a decision in the family?	% of *kartris*: non-economic issues								
	Children's education			Marriage			Family rituals		
	Rural (R)	Urban (U)	R + U	Rural (R)	Urban (U)	R + U	Rural (R)	Urban (U)	R + U
Can't say due to non-occurrence of the event recently	20.13	11.05	19.44	25.76	17.31	25.12	16.57	13.82	16.36
Kartri	12.10	12.81	12.16	7.92	8.46	7.96	8.35	11.47	8.59
Any other female member	2.53	0.30	2.36	0.79	0.51	0.77	10.82	1.63	10.13
Karta	27.13	37.75	27.93	22.72	32.40	23.45	20.51	27.55	21.04
Any other male member	8.48	3.28	8.09	6.46	4.67	6.33	5.29	4.53	5.23
All together	26.40	27.74	26.50	32.87	25.36	32.30	36.34	29.04	35.79
Others	3.23	7.07	3.52	3.48	11.29	4.07	2.12	11.91	2.86
Total	100.00	100.00	100.00	100.00	100.00	100.00	100.00	100.00	100.00

Table G64.2

Who takes a decision in the family?	% of *kartris*: economic issues								
	Agricultural activity			Land sale/purchase			Economic issues		
	Rural (R)	Urban (U)	R + U	Rural (R)	Urban (U)	R + U	Rural (R)	Urban (U)	R + U
Can't say due to non-occurrence of the event recently	23.91	43.58	25.40	36.02	45.80	36.76	11.43	11.00	11.40
Kartri	5.46	2.93	5.27	4.38	3.69	4.33	9.76	13.63	10.05
Any other female member	1.00	0.00	0.92	0.28	0.00	0.26	0.78	0.32	0.75
Karta	34.97	20.42	33.87	35.51	18.59	34.23	40.96	47.92	41.49
Any other male member	16.74	3.28	15.72	8.63	4.14	8.29	12.58	5.85	12.07
All together	14.40	10.99	14.14	12.36	9.28	12.13	20.89	17.10	20.60
Others	3.52	18.80	4.68	2.82	18.50	4.00	3.60	4.18	3.64
Total	100.00	100.00	100.00	100.00	100.00	100.00	100.00	100.00	100.00

Table G65

| Area of decision making | % of *kartris* reporting (rural and urban combined) authority of | | | | |
	Kartri and other females	*Karta* and other males	All involved	Others	Total
Non-economic					
Children's education	18.02	44.71	32.90	4.37	100.00
Marriage	11.66	39.77	43.14	5.43	100.00
Family ritual	22.38	31.41	42.79	3.42	100.00
Economic					
Sale and purchase of land	7.26	67.24	19.18	6.32	100.00
Agricultural activities	8.29	66.47	18.96	6.28	100.00
Economic matters in general	12.19	60.45	23.25	4.11	100.00

Table G66

| Caste and community affiliation | % of *kartris* suffered from 'teasing' | | |
	Rural	Urban	Combined
SC	12.02	14.70	12.22
ST	13.43	16.45	13.66
Muslim	27.90	33.26	28.30
Hindu general castes	11.36	16.07	11.90
Total	15.29	19.74	15.63

Table G67

| Age (in years) of a *kartri* | % of *kartris* | | |
	Rural	Urban	Combined
<30	19.81	27.17	20.37
0≤	13.32	16.60	13.57

Table G68

| Caste, class, formal education of a *kartri* | % of *kartris* visiting a PHC or a hospital | |
	Rural	Urban
Caste/community categories		
SC	75.40	94.12
ST	84.49	80.18
Muslim	87.53	87.33
Hindu general castes	74.49	81.12
Occupational class		
Lower	80.33	93.20
Middle	74.60	82.32
Upper	79.08	82.05
Formal education		
None	79.68	96.97
Class V or below	76.52	74.83
Class VI or above	81.88	77.70

Table G69

Public institutions (PI)	% of rural *kartris* having at least some form of contact with PI
Gram panchayat (GP)	82.49
Mahila samiti (MS)	77.57
Krishak sabha (KS)	73.01
Any other organization including library, club, etc. (or)	72.88
All combined	87.04

Table G70

| Caste and community affiliation | % of *kartris* in rural areas having contact with | | | | |
	GP	MS	KS	Or	Combined
SC	77.13	72.53	67.70	62.25	79.76
ST	89.57	78.81	73.20	82.22	93.58
Muslim	86.93	87.58	82.72	78.42	90.88
Other Hindu general castes	81.23	75.65	72.26	75.66	88.81

Table G71

| Level of formal education | % of *kartris* having contact with | | | | |
	GP	MS	KS	Or	Combined
None	80.08	74.68	69.04	70.61	84.86
Class V or less	87.47	85.24	82.78	77.89	91.01
Class VI or above	85.63	78.08	75.13	75.21	90.86

Table G72

| Voting decision | % of *kartris* | | |
	Rural	Urban	Combined
One's own	26.13	52.47	28.28
Discussion with husband/son	64.04	41.35	62.32
Others in the village	9.66	6.18	9.40
Total	100.00	100.00	100.00

Table G73

| Socio-economic characteristics | % of *kartris*: rural and urban combined* | | |
| | | Discusses with | |
	Self-reliant	Husband/son	Others in the village
Occupational class			
Lower	25.71 (35.45)	63.51	10.78
Middle	32.57 (57.82)	61.89	5.54
Upper	40.79 (71.87)	47.35	11.86
Caste and community			
SC	30.90 (37.45)	58.46	
ST	20.09 (46.82)	61.90	10.64
Muslim	21.47 (43.61)	74.54	18.01
Hindu non-SC Castes	33.92 (64.59)	59.14	3.99
Level of formal education			
None	24.62 (39.09)	64.16	11.22
Class V or less	32.01 (64.72)	61.55	6.44
Class VI or above	37.56 (62.45)	56.25	6.19

Note: * % with urban *kartris* in brackets.

Table G74

Expected age of daughter's marriage (in years)	% of *kartris*: rural and urban combined
Less than 18	31.22
18–22	56.43
More than 22	12.35
Total	100.00

Table G75

Whether dowry should be taken at son's marriage	% of *kartris*		
	Rural	Urban	Combined
No	62.29	52.90	61.58
May be taken as a token for 'give and take'	37.71	34.45	37.47
Yes	0.00	12.65	0.95
Total	100.00	100.00	100.00

Table G76

	% of *kartris*	
Frequency	Performance of *brata*: rural and urban combined	Lighting a lamp in front of *Tulsi* plant
None at all	28.24	23.94
Very rarely	10.58	10.63
Time-to-time or as and when required	21.16	19.79
Often/regularly	40.02	45.64
Total	100.00	100.00

Table G77

	% of *kartris*					
	Women should be more tolerant and patient			Women should first think of others in the family than about herself		
Response	Rural	Urban	Combined	Rural	Urban	Combined
Disagreed	18.13	10.15	17.53	18.84	6.18	17.88
Agreed	81.87	89.85	82.47	81.16	93.82	82.12
Total	100.00	100.00	100.00	100.00	100.00	100.00

Table G78

Social characteristics of *kartri*	% of rural *kartris* reporting expected age of daughter's marriage			
	Less than 18	18–22	More than 22	Total
Caste and community affiliation				
SC	37.57	59.39	3.04	100.00
ST	31.12	63.39	5.49	100.00
Muslim	47.91	49.50	2.59	100.00
Hindu general castes	17.42	68.94	13.64	100.00
Level of formal school education				
None	40.29	55.50	4.21	100.00
Class V or below	20.29	69.10	10.61	100.00
Class VI or above	17.12	72.98	9.90	100.00

Table G79

Social characteristics of *kartri*	% of *kartri* performing a *brata*	
	None	Regularly/often
Level of formal education		
None	36.24	29.74
Class V or below	16.54	56.14
Class VI or above	16.54	50.41
Caste and community affiliation		
SC	28.28	38.82
ST	49.72	19.33
Muslim	41.54	17.36
Hindu general castes	8.83	64.86

Table G80

Possibilities of legal redressal of women's grievances or any act to that effect	% of *kartris* aware			% of *kartris* aware by level of formal education		
	Rural	Urban	Combined	None	Class V or below	Class VI or above
Same wage for same work	52.98	43.89	52.29	49.59	55.19	59.57
Physical and mental torture	27.80	39.79	28.71	20.05	40.44	48.15
Dowry	26.09	48.70	27.80	18.12	39.62	51.63
Age at marriage	22.22	44.43	23.90	14.68	35.63	45.84
Divorce/separation	23.32	44.43	24.91	16.63	37.43	41.41
Maintenance	35.56	44.26	36.22	31.97	40.91	47.47
Hindu marriage act	5.63	17.95	6.56	2.54	12.67	14.47
Special marriage act	3.24	13.35	4.00	1.91	5.47	10.96
Maternity benefits	1.09	12.86	1.98	0.22	3.66	7.05
Succession/inheritance of property	15.27	27.85	16.22	12.94	21.01	22.97
Representation in elections	1.17	11.95	1.98	0.35	3.70	6.48

Table G81

Possibilities of legal redressal of women's grievances or any Act to that effect	% of *kartris* aware by caste/community affiliation				% of *kartris* aware by occupational class		
	SC	ST	Muslim	General	Upper	Middle	Lower
Same wage for same work	57.59	52.37	41.66	53.43	56.26	50.79	52.60
Physical and mental torture	19.27	34.12	18.17	43.06	44.96	39.92	24.98
Dowry	16.30	28.95	23.78	42.49	52.81	40.96	23.25
Age at marriage	10.89	28.95	15.71	40.85	45.73	40.46	18.45
Divorce/separation	12.66	31.33	20.06	38.06	38.56	41.02	19.85
Maintenance	27.94	51.20	30.16	42.98	34.13	43.60	34.15
Hindu marriage act	2.44	5.22	2.15	14.76	15.63	15.14	3.81
Special marriage act	3.95	2.05	1.26	6.96	13.97	7.22	2.78
Maternity benefits	0.32	0.00	0.25	6.06	11.87	5.53	0.66
Succession/inheritance of property	10.56	19.79	11.71	23.44	23.35	21.02	14.61
Representation in election	0.47	0.00	0.77	5.57	11.60	5.35	0.72

Policy Recommendations

Demography

- High population density and growing urbanization usually give rise to a host of problems that have adverse consequences for the everyday life of women. Provision of basic amenities, such as water supply, sanitation and affordable shelter, should be a priority concern for civic authorities. Special schemes need to be drawn up for constructing *sulabh* toilets for women in downtown areas and marketplaces of cities and small towns. A safe and crime-free neighbourhood is necessary so that women's mobility and sense of security are not compromised.

- Older women (aged 60 and above) constitute a vulnerable segment of society, who are growing in number with an enhanced expectation of life. We require a reliable database for this group so that their need for economic sustenence and medical care can be properly assessed and addressed.

- For the substantial proportion of older women who are widows, a more detailed enumeration of female-headed households for compiling information on households headed by widows is necessary. Provision for asset-less widows and female-headed/widow-headed households in women-oriented programmes and projects needs to be made. Collection of information on trends in widow remarriage to assess social change favouring women is essential.

- A more determined campaign has to be mounted against the rampant abuse of medical techniques catering to pre-birth sex-selection and consequent female foeticide. This campaign has to be multi-pronged and it has to percolate to the grassroots level—beginning with movements for awareness building and more stringent law enforcement

- West Bengal has consistently had lower levels of infant and child mortality as compared to national averages. It should be possible to identify clusters of high IMR (infant mortality rate) locations in the districts of West Bengal. Certain ameliorative steps like spreading health awareness at the household level and strengthening antenatal, natal and post-natal care delivery systems at the village level should be taken. Close attention must also be paid to the observed rural–urban disparity in infant mortality levels.

- Recent research has drawn attention to a marked gender gap in under-five mortality, particularly in urban localities. Now that it is possible to identify districts where mortality rates for under-five girls exceed those for their male counterparts, area-specific policy interventions are called for. As compared to the rural population, urban residents are ordinarily expected to be less affected by gender bias and enjoy better access to facilities that promote child health and child survival. Therefore, the factors that give rise to gendered child mortality patterns will have to be probed first so that steps can be taken to meet the specific needs of specific urban pockets.

- Vigorous awareness generation and education programmes need to be designed and propagated in districts/blocks that systematically report marriages of girls at ages below the legal minimum.

- Reproductive rights for women are now seen as an integral part of demographic discourse. Policies and programmes concerned with women's well-being must strive to ensure that physical relationships experienced by women are free of coercion and risk of disease; childbirth for women needs to be medically safe and a consequence of their voluntary decision; and women have access to informed options in matters relating to reproduction.

- The importance of female literacy and education cannot be over-emphasized, particularly in view of its contribution towards lower fertility rates, better childbirth and child health practices and better survival prospects for girl children, as brought out in many studies. There are several dimensions to female literacy and education for which appropriate task forces and teaching aids have to be developed. These include literacy and education programmes for rural women in general and for adult women who are illiterate, special educational programmes for tribal women and scheduled caste women living in backward areas, continuing education programmes for preserving the gains made by neo-literate women, and vocational education programmes for women's skill building that leads to opportunities for income generation.

Health and Nutrition

- The paucity of quantitative data relating to certain aspects of women's health, particularly nutritional status of women is a cause for serious concern in West Bengal. Concerted efforts need to be made to compile gender-differentiated data on incidence of malnutrition with as much spatial disaggregation as practicable. Such data at the block level, for example, can lead to more focussed policy intervention for dealing with malnutrition—a major cause behind common but preventable health risks affecting women and children, such as iron deficiency, vitamin-A deficiency, low BMI (body mass index) status and complications arising in connection with childbirth.

- A general rise in food availability may not necessarily be translated into proper food intake by women and children. If we have the required background data, adequate arrangements can be made to supply nutritional supplements to under-nourished women and children in poverty-prone localities. This important step should help to curb widespread protein-energy malnutrition observed among women, as also the prevalence of low birth-weight among the newborn.

- As in other areas, female sterilization continues to be the most prominent 'modern' family method in West Bengal. Here, male sterilization as a percentage of 'modern'

methods appears to be less than 3 per cent and according to the National Family Health Survey-2, use of male condoms accounts for only about 6 per cent. This serious anomaly has to be addressed on a priority basis through assiduous awareness and motivational campaigns so that male-centred contraception can be popularized and adopted on a much larger scale throughout the state.

- Awareness campaigns are also needed to prevent experimental use of risky modes of female contraception in the form of injectibles and implants.

- The existing network of pre-natal, natal and post-natal care have to be extended and strengthened, both in terms of institutional and home-based care, to reach out to a much larger segment of women of childbearing age.

- Available data suggest that between 11–14 per cent of all maternal deaths in rural India during 1990–94 could be attributed to complications arising from induced abortion. Though such data are not easily available for West Bengal, there is no doubt that large numbers of women are compelled to take recourse to unsafe abortion and this obviously poses a grave health hazard for them. As our study brings out, government health centres in West Bengal are plagued by a great dearth of medical personnel trained in MTP and medical apparatus needed for MTP. This state of affairs requires a detailed survey of existing facilities for MTP so that these can be modernized and extended as far as possible and women in need of it do not have to resort to unsafe procedures. Awareness campaigns at the grassroots level is also necessary to make women aware of the facilities available in government hospitals related to MTP.

- We need to expand our access to reliable data on weight and height of newborn babies. It appears that compared to other states, there is a dearth of portable equipment which the Anganwadi workers can use for this purpose in West Bengal. It should not be difficult to at least substantially remedy this shortfall.

- In West Bengal, less than half of the children aged 12–23 months appear to be fully immunized. Therefore, the drive for child immunization has to be vigorously sustained till full coverage is achieved in urban as well as rural areas.

- Women in West Bengal are found to lack awareness about reproductive tract infection and sexually transmitted infection as compared to men. This has to be taken note of and suitable awareness generation programmes have to be devised and implemented.

- Like the rest of the country, West Bengal is also threatened by the spectre of HIV/AIDS, but it has been found that here women lag behind 10 major states in awareness with respect to the disease. This calls for specifically designed schemes for dissemination of HIV/AIDS-related information as well as medical assistance.

School Education

- The gender gap that has persisted in spite of all the changes will have to be addressed as a special social malady. The external obstacles that come in the way of girls and women being educated need committed attention.

- The number of female teachers needs to be increased at the primary school level. The teacher–student ratio has to be looked into.

- Gender sensitization training needs to be given to teachers, whether male or female. Teachers must have proper understanding of the special needs of school children, especially girls who come from poor and deprived families or those who may be physically handicapped.

- Up to elementary level, all girls should have a school which is easily accessible. Wherever such arrangements cannot be made, a hostel should be set up.

- Each school must have safe drinking water and toilets that are clean and hazard-free.

- School uniforms, textbooks and mid-day meals should be made available at the right time. Active cooperation with the women members of the panchayats to be sought. Pro-active NGOs and youth clubs should be made partners of the state government to make school education a success.

- Teachers must liaise with the families of schoolgoing children and village education committees and solicit their cooperation in the children's education.

- Vocational education should be introduced from the post-elementary secondary and higher-secondary stages so that school education is not considered redundant.

- With increasing privatization of education it has become necessary to find ways of mainstreaming students who go to non-formal schools.

- The rising trend of taking and giving of dowry cannot be delinked with the fact that parents are less inclined to invest in a girl child's (especially adolescent girl child's) education and would rather invest in her marriage. Intensive campaigns are necessary to counter this trend in general. Dowry, which was not prevalent even a generation ago among Muslims, is now a deterrent towards educating Muslim girls. Special awareness campaigns also need to be designed to propagate the fact that giving and taking of dowry is not consistent with Islamic culture.

- Muslim girls should be offered special space to retain and broaden their cultural identity.

Higher and Technical Education

- In the fields of non-technical higher education an environment needs to be created where more and more women, in particular, and all persons, in general, are able to translate their educational attainments into income generation. For this, required changes must be made in the syllabi, teaching techniques, extra-curricular orientation courses, and in examination and marking procedures wherever necessary. Vocational courses allied to and complementary to particular subjects may also be designed and offered to this end.

- To increase female enrolment in engineering degree courses, especially in the so-called hardware engineering fields, like mechanical, civil, electrical etc., gender sensitization programmes have to be introduced for prospective employers and for those in senior, decision making positions in administration and management, in offices and factories and for society in general. This should aim to remove existing prejudices, misconceptions and biases which have serious negative impacts on female employability and enrolment in these engineering fields. One such myth is that women are not suitable for studying mechanical engineering because they are unable to handle heavy equipment. The fact is that, even as students, moving heavy machinery is not necessary because there are technical assistants to help in this. In the work field, officers do not move or carry heavy machinery. Besides, much of the work done by mechanical engineers in their work sphere is in the nature of design, sales and technological development. Besides, women are not recruited as mechanical, chemical, electrical or civil engineers because during night shifts they apparently distract the men and also because it involves risks of sexual abuse for the women. These so-called problems are not physical, legal or efficiency problems, but are problems of gender-based conditioning of the psyche and should be removed by gender sensitization programmes.

- Increasing the number of courses offered may help increase female enrolment in technical diploma and certificate courses specially in the industrial training institutes, where female enrolment is very low. In the initial stages, some courses which are traditionally attractive to women may help. Gradually, women may be motivated to join other types of courses as well.

- Dissemination of information regarding the technical courses available and their prospects for women's income generation is necessary because the target students come from low-middle or low socio-economic backgrounds who usually do not have any perception or knowledge of these possibilities. The low female enrolment in ITIs and short-term vocational training courses (STVTs) points towards this need.

- Employment opportunities for women must be increased if women are to be motivated to join the technical courses available. Without employability, enrolment quotas are ineffective in the long run. A two-pronged effort is needed—first, to increase jobs for technically trained women, in which government organizations and undertakings can play an important role; second, to increase self-employment opportunities for technically trained women by making available contemporary inputs, such as land, capital, credit, materials, information, all of which are necessary for self-employment projects. Marketing channels for the products produced by women entrepreneurs need to be effectively worked out.

- Currently, the number of women's hostels for polytechnics and ITIs are reasonably sufficient to meet the demand. But as enrolment increases, the need for more training institutes and polytechnics, both co-educational and for women only, will arise and so in anticipation of this fast-changing situation, we need to set up more hostels for women.

- Open and distance education may play an effective role in promoting higher and technical education for women because of its flexibility with regard to location, timing and content. For this, the courses must be designed and run keeping in mind the particular needs, constraints and possibilities of prospective women students in area-specific, age-specific and class-specific fashion, as far as possible.

- As subsidies are reduced or removed from higher education and professional courses, and capitation fees of different hues and shades become the norm, middle class families may find it increasingly difficult to provide higher education to all their children. Given patriarchal norms, a family's need to prioritize may lead to many deserving girl students dropping out from higher education and professional fields in favour of their even less-deserving brothers. Awareness campaigns must be stepped up to remove gender bias from our individual, familial and social psyche so that a family's resource allocation on children's higher education is based on their interests, aptitude and ability, and not on the basis of their gender.

- In these days of globalization and market economy, where there is an increasing tendency to consider education only as 'investment' in human resources for purposes of manpower planning and where curricula are being revised to include only that which 'sells' in the market, it is critically important that we do not lose sight of the character of education as a holistic process of personality building, development of critical faculties, awareness generation, and sensitization with respect to inequities that prevail in society, be it of class, caste, tribe, religion or gender. So, when designing curricula and teaching approaches, along with income generation prospects, this broader and more fundamental role of education must be kept in view. Otherwise, an educational system may evolve which will certainly not help in generating a just and equal society with respect to gender or otherwise.

Economic Empowerment

- Women in the civil services show a very low rate of participation in West Bengal compared to other states. To encourage more participation of women in this sector, proper tutorial centres to guide students for the civil services examinations need to be set up in the state, with residential facilities in some of these.

- A rise of earning middle class women has been registered over the last few years, but this rise has been very small. The rise has been only 1 per cent between 1995 and 1999. This does not corroborate the rise in educational attainment of women in the state and hints at the increasing trend of educated unemployed women.

Therefore, a baseline survey needs to be conducted to enumerate the reasons for unemployment of educated middle class women and policy measures taken accordingly.

- Keeping in mind the displacement of female labour in agriculture, opportunities for off-farm agricultural employment need to be created.

- Stereotyping and gender-based occupational segregation need to be addressed. There is an urgent need to promote occupational diversification in order to avoid excess supply of the same products. Training for new jobs and skill attainment need to be organized for women.

- For small manufacturers and home-based workers, access to easy credit through development of micro-finance groups needs to be organized. There should not be any problem at the policy level of providing training as well as giving loans through micro-finance groups to the same woman so that she may convert the training into reality. Besides, a proper method of enlisting BPL (below-poverty-line) population must be developed so that women who need it most are not deprived of the opportunities of credit etc.

- The male–female wage disparity for equal amount of work should be removed immediately through legislation, and non-implementation of equal wage rates should be penalized.

Political Participation

- Awareness programmes on equal rights of men and women, on existing provisions in the law and the Constitution reinforcing such rights should be continuous and a lot more extensive and should address both men and women.

- Sensitization of leading cadres of all political parties to share household chores with their wives, mothers and sisters, so that the latter may play a more active part in economic, social and political life of the country, should be advocated.

- An increase in participation of women in all decision making bodies of the state government, including the West Bengal State Planning Board needs to be advocated, and lobbying for including women cadres in decision making, policy making and implementing bodies at all levels should be continually carried on.

- Manifold extension of support systems such as crèches and *balwadis*, mid-day meals, etc., for children of all working mothers in rural and urban areas, including the elected members of panchayats and municipalities should take place.

- The State Women's Commission should take an initiative in making concrete recommendations to remove all traces of discrimination in the criminal and civil laws of the country that is in violation of CEDAW, the UN Charter of Human Rights or the Charter of Child Rights, to the state government, the central government as well as the National Commission for Women.

- Every political party which claims to support the 81st Constitution Amendment Bill on one-third representation of women in the Lok Sabha and the state Vidhan Sabhas should be asked to issue a whip to their MPs to support the Bill.

- More effective campaigns against child marriages and necessary amendments in the preventive laws need to be carried out.

- The programme of action adopted at the Fourth UN International Women's Conference at Beijing should be effectively implemented.

Law and Violence

- Amendments in existing laws to be carried out on the basis of recent Supreme Court judgements, which apart from addressing discriminations also ensures less harassment for the victims including reducing the delay in removing wrongs.

- Awareness raising campaigns need to be intensified regarding the different forms of violence practised against women in everyday life, and the police and bureaucracy need to be continually sensitized regarding handling of crimes committed against women.

- Codification of various personal laws on the basis of Declaration of Human Rights, 1948, and other international covenants discussed in this status report needs to be done.

- A network of counselling centres should be established.

- Amendment to different laws need to be carried out with a view to bring 50 per cent women into various state committees as a process of empowerment of women.

- Irretrievable breakdown of marriage should be made a ground for divorce and both parents to be considered natural guardians.

- Testamentary successions should in all cases make a provision for maintenance of the wife.

- Right to maintenance for Christian women to be advocated.

- Punishment for an offence under Section 498A should be raised up to 10 years and the fine determined accordingly. Section 354 IPC to be made non-bailable, non-compoundable and the quantum of punishment be raised up to 10 years or fine according to the gravity of the offence.

- Age of consent in case of rape be increased to 18 years and age of repudiation of marriage be increased to above 18 years.

- Children born through the use of reproductive process adopted in many modern expert laboratories these days should be known by their mothers. A suitable law is immediately needed to this effect.

- To look after the interests of disabled women, it is recommended that representatives of both NCW and SCW should be included in the Central Coordination Committee and the State Coordination Committee set up to protect the rights and opportunities of persons with disabilities.

- There is an urgent need to set up more drop-in centres, short-stay homes and day-care centres for adolescent girls, in particular, and women in distress, in general. These may be set up by the government or the State Women's Commission in collaboration with NGOs and voluntary organizations, especially in the suburban towns of West Bengal apart from Kolkata.

- Compulsory registration of marriages should become a reality.

- Special benches and fast-track courts need to be instituted for speedy redressal of crimes against women.

Culture

- Special publication programmes for women writers, special encouragement to women filmmakers and special awards for women theatre persons and directors need to

be instituted. Prizes may also be instituted for themes and content dealing with gender issues.

- There should be a mechanism to ensure parity in the emoluments received by men and women artists.

- Festivals, exhibitions, seminars and discussions to highlight the contribution of women artists should be organized with direct or indirect initiative of the state government.

- Programmes of vocational training in visual arts, music, dance, editing, film production and short courses in the audiovisual media should be introduced at the school level to enable those girl students with aptitude to avail themselves of these.

- Audiovisual literacy courses should be organized to enable the public to look more critically at the ways in which women are portrayed in the media.

- Appropriate authorities should evolve an efficient and sensitive mechanism to prevent texts and images that are derogatory to women from flooding the market.

- Documentary films, poster exhibitions and informative leaflets should be produced by the government in consultation with experts to raise public awareness on gender issues. Such material should be accessible not only to the urban middle class but to neo-literates from the poorer sections, in rural and urban areas.

- Training should be given to women rural artists to upgrade their skills and market their products and they should be provided with accessories like dress, musical instruments and free performing space to the extent possible.

- There should be a sustained campaign, directly and indirectly, by the government to discourage neglect of the girl child, prosecution of witches, oral *talaq*, dowry etc., at a massive scale.

- State commissions should create opportunities for interaction with members of the Censor Board to ensure that films uphold the dignity of women. The Censor Board needs to be made aware of the implication of the depiction of certain images on issues like violence on women.

- Steps should be seriously initiated to curb both the illegal and 'legal' screening of 'A' films which are pornographic in nature. Even posters for such films, which are quite offensive, should be banned.

- Gender awareness or sensitization workshops should be conducted by the State Commission for Women for journalists in the print and electronic media.

- The State Women's Commission should demand a closer interaction with the framers of the syllabi for Madhyamik and Uccha Madhyamik Examinations. Serious problems exist in educational materials which need to be addressed. The Commission could also organize workshops for implementing changes in syllabi at the university level.

Tribal Women

- In all districts/blocks of the state and especially in districts/blocks with a relatively high share of scheduled tribes in the population, adequate databases need to be built that throw light on the socio-economic condition of women from various tribal communities. The same applies to the relatively backward sections among scheduled caste communities.

- Setting up more schools for girls in tribal areas is urgently recommended. The percentage of such schools with hostel facilities also need to go up substantially.

- Setting up of crèches with pre-school education facilities in tribal villages is absolutely necessary. Children can be looked after in community crèches in which the elderly people of the villages can be roped in as babysitters.

- Rising cases of witch-hunt must be dealt with on a priority basis. Witch cult is rooted in the tribal ethical structure which deprives women a share in the magico-religious knowledge. It is used to establish male control over women. The police must be sensitized to timely intervene in cases of witch-hunt.

- Providing basic health facilities to tribal women in West Bengal craves immediate attention. Implementing ICDS projects in tribal areas may help the situation. Lack of basic health facilities renders the tribal society helpless. In the face of a disease, where prevention and cure is not easily available, superstition takes over and women are accused of being witches and held responsible for any death in the community.

- Rapid electrification of tribal areas and building proper roads should be a priority.

- Development processes need to be women-sensitive. Involving women in planning is essential. For this, village-level institutions such as panchayats and Forest Protection Committees need to be gender-friendly.

- Strong taskforces under district magistrates need to be organized to monitor the proper implementation of government schemes for tribals. Involving local groups and NGOs in such taskforces is necessary. It should constantly monitor development activities for tribals, and members of these taskforces need to be properly sensitized as well.

- The *benami* and illegal sale of ancestral lands by tribals of the plains to non-tribals make them landless and even more wretched. A strong taskforce under district magistrates should monitor this practice to end it.

Select Bibliography

General

Reports (English)

Gopalan, Sarala, *Towards Equality: The Unfinished Agenda. The Status of Women in India 2000*, NCW Publication, New Delhi, 2002.

Human Development Report. UNDP, 1995.

Human Development Report: India, 2002. Planning Commission, 2002.

Men and Women in India: 2000. CSO, 2000.

National Perspective Plan for Women (1988–2000).

Selected Socio-Economic Statistics, CSO, 1998.

Shram Shakti. Report of the National Commission on Self-Employed Women and Women in the Informal Sector, New Delhi, 1988.

Status of Women in Maharashtra: A Situational Analysis 1981–95. Maharashtra State Commission for Women, Mumbai, 1997.

Towards Equality. Report of the Committee on Status of Women in India. New Delhi, 1974.

Women in India: A Statistical Profile—1997. Department of Women and Child Development, Government of India, 1997.

Books (English)

Agarwal, Bina, *A Field of One's Own: Gender and Land Rights in South Asia.* Cambridge University Press, New Delhi, 1994.

Bagchi, Jasodhara (ed.), 1995. *Indian Women: Myth and Reality.* Sangam Books, Hyderabad, 1995.

Basu, Aparna, 'Women's History in India: An Historiographical Survey', in Karen Offen (ed.), *Writing Women's History: International Perspectives*, Macmillan, London, 1991.

Dasgupta, Kalpana (ed.), *Women on the Indian Scene, an Annotated Bibliography.* Abhinav, New Delhi, 1976.

Desai, Neera, *Women in Modern India.* Vora and Co, Bombay, 1957.

Forbes, Geraldine. *Women in Modern India.* Cambridge University Press, New Delhi, 1998.

Jain, Devaki, *Indian Women.* Publications Division, Ministry of Information and Broadcasting, New Delhi, 1975.

Kumar, Radha, *The History of Doing.* Kali for Women, New Delhi, 1993.

Menon-Sen, Kalyani and A.K. Shiva Kumar, *Women in India: How Free? How Equal?* India Office, United Nations, 2001.

Nanda, B.R., *Indian Women: From Purdah to Modernity.* Vikash Publishing House, New Delhi, 1976.

Ray, Bharati and Aparna Basu, *From Independence towards Freedom: Indian Women since 1947.* Oxford University Press, New Delhi, 1999.

Saraswati, Raju, et al., *Atlas on Men and Women in India.* Kali for Women, New Delhi, 1999.

Sen, Gita and Caren Grown, *Development, Crises and Alternate Visions: Third World Women's Perspectives.* DAWN, 1985.

Women in India: A Bibliography. Nehru Memorial Museum and Library, New Delhi, 2001.

Directories and Reports (English)

20 Years of ICDS in West Bengal, 1975–95. Ministry of Health, Government of West Bengal.

Bagchi, Jasodhara (ed.), *Calcutta for Women: Organizations Working for Women within Municipal Calcutta.* School of Women's Studies, Jadavpur University, Kolkata, 1990.

List of Juvenile Homes and Voluntary Organizations, Department of Social Welfare, Government of West Bengal.

Support Services to Counter Violence against Women in West Bengal: A Resource Directory. Sanhita and Unifem, Kolkata, 2002.

Journal Articles (English)

Nair, Janaki, 'Reconstructing and Recasting the History of Women in India', *Journal of Women's History*, 3 (1), Spring, 1991.

Sen, Amartya, 'Many Faces of Gender Inequality', *Frontline*, 27 October–9 November, Chennai, 2001.

Demography

Books (English)

Agnihotri, S.B., *Sex Ratio Patterns in the Indian Population: A Fresh Exploration.* Sage Publications, New Delhi, 2000.

Basu, Alaka Malwade, *Culture, Status of Women and Demographic Behaviour*. Clarendon Press, Oxford, 1978.

Krishnaraj, Maithreyi, et al. (eds), *Gender, Population and Development*. Oxford University Press, New Delhi, 1998.

Mazumdar, Vina and N. Krishnaji (eds), *Enduring Conundrums: India's Sex Ratio, Essays in Honour of Asok Mitra*. Rainbow Publications, New Delhi, 2001.

Miller, Barbara, *The Endangered Sex*. Cornell University Press, Ithaca, 1981.

Mitra, Asok, *Implications of India's Declining Sex Ratio*. ICSSR Programme of Women's Studies, New Delhi, 1979.

Murthy, Mamata, et al. 'Mortality, Fertility and Gender Bias in India', in Jean Drèze and Amartya Sen (eds), *Indian Development: Selected Regional Perspectives*, Oxford University Press, New Delhi, 1996.

National Population Policy: Perspectives from the Women's Movement. CWDS, 1997.

Presser, Harriet B. and Gita Sen (eds), *Women's Empowerment and Demographic Process: Moving Beyond Cairo*. Oxford University Press, New Delhi, 2000.

Timaeus, Ian, *Principles of Population and Development: With Illustration from Asia and Africa*. Oxford University Press, Oxford, 1957.

Uberoi, Patricia, *Family, Kinship and Marriage in India*. Oxford University Press, New Delhi, 1993.

Periodicals/Journals (English)

Bhat, P.N. Mari, 'On the Trail of Missing Indian Females', Parts I and II, *Economic and Political Weekly*, 21 and 28 December 2002.

Guilmoto, Christopher and S. Irudaya Rajan, 'District Level Estimates of Fertility from India's 2001 Census', *Economic and Political Weekly*, 16 February 2002.

Kynch, Jocelyn and Amartya Sen, 'Indian Women: Well-being and Survival', *Cambridge Journal of Economics*, 7 (3–4), 1983.

Rajan, S. Irudaya and P. Mohanachandran, 'Infant and Child Mortality Estimates for Scheduled Castes and Scheduled Tribes, based on the 1991 Census', *Economic and Political Weekly*, 33 (19), 2001.

Sen, Amartya and Sunil Sengupta, 'Malnutrition of Rural Children and the Sex Bias', *Economic and Political Weekly*, 19, Annual No., 1983.

Visaria, Pravin. 'Demographic Aspects of Development', in *Indian Journal of Social Science*, 6 (3), 1993.

'Women and Ageing', Special Issue, *Economic and Political Weekly*, 30 October 1999.

'Demographic Change and Family Health', Special Issue, *Economic and Political Weekly*, October 16–22/23–29, 1999.

'India's Population: Heading towards a Billion', Special Issue, *Economic and Political Weekly*, 17–24 December 1994.

Health

Books (English)

Anita, N.H. (ed.), *People's Health in People's Hands*. The Foundation for Research in Community Health, Bombay, 1993.

Banerjee, D., *Family Planning in India: A Critique and A Perspective*. People's Publishing House, New Delhi, 1971.

Baru, Rama V., *Private Health Care in India: Social Characteristics and Trends*. Sage Publications, New Delhi, 1998.

Batliwala, S., 'Women in Poverty: The Energy, Health and Nutrition Syndrome', in Devaki Jain and Nirmala Banerjee (eds), *Tyranny of the Household: Investigative Essays on Women's Work*, New Delhi, Shakti Books, 1985.

Correa, Sonia, *Population and Reproductive Rights: Feminist Perspectives from the South*. Kali for Women, New Delhi, 1994.

Dasgupta, Monica (ed.), *Women's Health in India: Risk and Vulnerability*. Oxford University Press, New Delhi, 1998.

Davar, Bhargavi V., *Mental Health of Indian Women: A Feminist Agenda*. Sage Publications, New Delhi, 1999.

Desai, A.R., *Urban Family and Family Planning in India*. Popular Prakashan, Bombay, 1980.

Devi, Laxmi (ed.), *Women as Human Resources: Health, Nutrition, Education and Programmes*. Anmol, New Delhi, 1998.

Ginsberg, D. Faye and Rayna Rapp (eds), *Conceiving in the New World Order*. University of California Press, Berkeley, 1995.

Gittel John, Joel, et al., *Listening to Women Talk about their Health: Issues and Evidence from India*. Har-Anand, New Delhi, 1994.

Gupta, Jyotsna Agnihotri, *New Reproductive Technologies: Women's Health and Autonomy, Freedom or Dependency*. Sage Publications, New Delhi, 2000.

Jejeebhoy, Shirin J., *Women's Education, Autonomy and Reproductive Behaviour: Experience from Developing Countries*. Clarendon Press, New York, 1995.

Mukhopadhyay, Swapna (ed.), *Women's Health, Public Policy and Community Action*. Manohar, New Delhi, 1998.

Mukhopadhyay, Swapna and R. Savithri, *Poverty, Gender and Reproductive Choice: An Analysis of Linkages*. Manohar, New Delhi, 1998.

Nilanjana, *Status of Women and Family Welfare*. Kanishka, New Delhi, 2000.

Oakley, Ann, *Essays on Women, Medicine and Health*. Edinburgh University Press, Edinburgh, 1993.

Partha Sarathy, G. (ed.), *Mother and Child Care*. Har-Anand Publications, New Delhi, 1998.

Reddy, M.M. Krishna, *Health and Family Welfare: Public Policy and People's Participation in India*. Kanishka, New Delhi, 2000.

Seal, Arna, *Negotiating Intimacies: Sexualities, Birth Control and Poor Households*. Stree, Kolkata, 2000.

Book (Bengali)

Bandyopadhyay, Krishna, *Swasther Adhikar Nijer Hathe Nebar Pathey*. School of Women's Studies, Jadavpur University, Kolkata, 1996.

Reports (English)

Bulletin of the Department of Health and Family Welfare. Government of West Bengal, Kolkata, 1986.

Gopalan, Sarala and Mira Siva (eds), *National Profile on Women, Health and Development: A Country Profile—India*. Voluntary Health Association of India and WHO, New Delhi, 2000.

Health on the March, West Bengal 2000–2001. Government of West Bengal, Kolkata, 2001.

Karkal, Malini, *National Family Heath Survey. Revisited from Women's Perspectives*. Women's Studies Research Centre, M.S. University of Baroda, Vadodara, 1999.

NSSO, Morbidity and Utilization of Medical Services, Report No. 364, National Sample Survey Organization, Government of India, New Delhi, 1987.

Report on Development on Health Facilities among Women Belonging to Scheduled Tribe Communities. National Commission for Women, New Delhi, 1996.

Working towards Right to Health and Health Care. CEHAT, Mumbai, 2001.

World Development Report 1993: Investing in Health. Oxford University Press, New York, 1993.

Journals/Magazines (English)

Chatterjee, Biswajit, 'Poverty in West Bengal: What have we learnt?' *Economic and Political Weekly*, 33 (47 and 48): 3003–3014, 1998.

Patel, Tulsi, 'The Sterilization Decisions and Family Structures: Case Study of an Indian Village', *Indian Journal of Sociology*, 23–25 December 1990.

Prakash, Padma, 'Identifying Health Needs of Women', *The Hindu Magazine*, 27 October 1991.

Education

Books (English)

Kumar, Narendra and Chandrima Jai, *Educational Television in India*. Arya Book Depot, New Delhi, 1967.

Loening, Arian, *The Roots of Heaven*. Calcutta, 1990.

Mehta, Madhavi and Maithreyi Krishnaraj, *Survey of Non-Working Women: Post-Graduate Science Degree Holders in Bombay 1979–81*. S.N.D.T. Women's University, Mumbai.

Newman, R.S., *Grassroots Education in India: A Challenge for Policy Makers*. Sterling, New Delhi, 1989.

Nuna, Sheel C., *Women and Development*. National Institute of Educational Planning and Administration, New Delhi, 1990.

Panchamukhi, P.R. (ed.), *Studies in Educational Reform in India. Vols 1– 5*. Bombay Himalaya, Bombay, 1989.

Parikh, S. Kirit (ed.), *India Development Report 1999–2000*. Oxford University Press, New Delhi, 1999.

Public Report on Basic Education in India. Oxford University Press, New Delhi, 1999.

Rao, Sudha V, *Education and Rural Development*. Sage Publications, New Delhi, 1985.

Shukla, P.D., *Towards the New Pattern of Education in India*. Sterling, New Delhi, 1987.

Swaminathan, Mina, *The First Three Years: A Sourcebook on Early Childhood Care and Education*. UNICEF, paris, 1991.

Reports (English)

Annual Report of the Department of Higher Education. Government of West Bengal, Calcutta, 1997.

Annual Report 1998–99. West Bengal District Primary Education Programme, Department of Education, Government of West Bengal.

An Asian Model of Educational Development: Perspectives for 1965–80. UNESCO, Paris, 1966.

A Brief Status Report on Primary Education: Burdwan. West Bengal, 1998.

Bag, Dulal Chandra, *Impact of Education on Some Backward Communities of West Bengal: Study based on West Dinajpur*. OPS Publications, Calcutta, 1984.

Bengal Moslem Education: Advisory Committee Report, 1934.

Chandrakant, L.S., *Technical Education in India Today*. Ministry of Scientific Research and Cultural Affairs, New Delhi, 1963.

Children in South Asia: Securing their Rights. Amnesty International, London, 1998.

Chitnis, Suma, *A Long Way to Go: Report on a Survey of Scheduled Caste High School and College Students in Fifteen States of India*. Indian Council of Social Science Research, Allied Publishers, New Delhi, 1981.

Country Report: Fourth World Conference on Women, Beijing. Department of Women and Child Development, Government of India, 1995.

Education for All: The Indian Scene Widening Horizons. Ministry of Human Resource and Development, Department of Education, New Delhi, 1993.

Education India: The Next Millennium Report (Part III). S.C.E.R.T., New Delhi, 1997.

Education of Girlchild in India: A Factsheet. NCERT, New Delhi, 19.

Educational Statistics at a Glance: 1969–74/75. Ministry of Education, New Delhi.

Educational Statistics Districtwise: 1965–66. Ministry of Education, New Delhi, 1969.

Educational Statistics Districtwise: 1976–77. Department of Education, New Delhi, 1978.

Educational Statistics Districtwise: 1981–82. Department of Education, New Delhi, 1986.

Enrolment Trends in States: 1968–69/1978–79. Education and Social Welfare, Ministry of Education in India, The Author, New Delhi, 1979.

External Evaluation of the Post-Literacy and Continuing Education Programme: North 24 Parganas. Zilla State Level Samity, Government of West Bengal, 1995.

Fifth All-India Education Survey Reports, Vols 1–2. N.C.E.R.T., New Delhi, 1992.

Fourth All-India Education Survey 1978–79. N.C.E.R.T., New Delhi, 1980.

Ghara, T.K., *Critical Analyses of DISE. Bankura District*. West Bengal District Primary Education Programme. Department of Education, Government of West Bengal, 1999–2000.

———, *Critical Analyses of DISE. Birbhum District*. West Bengal District Primary Education Programme, Department of Education, Government of West Bengal, 1999–2000.

———, *Critical Analyses of DISE. Cooch-Behar District*. West Bengal District Primary Education Programme, Department of Education, Government of West Bengal, 1999–2000.

———, *Critical Analyses of DISE. Murshidabad District*. West Bengal District Primary Education Programme, Department of Education, Government of West Bengal, 1999–2000.

———, *Critical Analyses of DISE. South 24 Parganas District*. West Bengal District Primary Education Programme, Department of Education, Government of West Bengal, 1999–2000.

Girl Child: A List of Holdings. School of Women's Studies, Jadavpur University, 1998.

The Girl Child in India: A Data Sheet. SAARC decade of the Girl Child, SAARC Documentation Centre, New Delhi, 1991–2000.

The Girl Child in India: A Data Sheet. SAARC Year of the Girl Child SAARC Documentation Centre, New Delhi, 1990.

Glimpses of Girlhood in India. UNICEF, New Delhi, 1994.

A Handbook of Educational and Allied Statistics. Ministry of Education and Culture, Government of India, New Delhi, 1980.

Human Development Report: 1995, 1996, 1997. UNDP.

The ICDS and other Child Care Programme in India: A Data Sheet. Department of Women and Child Development, Ministry of Human Resource Development, Government of India, New Delhi, 1991.

The Lesser Child: The Girl in India. GOI Department of Women & Child, Ministry of HRD with assistance from UNICEF, New Delhi, 1990.

Literacy Campaign in West Bengal. Directorate of Mass-Education Extension, Government of West Bengal, 8 September 1999.

Literacy Campaign in West Bengal. Directorate of Mass-Education Extension, Government of West Bengal, 8 September 2000.

Minault, Gail, *Secluded Scholars: Women's Education & Muslim Social Reform in Colonial India*. Oxford University Press, New Delhi, 1998.

Mukherjee, R.K., *Field Studies in Sociology of Education*. The Report on West Bengal. NCERT, New Delhi, 1979.

Pashchimbanga Rajya Prathamik Siksha Unnayan Sanstha Annual Report 1996–97. Bikash Bhavan, Calcutta.

Political and Social Mobilization for Education for All: The Indian Experience, Country Paper 29, Second Ministerial Review Meeting. Islamabad, 1997.

Premi, Mahendra Kumar, *Educational Planning in India: Implications of Population Trends*. Sterling Publications, New Delhi, 1972.

Primary Education in India—Development in Practice. A World Bank Publication, Washington, D.C., 1992.

Primary Education in Rural India. Agricultural Economics Research Centre, University of Delhi, Tata McGraw-Hill, New Delhi, 1971.

Primary Education in West Bengal: A Profile. Directorate of School Education, Government of West Bengal, 1995.

Raza, Moonis and Nirmal Malhotra, *Higher Education in India—A Comprehensive Bibliography*. Concept Publishing Company, New Delhi, 1991.

Report of the Education Commission. S.C.E.R.T., Government of West Bengal, 1992.

Report of the Working Group on Elementary Education, Non-Formal Education, Early Childhood Education and Teacher Education for the Nineth Five Year Plan. Ministry of Human Resource & Development, Department of Education, New Delhi, 1996.

SAARC Decade of the Girl Child: Status of Children in West Bengal. Relief and Welfare Department, Government of West Bengal, 1991.

Saldanha, D., *The Area Intrusive Education Project for Human Resource Development: A Rapid Assessment*. Tata Institute of Social Sciences, Mumbai, 1996.

Selected Educational Statistics. Department of Education, Government of India, New Delhi, 1976.

Sixth All-India Education Survey Reports. Vols 1–4. N.C.E.R.T. and National Informatics Centre, New Delhi, 1998.

State Plan of Action for Children: Education. Government of West Bengal, 1993.

State Plan of Action for Universalization of Primary Education in West Bengal. Directorate of School Education, Government of West Bengal, 1994.

The Status of Primary Education in West Bengal. Vols 1–2. I.I.M., Calcutta, 1998.

Thomas, Jean, *World Problems in Education: A Brief Analytical Survey*, UNESCO, Paris, 1975.

Total Literacy Programme: Howrah District. Howrah Zilla Sarbik Parishad, West Bengal, 1992.

Towards Ability. A Survey of Organizations Working on 'Special' Children in Calcutta, North and South 24 Parganas, CINI, Calcutta, 1988.

Tyagi, K.G. (ed.), *Indian Education Index (1947–1978)*. Archan Prakash, New Delhi, 1980.

UNICEF and Education in South Asia: Paper presented to the meeting of the Education Cluster. UNICEF, New York, 1995.

Wazir, Rekha (ed.), *The Gender Gap in Basic Education. NGOs as Change Agents*. Sage Publications, New Delhi, 2000.

West Bengal Commission for Planning of Higher Education Report. Education Department, Government of West Bengal, 1984.

Journals/Periodicals (English)

Bagchi, Amiya Kumar, 'Amartya Kumar Sen and the Human Sciences of Development', *Economic and Political Weekly*, 5 December 1998.

Bhatt, R. Ela. 'Women and the Second Freedom: Convocation Address', *University News*, 37 (30), 26 July, 1999.

Chinara, Benudhar, 'Gender Disparity and Education in Post-Independence India: A Situational Analysis', *University News*, 38 (5), 31 January 2000.

Desai, A.S., 'Women in Higher Education and National Development: Convocation Address', *University News*, 37 (3), 1 March 1999.

Gopalan, Sarala, 'The Empowerment of Women: Convocation Address', *University News*, 34 (13), 25 March 1996.

Indiressan, Jaya, 'Do We Need an Exclusive Women's College: Perceptions in the Indian Context', *University News*, 37 (24), 14 June 1999.

Kulandaiswamy, V.C., 'Women's Studies', *University News*, 37 (49), 6 December 1999.

Kumar, Virendra, 'Management Education for Women', *University News*, 35 (11), 17 March 1997.

Pandya, Rameshwari. 'Higher Education for Girls: Myth and Reality', *University News*, 37 (30), 23 August 1999.

Sharma, P.B., 'Technical Education for the Next Millennium', *University News*, 38 (6), 7 February 2000.

Singh, Nisha, 'Women's Education: Reflection on National Documents', *University News*, 38 (7), 14 February 2000.

Singh, Yashpal and Anju Agarwal, 'Research on Gender based Basics in Education', *University News*, 38 (4), 24 January 2000.

Tripathi, R.S., 'Access of Female Students to Higher Education', *University News*, 35 (19), 12 May 1997.

'Compulsory Primary Education in India', *The Lawyers Collective*, 13, N.H. April 1998.

'Women's Education: Key to National Development', *Social Welfare*, 36 (9), December 1989.

Books (Bengali)

Bethune Vidyalaya Sardhashatabarsher Smarak Grantha: 1849–1999. Bethune Vidyalaya Sardha satabarsha Udjapan Committee, Kolkata, 1999.

Ray, Bharati (ed.), *Shekaler Nari Shiksha Bamabodhini Patrika (1270–1399)*, Women's Studies Research Centre, Calcutta University, 1998.

Reports (Bengali)

Singha Abha, *Kusum Photar Chhora*. Book Club, Calcutta, 1993.

Siksha Darpan, *Siksha Bibhag Samuher Trai-mashik Mukhopatra*. Naba Parjyay, Prathom Varsha, Choturtho Sankhya, February 2000.

———, *Siksha Bibhag Samuher Trai-mashik Mukhopatra*. Naba Parjyay, Dwitiyo Varsha, Pancham Sankhya, May 2000.

———, *Siksha Bibhag Samuher Trai-mashik Mukhopatra*. Naba Parjyay, Dwitiyo Varsha, Tritya Sankhya, September 2000.

Economic Empowerment

Books (English)

Banerjee, Nirmala, *Women Workers in the Unorganized Sector: The Calcutta Experience*. Sangam, Hyderabad, 1985.

———, (ed.), *Indian Women in Changing Industrial Scenario*. Sage Publications, New Delhi, 1991.

Bhatt, Ela, 'The Invisibility of Home-based Work: The Case of Piece Rate Workers in India', in Singh, Menefee and Kelles-Vittaneu (eds), *Invisible*

Hands Women in Home-based Production: Women and the Household in Asia, Volume 1, Sage Publications, New Delhi, 1987.

Gopalan, Sarala, *Women and Employment in India*. Har-Anand Publications, New Delhi, 1995.

Institute of Social Studies Trust, *Women at Work in India: An Annotated Bibliography*. Sage Publications, New Delhi, 1994.

Jain, Devaki and Nirmala Banerjee (eds), *Tyranny of the Household: Investigative Essays on Women's Work*. Shakti Books, Vikas Publishing House, New Delhi, 1985.

Jose, A.V. (ed.), *Limited Options: Women's Work in Rural India*. ILO, New Delhi, 1989.

Mitra, Asok, *Status of Women: Literacy and Employment*. ICSSR Programme of Women's Studies, New Delhi, 1979.

———, *Status of Women: Household and Non-household Economic Activity*. ICSSR Programme of Women's Studies, New Delhi, 1979.

Mukherjee, Mukul, 'Impact of Modernization on Women's Occupations: A Case Study of the Rice Husking Industry of Bengal', in J. Krishnamurthy (ed.), *Women in Colonial India: Essays on Survival, Work and the State*, Oxford University Press, New Delhi, 1989.

———, 'Women and Work in India: A Collage from Five Decades of Independence', in Bharati Ray (ed.), *From Independence to Freedom: Indian Women since 1947*, Oxford University Press, New Delhi, 1999.

Papola, T.S. and A. Sharma (eds), *Gender and Employment in India*. Vikas Publications, New Delhi, 1999.

Standing, Hilary, 'Resources, Wages and Power: The Impact of Women's Employment on the Urban Bengali Household', in H. Afshar (ed.), *Women, Work and Ideology in the Third World*, Travistock, New York, 1985.

Journal/Periodicals (English)

Banerjee, Diptesh, 'West Bengal: Detours of Stagnation', *Economic and Political Weekly*, 21 (19): 975–76, 1984.

Jain, Devaki, 'Valuing Work: Time as a Measure', *Economic and Political Weekly*, 26 October 1996.

Krishnaraj, Maithreyi, 'Women's Work in Indian Census: Beginnings of Change', *Economic and Political Weekly*, 1–8 December 1990.

'Changing Patterns of Women's Work', Special Issue, *Economic and Political Weekly*, 4 April 1989.

'Women, Work and Health', Special Issue, *Economic and Political Weekly*, 25–31 October 1997.

'Women, Work and Markets', Special Issue, *Economic and Political Weekly*, 26 October–1 November 2002.

Book (Bengali)

Ghosh, Saswati, *Ardhek Arthanithi*. Ananda Publishers, Kolkata, 1997.

Political Participation

Books (English)

Basu, Aparna and Bharati Ray, *Women's Struggle: A History of the All-India Women's Conference 1927–1990*. Manohar, New Delhi, 1990.

Bystydzienski, M. Jill and Joti Seklion, *Democratization and Women's Grassroot Movement*. Kali for Women, New Delhi, 2002.

Chakrabarti, Shanti (ed.), *Rural Women's Claim to Priority—A Policy Debate: 1975–85*. CWDS, New Delhi, 1985.

Chakravartty, Renu, *Communists in Indian Women's Movement: 1940–50*. People's Publishing House, New Delhi, 1980.

Chattopadhyay, Manju, *The Trail-Blazing Women Trade Unionists of India*. AITUC Publication, 1995.

Dutta, Satyabrata, *Impact of Women's Empowerment: A Pilot Study of West Bengal Panchayats*. Joshi Adhikari Institute of Social Studies, West Bengal.

Engineer, Asgar Ali, *Problems of Muslim Women in India*. Orient Longman, New Delhi, 1995.

Gokilvani, S., *Women, Politics and Empowerment*. Department of Women's Studies and Centre for Women's Studies, Alegappa University, Karaikudi, n.d.

Kamrava, Mehran, *Politics and Society in the Third World*. Routledge, London, 1993.

Kaushik, Susheela, *Panchayati Raj in Action, Challenges to Women's Role*. Friedrich Ebert Stiftung, New Delhi, 1996.

———, *Knocking at the Male Bastion: Women in Politics*. NCW, New Delhi, 1997.

Lieten, G.K., *Development, Devolution and Democracy: Village Discourse in West Bengal*. Sage Publications, New Delhi, 1996.

Mandal, Tirtha, *Women Revolutionaries of Bengal: 1905–39*. Minerva, Kolkata, 1991.

Mazumdar, Vina (ed.), *Symbols of Power: Studies on the Political Status of Women in India*. Allied Publishers, Bombay, 1979.

———, *The Non-Aligned Movement and the International Women's Decade*. Centre for Women's Development Studies, New Delhi, 1983.

Mukhopadhyay, Ashim, *Coming of Women into Panchayati Raj*. School of Women's Studies, Jadavpur University, Kolkata, 1996.

Reaching for Half the Sky: A Reader in Women's Movement. Antar Rashtriya Prakashan, Baroda, 1985.

Sen, Manikuntala, *In Search of Freedom*. Stree, Kolkata, 2001.

Government Reports/Publications

Confronting Myriad Oppressions: Voices from the Women's Movement in India. A Report of a Consultation in Bombay, CWDS, New Delhi, 1995.

India in the Search for Freedom. Government of West Bengal, Kolkata, 1986.

Mishra, Surya Kanta, *An Alternative Approach to Development: Law Reforms and Panchayats*. Government of West Bengal, Kolkata, 1991.

Mukherjee, Nirmala and D. Bandyopadhyay, *New Horizons for West Bengal Panchayats*. Government of West Bengal, Kolkata, 1993.

Report of the Committee on Panchayati Raj Institutions. Government of India, New Delhi, 1978.

Books (Bengali)

Begum, Maleka. *Ila Mitra*. Agami, Dhaka, 1986.

Chattopadhyay, Manju, *Sramik Netri Santoshkumari*. Manisha, Kolkata, 1983.

Chattopadhyaya, Maitreyee, *Badhan Cherar Sadhan*. Pratikshan, Kolkata, 1999.

Das, Bina, *Srinkhal Jhankar*. Jayasree, Kolkata, 1995.

Dasgupta, Kamala, *Rakter Akshare*. Navana, Kolkata, 1954.

———, *Swadhinata Sangrame Banglar Nari*. Vasudhara Prakashan, Kolkata, 1963.

Gangopadhyay, Aroti, *Banglar Itihase Narir Bhumika O Sangram*. Unnayan Parshad, Kolkata, 1992.

Ghosh, Saswati, *Samatar Dike Andolane Nari*. Progressive, Kolkata, 1999.

Gupta, Jayati, *Jami, Ain O Meyera*. Sachetana Information Centre, Kolkata, 2001.

Mukherjee, Kanak, *Nari Andoloner Nana Katha*. Eksathe, Kolkata, 1995.

———, *Nari Mukti Andolan O Amra*. National Book Agency; Kolkata, 1999.

Singha, Abha, *Noa Khalir Durjoger Diney*. Naya Udyog, Kolkata, 1999.

Booklets (Bengali)

Gramin Mahilader Baithake. Sachetana Information Centre, Kolkata, 2000.

Gramin Nari O Shishubikash Karmasuchi. State Institute of Panchayat and Rural Development, Kalyani, West Bengal, 1996.

Khudra Reen. Sachetana Information Centre, Kolkata, 1999.

Nari O Shishu Unnayan O Panchayati. State Institute of Panchayat and Rural Development, Kalyani, West Bengal, 1995.

Culture

Books (English), Literature

Banerji, Himani, *The Mirror of Class: Essays on Bengali Theatre*. Papyrus, Kolkata, 1998.

Baruah, U.L. *This is All India Radio*. Publications Division, Ministry of Information and Broadcasting, Government of India, New Delhi, 1983.

Bathla, Sonia, *Women, Democracy and the Media*. Sage Publications, New Delhi, 1998.

Chaki Sirkar, Manjushri, *Feminism in a Traditional Society: Women of the Manipur Valley*. Shakti Books, New Delhi, 1984.

Chatterjee, Maitreyee, 'The Bengali Press', in Ammu Joseph and Kalpana Sharma (eds), *Whose News? The Media and Women's Issues*, Sage Publications, New Delhi, 1999.

Chatterjee, Shoma A., *The Indian Women's Search for an Identity*. Vikas, New Delhi, 1988.

Dasgupta, Madhusraba, *Samsad Companion to the Mahabharata*. Samsad, Kolkata, 2000.

Ganguly, Swati and Sarmistha Dutta Gupta (eds), *The Stream within: Short Stories by Contemporary Bengali Women*. Stree, Kolkata, 1999.

Luthra, H.R., *Indian Broadcasting*. Publications Division, Ministry of Information and Broadcasting, Government of India, New Delhi, 1986.

Subramaniyam, Vimala, *Mirror Image: The Media and the Women's Question*. CED, New Delhi, 1988.

Tharu, Susie and K. Lalitha, *Women Writing in India Vol 1*. Oxford University Press, New Delhi, 1991.

———, *Women Writing in India: The 20th Century Vol 2*. Oxford University Press, New Delhi, 1993.

Books (Bengali), Literature

Akhtar, Shaheen and Moushumi Bhowmick (eds), *Zenana Mehfil: Bangali Musalman Lekhikader Nirbachita Rachana 1904—1938*. Stree, Kolkata, 1998.

Ayub, Gauri, *Tuccha Kichu Sukh-Dukkho*. Dey's, Kolkata, 1986.

Bandopadhyay, Kalyani, *Dharma O Nari: Shekal O Ekal*. Allied, Kolkata, 1998.

Bashak, Sheila, *Banglar Brataparban*. Pustakbipani, Kolkata, 1998.

Basu, Jayati, *Care Kari Na / Robot Kupokat*. Dey's, Kolkata, 1997.

Basu, Purabi and Shafi Ahmed (eds), *Bangladesher Nari Andolaner Galpo*. Anushtup, Kolkata, 1996.

Bhattacharya, Malini, *Meye Dile Sajiye*. Sachetana, Kolkata, 1984.

———, *Gananatya Andolan: Natya Kalar Rupantar Bhavna*. Pratikkhan, Kolkata, 1990.

———, *Nirmaner Samajikata O Adhunik Bangla Upanyash*. Dey's, Kolkata, 1996.

Bhattacharya, Sukumari, *Pracheen Bharat: Samaj O Sahitya*. Ananda, Kolkata, 1987.

———, *Ramayana*. Sahitya Samsad, Kolkata, 1994.

———, *Ramayan O Mahabharat Anupatik Janapriyata*. Cama, Kolkata, 1996.

———, *Bibaha Prasange*. Camp, Kolkata, 1998.

———, *Veder Yuge Khudha O Khadya*. Chirayat, Kolkata, 1998.

Bhattacharya, Sutapa, *Rokeya*. Papyrus, Kolkata, 1996.

———, *Bangali Meyer Bhavna Gadya*. Sahitya Academi, Kolkata, 1999.

———, *Meyeli Path*. Pustakbipani, Kolkata, 2000.

Chattopadhyay, Ratnabali and Goutam Neogi, *Bharat Itihashe Nari*. K.P. Bagchi, Kolkata, 1989.

Chattopadhyay, Ratnabali, *Darbari Shilper Swarup: Mughal Chitrakala*. Thema, Kolkata, 1999.

Chowdhuri, Anjali, *Picasso: Jibon O Shilpo*. Sharat Publishing House, Kolkata.

Das, Abhi, *Kanya Janma Kanya Bisharjan*. Ananda, Kolkata, 1992.

Das, Krishna Bhamini, *England E Banga Mahila*. Stree, Kolkata, 1996.

———, *Surma Nadir Deshe*. Anushtup, Kolkata, 2000.

Dasi, Binodini, *Nati Binodini Rachana Samagra*. Sahitya Sanstha, Kolkata, 1986.

———, *Aamar Katha O Onyanno Rachana*. Subarnarekha, Kolkata, 1987.

Deb, Chitra, *Abarane, Abharane Bharatiya Nari*. Dey's, Kolkata, 1983.

———, *Artahpurer Atmakatha*, Kolkata, 1984.

——— (ed.), *Nirjharini Sarkar Rachana Sangraha*. Ananda, Kolkata, 1991.

———, *Thakurbarir Andarmahal*. Ananda, Kolkata, 1992.

Dev Sen, Nabaneeta, *Sita Theke Suru*. Ananda, Kolkata, 1996.

Dey, Bela, *Amar Jibon, Amar Akashvani*. Allied Books Distribution, Kolkata, 1999.

Dutta, Kalyani, *Pinjare Basiya*. Stree, Kolkata, 1998.

Dyson, Ketaki Kushari, *Antahpurer Atmakatha*. Ananda, Kolkata, 1984.

———, *Rabindranath O Victoria O Kampor Sandhane*. Dey's, Kolkata, 1997.

Gangopadhyay, Arati (ed.), *Dui Shataker Lekhikader Nari Jiban Niye Rachita Galpo Sankalan*. Calcutta University Women's Studies Research Centre, Kolkata, 1989.

Ghatak, Surama, *Ritwik: Padma Theke Titash*. Anushtup, Kolkata, 1995.

———, *Surma Nadir Deshe*. Anushtup, Kolkata, 2000.

Ghoshjaya, Sailabala, *Shekh Andu*. Antaranga, Kolkata, 1994.

Guha, Phulrenu, *Bangalir Samaj Chitra: Raja Rammohan Roy Theke Swami Vivekananda*. Calcutta University, Kolkata, 1973.

Kar, Debrani, *Kolkatar Nagar Nati*. Mitra O Ghosh, Kolkata, 1995.

Lahiri, Swati, *Group Theatre Sandhane*. Jatiya Sahitya Parishad, Calcutta, 19.

Mitra, Saonli, *Katha Amrita Saman*. M.C. Sarkar, Kolkata, 1991.

———, *Didrikkha*. Ananda, Kolkata, 1992.

Mitra, Tripti, *Boli, Indur, Sutorang*. Karuna Prakashani, Kolkata, 1986.

———, *Natak Samagra*. Mitra O Ghosh, Kolkata, 1996.

———, *Ei Prithibi Rangalaya*. Mitra O Ghosh, Kolkata, 1987.

———, *Tarpan*. Ananda, Kolkata, 1998.

———, *Vranti Kaal*. Mitra O Ghosh, Kolkata, 1999.

———, *Mukure Mukh Na Mukhosh*. Mitra O Ghosh, Kolkata, 1998.

———, *Sombhu Mitra O Satnatya*. Mitra O Ghosh, Kolkata, 1999.

———, *Nathabati Anathbat*. M.C. Sarkar, Kolkata, 1993.

Mukhopadhyay, Meera, *Biswakarmar Sandhane*. Deepayan, Kolkata, 1993.

———, *Meera Mukhopadhyaer Diary*. Deepayan, Kolkata.

Nag, Shanta, *Purba Smriti*. Papyrus, Kolkata, 1983.

Nasreen, Taslima, *Nirbachita Kalam*. Ananda, Kolkata, 1994.

Ray, Binoybhusan, *Antahpurer Stree Shiksha*. Naya Udyog, Kolkata, 1998.

Ray Chowdhury, Reba, *Jibaner Taane Shilper Taane*. Thema, Kolkata, 1999.

———, *Sangram: Ghare Baire*. Unit Theatre, Kolkata, 1999.

Sahana Debi, *Smritir Kheya*. Prima, Kolkata, 1982.

Sen, Ashalata, *Shekaler Katha*. Naya Udyog, Kolkata, 1990.

Sen, Kshitimohan, *Pracheen Bharate Nari*. Visva-Bharati Gabeshana Prakashan Samiti, Santiniketan, 1982.

Sen, Minakshi, *Jeler Bhetor Jel*. Pratikkhan, Kolkata, 1994.

Sen, Shova, *Smarane Bismarane: Nabanna Theke Laldurga*. M.C. Sarkar, Kolkata, 1993.

Sengupta, Mallika, *Streelinga Nirman*. Ananda, Kolkata, 1994.

Sripantha, *Keyabat—Meye*. Ananda, Kolkata, 1988.

Tagore, Malabi, *Shilpi Sunnayani Devi*. Sundaram, Calcutta.

Law and Violence against Women

Books (English)

Agarwal, Bina, *A Field of One's Own: Gender and Land Rights in South Asia*. Cambridge University Press, UK, 1994.

———, *Gender and Legal Rights in Landed Property in India*. Kali for Women, New Delhi, 1999.

Agnes, Flavia, *Journey to Justice: Procedures to be Followed in a Rape Case*. Majlis, Bombay, 1990.

———, *Give Us This Day Our Daily Bread: Procedure and Case Law on Maintenance*. Majlis, Bombay, 1992.

———, *Law and Gender Inequality: The Politics of Women's Rights in India*. Oxford University Press, New Delhi, 1999.

Ahuja, Ram, *Violence Against Women*. Rawat, New Delhi, 1998.

Ahuja, Sangeeta, *People, Law and Justice: A Casebook of Public Interest Litigation*. Orient Longman, New Delhi, 1997.

Bajpai, Anju and P.K. Bajpai, *Female Criminality in India*. Rawat, New Delhi, 2000.

Bala, Raj, *The Legal and Political Status of Women in India*. Mohit, New Delhi, 1999.

Balasubrahmanyan, Vimal, *In Search of Justice*. S.N.D.T. Research Centre for Women's Studies, Subhadra Prakashan, Bombay, 1990.

Basu, Durga Das, *Criminal Procedure Code, 1973 (Act No. 2 of 1974)*. Prentice-Hall of India, New Delhi, 1993.

Basu, Monmayee, *Hindu Women and Marriage Law: From Sacrament to Contract*. Oxford University Press, New Delhi, 2001.

Chatterjee, Partha and Pradeep Jagannathan (eds), *Community, Gender and Violence*. Ravi Dayal, New York, 2000.

Datar, Chhaya (ed.), *The Struggle against Violence*. Stree, Kolkata, 1993.

Devasia, V.V. and Leelamma Devasia, *Women, Social Justice and Human Rights*. A.P.H. Publishing Corporation, New Delhi, 1998.

Dhagamwar, Vasudha, *Law, Power and Justice: The Protection of the Personal Rights in the Indian Penal Code*. Sage Publications, New Delhi, 1992.

Dhanda, Amita and Archana, Parashar, *Engendering Law: Essays in Honour of Lotika Sarkar*. Eastern Book Co., Lucknow, 1999.

Faiyaz, Nasreen (ed.), *Growing Poverty and Violence among Women*. NAWO, New Delhi, 2000.

Fyzee, Asaf A.A., *Outlines of Mohammedan Law*. Oxford University Press, New Delhi, 1949.

Ghosh, S.K., *Torture and Rape in Police Custody: An Analysis*. A.P.H., New Delhi, 1993.

Haksar, Nandita and Anju Singh, *Demystification of Law for Women*. Lancer Press, New Delhi, 1986.

Jaising, Indira (ed.), *Justice for Women: Personal Laws, Women's Rights and Law Reforms*. The Other India Press, Goa, 1996.

Jethmalani, Rani (ed.), *Kali's Yug: Empowerment, Law and Dowry Deaths*. Har-Anand Publications, New Delhi, 1993.

Kapur, Ratna and Brenda Crossman, *Subversive Sites: Feminist Engagements with Law in India*. Sage Publications, New Delhi, 1996.

Kulsreshtha, Sudhir, *Fundamental Rights and the Supreme Court: With Special Reference to Article 14 to 22*. Rewat, New Delhi, 1995.

Lingat, Robert, *The Classical Law of India*. Oxford University Press, New Delhi, 1998.

Moitra, Shefali. (ed.), *Women, Heritage and Violence*. Papyrus, Kolkata, 1996.

Mukherjee, Geetanjali, *Dowry Death in India*. IPD, New Delhi, 1999.

Mukherjee, Roma, *Legal Status and Remedies for Women in India*. Deep and Deep Publications, New Delhi, 1997.

Mukhopadhyay, Maitreyee, *Legally Dispossessed: Gender, Identity and the Process of Law*. Stree, Kolkata, 1998.

Nair, Janaki, *Women and Law in Colonial India: A Social History*. Kali for Women, New Delhi, 1992.

Omvedt, Gail, *Violence Against Women: New Movements and New Theories in India*. Kali for Women, New Delhi, 1990.

Parashar, Archana, *Women and Family Law Reforms in India: Uniform Civil Code and Gender Equality*. Sage Publications, New Delhi, 1992.

Pearl, David and Werner Menski, *Muslim Family Law*. Evert & Maxwell Ltd., London, 1998.

Prutho, Raj Kumar (ed.), *Encyclopaedia of Status and Empowerment of Women in India; Vol. 3, Women in Law and Politics*. Mangal Deep Publications, Jaipur, 1999.

Qureshi, Muhammad Ahmed, *Muslim Law of Marriage, Divorce and Maintenance*. Deep and Deep Publications, New Delhi, 1992.

Rajendra, Mangari, *The Publication of Human Rights Act, 1993 and Relating Laws*. Law Book, Hyderabad, 1999.

Saharay, H.K., *Laws of Marriage and Divorce*. Eastern Law House, Kolkata, 1992.

Sarkar, Lotika and B. Sivaramayya (eds), *Women and Law: Contemporary Problems*. Vikas Publishing House, New Delhi, 1994.

Sivaramayya, B., *Matrimonial Property Law in India*. Oxford University Press, New Delhi, 1999.

Sleightholme, Carolyn and Indrani Sinha, *Guilty Without Trial: Women in the Sex Trade in Calcutta*. Stree, Kolkata, 1996.

Subbamma, Malladi, *Atrocities on Women*. Translated by M.V. Ramamurty. AIWC (3), Sarojini House, New Delhi, 1987.

Support Services to Counter Violence against Women in West Bengal: A Resource Directory. Sanhita and Unifem, Kolkata, 2002.

Tope, T.K., *Constitutional Law of India*. Eastern Book Co., Lucknow, 1992.

Violence against Women: A Select List of Books and Websites. American International Resource Centre, Kolkata, 2001.

Reports/Proceedings (English)

Bandyopadhyay, D., *Law Reforms in West Bengal*. Government of West Bengal, Kolkata, 1980.

Crime in India 1999. National Crime Records Bureau, New Delhi.

Crime in India 2000. National Crime Records Bureau, New Delhi.

Justice Delivery through Family Courts: Proceedings of the National Conference. New Delhi, 1994.

Report of the Workshop on Gender Justice: Forging Partnership with Law Enforcement Agencies. National Commission for Women, New Delhi, 2000.

Societal Violence on Women and Children in Prostitution: A Report. National Commission for Women, 1995–1996, National Commission for Women, New Delhi, 1996.

Books (Bengali)

Adhikari, Nishith, *Narir Odhikar O Ain*. Dip Prakashan, Kolkata, 1999.

Ain O Narir Sahayata. Voluntary Action Bureau, West Bengal Social Welfare Board, Calcutta.

Aine Narir Adhikar. Unnayani, Calcutta, 1993.

Bagchi, Jasodhara and Anindita Bhaduri, *Meyeder Chokhe Ain O Ainer Chokhe Meyera*. West Bengal Commission for Women, Kolkata, 2001.

Balyabibaha Nirodhak Ain, 1929. West Bengal Commission for Women, Calcutta.

Bhattacharya, Malini and Smita Khator, *Dharshan O Ain* (Sexual Violence and Law). West Bengal Commission for Women, Kolkata, 2002.

Gupta, Jayati, *Jami, Ain O Meyera*. Sachetana Information Centre, Kolkata, 2000.

Mondal, Manabendra (ed.), *Bibaha Ain*. Women's Socio-legal Aid Research and Training Centre, Calcutta, 1997.

Sen, Subrata, *Panpratha Shastre O Samaje*. Ananda, Kolkata, 1998.

Tribal Women

Books (English)

Alam, Jayanti, *Tribal Women Workers: A Study of Young Migrants*. Raj, New Delhi, 2000.

Antony, Piush, *Towards Empowerment: Experiences of Organizing Women Workers*. International Labour Organization, New Delhi, 2001.

Bakshi, S.R. and Kiran Bala (eds), *Women, Children and Weaker Sections: Social and Economic Development of Scheduled Tribes*. Deep and Deep Publications, New Delhi, 1999.

Banu, Zenab, *Tribal Women's Empowerment and Gender Issues*. Kanishka, New Delhi, 2001.

Chaudhuri, Buddhadev (ed.), *Tribal Development in India: Problems and Prospects*. Inter-India, New Delhi, 1982.

———, (ed.), *Tribal Health: Socio-Cultural Dimension*. Inter-India, New Delhi, 1986.

———, (ed.), *Tribal Transformation in India*. Volumes 1 to 5. Inter-India, New Delhi, 1992.

Chauhan, Abha, *Tribal Women: Continuity and Change*. A.C. Brothers, New Delhi, 1999.

Choudhary, Damina, *Tribal Girls: Aspiration, Achievement and Frustration*. Pointer, Jaipur, 2000.

Das, Amal Kumar, *Glimpses of the Development of Scheduled Castes and Tribes through Decades in West Bengal in Fifty Years of Independence*. Government of West Bengal, 1997.

Dasgupta, Malabika (ed.), *Status of Tribal Women in Tripura*. Vikas, New Delhi, 1993.

Devasia, V.V. and Leelamma Devasia. *Women, Social Justice and Human Rights*. APH, New Delhi, 1998.

Fernandes, Walter and Geeta Menon, *Tribal Women and Forest Economy: Deforestation, Exploitation and Social Change*. Indian Social Institute, New Delhi, 1987.

Ghatak, Maitreya (ed.), *Dust on the Road. Activist Writings of Mahasweta Devi*. Seagull, Kolkata, 1999.

Hans, Asha, *Tribal Women: A Gendered Utopia? Women in the Agricultural Sector*. South Asia Publishers, New Delhi, 1999.

Majumdar, D.N. and B. Datta Ray, *Tribal Occupational Mobility*. Research India Publication, Kolkata, 1984.

Sahay, Prasad Sushama, *Tribal Woman Labourers: Aspects of Economic and Physical Exploitation*. Gyan, New Delhi, 1998.

Sarkar, Chanchal, *Tilting against Odds, Bankura's Rural Women Organize for Empowerment*. Centre for Women's Development Studies, New Delhi, 1998.

Seth, Mira, *Women and Development: The Indian Experience*. Sage Publications, New Delhi, 2001.

Singh, K. Suresh (ed.), *Tribal Situation in India*. Indian Institute of Advanced Studies, Simla, 1972.

Singh, K.S. (ed.), *Economies of the Tribes and their Transformation*. Concept Publishing, New Delhi, 1982.

———, (ed.), *Tribal Movements in India*. Vol. 2. Manohar, New Delhi, 1982.

Tappo, S.R., *Tribes in India*. SR Publication, New Delhi, 2000.

Tripathy, S.N., *Tribal Women in India*. Mohit Publications, New Delhi, 2002.

Journals/Periodicals (English)

Beteille, Andre, 'Question of Definition', *Seminar*, 14 October 1960.

Desai, A.R., 'Tribes in Transition', *Seminar* 14 October 1960.

Gupta, Ratna (ed.), Profiles of Tribal Women in West Bengal—Special Series 34. Bulletin of the Cultural Research Institute, Scheduled Castes and Tribes Welfare Department, Government of West Bengal, Kolkata, 1990.

Haimendorf, Christoph von Furer, 'The Problem', *Seminar*, 14 October 1960.

Reports/Surveys

Census of India 1971. Series 22, West Bengal, Special tables for Scheduled Castes and Scheduled Tribes, Part-IVA.

Census of India 1981. Series 23, West Bengal, Primary Census Abstracts of Scheduled Castes and Scheduled Tribes.

Census of India 1991. Series 26, West Bengal, Primary Census Abstracts (Scheduled Castes/Tribes), Part-IIB.

Development of Man-Forest Symbiotic Living System in West Bengal: A Project on Joint Forest Management Performance Report: 1996–99. Ramakrishna Mission Loka Shiksha Parishad, West Bengal.

Performance Report on Joint Forest Management Project (1991–94). Ramakrishna Mission Loka Shiksha Parishad, West Bengal.

Report on Tribal Women and Employment. National Commission for Women, New Delhi, 1998.

Science and Technology for Tribal Women (Conference Report). National Commission for Women, New Delhi.

Book (Bengali)

Baske, Dhirendra Nath, *Pashchimbanger Adivasi Samaj* (Vol. I). Subarnarekha, Kolkata, 1993.

Index

About the Editor and Contributors

The Editor

Jasodhara Bagchi is Chairperson, West Bengal Commission for Women and Founder Director of the School of Women's Studies, Jadavpur University. She was born in 1937 and educated at Presidency College, Kolkata, Somerville College, Oxford, and New Hall, Cambridge. The larger part of her working life was spent at Jadavpur University, where she was Professor of English. In 1988 she became the Founder-Director of the School of Women's Studies at Jadavpur University, in which capacity she led the activities of the centre until her retirement in 1997. She is also one of the founder-members of the feminist organization Sachetana in Kolkata. Her focus areas of research include women's studies, women's writing, 19th-century English and Bengali literature, the reception of Positivism in Bengal, motherhood, and the Partition of India. Among her numerous authored, edited, and co-edited volumes are *The Trauma and the Triumph: Gender and Partition in India* (2003), *Thinking Social Science in India: Essays in Honour of Alice Thorner* (2002), *Gem-like Flame: Walter Pater and the 19th-Century Paradigm of Modernity* (1997), *Loved and Unloved: The Girl Child in the Family* (1997), *Indian Women: Myth and Reality* (1995), and *Literature, Society, and Ideology in the Victorian Era* (1992), and . She initiated and spearheaded the pioneering Bengali Women Writers Reprint Series edited by the School of Women's Studies, Jadavpur University, which continues to bring out new editions of writers such as Jyotirmoyee Devi. She is currently Chairperson of the West Bengal State Women's Commission.

The Contributors

Suraj Bandyopadhyay has retired as Professor, Sociological Research Unit, Indian Statistical Institute, New Delhi.

Nirmala Banerjee was a Professor of Economics at the Centre for Studies in Social Sciences, Kolkata and Director, Sachetana Information Centre, Kolkata.

Malini Bhattacharya is former MP from West Bengal, member of the West Bengal Commission for Women and former Director, School of Women's Studies, Jadavpur University.

Anuradha Chanda teaches history at Jadavpur University and is former Director, School of Women's Studies, Jadavpur University.

Kamal Kumar Chattopadhyay has taught education at the SCERT.

Ratnabali Chattopadhyay teaches Islamic history at Calcutta University and is former Director, Women's Studies Research Centre at the same university.

Atis Dasgupta is Head, Sociological Research Unit, Indian Statistical Institute.

Maitreya Ghatak was an independent researcher with Development Research Group, Kolkata.

Jaba Guha is former Head of the Department of Economics, Jadavpur University.

Manjari Gupta is an advocate at the Calcutta High Court and former President, All India Democratic Women's Association.

Mukul Mukherjee has taught economics in Delhi and is associated with the Women's Studies Research Centre, Calcutta University.

Ishita Mukhopadhyay heads the Women's Studies Research Centre, Calcutta University.

Vidya Munshi is a veteran political activist with the Communist Party of India and the National Federation of Indian Women.

Dipali Nag has retired as Lecturer, College of Education for Women, Hastings House, Kolkata.